LOVE, WORK, AND DEATH

T0369727

THE LITTMAN LIBRARY OF
JEWISH CIVILIZATION

Dedicated to the memory of
LOUIS THOMAS SIDNEY LITTMAN
*who founded the Littman Library for the love of God
and as an act of charity in memory of his father*
JOSEPH AARON LITTMAN
and to the memory of
ROBERT JOSEPH LITTMAN
who continued what his father Louis had begun
יהא זכרם ברוך

'*Get wisdom, get understanding:
Forsake her not and she shall preserve thee*'
PROV. 4: 5

*The Littman Library of Jewish Civilization is a registered UK charity
Registered charity no.* 1000784

Love, Work, and Death

Jewish Life in Medieval Umbria

◆

ARIEL TOAFF

Translated by
JUDITH LANDRY

London
The Littman Library of Jewish Civilization
in association with Liverpool University Press

The Littman Library of Jewish Civilization
Registered office: 4th floor, 7–10 Chandos Street, London, W1G 9DQ

in association with Liverpool University Press
4 Cambridge Street, Liverpool L69 7ZU, UK
www.liverpooluniversitypress.co.uk/littman

Managing Editor: Connie Webber

Distributed in North America by
Oxford University Press Inc, 198 Madison Avenue,
New York, NY 10016, USA

First published in Italian © Società Editrice Il Mulino, Bologna 1989
English translation © The Littman Library of Jewish Civilization 1996

English translation first published in hardback 1996
First published in paperback 1998

All rights reserved.
No part of this publication may be reproduced,
stored in a retrieval system, or transmitted, in any form or by
any means, without the prior permission in writing of
The Littman Library of Jewish Civilization

This book is sold subject to the condition that it shall not,
by way of trade or otherwise, be lent, re-sold, hired out or
otherwise circulated without the publisher's prior consent in any
form of binding or cover other than that in which it is published
and without a similar condition including this condition
being imposed on the subsequent purchaser

Catalogue records for this book are available from the
British Library and the Library of Congress

ISBN 978-1-874774-33-4

Publishing co-ordinator: Janet Moth
Index: Andrew Hawkey
Cover design: Pete Russell, Faringdon, Oxon.

Printed and bound in Great Britain by
CPI Group (UK) Ltd., Croydon, CR0 4YY

Contents

List of Figures

List of Tables

Abbreviations

AC	Archivio Comunale (town archive)
Add.	Addictiones (supplements and appendices to the statutes)
Arch. Segr.	Archivio Segreto (archive of the court with jurisdiction over cases involving public order and the security of the city)
AS	Archivio Statale (state archive: record office and central archive for a district)
AV	Archivio Vaticano (Vatican archive)
coll.	*collactio* (serial number)
Con. e Rif.	Consigli e Riformanze (debates, proceedings, and resolutions of the town or city council)
contr.	contract
env.	envelope (attached to a folder)
Giud.	Giudiziario (archive of criminal records)
ind.	index
Not.	Notarile (archive of notarial acts)
orig.	original document (not a copy)
prot.	*protocollo* (register)
prot. sine coll.	*protocollo sine collactione* (register without serial number)
Prov.	Provveditorato (administrative archive)
reg.	register
Rif.	Riformanze (resolutions of the town or city council)
Stat.	Statuti (statutes or constitutions of a city or town)

Note on Currency, Weights, and Measures

CURRENCY

ducato (ducat), *fiorino* (florin), *scudo*
all names for a gold coin weighing *c.*3.5 g. and equivalent to
approximately £300 sterling at present-day values

baiocco	100 *baiocchi* = 1 *scudo*
bolognino	40 *bolognini* = 1 *fiorino*
denaro	960 *denari* = 1 *fiorino*
lira	4 *lire* = 1 *fiorino*
quattrino	400 *quattrini* = 1 *scudo*
soldo	80 *soldi* = 1 *fiorino*

WEIGHTS AND MEASURES

Dry

libbra	0.33 kg.
quintale	100 kg.
salma, soma	68.5 kg.

Liquid

caldarello	25 litres
foglietta	0.35 litres
modiolino	9 litres

Area

moggio *c.*320 square metres

Jewish settlements in Umbria (13th–16th centuries)

Monterchi○ Citerna
Lippiano○ ○
Gioiello○ ▲ **Città di Castello**
○ Monte S. Maria

○ Montone

Fratta○

● **Gubbio**

Tiber

Lake
Trasimene

Gualdo Tadino○
Casa Castalda

PERUGIA ■

Nocera○

Bastia○ ● **Assisi**
Bettona
○ Cannara
Città della Pieve ○ Deruta ● **Spello**
Cerqueto ○ ▲ **Foligno**
Marsciano ○ Gualdo ● **Bevagna**
Cattaneo○ ○ Montefalco
Bastardo○ ● **Trevi**
Giano○ Sellano
○
Castel Ritaldi ○ Cerreto
● **Todi**

Orvieto ● ▲ Spoleto ● **Norcia**

Acquasparta○ Montesanto
○ ○ Cascia
Monteleone ○
Sangeminio Ferentillo ○
Amelia● ○ Arrone
Terni ▲
● **Narni**

■ More than 100 Jews
▲ Fewer than 100 Jews
● Fewer than 50 Jews
○ Fewer than 20 Jews

Introduction

FOR some time now the latter part of the thirteenth century has been seen as a key period in the history of Italian Jewry. During that time many Jewish communities sprang up in the regions of central and northern Italy: their appearance marked a turning-point after which Jewish history ceased to be purely that of the Jews of Rome and southern Italy.

The growth of these new communities, which archival documentation shows to have been surprisingly rapid and widespread, had its origin in the northward migration from Rome of Jewish merchants engaged in the money trade. From the last quarter of the thirteenth century onwards, singly or in groups, Jews moved from Rome along the great consular roads towards the towns of central and northern Italy, invited by the rulers of the communes to invest their capital on the local credit markets alongside or as a substitute for that of the great Tuscan or Lombard companies. This wave of migration spread rapidly through Latium, Umbria, the Marches, and Tuscany, creating communities in areas where Jews had never previously settled, or where their appearance had hitherto been brief and sporadic. These communities had many features in common, and developed a vigorous cultural, religious, and also to some degree linguistic identity which was to persist over time.

The results of the research presented here into the everyday life of the Jews of Umbria—one of the earliest regions of settlement by the 'Roman' wave of migration—can therefore act as a template for the reconstruction of the world-view of much of Italian Jewry in the late Middle Ages and for determining how people lived and the traditions and culture they shared.

This continuing research and reconstruction is important because usury and antisemitism still seem to be virtually the only aspects of the Jewish presence in Italy that medievalists have taken an interest in, and even recent studies have failed to provide historians with new information with which to draw a more accurate picture of medieval Jewish life. Such histories as do exist often seem to have been based on secondary sources, themselves based largely on Christian documents which by definition are unlikely to present the Jewish world accurately: here, Jewish communities are presented as monochromatic and one-dimensional—closed and passive, and free from internal division and discord. In fact, the reconstruction of Jewish society in all its complexity can only be accomplished by correlating and comparing civic archives with contemporary internal Jewish sources—the only possible key to understanding a world which would otherwise be seen only through the eyes of outsiders. The important point is the comparison and correlation: just as secondary sources taken by themselves are unsatisfactory, primary Jewish sources also need to be treated with caution. A synagogue sermon or a model letter, written in an intricate style and steeped in biblical allusions, does not always give a reliable picture of the material conditions of Jewish social life, and is not necessarily to be preferred to a series of notarial deeds which give a contrary picture. Many Jewish documents of the period also contain a certain amount of wishful thinking: there is always some degree of discrepancy between the objective situation of a Jewish community, with its real individual and collective behaviour, and the image it liked to present of itself in propaganda, polemical treatises, and edifying speeches. The cautious historian should therefore be able to sense discrepancies and divergencies between the history of the real social relationships experienced by Jews and the value-systems through which they liked to present and interpret that experience.

The picture of medieval Italian Jewry that emerges from a thorough study of all the sources is lively and varied: full of subtleties and contradictions and thus more difficult to interpret, but ultimately far more revealing. Here the moneylender is no longer the undisputed protagonist, but plays second lead; money is handled not only in banks, but in shops and workplaces, at markets and fairs; and antisemitism is hardly ever endemic, at least in late medieval Italy.

The power and attraction of Christian society were felt at almost every level. Any direct and overt clash would clearly have been counterproductive, and Jewish society had to develop a capacity for accommodation—at least outwardly—in order to survive. Thus, the images and models of Christian society were partially integrated into the Jewish system, altered to lessen their friction and tame their disruptive power. The pursuit of the compromise, the desire to make the best of both worlds, proved extraordinarily effective. Though many aspects of Christian society encroached on the Jewish way of life at this period, they rarely amounted to a brutal intrusion and were more usually felt as a constant and insidious influence, born of the unequal power-struggle between the opposing societies. It is in this context, for instance, that we should view the Jewish communities' attempts to safeguard Jewish dietary laws, especially those concerning meat and, to some degree, wine.

A Jewish presence in any community appears to have been directly linked to the possibility of their being allowed to prepare and eat kosher food. This was not usually a problem, but it is no surprise that the circles hostile to Jewish settlement, in particular the Franciscans, freely used the prohibition on ritual slaughter or the preparation of wine 'pressed by the Jews' to pursue their aims.

The attempt to fit in brought with it not only a dawning awareness of the gulf that separated the Jew from his or her Christian counterparts but also a heightened sense of the divisions within the Jewish community itself. Those at the top of the hierarchy worked hard to maintain their position and to repress social climbing by the lower orders; they also had an eye to their position *vis-à-vis* Christian society, encouraging good relations with its leaders, and justifying their privileged position to their own community by presenting their interests as identical with those of Jewish society as a whole.

The position of the banker at the top of the Jewish social tree was absolute. His fortune guaranteed the survival of the community which he had fostered and for which he felt responsible, and he defended it with strategies which were the outcome of lengthy adaptation to shifting political conditions and which had stood the test of time. The banker's mode of operation was based on the experience and success of his predecessors in the money trade, who had understood its mechanisms, amending and directing them as need be, but above all keeping an eye on the future. Jewish society lived in fear of new developments which might endanger the balance of this system, and defended its bankers as a privileged minority which offered itself as guarantor of the survival of the whole community.

So-called fraudulent marriages are another example of perceived threats to this social order and reveal the divisions within an apparently united community. The control exercised by rich families over their children's matrimonial choice, and the careful investment of their dowries, were defended by threatening interdicts against the claims of the disinherited or fortune-hunters, real or alleged, and by innumerable rabbinical responsa. The immediate concern was, of course, loss of status and fortune, but the underlying justification was the need to protect the long-term stability and prosperity of the community as a whole.

A true picture of Jewish community life in medieval Italy must therefore take account of many pressures and contradictions acting from within and without. Above all, it is important to be open to what the archival and notarial sources tell us—even when they contradict the widely accepted vision of a community that was basically hostile to the models of the surrounding Christian society and hermetically sealed against them. It is not acceptable to disqualify such sources as tendentious, or to disallow them by disputing their typicality, or to falsify them through intentionally reductive interpretations, in order to give credence to the image of a homogeneous Jewish society, isolated and beleaguered, whose main preoccupation was to maintain its own world-view as a complete and all-inclusive system within the political and economic structures imposed by a basically alien outside world. This ideological version of late medieval Jewish society, which has its hardened champions today, provides only a simplified, schematic image of the reality of Jewish social organization; it overlooks or minimizes subtleties, overlappings, influences, and contradictions, since its main purpose is to draw a mythical picture of a heroic society drowning in a sea of sorrows and illuminated only by Providence.

A.T.

I

Sex, Love, and Marriage

LOVE: ACCIDENT OR DESIGN?

THE Jewish presence in Italy in the late Middle Ages was distinguished by the breadth of its dispersal; settlements, often limited to single families, were spread over a considerable number of city-states, walled towns, and villages, linked by poor or inconvenient communications. The Jewish population of Umbria between the fourteenth and sixteenth centuries could hardly have numbered more than 500 people, and was scattered over fifty centres of various sizes, on the shores of Lake Trasimene, in the Tiber valley, and up the slopes of the Apennines. Jewish families were often only given temporary permits of residence by the authorities in these areas. Their choice of precisely where to settle was linked to their professional skills—for example, as bankers or as managers or employees with the local pawnbroker. If they wanted to retain their Jewish identity, their social life was limited to mixing mainly with other Jews, and they were therefore cut off to some degree from the surrounding world. However, many Jews wanted to strike a satisfactory balance between their particular needs as a religious minority and the attractions of Christian society, in which they wanted to participate, and whose influence made itself felt in all aspects of their everyday life.[1]

The problem was undoubtedly more acute for young people, and especially young men, than for those who had moved into a new locality already married and with a dependent family. Indeed, young men were

---

[1] On the dispersal of the Jewish nucleus throughout Italy at this period and the reasons behind it, see e.g. V. Colorni, 'Prestito ebraico e comunità ebraiche nell'Italia centrale e settentrionale', *Rivista di Storia del Diritto Italiano*, 8 (1935), 1–55; A. Milano, 'I primordi del prestito ebraico in Italia', *La Rassegna Mensile di Israel*, 19 (1953), issued in instalments: 221–30, 272–80, 306–19, 360–71, 450–60; L. Poliakov, *Jewish Bankers and the Holy See* (London, 1977), 53–70; R. Bonfil, 'Jewish Emigration to Italy in the Late Middle Ages' (Heb.), in A. Shinan (ed.), *Emigration and Settlement in Jewish and General History* (Jerusalem, 1982), 139–53; A. Toaff, 'Gli ebrei romani e il commercio del denaro nei comuni dell'Italia centrale alla fine del Duecento', in *Italia Judaica*, proceedings of the first international conference held at Bari, 18–22 May 1981 (Rome, 1983), 183–96.

aware that their very future as Jews was conditional upon their choosing a Jewish wife, as required by the religious rules by which they felt themselves bound; but their natural sexual impulses could find no release within the local Jewish microcosm, often limited to a few families. Thus 'spontaneous' love between a Jewish boy and girl would be, at best, extremely rare. Rather, in everyday life, it was the young Christian girls whom they met at market, in the piazza, on the town streets, and in neighbours' houses who attracted their attention. Fashionably dressed on feast days, it was these girls who stirred up fantasies and desires. These were the circumstances where love was born and flourished, despite prohibitions and injunctions.

Thus the young Jewish man gradually became aware that his first sexual encounters would not take place in a Jewish environment, and that love and marriage ran on parallel tracks, usually with little relation between them. Love was the spontaneous fruit of youthful urges; marriage remained a matter for family choice, linked to strategies and policies of an economic and religious nature. The woman you married was not necessarily the woman you loved. Marriages were worked out and haggled over by Jewish families with great prudence. Money held sway in the choice of a spouse: rather than love each other, the young people needed to make the best possible financial match. For the young Jewish male, as often for his Christian counterpart, love came after marriage, at best, and very often continued to be extraneous to it.[2]

The case of the young son of Mosè da Bevagna, a merchant from Spoleto, may be regarded as typical: in 1480 he was popularly described as 'courting Caterina', a young and shapely local beauty. Flying in the face of rabbinic injunctions and family censure, the young Venturello met Caterina on frequent amorous encounters in the vineyards and woods on the slopes of Monteluco, not attempting to conceal his ardent, star-crossed love. Yet that did not prevent him, a few years later,

---

[2] In this connection Cassuto maintains that marriage for love was considered exceptional in Renaissance Jewish society; see *Gli ebrei a Firenze nell'età del Rinascimento* (Florence, 1918), 221. However, the phenomenon does not seem to have been restricted to Jewish society, but was also characteristic of the host society of the period; see J. Solè, *Storia dell'amore e del sesso nell'età moderna* (Bari, 1979), 30–5; talking of Christian society (and his remarks are all the more applicable to Jewish circles) Solè rightly notes that 'by seeking to hold out against fleeting youthful impulses and personal inclination, marriage became the collective creation of relatives and friends; it usually brought together two strangers who shared a single rational desire to found a socially and economically balanced family.' See also J. Rossiaud, *Medieval Prostitution* (Oxford, 1988), 15.

from making an acceptable marriage in his native Bevagna to Stella, the daughter of a Jewish banker from Bologna. Love and marriage had no doubt constituted two separate phases in the young man's life, as in those of so many of his Jewish contemporaries.[3] Problems certainly existed on both the Jewish and Christian sides. Canon law forbade sexual relations between Christians and Jews and punished them severely. The Perugia statutes of 1342 (and the principle is found again unchanged in those of 1523) compare such relationships to those with lepers and state 'that no Jew shall presume to lie with any Christian woman and to know her carnally, and that no Christian woman shall yearn to lie with a Jew, lending her body to copulation with him. In the case of the violation of these regulations the transgressors shall be punished with a fine of 1,000 *lire*, and in case of insolvency they shall be burned in the fire until dead. The same punishment shall be meted out to the Christian who has had carnal knowledge of a Jewish woman.'[4] But in practice things were different; and if there were indeed numerous Jews who incurred the rigours of the law in this context (always resolved with the payment of fines, whose size usually depended on the relative wealth of the accused), those who managed to elude it in one way or another must have been even more numerous. Nor did Christian society usually react particularly strongly to a phenomenon which must have been fairly general and hence, *de facto*, considered normal. For this reason the suggestion of the Mantuan justices, questioned in 1569 as to the punishment to be applied to Jews guilty of sleeping with Christian women,

---

[3] AC Spoleto, Not., Giuliano da Monte Publico, 137/II, fo. 57^r (trial of Venturello di Mosè da Bevagna for having had sexual relations with Caterina da Imola, a Christian girl, 30 Apr. 1480); AC Bevagna, Not., Crescimbene di Pietro di Percivalle, 1539, fo. 44^v.

[4] *Corpus statutorum italicorum*, i/4. *Statuti di Perugia del 1342*, ed. G. degli Azzi (Rome, 1913), 380–4; AS Perugia, Stat., 3, fo. 34^v; B. Giliani, *Compendium iuris municipalis civitatis Perusiae* (Perugia, 1635), 166; A. Fabretti, *La prostituzione in Perugia nei secc. XIV e XV* (Turin, 1885), 6; A. Toaff, *Gli ebrei a Perugia* (Perugia, 1975), 49. As is well known, from the second half of the 13th cent., statutes and local laws bracketed Jews, lepers, and prostitutes together as social outcasts, even if in practice the restrictive regulations concerning them were generally very leniently applied; see N. Coulet, 'Juif intouchable et interdits alimentaires', in M. de Combarieu *et al.*, *Exclus et systèmes d'exclusion dans la littérature et la civilisation médiéval: Sénéfiance* (Aix-en-Provence, 1978), 207–21; M. Kriegel, 'Un trait de psychologie sociale dans les pays méditerranéens du bas Moyen Âge: Le Juif comme intouchable', *Annales ESC*, 31 (1976), 326–30; id., *Les Juifs à la fin du Moyen Âge dans l'Europe méditerranéenne* (Paris, 1979), 39–59; Rossiaud, *Medieval Prostitution*; S. S. Nigro, *Le brache di San Griffone: Novellistica e predicazione tra '400 e '500* (Bari, 1983), 24.

strikes me as written more in jest than earnest: 'that in this case their testicles shall be cut off, which would provide a fine carnival spectacle.'[5]

Almost everywhere in Umbria we find Jews sentenced to financial punishment for having sexual relations with Christian women—in Spoleto, Gualdo, Città di Castello, and, of course, in Perugia, the centre with the largest and most energetic Jewish community.[6] A survey of the other Italian regions with centres of Jewish settlement reveals a similar picture at this time. In fifteenth-century Tuscany, for example, thirty-four offences against public morals committed by Jews were recorded, including three cases of rape, twenty-six of intercourse, and five of corruption of minors and of sodomy.[7] Only rarely did there seem to be any possibility that the accusation might be punished by anything more than a fine. And even these were special cases, where sexual relations between a Jew and a Christian were accompanied by aggravating circumstances of various kinds. One such case concerned the banker Angelo di Guglielmo: he underwent trial in Perugia in 1467 for having had

[5] See Sh. Simonsohn, *History of the Jews in the Duchy of Mantua* (Jerusalem, 1977), 115.
[6] AC Spoleto, Not., Giuliano da Monte Publico, 137/II, fo. 57ʳ; L. Fumi, 'I registri del Ducato di Spoleto', *Bollettino della Deputazione di Storia Patria per l'Umbria*, 4 (1898), 142; AC Città di Castello, Prov. (1489), fo. 37ᵛ; AS Perugia, Giud., Sentenze del Podestà, I, fos. 222ʳ–224ʳ; ibid. 1462, fo. 11ᵛ; ibid. 1467, fo. 73ʳ; Toaff, *Ebrei a Perugia*, 92–3.
[7] See M. Ciavarini, *I banchieri ebrei in Firenze nel secolo XV* (Borgo S. Lorenzo, 1907), 10–12; M. Luzzati, 'Per la storia degli ebrei italiani nel Rinascimento: Matrimoni e apostasia di Clemenza di Vitale da Pisa', *Studi sul medioevo cristiano offerti a Raffaello Morghen* (Rome, 1974), 455–6. In other regions, too, the offences committed by the Jews against public morality fell essentially into the field of sexual relations with Christian women. See B. Ghetti, 'Gli ebrei e il Monte di Pietà in Recanati nei secoli XV e XVI', *Atti e memorie della R. Deputazione di Storia Patria delle Marche*, 4/2 (1907), 34–5; A. Balletti, *Gli ebrei e gli Estensi* (Reggio Emilia, 1930), 53, 55; Sh. Simonsohn, 'Alcune note sugli ebrei a Parma nel '400', in E. Toaff (ed.), *Studi sull'ebraismo italiano in memoria di Cecil Roth* (Rome, 1974), 235–6, 256–9; id., *Jews in the Duchy of Mantua*, 112, 208–18, 774; id., *The Jews in the Duchy of Milan* (Jerusalem, 1982), i. 19–20, 171, 229–30, *et passim* (in 'Alcune note' Simonsohn refers to the 'disproportionate number of documents concerning this matter to be found among those of the second half of the 15th cent., not only as regards Parma, but also the whole duchy of Milan'); A. Antoniazzi Villa, *Un processo contro gli ebrei nella Milano del 1488* (Bologna, 1986), 35–6; A. Esposito, 'Gli ebrei a Roma tra Quattro' e Cinquecento' *Quaderni Storici*, 18/54 (1983), 828; R. Segre, *The Jews in Piedmont* (Jerusalem, 1986), i. 354. In 1580 the leaders of the Jewish community in Padua were still complaining 'that the number of scoundrels who go to bed with Christian women is multiplying daily in our community, arousing the wrath of God and men, since apart from transgressing against our laws, they put themselves in danger and all of us in a bad light in the eyes of those who govern us' (see *Minutes-Book of the Council of the Jewish Community of Padua* (Heb.), ed. D. Carpi (Jerusalem, 1973), i. 117).

sexual relations with a Christian serving-girl.[8] The clerk of the court specified that Marta Margherita, 'a woman of lowly estate, ill repute, and reprehensible conduct', had been taken on as a wet-nurse for Angelo's daughter and had subsequently had a close relationship of friendship and goodwill with Angelo himself. The nature of this friendship and goodwill is spelled out for us in abundant detail in the records of the trial: the woman 'had had the effrontery to lend her body for copulation with the Jew Angelo, and he had dared to know the Christian woman carnally several times and at various intervals'. The young wet-nurse had become pregnant and had had an illegitimate daughter. The hapless Marta Margherita, fearing her parents' beatings and indeed not being any too certain of the identity of the child's real father, since she had had relationships with various men during that same period, decided to kill her unwanted child. With the discovery of the crime, Angelo was in deep trouble: it required considerable effort on his part to prove his own lack of involvement in the child's killing and to convince the judges that his very paternity was to be regarded as highly doubtful. The limitation of his confession to an admission of having had sexual intercourse with a Christian woman constituted his line of defence in a difficult and hazardous trial. He was very fortunate that the judgment, when it came (partly mitigated by the intervention of the papal legate, who had pleaded his cause), was limited to a heavy fine.[9]

Another trial in Perugia, different in nature but equally serious in its potential consequences, concerned Gabriele di Musetto, a Jew who lived at Castel delle Forme in the countryside near Perugia.[10] The young man was accused of the rape of a Christian widow. In this case too the clerk of the court did not skimp on spicy details of sexual misdeeds. Gabriele, 'after sunset and before sunrise, seized with lustful appetites, had assailed the widow, donna Margherita, near the boundary ditch of il Francia, in the territory of Castel delle Forme'. Then, intent on assaulting the woman's honour and integrity and robbing her of her good name, he had—still in the words of the clerk of the court—'taken her by the neck and thrown her to the ground in order to have carnal knowledge of her,

---

[8] AS Perugia, Giud., Sentenze del Podestà, 1467, fo. 73ʳ; ibid., 'Copiae condemnationum pro mensibus novembris et decembris', 1467, fo. 7ʳ.

[9] On 9 Dec. 1467 Angelo was sentenced to a fine of 150 florins. His brother Aleuccio had previously presented the judges with a letter from bishop Ermolao Barbaro, the governor of Perugia, in which he pleaded warmly in favour of the accused (see Toaff, *Ebrei a Perugia*, 92–3).

[10] AS Perugia, Giud., Sentenze del Podestà, 1462, fo. 11ᵛ; ibid., 'Copiae condemnationum pro mensibus januarii et februarii', 1462, fo. 19ʳ.

while the woman struggled and fought him off courageously'. Gabriele's arrest and severe punishment were inevitable; however, he managed to escape from Perugia prison, where he was being held pending trial. He subsequently arrived at a surprising accommodation with the authorities by proffering justifications whose nature is unknown to us, but which clearly proved extremely convincing, and obtained his freedom upon payment of a modest fine.[11]

Sex and violence also figure in the proceedings of the trial, in 1245, of the Frenchman Abramo de la Bachelerie, an inhabitant of Perugia. Abramo had struck up an amorous relationship with a married Christian woman, who had abandoned her husband and family and gone to live with him. At first the woman's husband had turned to the Perugian authorities, complaining that Abramo 'had carried off his wife and was keeping her at his side, knowing her carnally'. Then, seeing the futility of his protests, he decided to take the law into his own hands, assaulting his rival and wounding him with a dagger. Abramo was finally sentenced to a fine of 100 *lire* for adultery, while the wielder of the dagger, who had clearly earned the judge's sympathy, had to pay one of 25 *lire*.[12]

Homosexuality and sodomy, which in the late medieval period were associated with witchcraft and heresy, and which the Observant friars often preached against in their sermons, do not seem to have been unknown in Jewish circles.[13] All these ingredients, and others besides, figure in the accusations made before the papal authorities between 1322 and 1323 in relation to Abramo, a Jew from Gualdo Cattaneo in the duchy of Spoleto. Abramo was accused of having had amorous relations with a Christian woman from Gualdo and, later, of having homosexual relations with a Christian man from the same town. For this deviant behaviour he was sentenced to pay a fine of 100 *lire* to the Apostolic Camera. However, it would seem that Abramo da Gualdo was actually an eccentric and anti-social character, indeed a sexual psychopath, known throughout the duchy of Spoleto for his heretical and sacrilegious behaviour, 'accustomed to appear naked, with a mitre on his head, in the churches of Montefalco, Gualdo Cattaneo and the whole region'. At the

[11] Gabriele was sentenced by default on 9 Feb. 1462 to a fine of 500 *lire*. On 21 May 1468 the sentence was annulled after Gabriele had paid the derisory sum of 35 *lire* to the apostolic treasury of Perugia; see Toaff, *Ebrei a Perugia*, 92.

[12] AS Perugia, Giud., Sentenze del Podestà, I, fos. 222^r, 224^r.

[13] See Solè, *Storia dell'amore*, 235–48; Rossiaud, *Medieval Prostitution*, 114–15; N. Cohn, 'The Myth of Satan and his Human Servants', in M. Douglas (ed.), *Witchcraft* (London, 1970), 3–6.

end of 1322 he was sentenced for having addressed injurious words to the pope, and had to pay a fine of 100 florins.[14]

Clearly, I would not for a moment maintain that cases like those of Angelo, Gabriele, Abramo de la Bachelerie, or Abramo da Gualdo were common, far less that they were typical. I simply wish to point out that infanticide, rape, adultery, and sexual assault were exceptional and unusual aspects of the phenomenon—itself widespread—of sexual relations between Jews and Christians, and that the extent and frequency of these relations are only partly revealed by the archival material that has come to light, considerable though this is. It is a fact that cannot be ignored by anyone who wants to form an accurate picture of everyday relationships between Jews and Christians in late medieval Italy. Jewish documents in particular put the issue beyond doubt. When delegates of the Jewish communities of central Italy met in Forlì in 1418, one of the main topics on their agenda was the problem of sexual relationships between Jews and Christians.[15] These relationships, which often produced illegitimate children, threatened to weaken the fabric of Jewish society and undermine its moral integrity. The meeting proposed ways to curb the growth of such relationships, but where canonic prohibitions and city statutes had failed, it was unlikely that rabbinical interdicts would fare any better. It was everyday life—daily dealings with the surrounding Christian society of city, town, and village—which spurred the Jewish minority to try to find pragmatic solutions to the problem. Though these inevitably involved compromises, they offered potential long-term protection of Jewish religious identity in difficult circumstances.

In the long term a Jewish marriage was always the ideal, and the Jewish family steered its children in this direction firmly and unhesitatingly; it was a goal that concerned both the family and the entire community, and non-compliance was out of the question. A young man had to abandon youthful dreams and let himself be guided by the experience of those who had his future at heart. But in his sexual education—his first love affairs and so-called marriage apprenticeship—he was left to his own devices; in the view of many parents, there was nothing to prevent these encounters

---

[14] AV, Camera Apostolica, Registri del Ducato di Spoleto, Entrate e Uscite, 21, fo. 124ᵛ (15 Sept. 1322) and fo. 126ʳ (11 Oct. 1322); ibid. 22, fo. 136ʳ (13 Mar. 1323) and fo. 153ᵛ (6 Nov. 1323). See L. Fumi, 'I registri del Ducato di Spoleto', *Bollettino della Deputazione di Storia Patria per l'Umbria*, 4 (1898), 141, 144; ibid. 5 (1899), 142, 148; Ch. Reydellet-Guthinger, *L'Administration pontificale dans le Duché de Spolète* (Florence, 1975), 73.

[15] See L. Finkelstein, *Jewish Self-Government in the Middle Ages* (New York, 1964), 281–95.

taking place with his Christian counterparts, since Jewish society was in
no position to provide them.[16] As Roberto Zapperi has aptly observed, in
the urban world of the late Middle Ages, no social activity was conceiv-
able which did not assume some preliminary apprenticeship.[17] In the case
of marriage this was twofold, involving, first, procreation, where it was
considered essentially, though not exclusively, the man's role to take the
lead; and, second, running a household, which required initiative and
experience, both also regarded as male attributes.

The young man's first amorous experiments tended to be with the
serving-girl, the wet-nurse of his younger siblings, or the maidservant
(who, as we have seen, could also be his father's mistress), often under
the colluding eye of his parents, if not with their explicit approval.[18]
Often it was the young man's father who provided money for gaming,

[16] Solè, *Storia dell'amore*, 21, stresses that 'in the West, premarital relations, guaranteeing the future and later union and cementing the institution of marriage, were a
custom rather than a disruptive element, and certainly not a scandalous exception,
except in the eyes of priests'. Examining the decrees of the Jewish communities in the
Po valley of 1507, which attempted to put a brake on the customs, widespread among
Jewish girls, of frequenting public baths (where they had contact with young Christian
men of their own age) and of taking part in dances, scantily clad, Robert Bonfil won-
ders ingenuously 'whether these were practices which the rabbis hoped to extirpate,
or whether they wished only to express their alarm at the danger that Jewish girls
might be seduced by immoral behaviour in Christian society, opening up a breach in
the closed world of Jewish modesty'. ('Aspects of the Social and Spiritual Life of the
Jews in the Venetian Territories at the Beginning of the XVI Century' (Heb.), *Zion*,
41 (1976), 83, 95–6.) Later in the same article he appears less uncertain, maintaining
that 'the picture painted [by the decrees] presents allusions to the everyday life [of the
Jews], and to personal hygiene, which sometimes arouse the fleeting suspicion that
perhaps this physical cleanliness was accompanied by a certain uncleanness of spirit,
and all this in the context of conflict with the habits and customs of the surrounding
Christian society, and of the evident tension between two diametrically opposed tendencies: of being similar to that society yet distinct from it'. It is surprising that such
conclusions should have been reached precisely on the basis of documents which seem
to prove the contrary and where there is certainly no allusion, either implicit or explicit, to conflict between Jewish and Christian society in Italian Renaissance life as far as
manners and morals were concerned. The phenomenon of premarital relations
between young Jews and their Christian contemporaries is also played down by
Cassuto, who claims to be convinced 'that occasional youthful misdeeds did nothing
to impair the structure of the Jewish family, so justly famed' (*Ebrei a Firenze*, 29–30).
At all events, in 1580 the heads of the Jewish community in Padua once again felt
obliged severely to prohibit 'the boys of our community from going dancing with
those who do not belong to our religion . . . whether at dances in Jewish houses, or in
Christian ones' (see *Minutes-Book of the Council of the Jewish Community of Padua*, i.
117).
[17] See R. Zapperi, *The Pregnant Man* (London, 1991).
[18] The sexual apprenticeship of the young Jew did not differ much from that of his

wine, and girls; in the larger towns, recourse to prostitutes was also tolerated as a necessary enhancement of the young man's sexual education
and aid to his future choices.[19] His susceptibility to the dictates of the
heart or the pleasures of the flesh placed no real obstacle in the path of his
family's long-term plan to marry him off to a Jewish woman of good
family and in possession of a modest fortune.

DOWRIES AND DYNASTIC MARRIAGES

During the century of demographic growth (1450–1550), it seems that
the average marital age remained fairly stable, among Italian Jews as elsewhere. For men it was around 24 to 25, while for women it was around
20 to 21.[20] But if we look at marital age in the Jewish communities of
Umbria from the socio-economic viewpoint, we can see that there is an
inverse relationship between marital age and social status. In other
words, in the richer Jewish families we see a tendency to marry earlier,
while members of less well-off families tend to marry later. It is thus
possible to calculate that, for the rich, marriage took place generally
before the ages of 22 for men and 20 for women, while for the poor,
men usually married at around 26 to 27 and women at 22 to 23. So, for
example, in Spoleto in, 1469, the son of the banker Mosè da Camerino,

---

Christian contemporary (Solè, *Storia dell'amore*, 21–4; Rossiaud, *Medieval Prostitution*, 135–8).

[19] On brothels and prostitution in Perugia and Umbria see Fabretti, *La prostituzione in Perugia* and, more recently, A. Grohmann, *Città e territorio tra medioevo ed età moderna: Perugia, secc. XIII–XVI* (Perugia, 1981), ii. 313–28. During this period Jewish prostitutes plied their trade in various Italian cities, including Florence, Mantua, and Rome; see Simonsohn, *Jews in the Duchy of Mantua*, 543–4; Cassuto, *Ebrei a Firenze*, 229; A. Shulvass, *The Jews in the World of the Renaissance* (Leiden, 1973), 165. The 1526–7 census of the population of Rome reveals that, along with 1,500 Roman prostitutes, about thirty Jewish women were engaged in the world's oldest profession (see Esposito, 'Ebrei a Roma tra Quattro' e Cinquecento').

[20] On the average marital age in Italian and European society in the late Middle Ages see e.g. D. Herlihy, 'Vieillir au Quattrocento', *Annales ESC*, 24 (1969), 1338–52; D. Herlihy and Ch. Klapisch, *Tuscans and their Families* (London, 1985), 203–4; Rossiaud, *Medieval Prostitution*, 15; Ernst Hinrichs, *Alle origini dell'età moderna* (Bari, 1984), 3–20; M. Barbagli, *Sotto lo stesso tetto* (Bologna, 1984), 143–4. For Jewish society see Shulvass, *Jews in the World of the Renaissance*, 159–68; Luzzati, 'Storia degli ebrei italiani', 427–73; S. DellaPergola, *La trasformazione demografica della diaspora ebraica* (Turin, 1983), 174–83; R. Bachi and S. DellaPergola, 'Gli ebrei italiani nel quadro della demografia della diaspora', *Quaderni Storici*, 19/55 (1984), 155–91.

who had been left an orphan under the guardianship of his mother, was able to marry a rich girl from Fermo before he was even 20,[21] while Giacobbe di Vitale da Perugia, a house-painter and decorator by profession, married for the first time at the age of 32, in 1514. Giacobbe's wife, Gentile, who came from Castiglione Aretino, brought him a small dowry of 21 ducats, indicating the couple's low social status.[22] These are just two examples, but there is no doubt that they represent a general tendency.

Jewish society, divided like its Christian counterpart into classes, practised what Emmanuel Le Roy Ladurie, referring to the agrarian society of Occitania, has called 'class endogamy'. Young men married into their own circles, gravitating towards their own levels of wealth and prestige, and property was a key element in their choice of partner.[23] For the Italian Jewish male of the Middle Ages and Renaissance, marriage was therefore a business deal, a contract, which was carefully drawn up by the entire family, and whose conditions were studied in the minutest detail. Nothing was left to chance. After the choice of a Jewish bride whose social and economic status corresponded to the aspirations of the husband's family, amateur and professional middlemen, relatives, friends, and rabbis, who knew one or both parties, all closed in to bring the undertaking to a speedy and successful conclusion.[24] All parties realized that a great deal was at stake, from the future wealth and economic success of the family to its social position and role within the community. Linking two wealthy families through marriage was an extremely important form of investment, and, like all investments, it had its attendant risks. It could be the means of consolidating a fortune, since each of the two parties brought their capital to it in support of the marital union, which was thus doubly reinforced;[25] but it could also spell

21 AC Spoleto, Not., Ponziano di Giordano, 118, fos. 5ʳ, 15ᵛ; ibid., Not., Giovanni di Luca, 11, bundle B, fos. 116ʳ, 118ʳ, 126ʳ.

22 AS Perugia, Not., Pietro Paolo di Domenico, 571, fo. 117ʳ.

23 See E. Le Roy Ladurie, *Love, Death and Money in the Pays d'Oc* (London, 1982), 142.

24 Such aspirations are summarized in the will of the banker, Giacobbe di Elia di Francia (Perugia, 8 Dec. 1445): 'I urge that my daughter Ricca should marry a Jew, that he should be of good estate and should enjoy the approval of his parents and relatives' (AS Perugia, Not., Mariano di Luca di Nino, 114, fo. 105ᵛ).

25 On this subject see D. Herlihy, 'The Medieval Marriage Market', *Medieval and Renaissance Studies*, 7 (1976); G. Bruckner (ed.), *The Society of Renaissance Florence: A Documentary Study* (New York, 1977), 29–31; G. Huppert, *Les Bourgeois Gentilshommes* (London, 1977); Barbagli, *Sotto lo stesso tetto*, 144, 197–8; Ch. Klapisch-Zuber, *Women, Family and Ritual in Renaissance Italy* (Chicago, Ill., 1985).

his house for one year, until the day when the marriage was to be consummated.[29] In this case the woman's family was clearly using the expedient of keeping the other party committed for a fixed period, to give them time to assemble the agreed dowry.

If the dowry was very large and the couple's families of high social standing, the wedding ceremony had to be sufficiently lavish to impress the entire community, who would in all likelihood have followed the various phases of the negotiations and be acquainted with the assorted backstage manœuvrings. For instance, in Ferrara in the fifteenth and sixteenth centuries it was common practice for all the Jewish banks in the city to close their doors for the day as a sign of celebration when a banker had a wedding in his family.[30] On such occasions the *nouveaux riches* spared no expense in their imitation of the princely festivities common in Christian society, making great play of what they regarded as the distinctive elements of their own status: an elegant house, preferably turreted like those of the main nobles and merchants, jewels, fashionable clothing, elaborate weapons, and an impressive guest-list.[31] Often this eagerness to cut a figure went beyond the limits of good taste. The many sumptuary laws issued by the communes, either on their own account or under pressure from the preaching friars, proved blunt instruments. Linked as they were to contemporary social changes, these laws aimed to contain the aspirations of the newly rich, both Jewish and Christian, eager to outshine the old families with their displays of luxury, and sought unsuccessfully to uphold the existing social order by imposing a link between dress and festive customs and social position.[32] The Jewish communities had no more success than the Christians when they asked their members to adhere to these laws, and their repeated and often unenthusiastic attempts to humour city authorities and mendicant orders proved fruit-

[29] The betrothal of Giuditta di Salomone to Raffaele di Abramo da Imola was made official on 2 Jan. 1528 by Deodato, the woman's brother, and Salomone her father, handing a ring to her fiancé (AC Spoleto, Not., Simone Tigrini 146/1, fo. 30ʳ). The phenomenon of a husband putting off cohabitation with his wife until the entire dowry had been made over by her relatives was not uncommon in Italian society at this time; see S. Chojnacki, 'Dowries and Kinsmen in Early Renaissance Venice', *Journal of Interdisciplinary History*, 5 (1975), 571–600.

[30] See Y. Boksenboim (ed.), *Parashiot: Some Controversial Affairs of Renaissance Italian Jews* (Heb.) (Tel Aviv, 1986), 91.

[31] One chronicler reports, for instance, that in June 1542 the banker Bonaiuto da Modena, 'in giving a husband to his niece, opened his house to so many Christians and nobles, men and women, who gathered there in his honour, that they could not fit into the room' (see Balletti, *Gli ebrei e gli Estensi*, 138).

[32] See J. Le Goff, *Medieval Civilization* (Oxford, 1988), 358.

ruin for the husband's family if the wife's dowry outweighed the wealth contributed by her husband to their common estate or if their money was badly invested in the husband's business. Thus in the medium or long term an excessive dowry could be as much of a threat as a dowry put to unwise use. The burden of the restitution of the dowry hung like the sword of Damocles over the estate of a husband who died before his wife. Thus the warning given by Giovanni Morelli, at the beginning of the fifteenth century, in his book of family records, becomes understandable, if a little excessive: he advises against asking for too large a dowry from the wife's parents because 'no good ever came of a dowry; and should you have to return it, they will undo you'.[26] With this danger in mind the rabbis of Padua recommended, in the ordinances they issued in 1507, that the supplement traditionally added by the husband to the wife's dowry should not amount to more than 50 per cent of the value of the same, and that in any event dowry plus supplement should not exceed 150 ducats. The rabbis made this recommendation 'bearing in mind the future well-being of the children to be born of the couple', convinced that the possible restitution of an excessive dowry to the mother's family could lead to the complete economic ruin of the blameless children.[27]

An offer of marriage was usually solemnized by the husband's family by sending gifts and jewels to the fiancée and her family, either directly or through envoys specially appointed for the task. This amounted to a binding engagement, of whose importance both families were aware.[28] Commitment took a variety of forms, and was sometimes made official through notarial deeds. We have evidence of one of these agreements in Spoleto in 1528, where the girl's father and older brother handed over the engagement ring to the future husband, who bound himself to regard it as 'a sign of true and legitimate matrimony', though deferring cohabitation *more uxorio* with the bride until the moment when he received the whole dowry. For his part, the bride's brother undertook to keep her in

[26] Quoted in P. Cammarosano, 'Aspetti delle strutture familiari nelle città dell'Italia comunale: Secoli XII–XIV', in G.·Duby and J. Le Goff (eds.), *Famille et parenté dans l'Occident médiéval* (Paris, 1977), 113.

[27] See Bonfil, 'Aspects of Social and Spiritual Life', 71, 78–82, and its extensive bibliography.

[28] On marriage in Jewish law and the practices of the Jewish communities of the period, see e.g. V. Colorni, *Legge ebraica e leggi locali* (Milan, 1945), 182–3, and Cassuto, *Ebrei a Firenze*, 220–1. On marriage in the surrounding society see the summary by Sh. Shahar, *The Fourth Order: A History of Women in the Middle Ages* (Heb.) (Tel Aviv, 1983), 66–114, 159–64, 198–204.

less. At best, the richest Jewish families paid no heed to them; at worst, they openly derided them.

The sumptuary laws issued by the assembly of the Jewish communities of central Italy that met in Forlì in 1418 are surprisingly similar in form, and for the most part in content, to the so-called statutes of S. Bernardino of Siena, drawn up in Perugia in 1425.[33] As far as marriage celebrations were concerned, the representatives of the Jewish communities called for moderation and limitation within an acceptable framework, worried as they were about the consequences of any excessive and harmful exhibitionism:

We often witness nuptial banquets of brazen luxury, well exceeding the economic resources of those involved and indeed of the richest Christians who live in the society around us; and among many other things this entails quite unnecessary expenditure. We therefore decree that, from the end of the month of Siwan 5178 [June 1418] no Jew of our communities should be allowed to invite more than twenty men to a wedding banquet at one time, together with ten women and five girls, and that this number should include both local guests and those from elsewhere. Relatives, down to those of the third generation, may be invited without restriction. In cases when the bride comes to the wedding on horseback, we decree that she may be accompanied on her entry into the city by no more than ten horsemen and four men on foot. Should the woman arrive by boat, she may not be accompanied to the house where the wedding is to take place by more than twelve men and twelve women.[34]

In practice everything continued as before, and indeed, when the occasion arose, bankers and other city notables did not hesitate to incorporate precise clauses into their charters safeguarding their right to hold feasts and banquets as they pleased and without any restrictions. At Terni, for instance, the sumptuary laws known as the statutes of St James of the Marches were issued by the commune in 1443, following this Minorite's preaching in the town. Among other things, they placed severe restrictions on the opulence and ostentation publicly displayed by the richer citizens during family festivities and particularly at wedding

---

[33] The text of the sumptuary laws passed by the 1418 assembly is published in Finkelstein, *Jewish Self-Government*, 281–95; the text of the 1425 statutes of S. Bernardino of Siena can be found in A. Fantozzi, 'Documenta Perusina de S. Bernardino Senensi', *Archivum Franciscanum Historicum*, 15 (1922), 103–54, 406–75. On this subject see S. Majarelli and U. Nicolini, *Il Monte dei Poveri di Perugia: Periodo delle origini (1462–1474)* (Perugia, 1962), 108–29; Toaff, *Ebrei a Perugia*, 60–1.

[34] See Finkelstein, *Jewish Self-Government*, 286.

banquets.[35] These measures affected not only Christian society, but also the wealthier Jews, who promptly took action to thwart them, using reasoning that was sophistical, to say the least. In the negotiations preceding the signing of the charter between the commune and Jewish bankers of the town in 1456, the latter did not hesitate to refer to the precepts of the Jewish religion to support their own right to hold festivities and wedding feasts without any restriction whatsoever, whether of expense or number of guests: 'Given that the Jews are ruled by laws and customs different from those of the Christians in so far as the celebration of their marriages is concerned, they may receive gifts of any kind and value on the occasion of their weddings, and equally they may invite as many Jews to their wedding feasts as they shall wish, without restriction. And this shall apply notwithstanding the customs, uses, laws, and other statutes in force in the city.'[36] This clause was repeated in the charter granted to the Jews of Terni in the following years, for example that of 1474.[37]

Usually it was the bride's family which took responsibility for the expenses of the wedding reception and banquet. This was no mean undertaking when the couple belonged to the wealthier classes of the local Jewish community, whatever its size. However, the woman was safeguarded against the irreversible loss of money outlaid in this way by having it included in the supplementary part of the dowry she brought her husband. In all cases in which Jewish and civil law provided for the restitution of the dowry, this sum would be reimbursed by the husband or his heirs. In 1467, on the occasion of the marriage of Ventura, the son of Abramo da Bettona, the foremost banker in Perugia, to Stella di Vitale da Camerino, a member of one of the main families of Tuscan Jewry, the wedding expenses reached the sum of 30 ducats, or about half the average dowry of the time. Stella's dowry, obviously, was much larger: 300 ducats in ready money, plus a further 100 ducats in wedding-presents and trousseau items. Her family was careful to include the cost of the reception in the value of the dowry, which was officially registered

[35] The text of the statutes of St James of the Marches is examined in A. Ghinato, 'Apostolato religioso e sociale di S. Giacomo della Marca di Terni', *Archivum Franciscanum Historicum*, 49 (1956), 106–42, 352–90. See also id., *Vita religiosa nel Quattrocento italiano* (Rome, 1956), 21–37, 70–7.

[36] AS Terni, Rif., 499/I, fo. 185ᵛ (26 Dec. 1456).

[37] Ibid. 503/III, fo. 84ᵛ (30 Nov. 1474). See also A. Ghinato, *Studi e documenti intorno ai primitivi Monti di Pietà: I primordi del Monte di Pietà di Terni (1464–1489)* (Rome, 1959), ii. 109–39.

by a notarial deed.[38] The dowry which Ricca di Israel da Cittaducale brought in 1493 to Mosè di Angelo da Camerino, a rich banker from Foligno, amounted to 332 ducats. Apart from 200 ducats in ready money, it included a trousseau to the value of 55 ducats, and 30 ducats'-worth of wedding-presents brought by the bride and her family and acquaintances. The expenses of the wedding banquet, also included as a supplementary part of the bride's dowry, amounted to 27½ ducats, a considerable sum, and an indication that the festivities had been lavish.[39]

The marriage between the scions of two other important families of Italian bankers from Umbria and the Marches, Lazzaro di Consiglio da Macerata and Benvenuta di Angelo da Camerino, celebrated in Foligno in 1505, was no less magnificent. The woman brought a dowry of 355 ducats, which included 185 ducats in ready money, 115 in jewels and articles of clothing, and 25 ducats'-worth of wedding-presents. In this case too the expense of the wedding feast, 'in accordance with the customs and practices of the Jews', amounted to 30 ducats, and as usual this sum was registered as part of the overall value of the bride's dowry.[40] It may be said that in general, when marriages took place between members of the Italian Jewish financial élite, the expenses for the wedding banquet or reception (always magnificent, as befitted the couple's rank) amounted to around a tenth of the overall value of the woman's dowry. This same proportion, though naturally at lower values, remains constant in marriages between Jewish families of lesser rank and means. The reception for the wedding of Gentile da Corneto and Benedetto di Leone, a modest second-hand clothes dealer, which took place in Foligno in 1484, cost the bride's family only 4 florins. But the dowry that Gentile brought her husband was also modest, with an overall value of only 46 florins.[41] In 1479 Daniele di Abramo da Bevagna received a dowry of 100 florins from his wife Fiore, 78 in ready money and 22 in trousseau items. To this was added a further 7½ florins, the equivalent of the cost of the

---

[38] AS Perugia, Not., Simone di Giovanni di Giacomo, 303, fo. 14ᵛ (*confessio dotis* 13 Feb. 1467).

[39] AS Foligno, Not., Taddeo Angelelli, 12/3, fo. 600ᵛ (*confessio dotis* 15 Nov. 1493). The bride's father, Israel di Abramo da Cittaducale, had interests in numerous loan banks in the Marches (Ancona, Fabriano) and in Tuscany (Cortona), and was also involved in the dealings of the banks which the groom's father, Angelo di Musetto da Camerino, managed at Foligno, Todi, and Spoleto (AS Foligno, Not., Taddeo Angelelli, 9/10, fos. 251ʳ–252ᵛ (3 Nov. 1486); ibid., 17/II, fo. 21ʳ (18 Sept. 1488).

[40] AS Foligno, Not., Taddeo Angelelli, 21/9, fo. 13ʳ (*confessio dotis* 7 Feb. 1505).

[41] Ibid. 9/1, fo. 313ʳ (*confessio dotis* 16 Dec. 1484).

wedding reception.[42] This was a modest figure, but it made considerable inroads into the value of the dowry as a whole.

As we have seen, the dowry which the bride brought to her husband also included the bridal trousseau. Its value was appreciable in the case of the wealthier families, and often accounted for over a third of the overall value of the dowry. This is explained by the high cost of women's clothing, often more than 10 florins per garment. The trousseau included enough clothing to serve the woman's needs for many years to come, so that such expenses need not weigh upon the household; this trousseau also ensured that the bride would be able to appear in public in clothes befitting her station. The banker Abramo di Isacco da Bevagna, in his will of 1484, urged his heirs to return the dowry of 100 ducats to his wife, Ricca, after his death. Abramo had invested this sum in the affairs of the three banks he owned at Bevagna, Assisi, and Amelia, with a net profit of 16 per cent a year. Abramo also reminded his heirs that, as well as the ready cash, his widow was to inherit 'all the linen and wool clothing, the jewels, bracelets, and belts of all kinds kept in the said donna Ricca's trunk'. In the same will Abramo recorded the dowry he had given to his daughter Graziosa, on her marriage to a Jew from Assisi. Its value was estimated at 200 ducats, of which at least half took the form of jewels and trousseau items: 'linen and woollen clothing, rings and bracelets, bodices and belts, kept in a trunk belonging to donna Graziosa.'[43] In 1462 Fiorina, the daughter of Mosè da Terni, a Jew living in Spoleto, was promised in marriage to a young man from Foligno. The girl's mother, Stella, informed the fiancé's father that she had given her a dowry of 150 florins and a fitting trousseau. She reviewed the contents of the trousseau trunk before a notary with legitimate satisfaction: 'two everyday dresses for the bride's personal use, another garment and a cloak for feast days, this latter of the value of a good 10 florins, and lastly a chest of underwear and linen.' With ill-concealed maternal pride Stella concluded: 'I have done all this according to the Jewish custom, in keeping with the rank and conditions of the bride and as required by the usage and customs of the Jews of Rome.'[44]

The bride's family was thus expected to provide the husband with dowry, trousseau, and wedding-presents, and to pay for all the wedding festivities. The documents of the period tell us that presents

---

[42] AC Bevagna, Not., Bartolomeo di Gasparre (1521), fo. 330ʳ (*confessio dotis* 3 Nov. 1479).

[43] Ibid., Not., Gasparre di Angelo (1523), fos. 47ᵛ–49ᵛ (will of 7 Mar. 1484).

[44] AC Spoleto, Not., Giovanni di Luca, II, fo. 124ʳ (*costitutio dotis* 23 May 1462).

were generally handed over by the guests to the newly-weds 'on the day of the wedding itself, immediately after the breakfast and before the consummation of the marriage; they were placed on the tables where the banquet had taken place'.[45] For the rich, this was a heaven-sent opportunity for a public exhibition of their wealth, for reinforcing the family's prestige or acquiring a position in the leadership of the Jewish community, and for cutting a figure in the eyes of merchants, men of rank, and rulers. Often a sumptuous marriage and a rich dowry could put the seal on a tricky and hard-won piece of social climbing, which was thus fittingly celebrated in the marriage feast.

For the less well off, not to mention the poor, usage and custom were serious problems, arousing disappointment and anxiety from the very birth of each new daughter. Without the money for the dowry and other expenses, there was no hope that the girl might be properly married off, and the possibility that she might be forced to grow old in her father's house, caring for her parents until an advanced age, was extremely real.[46] We cannot gauge the effectiveness of the solution offered by the unattractive dowries scraped together by the charity of the rich (by will or otherwise) for poor girls of marriageable age. But there is reason to doubt its success in a society where every eligible man could claim a fitting portion from the woman who was to be his companion for life. Class endogamy, practised as zealously and scrupulously by the Jewish world as by the contemporary Christian one, aimed to maintain the existing social order at all costs, and brooked no exceptions to its rules. Thus the poor, who knew that they were going to have to marry their own kind, were obliged to use cunning expedients to keep up appearances. While they could not entirely avoid respecting established customs, with their often considerable expense, they could at least try to get off as lightly as possible. The commonest expedient was that of 'inter-linked alliances', as defined by Le Roy Ladurie, between members of two families, with dowry contracts entered into simultaneously.[47] This was a stratagem which, when cleverly and discreetly handled by the notary, made it possible to avoid any real exchange of money from one side to the other. For the poor, this meant it was possible to contract several marriages at once, without the contracting parties actually having to

[45] See Luzzati, *Storia degli ebrei italiani*, 446–7.

[46] Certain rabbis did express regret at this state of affairs, which meant that 'the daughters of the poor were obliged to remain unmarried until their hair turned white'; see Shulvass, *Jews in the World of the Renaissance*, 160.

[47] See Le Roy Ladurie, *Love, Death and Money in the Pays d'Oc*, 75.

produce the dowry money. For example, on 29 May 1466 dowry contracts were signed relating to three marriages between the children of a Jew from Perugia and those of a Jew from Macerata. Deodato di Mosè, a dancing-master by profession, his brother Giuseppe, and his sister Stella declared their intention to marry respectively Dolcefiore, Stella, and Cresce, the three children of the second-hand clothes dealer Mosè da Macerata. The dowry for each of the three marriages was identical, amounting to barely 60 florins, so any actual exchange of money between parties must in this case have been minimal, if not non-existent.[48]

Usually the dowry money was handed over by the bride's family to the husband's father for the latter to manage, investing it in all probability in a bank or some other commercial or mercantile enterprise, and becoming responsible for it to his daughter-in-law. The involvement of the husband's father, whose role as head of the family was undisputed, placed considerable restrictions on the independence of the new husband, though these were usually accepted with good grace, since they freed him from risk and responsibility. The income from the dowry thus invested was normally used to pay for part of the couple's household expenses; sometimes it was registered as the sole property of the woman, who could use it as she wished. When the dowry was handed over to the husband's family, the woman's father would occasionally add the condition that part of the interest on that money should be made available to him each year.[49]

A study of dowry contributions is an important index of the distribution of wealth among Jews during this period. Anna Esposito has shown that the dowries of the Jews of Rome in the fifteenth and sixteenth centuries could be anything between 20 and 200 florins, with average values varying from 76 to 100 florins.[50] These are modest figures in them-

[48] AS Perugia, Not., Simone di Giovanni di Giacomo, 295, fo. 15ʳ (*confessio dotis* 29 May 1466).

[49] On 14 Apr. 1472 Salomone da Tolentino promised his daughter Allegrezza in marriage to David da Bologna, a resident of Città di Castello. The fiancé pledged himself before a notary to pay his father-in-law part of the income from his wife's dowry every year (AC Città di Castello, Not., Angelo di Battista di Angelo, 5, fo. 33ᵛ).

[50] See A. Esposito, 'Gli ebrei a Roma nella seconda metà del Quattrocento attraverso i protocolli del notaio Giovanni Angelo Amati', in S. Boesch Gajano (ed.), *Aspetti e problemi della presenza ebraica nell'Italia centrale–settentrionale (secoli XIV e XV)* (Rome, 1983), 47–51, 81–5, 112–13, 117; id., 'Gli ebrei a Roma tra Quattro' e Cinquecento', 825–8. The largest dowry discovered by Esposito is one brought by Perna da Rieti to her husband, the well-known papal chief physician Bonet de Lattes, in 1501. It amounted to some 230 ducats, distributed as follows: 112 ducats in ready money; 88 ducats in jewels and trousseau items; with the rest given in the form of an

selves, and to some degree contrast with the images of luxury and wealth associated with the life of Italian Jews in the Middle Ages and Renaissance. But elsewhere in Italy, even in Jewish communities of Roman origin, there seems to be evidence of dowries with higher average values, although we still have no systematic study of the subject based on a quantitative investigation of the make-up of dowries detailed in the relevant archival material.[51] The conclusions put forward here refer to the Jewish communities of Umbria in the fifteenth and sixteenth centuries (a period during which their numbers rarely exceeded 500) and are based on a sample of 111 dowry agreements.[52] The are taken from the notarial archives of Perugia, Spoleto, Foligno, Terni, and Città di Castello, centres where Jews were relatively numerous and active, and from those of other communes where their presence was sporadic and less significant, such as Todi, Assisi, Bevagna, Spello, Bettona, and Trevi. This sample, which is undoubtedly representative, provides a telling picture of the wealth of the Jewish families of the area. First, it indicates a concentration of dowries into three main value-groups, each of which presents a homogeneous pattern. The first consists of 89 dowries, or 80 per cent of the total, which range from 0 to 300 florins, with average values of around 50 to 150 florins (51 dowries). The second consists of 19 dowries, or 17 per cent of the total, varying between 300 and 650 florins, with average values of around 500 florins (9 dowries).

---

orchard in Trastevere (see Esposito, 'Gli ebrei a Roma tra Quattro' e Cinquecento', 826). Even in minor centres in Latium it seems that the values of the dowries of Jewish girls were more or less equivalent to those of Jewish girls in Rome, varying between 80 and 150 florins. See e.g. M. T. Caciorgna, 'Presenza ebraica nel Lazio meridionale: Il caso di Sermoneta', in S. Boesch Gajano (ed.), *Aspetti e problemi della presenza ebraica nell'Italia centrale–settentionale (secoli XIV e XV)* (Rome, 1983), 155; A. Luzzatto and A. Tagliacozzo, 'Gli ebrei a Bagnoregio', *Archivio della Società Romana di Storia Patria*, 101 (1978), 221–309.

[51] The group of Florentine dowries in the period 1475–95 studied by Luzzati (with the obvious exception of that of Clemenza di Vitale da Pisa) all had a value of at least 100 florins, and in one case of 230 ducats (see Luzzati, 'Storia degli ebrei Italiani', 412, 448). The dowries of the Jewish women of Cesena between 1475 and 1490 seem to have been even higher, often amounting to over 200, and in some cases to as much as 300, florins; see M. G. Muzzarelli, *Ebrei e città d'Italia in età di transizione: Il caso di Cesena dal XIV al XVI secolo* (Bologna, 1984), 131–2, 143–4, 151, 155. In wealthy Jewish circles in Bologna at the beginning of the 16th cent. girls were generally provided with dowries of more than 500 florins; see R. Rinaldi, 'Un inventario di beni dell'anno 1503: Abramo Sforno e la sua attività di prestatore', *Il Carrobbio*, 9 (1983), 320–1.

[52] The documents concerning this sample, transcribed or summarized, appear in my *Jews in Umbria*, 3 vols. (Leiden and New York, 1993–4).

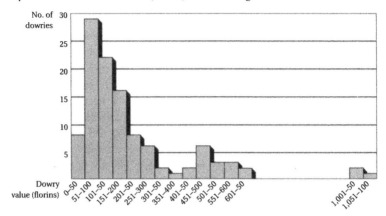

FIG. 1.1 Dowries of Jewish women in Umbria (14th–16th centuries)

Note: Total number of dowries = 111

The third consists of 3 dowries, or 3 per cent of the total, of between 1,000 and 1,100 florins, considerably more than even the immediately preceding group.

So, although it is true that for the most part the level of the dowries of Jews in Umbria did not differ much from those of the Jews of Rome, it is also the case that some 20 per cent of the total number of dowries had a higher value. This certainly indicates greater economic well-being among the Jews of Perugia and the other Umbrian centres than among those living in Rome, their city of origin, in the same period. But another fact emerges extremely clearly, namely the lack of economic uniformity in the Umbrian Jewish nucleus. Alongside a majority of families of limited or average means, which generally made do with dowries of around 100 florins, and rarely of more than 300, we have a notable and probably influential minority of rich Jews who could afford dowries with average values of around 500 florins.[53] These two groups form respectively 80 per cent and 16–18 per cent of the Jewish population. For obvious reasons these figures are inversely proportionate to the quantity of archival documentation that has come down to us concerning the two groups, and this has often misled historians into errors of interpretation. Thirdly, we have a small minority of Jews, made up of the richer and more influential bankers who were hand in glove with authority, who reveal

[53] Cassuto maintains that among the wealthier Jews of Florence the average dowry was around 500 florins (*Ebrei a Firenze*, 222). Luzzati agrees with this estimate ('Storia degli ebrei italiani', 442).

their status through dowries of 1,000 florins and over, on a level with the urban and rural nobility and with large merchants who had scaled the heights of the city social hierarchy. The dowry which Gentile da Bologna brought to Angelo di Musetto da Camerino, the chief Jewish banker of Foligno, in the latter part of the fifteenth century, for example, amounted to 1,000 florins,[54] and in 1514 Sarra, sister of the famous Daniele da Pisa and daughter of Isacco di Vitale, brought Abramo di Ventura, the chief banker of Perugia, a dowry of 1,100 florins.[55] These were considerable sums, which defined a family's rank not only within the Jewish community, but also in relation to the town nobility.

If it is perfectly clear that marriages were strictly dynastic among this small group of highly placed families, this is also true for the majority of the second group, the Jews of average means. The members of the family of Abramo di Ventura da Perugia chose their partners from among the main Italian Jewish banking families, such as the da Pisa and the da Camerino.[56] In the first half of the sixteenth century the children of the chief physician of Perugia, Laudadio de Blanis, married members of the da Montolmo family, bankers from the Marches who were also their business partners.[57] There are numerous examples of such marriages, confirming that wealthy families' matrimonial choices were always strategic affairs with clear-cut and inflexible implications.[58]

MARITAL CRISES AND MULTIPLE MARRIAGE

A young bride-to-be, a desirable dowry, and the prospect of dizzy and rapid social climbing were all formulas for attracting swindlers and

[54] AC Foligno, Not., Taddeo Angelelli, 17/II, fo. 21ʳ.

[55] AS Perugia, Not., Pietropaolo di Ludovico, 824, fo. 212ʳ (*confessio dotis* 27 Oct. 1514). Isacco da Pisa had promised each of his daughters a dowry of 730 'large gold ducats'; see Rinaldi, 'Un inventario di beni', 321. Clemenza, sister of Isacco di Vitale da Pisa and aunt to Sarra, had received a dowry of 800 florins from her father in 1480: 300 in ready money, 300 in trousseau items, 100 in wedding presents, and 100 in jewels; see Luzzati, 'Storia degli ebrei italiani', 442.

[56] AS Perugia, Not., Simone di Giovanni di Giacomo, 303, fo. 14ᵛ; ibid., Not., Pietropaolo di Ludovico, 824, fo. 212ʳ.

[57] AS Perugia, Not., Teseo di Antonio di Baldella, 964, fos. 205ʳ, 266ʳ; ibid., Not., Giovanni di Battista di Niccolò, 1159, fo. 202ᵛ; ibid., Not., Ludovico Arrighi, 987, fo. 164ʳ. On the activity of Laudadio de Blanis, originally from Orvieto, see H. Friedenwald, *The Jews and Medicine* (Baltimore, Md., 1944), i. 47–8, 342; Toaff, *Ebrei a Perugia*, 149, 161–3.

[58] See Poliakov, *Jewish Bankers and the Holy See*, 117–26; Luzzati, 'Storia degli ebrei italiani', 442–3; id., *La casa dell'ebreo* (Pisa, 1985), 257–9.

fortune-hunters with an eye to the main chance.[59] The wealthier Jewish
families mounted a merciless war—of defence and often of offence—
against unscrupulous and impoverished dowry-hunters. In such cases
marriages were doomed, even before being solemnized. The official
rabbinate, almost always allied with the richer families, did not hesitate
to issue severe prohibitions against those who might use matrimonial
manœuvrings to jeopardize social conventions and established interests.
In their attempt to prevent a girl from making a legitimate marriage
with someone who was not to the family's liking, the rabbis required the
presence of at least one of the parents at the ceremony. Alternatively they
might allow the religious ceremony to take place if attended by two of the
bride's relatives or ten Jews unrelated to the groom. The rabbinical ordinances of the Po valley communities in 1507 open with the melancholy
and worrying consideration that 'many evil-doers among our own people
use tricks and ruses to deceive women and join with them in marriage in
defiance of all the rules'.[60] To forestall such abuses, they issued a severe
prohibition against anyone daring to transgress the rules which required
the consent of the woman's family at the wedding celebrations. But the
malpractice was not so easily eradicated, partly because the object of the
deceit was less the innocent bride than the rich family to which she
belonged. The game often seemed well worthwhile to fraudulent suitors.
Again in June 1554 the rabbis of Padua, Mantua, Rome, Ferrara,
Bologna, and the other communities of Emilia and Romagna who met
at Ferrara, were obliged to order severe punishments to be inflicted on
'anyone having the effrontery to marry a girl without at least ten Jews
being present at the ceremony and without the consent of her father and
mother'.[61]

---

[59] See Solè, *Storia dell'amore*, 30–5.

[60] See Bonfil, 'Aspects of Social and Spiritual Life', 70, 75–8. For examples of
fraudulent marriage of this type between Italian Jews and Jews of German
origin in the duchy of Milan in the latter part of the Quattrocento see A. Antoniazzi
Villa, 'Aspetti e momenti della presenza ebraica nell'Italia settentrionale del basso
medioevo: I banchieri dei domini sforzeschi', in J. Shatzmiller (ed.), *Les Juifs dans la
Méditerranée médiéval et moderne*, proceedings of a conference held at Nice, 25–6 May
1983 (Nice, 1986), 66–7; id., 'Di un falso matrimonio: Note di vita ebraica nella
Lombardia quattrocentesca', *Studi di storia medievale e di diplomatica*, 9 (1987),
165–92; Simonsohn, *Jews in the Duchy of Milan*, ii. 856, document no. 2053. Efforts
to prevent marriages from being used to deceive the wife's family are also found
outside Italy, in ordinances passed by the Spanish Jewish communities in Valladolid
in 1432; see Finkelstein, *Jewish Self-Government*, 364–5; Y. Moreno Koch, 'The
Taqqanot of Valladolid of 1432', *The American Sephardi*, 9 (1978), 142–5.

[61] See Finkelstein, *Jewish Self-Government*, 302.

The opposition of the rich families, assailed in their strongholds by the Trojan horse of fraudulent marriage, and the harsh stance taken by the religious leaders in support of the interests of these families, were of little avail unless the bride's family was prepared to take the extreme measure of disinheriting her. The alternative was to dispute the religious validity of such marriages by asking the rabbis to regard them as null and void, but this had complex legal implications, and a successful outcome was far from assured.

In Perugia in May 1534 Rosa, an orphan and heiress of the rich banker Giacobbe da Montalcino, appointed her brother Raffaele as proxy so that he might set the conditions for her marriage with a young Jew, a certain Isacco da Note, who had asked for her hand.[62] The agreement between the two parties was drawn up in writing in Perugia that same month, in the presence of witnesses. Subsequently, as was customary among Jewish families, an envoy, the rabbi Mosè da Novara, was sent by the young man to visit the family of the young woman, who was spending her holidays that summer at Chianciano, to hand over gifts in his name. The girl's mother, Brunetta, received a gold chain with precious stones, presented to her by the rabbi by way of deposit. But in the mean time events had moved fast. Under pressure from her mother and brothers, Rosa would no longer hear of marrying Isacco da Note, claiming she did not feel committed by the gifts her fiancé had offered her. He, however, maintained that Rosa's promise of marriage must be regarded as sacrosanct after his gifts had been accepted. The Italian rabbinical authorities from both the large towns and the smaller communities were invited to offer their judgement on the controversy, which soon developed from a minor local matter into a national dispute. Among those who intervened in favour of the unsuccessful suitor were the famous Paduan rabbi, Meir Katzenellenbogen, who was related to Isacco da Note, and Azriel Diena, the rabbi of Sabbioneta. On her side, Rosa da Montalcino had a line-up of most of the rabbis from Rome, Umbria, and the Marches (whose links with the influential Perugia family were very close), with the rabbi of Ferrara, Mosè Nissim da Foligno, and the rabbi of Ancona, Mosè Basola, at their head. The thorny controversy was resolved by a compromise signed by the two parties in the summer of 1535 in the villa of rabbi

---

[62] The Montalcino family figures among the most important Jewish bankers of central Italy between the 15th and 16th cents. They were related to the Pisa family and were active not only in Perugia and other Umbrian towns, but also in Tuscany, where they enjoyed the protection of the Medici; see Cassuto, *Ebrei a Firenze*, 246–9; Luzzati, 'Storia degli ebrei italiani', 442–3.

Chananel Sforno outside Porta S. Mamolo at Bologna, in the presence of
two Umbrian rabbis, Mosè Norsa and Mosè Nissim da Foligno. On the
basis of this compromise Isacco da Note, who had been offered financial
compensation, declared his willingness to cease to regard the piece of
jewellery he had presented to his recalcitrant fiancée as a binding commitment to the marriage. The young man (with how much conviction we
do not know) stressed that he had reached such a conclusion because his
gifts had not been accepted by Rosa herself, but by her mother, who was
said to have acted without her knowledge.[63]

Twenty-five years later, a similar controversy with vast repercussions
throughout Italian Jewry had as its protagonist another Jew of Umbrian
origin, Venturozzo da Perugia, a young man from Città di Castello
without any clearly defined profession, but who led a wandering
life in the cities of central and northern Italy. A student at the University
of Pisa at the time, Venturozzo decided to settle down and contract a
marriage of convenience. He found a suitable wife in the person of
Tamara, daughter of Iseppo de Dattolis, a Venetian doctor, who had a
considerable dowry of 1,000 ducats, in ready money, jewellery, and
trousseau items. In 1560 Venturozzo and Tamara celebrated their
engagement in Venice, in the house of the bride's father and, following
the Italian custom, at his expense, though the family belonged to the
German community. But when the real marriage negotiations began and
the economic aspects of the union came under scrutiny, an immediate
and definitive break occurred between the parties, since Venturozzo's
requirements were found by Iseppo to be exorbitant and unacceptable.
At this point the husband-to-be, fearing for the success of his marriage
plan, asked for and obtained the consent of the rabbinical authorities that
the betrothal ceremony should be regarded as binding for the purposes of
the marriage and, as such, according to rabbinic law, requiring formal
divorce should the family wish to cancel the agreement. After many
delays, harassed and threatened by the girl's family, Venturozzo eventually consented to such a divorce. But the farce had scarcely begun, and
was destined to assume gigantic proportions, with the heated involvement of most of Italian Jewry: immediately after the divorce, Venturozzo

[63] On the matrimonial controversy between Rosa da Montalcino and Isacco da
Note, see M. Mortara, 'Notizie di alcune collezioni di consulti MSS di rabbini ital-
iani', *Mosè*, issued in instalments: 5 (1882) and 6 (1883), see pp. 53, 133–4, 191–3; M.
Steinschneider, *Hebräische Bibliographie* (1879), xix. 136; Toaff, *Ebrei a Perugia*,
134–5, 155–6. The documents concerning the controversy are published in full in
Boksenboim (ed.), *Parashiot*, 29–41, 234–345.

contested its validity, maintaining that his consent had been extracted by violence.

Under pressure from Iseppo's family, the rabbis of Venice decided to declare the divorce valid, as did many other Italian rabbis. But the thwarted husband-to-be battled on to obtain acceptance of his marital status, and soon the main spiritual leaders of Italian Jewry were dragged into the dispute. Excommunications and interdicts flew between the parties, to no avail.[64] Between the end of 1566 and the beginning of the following year the controversy reached its peak, with both factions publishing libellous statements concerning their adversaries. By now the tone of the conflict had degenerated, as it spilled out from the rabbinical courts on to the streets and piazzas, where the Jewish supporters of the two parties did not hesitate to come to blows, for instance in Mantua where the city authorities were obliged to intervene. At the same time Iseppo was indignantly trying to convince the leaders of the Venetian republic that his aspiring son-in-law, 'an iniquitous evil-doer, malevolent and conceited, who brings dishonour upon himself with his deceit, falsity and fraud', should be banished from the city.[65] Venturozzo, however, enjoyed the protection of Cosimo I, duke of Florence, who put in a good word for him with the duke of Mantua. Further incidents occurred among members of the Jewish population of Ferrara and in this case too the police authorities had to intervene. The Church voiced its judgement on the dispute through the cardinals of Bologna and Ferrara and the Venetian Inquisition. Towards the middle of 1567 the dispute died down as suddenly as it had begun, and we know neither how it ended, nor anything about its possible repercussions. Apart from the sensation and scandal they caused, the marital misadventures of Rosa da Montalcino and Venturozzo da Perugia are typical of the merciless struggle which wealthier Jewish families waged against 'social climbers', who recklessly used marriages of convenience to threaten the established order.

In general, however, in her planned progress from the paternal

[64] On the dispute concerning the betrothal of Venturozzo and Tamara see e.g. Sh. Simonsohn, 'The Scandal of the Tamari–Venturozzo Divorce', (Heb.), *Tarbiz*, 28 (1959), 375–92; id., *Jews in the Duchy of Mantua*, 501–4; E. Kupfer, 'Further Clarifications Concerning the Scandal of the Tamari–Venturozzo Divorce' (Heb.), *Tarbiz*, 38 (1969), 54–60; Toaff, *Ebrei a Perugia*, 135–6, 156.

[65] The proceedings of the court case brought by Iseppo against Venturozzo before the Holy Office in Venice in 1565 have been published in P. C. Ioly Zorattini, *Processi del S. Uffizio di Venezia contro ebrei e giudaizzanti*, ii. *1561–1570* (Florence, 1982), ii. 49–66.

home to that of her husband, the position of the fifteenth- or sixteenth-century Jewish woman appears to have been passive and submissive. It was her father or, in his absence, her elder brother, a rich relative, a guardian, or her widowed mother who took control during the various phases leading from engagement to marriage. After marriage, it was her husband who took on the role of her protector–master. As Claude Lévi-Strauss has observed, a woman is always given by a man to another man.[66] Jewish women, like their Christian contemporaries, were perpetual minors, often victims of a deep emotional void in their marriages. Therefore it should come as no surprise that they might wish to escape a dull and loveless life through separation, divorce, sometimes even through conversion, or simply by awaiting a longed-for widowhood. Even a pious, virtuous, and hard-working woman, like the model in Proverbs,[67] usually found only material and domestic satisfaction in marriage. For his part, particularly if he was a member of the wealthier classes, the Jewish husband of the time did not regard his companion as a lover, but rather as a partner to a contract. The legitimate wife, 'a creature enslaved to the hearth' according to Le Goff's definition, was valued essentially as a machine for producing sons, and treated accordingly.[68] The case of the merchant from Terni who, in his will of 1461, left his wife the marriage-bed, a mute witness to their love, is rare and rather moving.[69] In point of fact, notarial documentation does not reveal a particularly high divorce rate among the Jews of Umbria, though it does show that second and even third marriages of widowers and above all of widows, with or without children, were widespread.[70] In many

---

[66] *Structural Anthropology* (London, 1968), 61.

[67] Prov. 31: 10–31.

[68] See Le Goff, *Medieval Civilization*, 285–7; Cammarosano, 'Aspetti delle strutture familiari', 112–13; Solè, *Storia dell'amore*, 30–5, 45–6.

[69] AC Spoleto, Not., Giovanni di Luca, 8, fo. 210ʳ (1–8 Dec. 1461). On the importance of the double bed as a symbol of the matrimonial bond in the Middle Ages, see D. Roche, 'Un letto per due', in G. Duby (ed.), *L'amore e la sessualità* (Bari, 1986), 169–74.

[70] Looking at the notarial documents concerning the Jews of Umbria in the 15th and 16th cents. I have come upon only five cases of divorce: in Perugia (AS Perugia, Not., Tomaso di Antonio, 391, fo. 151ᵛ, 14 Dec. 1457 and ibid., Not., Giovanni Battista di Niccolò, 1160, fo. 1000ᵛ, 27 Aug. 1551); in Spoleto (AC Spoleto, Not., Giovanni Battista di Moscato, 111, fo. 296ʳ, 8 May 1510); in Bevagna in 1482 (see Esposito, 'Ebrei a Roma nella seconda metà del Quattrocento', 50); and in Città di Castello (AC Città di Castello, Not., Antonio Fidanzi, 19, fo. 14ᵛ, 27 Nov. 1505). This certainly represents only a small portion of the divorces occurring within the Umbrian Jewish community of the period and of those registered by notaries upon the restitution of the dowry, but equally certainly it is much lower than the average

cases, as we have seen, widowhood offered a woman her first opportunity to decide her financial and emotional future for herself. This was
a chance which few were disposed to let slip, even if the next marriage
and subtraction of the dowry from the first husband's inheritance
entailed considerable economic problems for the woman's children. The
case of the beautiful Brunetta da Sarnano of Perugia is probably somewhat unusual: within the space of a few years she exploited her dowry to
the full, marrying three times between 1547 and 1554, after having
buried two husbands.[71] But it was even more unusual for a widow not to
remarry fairly soon after her husband's death, even if she was no longer
young and had grown-up children.

There are naturally numerous references to matrimonial crises in
notarial documents, some of them with surprising outcomes. In 1510 the
beautiful Ricca, wife of Abramo, the elderly local doctor of Montolmo in
the territory of Macerata, finding married life with her unattractive husband unbearable, abandoned the conjugal home and returned to the
house of her father, Raffaele, at Spoleto. However, the young woman
could not bear to be parted from her trousseau, clothing, and jewels,
and arranged to take them with her. After a meeting between her father
and the indulgent husband in the presence of a notary, her sense of
responsibility once more prevailed and agreement was soon reached.
Raffaele returned his daughter to Abramo, together with her personal
possessions, while the parties agreed that 'if after one year Ricca shall persist in her refusal to live and have marital relations with maestro Abramo,
the latter shall be obliged to grant her a divorce in accordance with Jewish
law, and to return her dowry, which amounts to 200 florins'.[72]

But the epilogue to the matrimonial crisis between Ricca's brother,
Servadio, and his wife Eva, was tragic: the last of their innumerable
wrangles, in November 1508, ended with her murder. During the trial
Servadio defended himself before the governor of Spoleto, maintaining
that he had killed her unintentionally and without premeditation.
He subsequently admitted that he had murdered his wife 'because

---

registered for the time within the Jewish community of Nuremberg, where two-thirds
of married couples subsequently divorced; see J. Juval, 'Ordinances against the
Frequency of Divorce in Germany in the Fifteenth Century' (Heb.), *Zion*, 48 (1983),
175–215.

[71] AS Perugia, Not., Giovanni Battista di Niccolò, 1151, fo. 226ʳ (15 Mar. 1547);
ibid. 1163, fos. 274ʳ, 814ʳ (13 Apr. 1553, 4 Sept. 1554).

[72] AC Spoleto, Not., Giovanni Battista di Moscato, 111, fo. 296ʳ.

Eva continually struck and beat him'.[73] We do not know how much this revelation moved the judges, whether it rendered them understanding and lenient before wounded male pride, or convinced them that the legitimate family hierarchy, whose logic dictated that, at most, it should be the husband who struck the wife, had been seriously breached.[74] At all events Servadio was fined 300 florins, a considerable sum, and banished from Spoleto for a year. His daughter Pazienza was committed to the guardianship of her father's family and continued to live in her father's house in the town.[75] On his return there in the winter of 1510, Servadio decided to remarry, taking as his lawful wife Fiorentina, a woman from a modest family in Recanati, who brought him a small dowry of 60 florins. To sweeten the prospect of life with a wife-murderer, his father Raffaele decided to increase this by 172 florins,[76] a clause which had certainly been agreed upon in advance with the bride's father. For Raffaele this meant more than tripling the actual dowry which his daughter-in-law brought to his son, but it is doubtful whether it helped to make Fiorentina's first night in the bridal bed any less sleepless and troubled.

CONVERSION AND MARRIAGE

Baptism offered a Jewish woman the only possibility of realizing her dream of love with a Christian suitor. The dispersal of Italian Jews over countless small centres, and the kind of lives led by the wealthier families, facilitated meetings between young Jews and Christians. Sometimes such meetings developed in unexpected ways, and parental intervention came too late to prevent conversion and the subsequent 'mixed' marriage.[77] While the extent of the phenomenon should not be

---

[73] AS Spoleto, Not., Pietro di Giovanni, 91, fo. 264ᵛ.

[74] See Nigro, *Brache di San Griffone*, 153–6. Broadly speaking, medieval communal ordinances anticipated and tolerated husbands who beat their wives for disciplinary reasons. According to the 1371 statutes of Narni, for instance, husbands were allowed to beat wives provided the beating was not excessive and did not draw blood; see R. Ceroni, *Legislazione statutaria e condizione femminile a Narni nel basso Medio Evo* (Terni, 1983), 13. On attitudes to the apparently unusual phenomenon of the violent woman, see S. F. Matthew-Grieco, 'Mogli ribelli e mariti picchiati nel sec. XVI', in G. Duby (ed.), *L'amore e la sessualità* (Bari, 1986), 321–31.

[75] AC Spoleto, Not., Pietro di Giovanni, 93, fo. 60ʳ.

[76] Ibid., Not., Giovan Battista alias Moscato, 109, fo. 266ʳ (*confessio dotis* 27 Feb. 1510).

[77] See Shulvass, *Jews in the World of the Renaissance*, 164–5; Luzzati, 'Storia degli ebrei italiani', 427–73.

exaggerated, it is important to note that it was far from infrequent, as is confirmed by the notarial documentation. As Cassuto points out, the conversion of a Jew to Christianity did not release her family from the financial obligations imposed on them by civil law.[78] A Jewish woman who had herself baptized in order to marry a Christian could claim a fitting dowry from her father and other relatives, notwithstanding their more or less active opposition.[79] None the less, the attempts of the convert's relatives to evade this obligation were sometimes successful, and the woman was then forced to turn elsewhere to scrape together a dowry, in the absence of which the fiancé would probably take flight.

Morbidella, the young niece of Vitale, a doctor in Spoleto, converted in 1394 to marry a Christian man of her own age. Her family, who lived at Amelia, managed to wriggle out of their obligation to provide her with a dowry for a marriage of which they disapproved, and did not return to Spoleto. All that Morbidella (who in the mean time had taken on the eastern-sounding name of Salome) could do was to appeal to the commune of Spoleto to obtain the help that was indispensable to her marriage. Her plea did not go unheeded and a modest dowry of 100 *lire* was provided for her from the assets of the Ospedale di S. Croce on via Flaminia.[80] The example set by Morbidella–Salome was followed in 1416 by another Jewish woman from Spoleto, who converted to marry a young Christian from the same town. Here too the woman's family succeeded in denying her a dowry and the commune, again called upon to intervene, produced the sum of 50 florins for the newly converted bride from the assets of the Ospedale della Stella.[81] A century or so later, in 1528, a similar case occurred at Perugia. Verena, the daughter of the Jewish second-hand clothes dealer Lazzaro, was baptized in order to marry a Christian, and took on the name Laurenzia. Her family managed to prove that they were unable to give her a dowry, and the onerous task thus fell upon the unenthusiastic commune of Perugia, which acquitted itself by granting the new convert a miserable dowry of 21 florins, in the

[78] Cassuto, *Ebrei a Firenze*, 203.
[79] See e.g. the numerous cases quoted by Simonsohn concerning Parma and the duchy of Milan in the second half of the 15th cent., in 'Ebrei a Parma', 237–8; see also id., *Jews in the Duchy of Milan*, i. 228.
[80] AC Spoleto, Rif., 12, fo. 87ʳ (1 July 1394), fo. 96ʳ (24 July 1394), fo. 109ʳ (11 Nov. 1394). On the assistance provided by the *ospedali* of Spoleto for the newly converted, see L. Fausti, 'Degli antichi ospedali di Spoleto', *Atti dell' Accademia Spoletina*, 1 (1922), 59–111; S. Ceccaroni, *La storia millenaria degli ospedali della città e della diocesi di Spoleto* (Spoleto, 1978).
[81] AC Spoleto, Rif., 24, fo. 393ʳ (11 Oct. 1416).

form of a loan without interest, taken from the coffers of the Ospedale di S. Giacomo.[82] The case of Stella, the orphaned daughter of Isacco, a Jewish banker from Spoleto, 'aged over 22 years and less than 25', who converted to Christianity in 1472, was somewhat different. Here the woman, who claimed a dowry of 230 florins on the basis of a fateful promise made in her father's will, had her request fully satisfied by her brother. Thus she was able to marry her suitor Pierangelo Mattei, a nobleman from Spoleto, who had awaited the conclusion of this important affair with righteous impatience.[83]

It was not only marriageable girls who turned to the baptismal font in order to be able to marry Christians. Widows with children were not above resorting to this expedient, in order to cope with difficult circumstances, or brighten up their emotional lives, seeking a companion Jewish circles had failed to provide. Another Stella had been widowed by the death of Venturello, a Jew from Bevagna, with whom she had had two sons, both married, and one daughter, about to marry a Jew from Foligno. She had herself baptized in 1486 in order to marry a local Christian, and took the name Mariangela. She succeeded in persuading her sons to return the dowry of 50 florins which she had brought to her first husband.[84] The case of Ricca, daughter of Isacco, a doctor from Cremona, was more dramatic.[85] Ricca had married Mosè, son of Aleuccio da Pesaro, a banker from Spello, with whom she had had one daughter. After his death, she remained in the house of her father-in-law 'for whom she felt great love and deep affection', as we are told by a notarial document of 1449. Furthermore, Ricca agreed that the banker should continue to administer her large dowry of 400 Venetian ducats, with the stated condition that it was to go to her daughter Gentile when the girl found a husband.[86] But the situation changed dramatically one year later, when Ricca fell in love with Bartolomeo, a Christian merchant from Spello, and decided to marry him. She converted to Christianity, taking the name Giubilea, and had her daughter christened Francesca into the bargain. At this point the new convert demanded that her father-in-law

[82] AS Perugia, Not., Severo di Pietro, 464, fo. 201ᵛ (6 Apr. 1528).

[83] AC Spoleto, Not., Giovanni di Luca, 11, fo. 392ᵛ (*confessio dotis* 24 Jan. 1472).

[84] AC Bevagna, Not., Crescimbene di Pietro di Percivalle, 1539, fo. 44ᵛ (26 May 1486), fo. 56ʳ (18 Sept. 1486).

[85] The doctor Isacco di Salomone, Ricca's father, enjoyed the protection of Francesco Sforza and was seen as the leader of the Jewish community of Cremona towards the middle of the 15th cent.; see Simonsohn, *Jews in the Duchy of Milan*, i. 24–7, 50, 70, 78–9, 84, 105.

[86] AC Spello, Not., env. 3, Niccolò di Bartolomeo, 2, fo. 100. + 49ᵛ (15 Dec. 1449).

should return her dowry, which Aleuccio da Pesaro had long held invested in the affairs of his bank. Faced with resistance and delaying tactics, Ricca–Giubilea and Bartolomeo reacted by asking the Podestà of Spello, and Spinello Spini, a delegate of pope Nicholas V, to intervene. One winter evening in 1450 the police rushed into Aleuccio's bank, in the Mezzote district, and proceeded to seize money and objects up to the value of the dowry, whose restitution had been demanded by the widow and her new husband.[87] Poor Aleuccio never recovered from the blow. The enforced seizure of the very considerable sum threatened the affairs of his bank, and a few months later it was forced to close its doors for good.

[87] Ibid., Not., env. 6, Francesco Giovanni di Antonio, 1, fo. 29ʳ (16 Dec. 1450); ibid., Pascuccio di Giacomo di Tommaso di Alessio, 3, fo. 98ʳ (23 Dec. 1450).

2

Love of Life and Intimations of Mortality

CEMETERIES OUTSIDE THE CITY WALLS

WHENEVER a group of Jews settled in a new area, permission was immediately and urgently needed from the authorities for a space which they could use to bury their dead. Sometimes this simply meant reusing an area which had previously been a cemetery, as at Terni, where in the second half of the fifteenth century the Jews then living there received permission to use the land which had housed the cemetery of other Jews from Rome some 200 years earlier.[1] More often it entailed the *ex novo* allocation of a field where burials might take place in accordance with Jewish law but without creating unnecessary complications for the authorities, such as eye-catching funerals proceeding along the main streets of the town, in front of churches and monasteries. The need for a cemetery was problematic but unavoidable; it was brought to the attention of the municipal authorities by the Jews themselves, who included it in the clauses of the charters that regulated their presence and activity within a town, and which constituted a sort of legal and official contract between the two parties. Thus we find Jews' right to have their own cemetery recognized, for instance, in the clauses of the charters of Terni (1456 and 1474), Foligno (1445 and 1456), Todi (1481), and Amelia (1426, 1430, and 1445).[2] But even when such clauses were not explicit, it is clear that their underlying intentions were always put into effect.

The ground the authorities allotted Jews for their cemeteries, the

---

[1] The loan charter granted to the Jews of Terni on 26 Dec. 1456 states that 'the Jews had a cemetery in the city of Terni where they buried their dead, but it has fallen into ruin and disuse'; Ghinato, *Studi e documenti*, ii. 111. The cemetery had probably served a large group of Jews from Rome, who had worked in the city at the end of the 13th cent.: see Toaff, 'Commercio del denaro ed ebrei romani a Terni (1296–1299)', *Annuario di Studi Ebraici*, 10 (1984), 247–90.

[2] See Ghinato, *Studi e documenti*, ii. 111; A. Messini, *Le origini e i primordi del Monte di Pietà di Foligno (1463–1488)* (Foligno, 1940), 7–11; AC Foligno, Rif., 26, fos. 100ʳ–103ᵛ (27 July 1445); AC Amelia, Rif., 14, fo. 285ᵛ (12 Mar. 1426); ibid.,

sepulture dei giudei, was always *extra muros*, at the edge of the town or in open countryside. To reach it—the route was sometimes lengthy and hazardous—the funeral cortège had to request the opening of the city gates, both in the daytime and, more often, at night, when the solemn ceremony presented fewer organizational problems for the participants. At Perugia the cemetery was situated outside Porta S. Pietro, at a place called Vigiano; at Foligno it was in the Campo di Francalancia, outside the walls; at Assisi it was outside Porta Perlici; at Spello, in the countryside outside the town, at Scorpitolo. At Spoleto it was outside Porta S. Pietro, and at Città di Castello it was in the countryside beyond Porta S. Giacomo.[3] Thus, while Christians chose their last resting-place *intra muros*, in the churches or in their adjacent cemeteries, Jews were allotted peripheral burial-places, well out of town.[4] This physical separation of the dead in some sense highlighted the difference in status between 'established' Christian citizens and Jews, who were merely tolerated and granted temporary citizenship.

The cemetery ground was usually recorded in the land register in the name of the chief Jewish family of the town, the one which had the smoothest relations with the authorities.[5] At Assisi from the second half of the fourteenth century it was registered in the name of the physician Sabatuccio di Manuele da Roma; at Spoleto in 1479 in that of the banker Raphael di Isacco de Pomis. At Perugia at the beginning of the fifteenth century it was recorded by the Jewish community as being in the city's land register in the name of rabbi Salomone di Manuello, known as Pisano; at Rieti in the same period it appeared among the

---

Rif., 15, fo. 277ᵛ (7 Aug. 1430) and fo. 283ᵛ (15 Aug. 1430); ibid., Rif., 38, fo. 74ʳ (15 July 1445); AC Todi, Rif., 82, fo. 43ᵛ (28 Feb. 1481).

[3] See Toaff, *Ebrei a Perugia*, 38–9, 96; id., *The Jews in Medieval Assisi (1305–1487)* (Florence, 1979), 82; Messini, *Origini e i primordi del Monte di Pietà*, 9; D. Dorio, *Historia della famiglia Trinci* (Foligno, 1636), 25ᵛ; AC Spello, Not., env. 5, Pascuccio di Giacomo di Tommaso di Alessio, 4, fo. 241ʳ; AC Spoleto, Not., Moscato di Giovanni, 96, fo. 85ᵛ; AC Città di Castello, Not., Bartolomeo di Antonio di Giovanni Bovari, 16, fo. 47ᵛ.

[4] The custom of assigning Jews cemeteries *extra muros* was widespread throughout Italy. In 1387, for example, when Gian Galeazzo Visconti, Conte di Virtù, granted the Jews of Pavia their charter, he directed that their cemetery be situated 'extra civitatem (. . . quod eis detur cimiterium extra civitatem et sinagogam in civitate)'. See Simonsohn, *Jews in the Duchy of Milan*, i. 2.

[5] On the Jewish presence in the land registers of the Italian communes in the late Middle Ages, see the observations by R. Segre, 'La società ebraica nel tardo Medioevo', *Italia Judaica*, proceedings of the first international conference, held at Bari, 18–22 May 1981 (Rome, 1983), 244–5.

properties of the doctor and rabbi Mosè di Gaio.[6] Where there was no land register for Jews, as at Spello, the cemetery was recorded as being part of the property of an obliging Christian. In 1457 the physician Gaio di Sabatuccio da Assisi, acting in the name of the town's Jews, formally rented the cemetery ground for nine years to a Christian colleague, who entered it in the town's land register in his own name.[7] For their part, the Jews undertook to pay the taxes on this property on behalf of the Christian doctor. In 1451 at Città di Castello the Jewish cemetery was owned by the friary of S. Domenico. It was rented to the family of the banker Ventura Longo, and the contract was renewed annually. In 1469 the Jews of the town finally managed to buy the land from the friars and entered it in the land registry in the name of Elia, the son of Ventura Longo.[8] Sometimes the custom of registering cemetery land under the name of an individual presented problems of its own, as at Foligno, where the Jewish community had had it entered in the town register in the name of the family of the merchant Leone di Angelo ever since they had first settled there. When he converted to Christianity with his wife and daughter in 1511, taking the name Feliciano, the Jews of the town were presented with a problem, as their burial-ground now legally belonged to a Christian. But a compromise was soon found: Leone's daughter, Caterina, was engaged to marry a local nobleman, and needed a large dowry worthy of her husband's rank and expectations. Acting on behalf of the Jews of Foligno, the banker Angelo da Camerino made his own contribution to the new convert's finances by redeeming the cemetery for a considerable sum and entering it in his name in the town's land register.[9]

We have seen that one of the first religious requirements of each Jewish community, whatever its size, was its own cemetery; equally clearly, the cemetery boundary expanded and contracted in line with the community's growth or decline. Any crisis in that community had short-term repercussions on the cemetery, extending its perimeter or restricting new burials within the existing space. The case of Perugia, the largest and most important Jewish community in Umbria until the

---

[6] See Toaff, *Jews in Medieval Assisi*, 82, 197; id., *Ebrei a Perugia*, table VII; AC Spoleto, Not., Ponziano di Giordano, 33, fo. 99ʳ (9 Nov. 1479); AS Perugia, Not., Simone di Giovanni di Giacomo, 295, fo. 7ʳ (17 Dec. 1466).

[7] AC Spello, Not., env. 5, Pascuccio di Giacomo di Tommaso di Alessio, 4, fo. 241ʳ (25 Nov. 1457).

[8] AC Città di Castello, Not., Bartolomeo di Antonio di Giovanni Bovari, 3, fo. 47ᵛ (3 Nov. 1451); ibid., 16, fo. 47ᵛ (26 Oct. 1469).

[9] AC Foligno, Not., Taddeo Angelelli, 22/22, fo. 42ᵛ (22–3 Oct. 1511).

latter part of the fifteenth century, is typical. Here the Jewish presence is documented from the mid-thirteenth century, and the Jews had owned their cemetery land since they first settled there. As I have mentioned, it was situated at a place called Vigiano on the outskirts of town.[10] The cemetery was first extended at the end of the fourteenth century, in 1391, and again in 1394, when the community was at its largest and when for the first time the land appears registered in the community's name (*Universitas Judeorum in urbe Perusie commorantium*).[11] In 1413 the perimeter was further enlarged, when the community purchased some land that bordered the burial-ground from the well-known illuminator, Matteo di ser Cambio.

Matteo di ser Cambio conveys in perpetuity to Abramo di Musetto and Genatano di Angeletto, Jews from Perugia, present and acting for the community of Jews of the city of Perugia, a farmhouse and an orchard in front of the said farmhouse, whose walls border upon the enclosure of the Jews' cemetery, situated on the outskirts of Perugia, outside Porta San Pietro, at the place called Vigiano. In this orchard stand two trees, namely a fig tree and an olive tree. The cemetery walls run along two sides of the orchard, while the other two are bounded by the property of Matteo and a house with an olive press, also belonging to him.[12]

The cemetery was enlarged again in 1435 with the purchase, by the community, of a vineyard and an olive grove bordering on the tombs. Consiglio di Abramo da Gubbio, the Jews' representative, paid the owner the sum of 125 florins, granting him permission to cut down the numerous elms and oaks on the land for firewood for up to two years from the date of the purchase. As stated in the notarial deed, the land had been bought 'for the tombs needed by the Jews when they pass on from this world'.[13] One year later the enlarged cemetery ground was registered on behalf of the community in the name of Salomone di Manuello, known as Pisano, one of the most important Jews in the city.[14]

[10] See p. 37 above.
[11] AS Perugia, Not., Cola di Bartolino, 21, fo. 22ᵛ (14 May 1391); ibid., 17, fo. 231ᵛ (23 Dec. 1394). See A. Toaff, 'Documenti sulla storia degli ebrei a Perugia nei secoli XIII e XIV', *Michael*, 1 (1972), 319–20, 324–5.
[12] AS Perugia, Not., Nello di Nicoluccio, 10, fo. 68ʳ (25 Nov. 1413). See also W. Bombe, 'Dokumente und Regesten zur Geschichte der Peruginer Miniaturmalerei', *Repertorium für Kunstwissenschaft*, 33 (1910), 114; Toaff, *Ebrei a Perugia*, 88–9, 119–20.
[13] AS Perugia, Not., Mariano di Luca di Nino, 110, fo. 85ᵛ (1 July 1435).
[14] AS Perugia, Catasto Antico, group 1, book 31, fo. 199ʳ.

After 1463, with the founding of the Monte di Pietà,[15] intensified anti-Jewish preaching by the Franciscans, and other restrictive and repressive measures, the community went into irreversible decline. Many Perugian Jews emigrated to more welcoming parts; others converted to Christianity, using baptism to help them escape doubts, quandaries, and difficulties which were now felt to be intolerable. Only a few Jews remained, and these tended to be the less well off.[16] The documents speak tellingly of them as the 'survivors of the former Jews who had lived and resided in the city of Perugia in the past'.[17] The fate of the cemetery outside Porta S. Pietro mirrors this crisis all too clearly. In 1484 the Jews rented a piece of land adjoining the cemetery to a peasant, feeling that they no longer needed it for the burial of their dead in view of the decline in the size of their community. The only conditions were that the peasant should allow funeral processions to pass freely across his land, and that 'he should not prevent the Jews from having access to the tombs of their dead'.[18] Meanwhile an unfriendly presence was looming: the new convent of the nuns of the Holy Trinity, later known as the Beata Colomba da Perugia (Blessed Colomba of Perugia), with its various properties. The first controversy arose in 1487: the pretext was a small boundary ditch which had skirted the Jewish tombs from time immemorial and which the nuns now claimed was a threat to their property when the water level rose during the winter months.[19] Many subsequent disagreements were to arise concerning what the documents now referred to as 'il sotterratoio de li Giudei' (the burial-place of the Jews) between the remaining Jews and the combative sisters. Finally, in 1567, the last Jews of Perugia decided to sell the still-unused portion of the burial-ground to the convent for a price of 132 *scudi*.[20] At around the same time another part of the ground was sold to the noble Perugian family of Vincioli for 80 *scudi*.[21] Later, even the area containing the

---

[15] The Monte di Pietà was a non-profit-making institution run at the public expense and obtaining other funds through pawnbroking for the benefit of the poor. It was founded by the Franciscans to replace Jewish moneylending, seen by them as usury.

[16] Toaff, *Ebrei a Perugia*, 78–9; Majarelli and Nicolini, *Monte dei Poveri di Perugia*, 80.

[17] AS Perugia, Not., Rinaldo di Bartolomeo, 565, fo. 278ʳ.

[18] Ibid., Not., Tancio di Niccolò di Tancio, 387, fo. 23ᵛ (12 Feb. 1484).

[19] Ibid., Not., Francesco di Giacomo, 218, fo. 506ʳ (25 Aug. 1487).

[20] Archive of the Collegio del Cambio, Perugia, div. I, various papers, sect. I, judicial acts, catalogue 5, enclosed in env. 140, fo. 8ʳ. See Toaff, *Ebrei a Perugia*, 305–6.

[21] AS Perugia, Not., Francesco Patrizi, 1361, fo. 378ʳ. On 25 May 1569, shortly

tombs, with their headstones and inscriptions, was swallowed up by the convent, becoming a victim of its tentacle-like development. But by then the cemetery was untended and deserted, overrun with weeds and brushwood. Its fate could not but reflect that of the Jewish community as a whole, which it had served for over three centuries, until both vanished.

WILLS AS PASSPORTS TO THE NEXT WORLD

A will was not only a private legal deed settling the inheritance of property; it was also a religious act through which the believer expressed his desire to be buried in the Jewish cemetery, acknowledged his sins, and redeemed them through appropriate bequests. As Philippe Ariès observes, from the late Middle Ages until the pre-industrial era wills consisted of two equally important parts—the pious clauses and the apportioning of the inheritance—and these followed one another in a set order. Yet on closer inspection, it is clear that the notarial clauses were far from fixed, being instead varied and flexible and revealing the thoughts and sensibilities of the notary's clients in all their individuality.[22]

Ariès' general point applies equally to the Italian Jews, an apparently

---

before their expulsion from the city, the Jews of Perugia sold a farmhouse they owned at the perimeter of their burial-ground (AS Perugia, Not., Francesco Patrizi (1365), fo. 415ʳ). The sale of cemeteries by the Jewish communities shortly before their expulsion from the Papal State was a widespread phenomenon. For example, on 20 Apr. 1569 the Jews of Fano sold a private individual 'the cemetery where the bodies of the Jews are buried, situated outside the walls and bordering upon the property of the monastery of S. Salvatore'. The new owner agreed not to plough or cultivate the area of ground where the tombs were, and to use it solely for harvesting hay; see D. Diotallevi, 'Ultimi momenti della presenza ebraica a Fano', *Fano*, 1/1 (1978), 85–96.

[22] See Ariès, *The Hour of our Death* (Harmondsworth, 1983), 196. The importance of the detailed analysis of wills—uniform and quantifiable as they are—as a source for the study of collective mentalities and sensibilities, is demonstrated in the excellent study by M. Vovelle, *Piété baroque et déchristianisation: Attitudes provençales devant la mort* (Paris, 1973). See also the interesting notes by G. Bois on the subject, 'Marxisme et nouvelle histoire', in J. Le Goff (ed.), *La Nouvelle Histoire* (Paris, 1978), and O. Amore, 'L'apporto degli atti privati alla conoscenza della società mediovale', *Studi Romani*, 28 (1980), 467–9. But we should also bear in mind the reservations put forward recently in this context by Tenenti, who regards wills as 'quite inadequate documents for the proper study of the manifold forms of the sense of death, since in a way they form not a series, but a mere mass'; see A. Tenenti, *Il senso della morte e l'amore della vita nel Rinascimento* (Turin, 1957), pp. xxv–xxvi.

uniform group, who frequently made use of Christian notaries.[23] A Jewish will, like a Christian one, began with a general, stereotyped profession of faith, stressing the soul's pre-eminence over the body and commending it to the mercy of God, but none the less asking that the body too should be accorded a certain amount of attention and given burial in the Jewish cemetery. 'First he commends his soul to almighty God; then he directs that his body should be buried in the customary place, outside Porta S. Pietro at Spoleto'; 'First she commends her soul to almighty God; then she directs that her body should be buried in the customary place where the Jews are buried at Spoleto' (testators: Mosè di Aleuccio da Terni and his mother Stella in 1500). 'First she commends her soul to almighty God and wishes her body to be buried in the cemetery with the other Jews' (Benvenuta di Giacobbe, a woman of Sardinian origin, at Perugia in 1546). 'He commends his soul to almighty God and directs that his body be buried outside Porta S. Pietro in the city of Spoleto, in the customary burial-place of the Jews, because he wishes his body to be buried there' (the banker Abramo di Bonaiuto, at Spoleto in 1524). 'First they direct that their bodies be buried in the customary burial-place of the Jews' (donna Rosa di Manuele da Pisa and her husband Elia di Mosè da Padova, at Perugia in 1487). 'Before all else he enjoins that his body should be laid to rest in the countryside outside Perugia, in that place which people call Piscille, where the other Jews are

---

[23] Jewish law allows recourse to Christian notaries for the drafting of wills, and this custom was apparently widespread among Italian Jews in the 14th–16th cents. (see Colorni, *Legge ebraica*, 213–21). One will, originally drafted in Latin before a Christian notary, is quoted in a Hebrew translation, faithfully reproducing the stereotyped formulas we have already encountered in a ritual request addressed to rabbi Jacob Diena (the responsum is dated Reggio Emilia, 14 Mar. 1550). Here, fearing that his sons might squander their inheritance through inexperience or mutual envy, the testator names his wife sole heir and usufructuary of all his goods. See Y. Boksenboim (ed.), *Responsa Mattanot ba-adam* (Tel Aviv, 1983), 442–5. On this subject see also Colorni, *Legge ebraica*, 220. The study of Jewish wills is still in its infancy and has so far considered only apparently less problematic periods, such as the 17th and 18th cents. See A. Milano, *Il Ghetto di Roma* (Rome, 1964), 363–84; C. Roth, 'Will and Bequests of a Woman of Verona in 1642' (Heb.), *Zion*, 2 (1937), 125–36; C. Boccato, 'Testamenti di israeliti nel fondo del notaio veneziano Pietro Bracchi seniore (secolo XVII)', *La Rassegna Mensile di Israel*, 42 (1976), 281–95; G. Nahon, 'Pour une approche des attitudes devant la mort au XVIIIème siècle: Sermonnaires et testateurs juifs portugais à Bayonne', *Revue des études juives*, 86 (1977), 3–123; P. C. Ioly Zorattini, 'Il testamento di Caliman Belgrado', *East and Maghreb*, 5 (1986), pp. vii–xxix. Typical examples of medieval Christian wills are to be found in A. Sapori, *Studi di storia economica* (Florence, 1962), i. 117–26, ii. 965–71.

customarily buried, that is, outside the walls of the city of Perugia' (the merchant Abramo di Isacco, at Bevagna in 1484). In 1494 the rich banker Ventura di Abramo was less specific as to his last resting-place. Perhaps his frequent changes of abode, for professional reasons, had prevented him from becoming sentimentally attached to any particular cemetery or family tomb in his city: 'First he directs that his body be buried in the Jewish cemetery of whichever city or region fate shall decree that the said Ventura should come to die in.'[24] The last wills of the most pious among the faithful expressed their desire to be buried wearing the *mortaglia* (*takhrikhim*), the special garments prescribed by Jewish law for the covering of the dead. Such a desire was expressed by the Frenchman, Giacobbe di maestro Elia, who lived at Perugia and Assisi, in his will of 1445, where the stereotyped formulas read like a translation from an original in Hebrew: 'Thanks be to almighty God, who gave the law unto Moses on mount Sinai . . . first he commends his soul to almighty God and asks that his body be clothed, at the moment of death, in the special garments prescribed by the Jewish rite and, thus clothed, that it should be taken to the place where the Jews of Perugia are buried.'[25]

The choice of burial-place is followed by the pious bequests, distribution of alms, and charitable foundations, which make up the real heart of the will. The imperishable blessings of the world to come were clearly thought to be more readily attainable for the believer who was generous with his wealth to the advantage of the poor and dispossessed. In order to obtain what Jacques Le Goff calls the 'passport to heaven', the testator asked God to secure eternal peace for his soul, paying tax and insurance in worldly coinage through pious bequests.[26] These also ensured that their beneficiaries would continue to pray and intercede for the soul of the deceased, helping it negotiate any possible rough patches on the

---

[24] AC Spoleto, Not., Moscato di Giovanni, 96, fo. 53ʳ (21 July 1500); ibid., fo. 84ᵛ (18 Dec. 1500); AS Perugia, Not., Giovanni Battista di Niccolò, 1149, fo. 232ᵛ (20 Mar. 1546); AC Spoleto, Not., Piergiovanni Ficeni, 206/IV, fo. 89ᵛ (1 Dec. 1524); AS Perugia, Not., Francesco di Jacopo, 226, fo. 284ᵛ (19 Oct. 1487); AC Bevagna, Not., Gaspare di Angelo, 1523, fo. 47ᵛ (7 Mar. 1484); AS Perugia, Not., Francesco di Jacopo, 226, fo. 398ʳ (2 May 1492). The same formula are repeated elsewhere, with slight variants. The doctor Amadio di Bonaventura da Castro began his will (Bagnoreggio, 1550) with the formula: 'since the soul is more noble than the body . . . he entrusts it to almighty God and commends it to the heavenly paradise'; see A. Luzzatto and A. Tagliacozzo, 'Gli ebrei a Bagnoregio', 257–8.

[25] AS Perugia, Not., Marino di Luca di Nino, 114, fo. 105ʳ (8 Dec. 1445).

[26] See Le Goff, *Medieval Civilization*.

way to Gan Eden, the earthly paradise. The main, though not sole, beneficiaries of these pious bequests were the synagogues, to which the believer would leave varying sums of money to renovate, restore, and adorn the place of worship, purchase holy ornaments (sometimes donated directly by the testator), and, above all, provide the lamps with oil. The constant mention of oil for synagogue lamps (*shemen lamaor*) betrays the believer's concern for his own soul, symbolically associated with the oil-lamps lit in the synagogues on his behalf. The more lamps there were, it was believed, the easier the soul's access to the undying joys of the next world.

The will of the banker Mosè di Abramo da Terni (Spoleto, 1461) is meticulous on this subject, and unintentionally informative concerning the synagogues of the Papal State and the duchy of Spoleto and Umbria in the mid-fifteenth century.[27]

Mosè di Abramo, a Jew from Terni living in Spoleto, sound of mind and memory through the grace of God, yet sick in body, fearing an impending death and aware of the condition of human frailty, not wishing to die intestate, in order that no scandal arise after his death concerning the property he leaves behind or because of it, here makes his will in the following form and enjoins and directs as follows: first, that when he shall come to die in Spoleto, his body shall be buried at Valiano in the Jewish cemetery, according to the Jewish rite. Furthermore, in accordance with the Jewish custom, he leaves a florin for his tomb. For the love of God, he leaves a florin to be distributed among the poor of Spoleto. He leaves a florin for the purchase of the oil which shall burn in the lamps of the synagogue of the Jews of Spoleto. He leaves a florin for the purchase of the oil which shall burn in the lamps of the synagogue of the Jews of Perugia. He leaves half a florin for the purchase of the oil which shall burn in the lamps of the synagogues of the Jews of Todi and another half florin to be distributed among the poor of Todi: one florin in all. He leaves a florin for the purchase of the oil that shall burn in the lamps of the synagogue of the Jews of Terni. He leaves half a florin for the purchase of the oil that shall burn in the lamps of the synagogue of the Jews of Rieti and another half florin to be distributed among the poor of that city: one florin in all. He leaves half a florin for the purchase of the oil that shall burn in the lamps of the synagogue of the Jews of Foligno and another half florin to be distributed among the poor of Foligno: one florin in all. He leaves half a florin for the purchase of the oil that shall burn in the synagogue of the Jews of l'Aquila and another half florin to be

---

[27] AC Spoleto, Not., Giovanni di Luca, 8, fo. 210ʳ (1–8 Dec. 1461).

distributed among the poor of that city: one florin in all. He leaves a florin to
purchase the oil that shall burn in the synagogue of the Jews of Rome.[28]

In her will of 1457 Ora di Giuseppe, a wealthy Spanish Jewess living
in Perugia in an elegant palazzo in the district of Porta S.

Angelo,
remembered not only the two synagogues of the Jews of Perugia, to
which she left valuable holy ornaments and oil to burn perpetually in
their lamps, but was also concerned for the prayers for her soul, religious services on the anniversary of her death, and special ceremonies in
the synagogues and cemetery.[29] Relatives, the poor, all the beneficiaries
of her generous bequests must forgather to ease her soul's entry into the
realm of the beyond, praying that her sins may be forgiven by almighty
God. The testatrix

enjoins firstly that her body be buried in the place where the Jews are buried
on the outskirts of Perugia . . . for the salvation of her soul, of that of her
deceased husband Isacco, and of Aleuccio, her present husband, in accordance with the Jewish law, she bequeaths to the synagogues of the Jews of
Perugia a holy book, containing the law of Moses, bound in white damask
and lined with blue linen. Equally she bequeaths to them a cloth of taffeta
and blue silk, with gold brocade embroidery with images of birds and faces,
with letters of silver and fringes of various colours; two small silver chains to
hold the synagogue lamps in accordance with Jewish custom; two silk tablecloths striped with gold, of which one is beautiful and in fine condition, the
other threadbare and torn; a covered seat for seating in the said synagogues
. . . she enjoins that, for the salvation of her soul and the expiation of her
sins, the sum of 100 florins should be distributed among the poor Jews of
Perugia, at a rate of 40 *bolognini* per florin . . . 50 florins shall be distributed

[28] The custom of making pious bequests to synagogues was extremely common in
the wills of the Jews of Rome in the 15th and early 16th cents., and here there do not
seem to be differences between local Jews and those from the Iberian peninsula, since
they all leave various sums for the purchase of holy ornaments, and above all for oil
for the synagogue lamps. See e.g. the wills of Emanuele di Salomone da Velletri
(1467), Perna di Salomone (1472), Mosè Abenaym (1501), Salomone Spagnolo
(1507), and many other Italian Jews living in Rome (see Esposito, 'Ebrei a Roma
nella seconda metà del Quattrocento', 104–7, 114; id., 'Ebrei a Roma tra Quattro' e
Cinquecento', 819). In the Papal State and central Italy in general, whose cities had
been 'colonized' by Jews of Roman origin, pious bequests to synagogues often appear
in Jewish wills, e.g. in those of Anna di Signoretto (Sermoneta, 1446) who, after
leaving a sum for her own tomb, made several bequests in favour of the synagogues
of Sermoneta and Rome (see Caciorgna, 'Presenza ebraica', 164), and of Salomone di
Aleuccio da Bertinoro (Cesena, 1473), who set aside sums for the purchase of oil for
the lamps of Cesena synagogue (see Muzzarelli, *Ebrei e città d'Italia*, 154).
[29] See Majarelli and Nicolini, *Monte dei Poveri di Perugia*, 218–22.

on the first anniversary of her death, of which 2 florins shall be used for the setting of her tomb on the day of the anniversary of her burial, and a further 10 florins shall be deposited in the poor-boxes in the synagogues . . . she enjoins that 3 *modiolini* of oil shall be purchased for each synagogue and distributed among the said synagogues to be burned in the lamps there, and that Giuseppe, her nephew, shall recite the office for the soul of the testatrix, as though she were his mother. She enjoins that a further 50 florins shall be invested by her nephew Giuseppe and her husband Aleuccio and that the interest on this sum shall be divided by the same among the poor Jews of Perugia.

The return on the capital which Ora bequeathed to her beneficiaries, the poor of the Jewish community, ensured the future celebration of the synagogue offices for the salvation of her soul. Here we have the beginning of a sort of perpetual cycle which, for Christian wills, Philippe Ariès describes as the 'cycle of endowment masses'.[30] Having no sons or brothers to recite the *kaddish*, the special Jewish religious doxology prescribed for the first year following a death and on anniversaries, the testatrix commits the task to her nephew, 'as though she were his mother', compensating him amply by making him sole heir to her *gemilut ḥasadim* estate.[31] The *gemilut ḥasadim*, a pious confraternity much spoken of in documents from the fifteenth century onwards, makes an indirect appearance in this will with the mention of certain almsboxes for offerings for the poor, which the testatrix mentions as being in the synagogues of the Jews of Perugia.[32]

In her will of 1450, Letizia di Guglielmo da Montefalco entrusts her heirs with the task of drawing 75 florins from her estate and investing them at 8 per cent interest. Each year, on the anniversary of her death,

---

[30] See *The Hour of our Death*, 179; Vovelle, *Piété baroque*, 119.

[31] In her will of 1501 another Jewess of Spanish origin, Setti, the widow of Giuseppe da Siviglia, living in Rome, pledged her heirs 'scrupulously to perform all the ceremonies prescribed by the ritual, concerning both the tomb and the synagogue services for the salvation of her soul' (see Esposito, 'Ebrei a Roma tra Quattro' e Cinquecento', 819).

[32] In his will the doctor and rabbi Mosè da Rieti left a sum for alms to be deposited 'in the Jewish poor-box of the town of Rieti': AS Perugia, Not., Simone di Giovanni di Giacomo, 295, fo. 7ʳ (17 Dec. 1466). On the activities of the pious Roman confraternity *gemilut ḥasadim* in the 16th cent. see Toaff, *The Roman Ghetto in the Sixteenth Century: Ethnic Conflicts and Socioeconomic Problems* (Heb.) (Ramat Gan, 1984). See also A. Farine, 'Charity and Study Societies in Europe of the Sixteenth to Eighteenth Centuries', *Jewish Quarterly Review*, NS 64 (1973–4), 16–47; D. B. Ruderman, 'The Founding of a Gemilut Hasadim Society in Ferrara in 1515', *Association of Jewish Studies Review*, 1 (1976), 234–58.

this interest 'shall be spent, for the love of God, upon the salvation of the soul of the said Letizia'. Fifty years later Letizia's descendants were still zealously attending to the salvation of her soul, distributing alms to the poor of Perugia on the anniversary of her death.[33] In a will made in Perugia in 1445 a banker from Assisi enjoined 'that for the salvation of his soul, for the love of almighty God and in expiation of his sins, 25 florins should be distributed among the poor'. In his will of 1420 another Jew from Assisi directed his heirs 'to dispose of and distribute his goods for charity, as they think fit, for the love of God'.[34] In his will of 1475 Gaio, son of the well-known Mosè da Rieti, a doctor in Narni like his father, duly made pious bequests to the Jewish cemetery, the poor and, of course, for the oil for the synagogue lamps, without which the soul of the testator seems to have been in some jeopardy.[35]

First, since the soul is worthier than the body, he commends his soul to almighty God and enjoins that for the grace of God and for the salvation of his soul, the sum of 10 florins shall be distributed among penurious Jews. Furthermore such money shall serve for repairs needed by the Jewish cemetery and for purchasing the oil for the synagogue lamps, in accordance with the Jewish custom. Should his heirs wish to give further alms for the salvation of his soul, this is a matter for their own consciences.

Other believers left sums for the restoration or rebuilding of synagogues, as did a second-hand clothes dealer from Perugia in 1558, while in her will of 1546 Benvenuta, a woman living in the same city, directed that '12 *scudi* should be used, for the love of God, for the restoration and rebuilding of the synagogue of the Jews living in Perugia'.[36] Abramo di Isacco, a merchant from Bevagna, directed in his will of 1484 that '5 florins from the property of the testator, at the rate of 50 *bolognini* per florin, should be spent for the benefit of the Jewish cemetery of Perugia, in whatever form his heirs shall deem fit', adding that '25 florins shall be spent from his estate, to be distributed in charity, as his heirs consider

---

[33] AS Perugia, Not., Francesco di Jacopo, 226, fo. 398ʳ.

[34] Ibid., Not., Mariano di Luca di Nino, 114, fo. 105ʳ (will of Giacobbe di Elia di Francia); Toaff, *Jews in Medieval Assisi*, 205–6 (will of Aleuccio di Salomone da Roma).

[35] AC Spoleto, Not., Antonio di Pietro, 142, fo. 24ʳ (Narni, 5 June 1475). On the doctor Mosè di Gaio da Rieti and his family see R. Sassi, 'Un famoso medico ebreo a Fabriano nel secolo XV', *Studia Picena*, 6 (1931), 113–20; Toaff, *Ebrei a Perugia*, 82–7, and its extensive bibliography, esp. p. 116.

[36] AS Perugia, Not., Simonetto di Eusebio, 1122, fo. 296ʳ (will of David di Gaio, 21 Oct. 1558); ibid., Not., Giovanni Battista di Niccolò, 1149, fo. 232ʳ (will of Benvenuta di Giacobbe di Sardegna, 20 Mar. 1546).

appropriate'. In his will of 1492 Ventura di Abramo, a banker from Perugia, duly mentioned the cemetery where he was to be buried, ordering that 'the sum of 25 florins should be left for the benefit of the cemetery where the body of the testator shall be buried'.[37] In his will of 1471 the banker Aleuccio di Guglielmo da Perugia directed that his elegant house in the district of S. Angelo, acquired for a sum of over 200 florins, should be turned into a synagogue after his death and used for worship by the Jews of the city.[38] In such cases, as André Vauchez remarks, the rich had a clear advantage in ensuring their salvation, able as they were to finance others to pray for them and thus building up continual merit before God with donations, pious works, and alms. Far from being a curse, wealth offered a distinct advantage in obtaining the eternal blessings of the next world. The weapons of the poor, such as they were, were far less effective.[39]

Other favoured beneficiaries of testators on the point of death were poor girls of marriageable age, who benefited from many pious contributions to the settlement of their dowries.[40] Ventura di Abramo's will directed 'that the sum of 50 ducats should be distributed, for the love of God, in favour of Jewish girls of marriageable age, in the following way: within one year of the day of the death of the testator, twenty-five poor Jewish girls of marriageable age should receive a subsidy of 2 ducats for their dowry'. At the end of his will this same Jew recommended that upon the death of his son, whom he had named sole heir, a third of his entire inheritance should be made over to the benefit of Jewish girls of marriageable age.[41] The will of a Jew from Foligno, made in 1488, is also significant in this context.

by the grace of almighty God being sound in mind, sense and intellect, in possession of a good and perfect memory, even if sick in body, facing impending death, which comes unknown to all and which none can foresee;

[37] AC Bevagna, Gaspare di Angelo, 1523, fo. 47ᵛ (Bevagna, 7 Mar. 1484); AS Perugia, Not., Francesco di Jacopo, 226, fo. 398ʳ (Perugia, 2 May 1492).

[38] AS Perugia, Giudiziario, Processus, env. 215, file 3.

[39] See A. Vauchez, 'Richesse spirituelle et matérielle du Moyen Âge', *Annales ESC*, 25 (1970), 1566–73.

[40] See Esposito, 'Ebrei a Roma nella seconda metà del Quattrocento', 104–7 (will of Emanuele di Salomone da Velletri, 1467), 107–8 (will of Daniele da Cori, 1467); id., 'Ebrei a Roma tra Quattro' e Cinquecento', 819 (will of Salomone Spagnolo, 1507); Muzzarelli, *Ebrei e città d'Italia*, 154 (will of Salomone di Aleuccio da Bertinoro, 1475).

[41] AS Perugia, Not., Francesco di Jacopo, 226, fo. 398ʳ (will of Ventura di Abramo, Perugia, 2 May 1492).

and given that nothing is more certain than death and nothing less certain than its hour, and hence it is written 'be vigilant, for you know neither the day nor the hour', not wishing to die intestate . . . [the testator] leaves 20 *soldi* for the salvation of his soul . . . and 40 florins at the rate of 50 *baiocchi* per florin, for the wife of the testator to distribute among the synagogues of the Jews, poor girls of marriageable age, and poor and destitute Jews.[42]

In many wills believers made bequests both in favour of girls to whom they were actually linked by ties of blood (nieces, cousins) and to more general acquaintances (servants, or the daughters of employees or bank workers). In one case in Perugia in 1445, the testator made his daughter's dowry conditional upon the fact that she should find a Jewish husband of 'good standing', whose choice would be approved by a committee of four trustworthy figures known to him, presided over by a rabbi.[43]

But it was not just religious confraternities, poor girls of marriageable age, synagogues, and cemeteries, all linked in some way or other to the microcosm of the Jewish community, which benefited from the pious bequests of Jewish testators. In his will of 1439 the doctor Gaio di Sabato da Assisi, a resident of Spello, made a bequest in favour of the town's hospital, to which he had been professionally linked for years.[44] In 1399 Angelo di Vitale, a Jew from Perugia, made a bequest in favour of the hospital of the confraternity of the flagellants of S. Maria Annunziata at Porta Eburnea, to provide new sheets and blankets for the

[42] AC Foligno, Not. Taddeo Angelelli, 17/II, fo. 21ʳ (18 Sept. 1488); ibid. 17/III, fo. 17ᵛ (22 Nov. 1493): wills of Angelo di Musetto da Camerino. In his *Sermo peroptimus de morte*, referring to the plague epidemic of 1464 in which many people had died throughout Italy and in Ferrara in particular, fra Roberto Caracciolo da Lecce (1425–95) addressed a similar exhortation to his readers: 'Et ideo clamo: vigilate, vigilate quia nescitis diem neque horam mortis . . .' [And therefore I proclaim: be vigilant, for you know neither the day nor the hour of your death . . .] (see Tenenti, *Il senso della morte*, 61).

[43] AS Perugia, Not., Mariano di Luca di Nino, 114, fo. 105ʳ (will of Giacobbe di Elia di Francia, 8 Dec. 1445).

[44] AC Spello, Not., env. 4, Bartolomeo di Domenico, 1, fo. 238ʳ (1 July 1439). In his will of 1467 the Roman Jew Emanuele di Salomone da Velletri, among other bequests, also left money to a hospital; but this was the Jewish hospital where the testator himself was lying ill (see Esposito, 'Ebrei a Roma nella seconda metà del Quattrocento', 104–7). The Roman banker Manuele di Genatano remembered his native city while living in Rimini: his will of 1392 contains two bequests, one 'to shore up the coast at Rimini, the city where he is living', and the other 'for the restoration of the walls of Rome, his native city': see H. Vogelstein and P. Rieger, *Geschichte der Juden in Rom* (Berlin, 1896), i. 319; P. Norsa, *Una famiglia di banchieri: La famiglia Norsa (1350–1950)* (Naples, 1953), 4.

patients.[45] And Angelo di Musetto da Camerino, the chief Jewish banker of Foligno, actually made a bequest to the Monte di Pietà, even though its creation might well have spelled his ruin.[46] Here, unless we attribute to him a sense of humour which did not desert him even on his deathbed, we must assume that in some cases Jewish believers felt it politic to balance their pious bequests to the charitable institutions of the Jewish world with others favouring their Christian equivalents. This was a wise strategy, which was to bear fruit later, when relations between the Jewish minority and the Christian majority were under strain. In some cases it amounted to a prudent life assurance for children and grandchildren.[47] Remembering the municipal authorities of Bevagna in his will, the merchant Abramo di Isacco openly states as much: 'I leave the sum of 10 florins to the municipality of Bevagna, at a rate of 40 *bolognini* per florin, to be spent for the purchase of two silver vases to be presented to the said municipality in its honour and for its use. I make this bequest mindful of the many kindnesses which I the testator have received from the municipality of Bevagna, and in the hope that such kindnesses may be repeated in the future and passed on to my children after my death.'[48] Abramo da Bevagna had played an open hand, but to little avail. Some months after his death his sons were arrested on charges of having crucified a local Christian child: after a difficult trial they were sentenced to a heavy fine and banished from Bevagna.[49]

The will was also a statement of the believer's awareness of himself and his own destiny, of his ability to distribute or redistribute the wealth he had accumulated as he wished and to decide the financial fate of the members of his family. At the moment his soul was about to leave his body for the dreaded journey to the next world, he kept his eyes lowered firmly upon the earth. His love of life and his desire for immortality could be fully expressed through the clauses of his will.[50] Whatever their importance, the objects of which he was fond had a place in his last wishes, which were sometimes described with a meticulousness which

[45] AS Perugia, Not., Jacopo di Buto, 45, fo. 133ᵛ (20 Dec. 1399).

[46] AC Foligno, Not., Taddeo Angelelli, 17/II, fo. 21ʳ (18 Sept. 1488); ibid. 17/III, fo. 17ᵛ (22 Nov. 1493).

[47] This may perhaps explain the bequest in favour of the town's bishop found in the will (1550) of doctor Amadio di Bonaventura da Castro, living in Bagnoregio. Alternatively it might have been a donation obligatory in all wills, both Jewish and Christian; see Luzzatto and Tagliacozzo, 'Ebrei a Bagnoregio', 257–8.

[48] AC Bevagna, Not., Gaspare di Angelo, 1523, fo. 47ᵛ (7 Mar. 1484).

[49] See Ch. 6.   [50] See Ariès, *The Hour of our Death*, 131.

astounds modern readers. These 'museums of everyday life'—another of Philippe Ariès' expressions—reveal the powerful hold that earthly life exerted upon the testator. Nor was there mention only of houses and landed property, of businesses and valuables. I have already mentioned the Jew from Terni who directed that his bed should go to his wife: 'To Stella, my wife, I leave the bed belonging to me the testator, the very one in which I am lying, complete with all that belongs to it and adorns it, namely its mattress, a feather bed, two large down bolsters, the seven pillows that are on it, two pairs of sheets and three blankets and bedcovers.'[51] In 1457 a woman from Perugia left her nephew a chest containing 'linen and woollen clothing and silk fabric'.[52] In 1461 the same Abramo da Terni enjoined that his wife should have two trunks, 'one Venetian and the other similar to those which the spinsters of Spoleto use for their trousseaux, with everything which is in them, on the death of the same'.[53] Particular mention is made in many wills of the books of prayers for the Jewish festivals (*machazor*), or of the bible which the testator had always taken to service in the synagogue. Often these were gifts, richly bound in leather or silver, which their wives had brought them on their wedding-day. 'I leave my son Mosè a book written in Hebrew characters on parchment, which contains the Jewish liturgical office for the whole year, a volume which is bound with wooden boards covered with leather and with silver bosses.'[54] 'I leave my nephew Mosè the book of the Bible, for everyday perusal, together with two volumes which comment upon the biblical text.'[55]

Male children generally inherited the greater part of their father's estate, while the girls had to make do with the sum left them as dowry, unless they had no brothers, in which case the will would be in their

[51] AC Spoleto, Not., Giovanni di Luca, 8, fo. 210ʳ (will of Mosè di Abramo da Terni, 1–8 Dec. 1461). In her will of 1472 Stella di Salomone from Rome left her 'down-filled bed' to her son Lodovico, and Emanuele di Salomone da Velletri (1467) gave his sister a double bed; see Esposito, 'Ebrei a Roma nella seconda metà del Quattrocento', 104–7, 114. On the importance of the double bed in popular urban culture see D. Roche, 'Un letto per due' in G. Duby (ed.), *L'amore e la sessualità* (Bari, 1986), 169–74.

[52] See Majarelli and Nicolini, *Monte dei Poveri di Perugia*, 218–22 (will of Ora di Spagna, 10 July 1457).

[53] AC Spoleto, Not., Giovanni di Luca, 8, fo. 210ʳ (will of Mosè di Abramo da Terni, 1–8 Dec. 1461). [54] Ibid.

[55] Ibid., Not., Antonio di Pietro, 142, fo. 24ʳ (Narni, 5 June 1475). In her will of 1472 Stella di Salomone, living in Rome, directed that a certain sum should be used to pay the salary of her nephew's tutor (see Esposito, 'Ebrei a Roma nella seconda metà del Quattrocento', 114).

favour. The testator often addressed himself to his children, forbidding
them to divide up the inheritance they had received until a specified
number of years had elapsed, his will being dictated by the concern
that the property built up over so many years of struggle should not be
dispersed or squandered through lack of foresight. Similarly, if the
children were minors (i.e. under 25), the testator's wife was made administrator or usufructuary of the estate going to his heirs, but on condition
that she should not remarry or that she should lead a chaste and honest
life.[56] As I have mentioned, a widow would frequently remarry shortly
after the death of her first husband, asking the heirs to return her dowry,
which she intended to use for a second time. If the dowry was large, this
might create a very considerable imbalance in the estate left by the testator to his heirs and affect their economic activity, which was often linked
to the bank where the money was invested. It is therefore understandable
that the enjoyment of the property he left his wife, and indeed the very
possibility that she might continue to live in his house, should be made
conditional upon a clear commitment on her part not to remarry.[57] In his
will the banker Abramo di Bonaiuto directed that his wife Stella should
be the usufructuary of his property 'as long as she lives chastely and
decently and retains her widowed state, but if she remarries she may not
remain in the house of the testator'. Not satisfied with this, Abramo
appointed two delegates, in the persons of his two brothers, to supervise
Stella's conduct and to ascertain that this clause was being scrupulously
observed.[58] The house–family–business unit, what Ernst Hinrichs calls
the 'house as aggregate', which had been the fulcrum of the testator's
earthly commitment and the measure of his success in this world, was not

---

[56] AS Perugia, Not., Mariano di Luca di Nino, 114, fo. 105^r (will of Giacobbe di
maestro Elia di Francia, 8 Dec. 1445); AC Spoleto, Not., Giovanni di Luca, 8, fo.
210^r (will of Mosè di Abramo da Terni, 1–8 Dec. 1461); ibid, Not., Moscato di
Giovanni, 96, fo. 84^v (will of Stella di Manuele, 18 Dec. 1500); AC Spello, Not., env.
4, Bartolomeo di Domenico, 1, fo. 238^r (will of Gaio di Sabatuccio da Assisi, 1 July
1439); ibid., Not., env. 3, Niccolò di Bartolomeo, 2, fo. 100^v (will of Mosè di Aleuccio
da Pesaro, 15 Dec. 1449); Toaff, *Jews in Medieval Assisi*, 204–5 (will of Abramo di
Musetto da Camerino, Assisi, 4 Sept. 1412).

[57] The picture presented by Christian wills of the period is not very different,
since here too the obligation to repay the dowry weighed heavily upon the estate of
the husband who died before his wife. Thus between the 14th and 16th cents., in
Italian merchants' domestic registers, information concerning marriages contracted
by members of the family is always accompanied by a specification of the exact
amount of the dowries, since relations of debit and credit are hereby implied; see
Cammarosano, 'Aspetti delle strutture familiari', 112–13.

[58] AC Spoleto, Not., Piergiovanni Ficeni, 206/IV, fo. 89^v (1 Dec. 1524). In the
wills of the Jews of Rome we find the same concern that the widow might remarry,

to be undermined at any price.[59] Similarly Angelo di Musetto da Camerino, a banker at Foligno, in his will of 1488, asked his wife and sons to continue to support the agents of the branches of their banks at Todi and Spoleto after his death, since they had served the family of the testator honestly and faithfully for many years.[60]

Although Jewish law gave precedence to the first son, directing that his portion of the inheritance should be twice that of his brothers, few wills in fact respected this rule. In general, in Jewish wills as in Christian ones, all male children were given an equal share in their father's inheritance.[61] Often even the conversion to Christianity of one of the heirs, or of the testator himself, does not seem to have brought about significant changes in the clauses, either to the detriment of the converts or of those members of the family who had remained Jewish. Concern for the unity of the family property, and an awareness of the need to keep it intact at all costs, were far stronger than resentment towards anyone choosing a different religious path, or persisting in his own when everyone else had abandoned it. Whether Jew or convert, the testator was aware that to behave any differently would serve only to add insult to injury and possibly lead to the economic ruin of his family, to which he continued

subtracting the dowry from the estate. In 1470, for instance, Elia Rosso named his wife usufructuary of all his goods 'as long as she shall continue to lead a chaste life, without other men, and shall not remarry' (see Esposito, 'Ebrei a Roma nella seconda metà del Quattrocento', 108–10). But actually in this context things were much the same the world over. E. Power recalls how William, earl of Pembroke, concluded his will of 1469 with this warning to his wife: 'and wyfe, ye remember your promise to me to take the ordere of wydowhood, as you may be the better mastre of your owne to performe my wylle' (*Medieval People* (London, 1946), 58).

[59] See Hinrichs, *Einführung in die Geschichte der frühen Neuzeit* (Munich, 1980), 25–6; J. Heers, *L'Occident aux XIVᵉᵐᵉet XVᵉᵐᵉ siècles: Aspects économiques et sociaux* (Paris, 1963), 256. These families were large and powerful; they included all the collateral kinsmen, had a joint estate, and often continued to give house-room to young couples after marriage: an extended family which enriched itself through a play of alliances and associations of all kinds.

[60] AC Foligno, Not., Taddeo Angelelli, 17/II, fo. 21ʳ (18 Sept. 1488); ibid. 17/III, fo. 17ᵛ (22 Nov. 1493).

[61] See Colorni, *Legge ebraica*, 213–14. In the many Jewish wills I have come across, I have found only two cases (both in the same family) where the first-born's share was greater than that of the other children. The wills are those of the doctor Gaio di Mosè, drafted at Narni in 1475 (AC Spoleto, Not., Antonio di Pietro, 142, fo. 24ʳ) and his father, the famous doctor and rabbi Mosè da Rieti, who died in 1460 (AS Perugia, Not., Simone di Giovanni di Giacomo, 295, fo. 7ʳ). On 17 Dec. 1466 the court of arbitration of the Jews of Perugia stated that 'in the inheritance of the said maestro Moisè . . . maestro Gaio might have a double share of everything because he was the first-born of the said maestro Moisè'.

to belong and whose fate continued to be dear to his heart. In his will of 1467, after having made several bequests in favour of the poor of the Jewish community in Rome, Mosè di Daniele da Cori named his son Filippo, who had converted to Christianity, heir to his estate.[62] Events at Bevagna in 1486 were even more telling. Stella, the widow of Venturello di Mosè, decided to have herself baptized and, probably with the intention of remarrying a Christian, claimed the restitution of her dowry from her sons, who had remained Jewish. But some months later she gave over much of this sum, duly received, to settle the dowry of her daughter Gentile, who had not converted and was marrying a Jew from Foligno.[63] The anomalies in these attitudes are purely superficial and seem to be quite separate from the often bitter and hurtful religious clashes that undoubtedly accompanied them: here what was all-important was the need to preserve the family patrimony intact at all costs.[64]

FRAUGHT FUNERALS, 'WIDOWS' WEEDS', AND ENFORCED MOURNING

The Jewish funeral was often quite an adventure. The strange procession accompanying the coffin beyond the walls of the city, intoning dirges so unlike those of Christian funerals, attracted general curiosity, not to say spite and irritation.[65] These processions sometimes aroused

[62] See Esposito, 'Ebrei a Roma nella seconda metà del Quattrocento', 107–8.

[63] AC Bevagna, Not., Crescimbene di Pietro di Percivalle, 1539, fo. 44ᵛ (26 May 1486); ibid., fo. 56ʳ (18 Sept. 1486).

[64] One interesting case is that of Salomone da Turano, a Jewish doctor from Bagnoregio, who converted to Christianity, taking the name Giovanni Luigi. In his will as a convert (27 Dec. 1557) he named his daughter Maddalena, who had been baptized along with him, as his sole heir. This did not prevent his wife, Laura, who had not converted, from being named usufructuary of his possessions until her death. He also left a bequest of 50 *scudi* to his sister Lea, who was marrying Salomone da Montolmo, a rabbi from the Marches. Equally surprising is the will's final clause: should his daughter Maddalena die without issue, half the testator's goods were to go to the Convent of S. Agostino at Bagnoregio, while the other half was to go to his brother Samuele, who had not converted (see Luzzatto and Tagliacozzo, 'Ebrei a Bagnoregio', 274–5). But there were also cases of evident ill feeling on the part of Jewish testators towards those heirs who had become Christian. Such ill feeling almost always gave rise to long and wasteful legal wrangles (see Simonsohn, 'Ebrei a Parma', 236–7).

[65] Leaving Città di Castello on his way to the Holy Land, the famous rabbi Obadiah (Servadio di Abramo) da Bertinoro spent several months in Sicily in the

people's most aggressive instincts, and on such occasions the Jews, for whom a funeral was a rare occasion to appear in public in relatively large numbers to celebrate a distinctive religious ceremony, became the target not only of insults, obscenities, and boorish comments, but of vicious and even fatal stonings. In Rome, even as recently as the end of the nineteenth century, it was not unusual for a Jewish funeral to be attacked by toughs, and for the participants to be beaten and injured.[66] In the fifteenth century the municipal authorities had devised various measures to avoid possible disputes during Jewish funerals, the most common being to have them take place in the small hours, in the hope that ill-wishers would be put off by sheer exhaustion. The funeral was often also accompanied by a motley assortment of municipal body-guards, bearing all manner of weapons and ready for any eventuality. But sometimes even these measures proved ineffective, and there would be a further toll of dead and wounded from both camps. This is how Graziani's chronicle of Perugia describes one such funeral, that of Elia di Giacobbe, a French Jew, in 1446:

Today, the thirtieth of July, saw the death of Elya the Jew, father of Jacobbe de Porta Sant' Angelo; and for the safety of other Jews who accompanied

---

summer of 1487, and recalled that in Palermo Jews 'take the body to the burial-place outside the city, starting from the door of the synagogue, while the officiants recite the psalms, beginning with Psalm 49, and sing with all their hearts until they reach the cemetery'; see A. Yaari, *Letters from the Land of Israel* (Heb.) (Ramat Gan, 1971), 106. The Greek historian Elia Capsali describes the funeral of Jehudà Minz, the head of the Talmudic Academy of Padua, which took place there in 1509 and at which he himself had been present: 'The leaders of the community approached the bier, and lifted the black cloth which covered it. Moving towards the cemetery, the notables took turns to carry the coffin, and this honour also befell all those, students and teachers, who had studied or taught in the talmudic academy run by the deceased . . . Arriving at the cemetery, we light the torches around the coffin, while the funerary eulogy of the deceased is recited, and lamentation and weeping is heard on all sides. A parchment manuscript of the Book of the Law [Torah] is put in a strong new amphora, and placed in the grave beside the head of the deceased. Lastly we bury him, to the deep anguish of the bystanders. When the torches have been extinguished, we accompany the children of the dead man to their house, into the room of mourn-ing, whose walls are covered with black hangings and draperies.' See E. Capsali, *Seder Eliyahu Zuta: History of the Ottomans of Venice and that of the Jews in Turkey, Spain and Venice* (Heb.), ed. A. Shmuelevitz (Jerusalem, 1977), ii. 253–5).

[66] On 1 Oct. 1879 the procession accompanying the coffin of a certain Rosa Sabatello to the Jewish cemetery in Rome was attacked by a large mob. The police intervened in the Jews' defence and were forced to use firearms, and to injure one of the assailants, in order to restore order (see G. Piperno Beer, 'Gli ebrei di Roma nel passaggio dal governo pontificio allo stato liberale italiano', in E. Toaff (ed.), *1870: La breccia del Ghetto* (Rome, 1971), 193).

him to their burial-place, near the Trinitade de Porta S. Pietro, fearing that they might be set upon by young lads, Monsignore sent us all the policemen of the Podestà and Capitanio [the *capitano di giustizia*, the highest-ranking official of the Commune in charge of criminal justice]; and the hour of his burial was 3 in the morning; and being at the foot of the place above the Trinitade, we glimpsed several youths at the turning to Porta del Pilo, and they began hurling great stones, and bellowing 'We want blood' so loudly that many of the people of Fontenova took up their weapons, not knowing what was going on. At last the said family and the other Jews were obliged to lay down the said bier, and take flight. And two guards of the Podestà were killed, and many of those of the Podestà and Capitanio were wounded, together with many Jews.[67]

Attacks on Jewish funeral processions cannot therefore have been unusual in Italian towns in the late medieval period.[68] In Foligno in 1456 the municipal authorities addressed a public appeal to the citizens to

[67] See Graziani, 'Cronaca della città di Perugia dal 1309 al 1491', in F. Bonaini, A. Fabretti, and F. Polidori (eds.), *Archivio Storico italiano*, 16/1. *Cronache e storie della città di Perugia dal 1150 al 1563* (Florence, 1850), 582–3.

[68] In his ritual responsa the rabbi Azriel Diena recounts an event which occurred in Pavia in 1514: 'When I was living in Pavia with my family, about fifteen years ago, I observed that the Jews of that place had no cemetery of their own, so that they were obliged to transport the bodies of their dead for burial to Cremona or to the towns around Pavia, such as Voghera. Naturally, this state of affairs was the cause of all manner of troubles and regrettable incidents. Indeed, a rich city landowner had not scrupled to put up a number of buildings upon the tombs belonging to the old Jewish cemetery of Pavia (dating from the period when the city had a Jewish community, subsequently expelled [in 1487] upon the orders of the father of the present duke of Milan). Thus the tombs were completely destroyed. When Jews returned to Pavia at the time of the French occupation [1500–22] they had no wish to quarrel with that landowner and left things as they were . . . But I managed to convince the Jewish community that it should at least buy another piece of land in the town to be used as a cemetery, so as to avoid transporting the dead hither and thither. This was indeed done after all the members of the community willingly agreed to tax themselves in proportion to their own wealth in order to collect the sum needed for the purchase of the cemetery. None the less, to our misfortune, when we tried to take our first deceased to burial, all the Christians living in those parts gathered around us, assaulting the funeral cortège with lances and swords. We were in such danger that the relatives of the dead man were forced to retrace their steps and take the bier back home in all haste. The poor man was then buried in the cemetery at Cremona, and the Jewish community has no cemetery of its own in Pavia to this day.' See Y. Boksenboim (ed.), *Responsa of Rabbi Azriel Diena* (Heb.) (Tel Aviv, 1977), i. 244–5. In Jan. 1470 a Jewish funeral at Piacenza met a similar fate. According to the chronicler, 'as the Jews were proceeding of a Sunday night . . . wishing to bury the corpse of one of their dead, they were assailed with weapons and stones in such a way that they were forced to abandon the said corpse, and a certain Isac was seriously wounded in the affray'; see E. Motta, 'Ebrei in Como ed in altre città del ducato

allow Jews 'to recite their office for the dead, and to allow their tombs to remain undisturbed, nor harmed in any way, either by day or by night'.[69] Just ten years earlier, in the charter of 1445, the Jews of that same town had received formal assurance 'that no newly appointed prior or ruler of the commune should have the right to extort money from them for licence for burial or for permission to open the gates of the city to go and bury their dead, whether by day or night, unless they are at war or because of some other state of *force majeure*'.[70] The charter granted to the Jews by the governors of Todi in 1481 included the assurance 'that the said Jews may possess and maintain a place for burial, and may bury their dead in the customary place, and say the office for their dead, as has always been done, and that their graves should not be disturbed or harmed in any way, either by day or by night'.[71] In 1456 the priors of Terni also solemnly promised the Jews that their cemetery would not be harmed or desecrated, but they were obliged to repeat this assurance in 1474, a sign that the situation had not improved in the mean time.[72] Clearly, rulers' promises and intentions were one thing, but their ability effectively to protect Jews from individual insults and the unseemly behaviour of the mob, incited by the clergy, was quite another.

In the thirteenth century many towns had a statutory regulation forbidding Jews, including close relatives of the deceased, to wear mourning-clothes during the funeral procession, since this was regarded as a 'dignity' which should not be extended to those who did not share the religious faith of the majority. The granting of such a right seemed scandalous and unthinkable at the time, because it would in some way imply that Jewish and Christian worship were on a par. But quite frequent

---

milanese', *Periodico della Società Storica per la provincia e antica diocesi di Como*, 5 (1885), 39. We have evidence of another assault on a Jewish funeral at Verona during these same years: see G. Castellani, 'Gli ebrei a Verona', *Studi Storici Veronesi*, 6–7 (1955–6), 73.

[69] See Messini, *Origini e i primordi del Monte di Pietà*, 9.

[70] AC Foligno, Rif. 26, fos. 100ʳ–103ᵛ (27 July 1445). At Catanzaro in the second half of the 15th cent. Jews were forbidden to bury their dead during Holy Week. The ruling was revoked in 1473 following protests by Jews forced to remain in their houses with the stench of the decomposing bodies of their dead. In 1476 the Jews of the communities of southern Italy complained of being disturbed while performing their funerary rites and asked to be allowed to bury their dead 'with no let or hindrance'; see O. Dito, *La storia calabrese e la dimora degli ebrei in Calabria dal sec. V alla seconda metà del sec. XVI* (Rocca S. Casciano, 1916), 229–30, 239.

[71] AC Todi, Rif., 82, fos. 43ᵛ–49ᵛ (28 Feb. 1481).

[72] See Ghinato, *Studi e documenti*, ii. 111, 140–1.

exceptions were made in the case of Jewish families who had earned
their city's gratitude through long and valued professional activity (doctors) or frequent financial largesse (bankers). In 1383, on the death in
Perugia of Matassia di Sabato, the most important Jewish banker of the
area, who had helped the city with valuable advice and above all
money in times of crisis, the grateful commune allowed his son and
two other close relatives to 'wear black mourning-garments with
impunity at the funeral of the said Matassia as a sign of grief and sorrow,
despite the contrary rulings of the statutes'.[73] In 1422 a similar
concession was granted by the commune of Città di Castello to the children and other relatives of the banker Bonaventura da Perugia.[74]
Bonaventura and his family were protégés of pope Martin V, who had
lavished privileges and concessions on them.[75] Once again, it was the
rich who were able to honour their dead in greater freedom, their grief
expressed in public through the wearing of appropriate clothes, and not
just through words and gestures. For the poor, the rich man's funeral
cortège was an opportunity to divide up offerings and alms, and to participate in the dead man's final charitable act by testifying to his virtues
and thus hastening his soul towards the eternal blessings awaiting it.
The funerals of the poor, by contrast, were necessarily modest, often
amounting to a tiresome but unavoidable obligation for the community
at large.

Quite apart from the solemn day of the funeral itself, mourning-
clothes in general were a positive obsession with the believer preparing
to take leave of this world. He made no secret of his desire that his relatives should remember him publicly, and for as long as possible,
expressing their grief and desolation through the clothes they wore. But
what strikes us today is the routine manner with which the testator stipulated these outward manifestations of grief, imposing them upon his
relatives so that they might stand out from the crowd.[76] This was indeed
a ritual practice, lacking spontaneity by its very nature. In many cases
the believer's reasons for imposing mourning on his wife after his death
were all too clear: namely, to prevent or postpone her remarriage for as
long as possible. Remarriage was often feared because of its implications

---

[73] AS Perugia, Con. e Rif., 31, fo. 229ʳ (14 July 1383). See Toaff, *Ebrei a Perugia*,
26–8, 229–30.

[74] See Toaff, 'Gli ebrei a Città di Castello dal XIV al XVI secolo', *Bollettino della
Deputazione di Storia Patria per l'Umbria*, 72/2 (1975), 6.

[75] See L. Fumi, *Inventario e spoglio dei registri della tesoreria apostolica di Città di
Castello* (Perugia, 1900), 24.

[76] See Ariès, *The Hour of our Death*, 325.

(economic, in part) for the family's balance and stability.[77] But it was not this alone. Society itself demanded that the close relatives of the dead man should wear mourning and, since this entailed a certain expense, it was right that the believer should make explicit reference to it in his will. Thus the vast majority of wills include detailed arrangements and bequests sufficient for the widow and close relatives to be provided with mourning-clothes, known as *vestes lucubrae*, or widow's weeds, which were often just as expensive as normal garments. Sometimes, indeed, we almost sense that there were 'fashions in mourning'.

In 1500 a Jew from Spoleto left 3 florins to his wife and sister so that they might be provided with *vestes lucubrae* after his death. In 1524 another Jew of the same city required mourning to be worn only by his wife, as did in 1445 a Jew of French origin who had lived in Perugia and Assisi, stressing that this should be done 'according to the Jewish custom'.[78] In his will of 1488 a banker from Foligno insisted on mourning-clothes for a whole host of relatives, including his wife, three married sisters, and five daughters, the eldest of whom was married, leaving each of them sums ranging from 6 to 10 florins to purchase the necessary wardrobe.[79] The will states that the widow 'shall be able to buy as many mourning-clothes as she shall deem fitting for the death of the testator'. Abramo da Terni stipulated mourning-garments not only for his wife, but also for his mother-in-law. He left 10 florins to the former for her to buy a mourning-cloak and dress 'in accordance with Jewish custom'; to the second just 5 florins for a black dress.[80]

Often, in connection with the observance of the funerary rites and customs, these wills make explicit reference to the practices of the Jews of Rome. In her will of 1462 Stella di Gaio da Rieti, from Spoleto, directed that the funeral cortège and accompanying rites 'should all proceed according to the usage and customs of the Jews of Rome'.[81] As we have seen, bequests favouring the synagogues of Rome and its Jewish community were also frequent. Here, too, we see the links between the Jews of Umbria, and of central Italy in general, with the

---

[77] See Cammarosano, 'Aspetti delle strutture familiari', 112–13, 122–3.

[78] AC Spoleto, Not., Moscato di Giovanni, 96, fo. 53ʳ (will of Mosè di Aleuccio da Terni, 21 July 1500); ibid., Not., Piergiovanni Ficeni, 206/IV, fo. 89ᵛ (will of Abramo di Bonaiuto, 1 Dec. 1524); AS Perugia, Not., Mariano di Luca di Nino, 114, fo. 105ʳ (will of Giacobbe di Elia di Francia, 8 Dec. 1445).

[79] AC Foligno, Not., Taddeo Angelelli, 17/II, fo. 21ʳ (18 Sept. 1488); ibid. 17/III, fo. 17ᵛ (22 Nov. 1493), will of Angelo di Musetto da Camerino.

[80] AC Spoleto, Not., Giovanni di Luca, 8, fo. 210ʳ (will of Mosè di Abramo da Terni, 1–8 Dec. 1461).   [81] Ibid. 11, fo. 124ʳ (23 May 1462).

mother community of Rome, from which they were directly descended or where their families had their roots. It should be remembered that the Jewish communities which grew up in centres as far north of Rome as the Po valley were largely made up of Jews of Roman origin, with their own robust cultural, religious, and, to some extent, linguistic and dialectal identity.[82]

[82] See Toaff, 'Convergenza sul Veneto di banchieri ebrei romani e tedeschi nel tardo medioevo', in G. Cozzi (ed.), *Gli ebrei e Venezia (secoli XIV–XVIII)*, proceedings of an international conference organized by the Istituto della Storia della Società e dello Stato Veneziano, and by the Cini Foundation, Venice, 5–10 June 1983 (Milan, 1987), 600–2.

3

Meat and Wine

THE NEED FOR MEAT

JEWS faced particular problems in what Fernand Braudel calls 'carnivorous Europe', where meat was eaten every day, servings were generous, and wine was drunk as though it were water.[1] For Jews, consumption of meat and wine was conditional upon their preparation according to strict rules. Meat in particular, excluding pork and horsemeat because of the well-known biblical taboos, could be eaten only when the animals had been slaughtered using a special technique, known in Hebrew as *shehitah*, which requires the trachea and oesophagus to be slashed with a very sharp knife so as to drain off all the blood. No animal could be eaten if it had been found to be unhealthy or in any way abnormal upon careful inspection after slaughter (*bedikah*). Even in those animals declared to be fit for consumption after ritual slaughter and inspection, there were many parts (blood, fat, and sinews) which still could not be eaten, particularly those from the hindquarters. Adherence to Jewish dietary law thus entailed waste: on the one hand, of animals which had been slaughtered and then found to be unfit, and on the other, of remains which could not in any circumstances be eaten by Jews. Thus a Jewish community needed a far greater supply of animals than a Christian one, irrespective of the appetites or financial means of individuals. The cost of a pound of kosher meat would have been prohibitive if the relevant butcher had not been able to sell the rejected parts to Christian customers. In summary, then, the presence of a Jewish community in any town was always dependent on the regular availability of kosher meat.[2] Jews required local authorities to allow

---

[1] See F. Braudel, *Capitalism and Material Life, 1400–1800* (New York, 1973), 127–9. Medieval and Renaissance Italian society is rightly regarded as one of hearty meat-eaters, at all social levels; see M. Montanari, *Campagne medioevali: Strutture produttive, rapporti di lavoro, sistemi alimentari* (Turin, 1984), 192–4.

[2] The problem of kosher slaughter in the Jewish community of Casale Monferrato is discussed in a special study by Segre, though he is concerned with a period later than that discussed here. See R. Segre, 'Gli ebrei e il mercato delle carni a Casale Monferrato nel tardo Cinquecento', in E. M. Artom, L. Caro, and S. J. Sierra (eds.), *Miscellanea di studi in memoria di Dario Disegni* (Turin, 1969), 219–37.

unrestricted ritual slaughter of animals; they also needed permission for town butchers to sell the residue and rejects to their Christian clients. This second condition protected Jews from the danger that the price of kosher meat might be higher than the general level fixed by the victualling laws.

Almost all the charters granted by Italian municipal authorities to Jews in the late Middle Ages contain clauses ensuring them a regular supply of kosher meat.[3] Traditional Jewish slaughter was so widespread that official documents and notarial deeds often rendered the Hebrew verb *lishḥot* (to slaughter ritually) with Latin and Italian terms such as *sciattare*, *sciaptare* and *assiactare*, newly coined but clearly widely understood. The charters drawn up with the Jews of Umbria in the fifteenth and sixteenth centuries are no exception to the general rule: we find examples in Todi in 1413, 1420, and 1481, Amelia in 1430, Perugia in 1439, Assisi in 1457, Foligno in 1456, Norcia in 1432, Spoleto in 1468, Terni in 1456 and 1474, Trevi in 1474, and in Città di Castello in 1485, 1500, 1510, 1521, 1531, and 1545, and there are certainly other examples.[4] The charter granted to the Jews of Città di Castello in 1485 is typical in this respect. It states that, at the Jews' request, every butcher in the town should allow the Jews to slaughter as many animals as they required and to sell them this meat at the same prices as to other citizens. Furthermore, the butchers' guild was not allowed to choose which of its members would host the slaughter and sale of the meat intended for Jews: the latter were allowed freely to choose their own butchers. Lastly, half of any fine meted out by the town authorities to

---

[3] Many historical monographs make reference to rules concerning ritual slaughter among Italian Jews in the late Middle Ages and Renaissance, though without mentioning them explicitly. See e.g. Cassuto, *Ebrei a Firenze*, 218–19; Balletti, *Gli ebrei e gli Estensi*, 177, 185; Simonsohn, *Jews in the Duchy of Mantua*, 348–9; id., 'Ebrei a Parma', 249; A. Ciscato, *Gli ebrei in Padova (1300–1800)* (Padua, 1901), 169–70, 274–6; Muzzarelli, *Ebrei e città d'Italia*, 151–3; Esposito, 'Ebrei a Roma nella seconda metà del Quattrocento', 45–6.

[4] AC Todi, Rif., 56, fos. 97ʳ–99ʳ (24 Oct. 1413); ibid. 58, fos. 52ʳ–54ᵛ (5 Nov. 1420); ibid. 82, fos. 43ᵛ–49ᵛ (28 Feb. 1481); AC Amelia, Rif., 15, fos. 283ᵛ–284ᵛ (15 Aug. 1430); AS Perugia, Con. e Rif., 75, fo. 72ᵛ (22 June 1439); AC Assisi, Rif., H, 14, fos. 111ʳ–112ᵛ (1 July 1457); AC Foligno, Rif., 30, fo. 94ᵛ (29 June 1456); AC Norcia, Con. e Rif., 4, fos. 135ᵛ–137ʳ (18 Aug. 1432); AC Spoleto, Rif., 44, fo. 57ᵛ (4 June 1468); AS Terni, Rif., 499, I, fo. 185ᵛ (26 Dec. 1456); 503, III, fo. 84ᵛ (30 Nov. 1474); AC Trevi, Tre Chiavi, env. 9, 139, fo. 4ʳ (11 Oct. 1474); AC Città di Castello, Annali Comunali, 52, fos. 118ʳ–124ʳ (12 Feb. 1485); ibid. 54, fos. 191ᵛ–196ʳ (21 Feb. 1500); ibid. 55, fos. 222ʳ–230ʳ (20 Sept. 1510); ibid. 56, fos. 148ʳ–150ʳ (1 Sept. 1521); ibid. 57, fos. 1ᵛ–3ᵛ (1 Sept. 1531); ibid. 57, fos. 166ʳ–168ʳ (10 Dec. 1545).

slaughterers caught flouting these regulations went to the Jewish community.[5] The clauses that were generally left implicit were made explicit in the regulations laid down by the priors of Spoleto in 1468 and of Terni in 1456 and 1474.[6] In these Jews were not required to take all the meat slaughtered for their use themselves, but were authorized to sell the residue and rejects to the town's butchers. In their turn, these butchers were authorized to sell the meat to the Christian population. However, the Terni charters stated, undoubtedly as a result of the pressure exerted by the local butchers' guild, that Jews could demand the slaughter of further heads of livestock only after the butchers' shops had completely sold out of the meat already slaughtered for them. Wrangles between Jews and the various butchers' guilds also touched on the selection and siting of the slaughterers serving the Jewish population and the level of retail prices, which the butchers naturally wanted to be higher than the officially controlled ones. In 1456 the consuls of the butchers' guild of Foligno assumed the right to choose 'one or more of the town's slaughterers' to be responsible for the slaughter and sale of kosher meat.[7] In Perugia in 1439 there were two slaughterhouses designated to serve the Jewish population, chosen because of their out-of-the-way position. The sale of kosher meat elsewhere was strictly forbidden:

First, no Jew or Jewess living in the town or outskirts of Perugia may in any way *sciattare* [ritually slaughter] any beast, or buy any sort of fresh meat, except in two slaughterhouses and no others, and the said slaughterhouses must be set up in a new place, where no slaughterhouse has been before; and this must be a convenient and decent place, public and set apart from other slaughterhouses . . . and these slaughterhouses may not sell meat at a lower price than in the large Christian slaughterhouse.[8]

In 1482 the butchers' guild of Foligno asked the authorities to abrogate the clause in the charter which allowed Jews to benefit from fixed prices when they purchased kosher meat. The butchers maintained that this clause caused them considerable economic damage, since the prepara-

[5] AC Città di Castello, Annali Comunali, 52, fos. 118ʳ–124ʳ. See Toaff, *Ebrei a Città di Castello*, 11.

[6] AC Spoleto, Rif., 44, fo. 57ᵛ; AS Terni, Rif., 499, I, fo. 185ᵛ; ibid. 503, III, fo. 84ᵛ. See Ghinato, *Studi e documenti*, ii. 23, 112, 140.

[7] AC Foligno, Rif., 30, fo. 94ᵛ (29 June 1456).

[8] AS Perugia, Con. e Rif., 75, fo. 72ʳ (22 June 1439). See A. Fabretti, *Sulla condizione degli ebrei in Perugia dal XIII al XVIII secolo* (Turin, 1891), 38–42; Toaff, *Ebrei a Perugia*, 96.

tion of kosher meat entailed a build-up of rejects which were hard to sell. Jewish reaction was immediate, and the banker Angelo da Camerino, the Jewish representative to the town authorities, appealed to the bishop, obtaining his support and thus preventing the passing of the measure.[9] But in 1438 the slaughterers of Todi were more successful. Their guild managed to establish the right to fix two price levels for the retail sale of meat within the town itself: the fixed price, endorsed by the victualling magistrature, and the price of kosher meat, which was 1 *denaro* more per *libbra*. 'Once a wether or any other animal has been slaughtered at the request of the Jews and with the permission of the consuls of the guild, the butchers of Todi may sell Jews the wether or part of it, asking a price of 1 *denaro* per *libbra* higher for their meat than is commonly asked of Christians.'[10] Here, too, Jewish reaction was not long in coming, and soon the price of kosher meat sold on the butcher's counter went back down to the fixed level.

The civil and ecclesiastical town authorities were both perfectly aware that a significant Jewish presence in any town or village was directly linked to the availability of regular supplies of kosher meat. Not surprisingly, antisemitic circles had no qualms about restricting the availability of kosher meat in order to further their ends. The preaching friars and Minorites were the shock troops in this struggle.[11] To make life impossible for Jews, it was not actually necessary to ban ritual slaughter in town slaughterhouses, or to forbid Jews to do it on their own premises. The friars' purpose was equally well served by the clever and effective expedient of forbidding Christians to eat kosher meat. This had the advantage of adhering to the letter of the law (the Jews' right freely to observe their dietary rules) while making it impossible to carry out in practice. Clearly, if butchers were not allowed to sell the rejects and residue of kosher slaughter to Christians, they had only two alternatives: to refuse to slaughter meat for Jews, or to raise retail prices for kosher meat to prohibitive levels. There was hardly a commune in

---

[9] AC Foligno, Not., Taddeo Angelelli, 12/6, fo. 20ᵛ (8 Jan. 1482).

[10] AC Todi, Stat., 4, Add. 224, fo. 335ʳ (27 June 1438); ibid., Rif., 62, fo. 420ʳ (4 Oct. 1438).

[11] On the Church's ban on Christians acquiring and consuming meat slaughtered by Jews, and its application in Europe during the 13th cent., see S. Grayzel, *The Church and the Jews in the Thirteenth Century* (New York, 1966), 72–3. See also W. C. Jordan, 'Problems of the Meat Market of Béziers, 1240–1247: A Question of Anti-Semitism', *Revue des études juives*, 135 (1976), 31–49; id., 'Jews on Top: Women and the Availability of Consumption Means in Northern France in the Mid-Thirteenth Century', *Journal of Jewish Studies*, 29 (1978), 39–56.

Umbria in the fifteenth century which, under pressure from the Observant friars, did not attempt to prohibit or restrict ritual slaughter and the public sale of kosher meat.[12] But these attempts rarely met with much success.

In 1439, following a sermon by fra Bernardino of Siena, the rulers of Perugia forbade the city's butchers to purchase meat slaughtered by Jews.[13] The decrees issued by the commune of Spoleto in 1451, 'at the instigation and request of the venerable friar Cherubino, of the order of Minorites', prohibited Jews from selling or even from giving Christians kosher meat. At the same time Christians were forbidden to purchase meat slaughtered by Jews.[14] The 1436 decrees of Todi forbade butchers to slaughter meat for Jews or sell the residue to Christian customers.[15] Similar measures were passed by the authorities of Norcia in 1442 and Terni in 1444.[16]

In the second half of the fifteenth century, just before and after the founding of the various Monti di Pietà, the Franciscan friars' anti-Jewish crusade again selected kosher meat as one of its favoured targets,

---

[12] In other Italian cities of the time we hear of frequent attempts by local authorities to restrict kosher slaughter. In 1441 at Reggio Christian butchers were forbidden to sell animals to Jews to slaughter themselves, unless they committed themselves in advance to buying the whole animal; see Balletti, *Gli ebrei e gli Estensi*, 26–7. In Padua in 1453 and 1488 the authorities ordered butchers to mark meat slaughtered for Jews with a yellow circle, so that Christians could recognize it as such and not buy it by mistake; see Ciscato, *Ebrei in Padova*, 169–70, 274–6. In Sicily meat slaughtered for Jews was marked with a red circle; see V. Lionti, 'La rotella rossa', *Archivio Storico Siciliano*, 8 (1883), 160. After 1457 an attempt was made to make the Jews of Cesena slaughter their animals as other citizens did, at the Saturday market, i.e. on a day when Jewish law forbade all work; see Muzzarelli, *Ebrei e città d'Italia*, 151–3. At Crema in 1480 the local authorities forbade butchers to sell their Christian customers the remains of animals slaughtered for Jews; see G. Albini Mantovani, 'La comunità ebraica in Crema nel secolo XV e le origini del Monte di Pietà', *Nuova Rivista Storica*, 59 (1975), 398. In 1488 the *capitano* of Agropoli in the province of Salerno gave the city's butchers permission to refuse to 'give or sell meat to the said Jews'; see C. Colafemmina, 'Documenti per la storia degli ebrei in Campania', *Sefer Yuhasim*, 2 (1988), 135. The repeated attempts made by Piedmontese cities to forbid kosher slaughter and the public sale of kosher meat, documented from 1409, are extensively registered by Segre, *Jews in Piedmont*, i. 4–5, 7, 25–7, 114, 249–50.
[13] 'No butcher may buy or sell any type of meat slaughtered in the said slaughter-houses by the Jews', AS Perugia, Con. e Rif., 75, fo. 72^r (22 June 1439). See Toaff, *Ebrei a Perugia*, 60–4.
[14] AC Spoleto, Rif., 36, fo. 205^v (13 Apr. 1451).
[15] AC Todi, Stat., 4, Add. 224, fo. 324^r (29 Mar. 1436).
[16] AC Norcia, Con. e Rif., 4, fo. 115^r (18 Feb. 1442); AS Terni, Rif., 497, fo. 69^r (11 Nov. 1444).

and measures against Jewish slaughter were dusted down and put forward for approval by city councils. This was done at Spoleto and Amelia in 1468, at Gubbio in 1483, and again at Spoleto in 1490, at the suggestion of the Minorite friar Andrea da Faenza. The text of the Gubbio *riformanze*, written in 1483 to justify measures against kosher slaughter, runs as follows: 'The meat slaughtered by Jews cannot be sold to Christians, as has hitherto been the case, offending against the Christian religion; mindful of their honour, Christians must abstain from eating it; butchers found selling such meat shall be punished by a fine of 10 lire; lastly, Jews shall not be allowed to set foot in the town's butchers nor in places where animals whose flesh is destined for sale are slaughtered.'[17] In 1473 the rulers of Spello resorted to the cunning ploy of prohibiting butchers from selling Jews quarters or half-quarters of animals.[18] Jews therefore had to buy the whole animal. The thinking behind such steps remained unchanged: 'to put an end to a situation where Jews refuse to eat the flesh of beasts slaughtered in accordance with the Christian rite, while Christians eat meat slaughtered for Jews indiscriminately';[19] 'because it is absurd and unacceptable that Jews, after having slaughtered their beasts by performing their own particular ceremonies, should then sell the residue and rejects to Christians; in this way Christians come to eat meat prepared by Jews, while the latter refuse to eat meat slaughtered by Christians at any price'.[20] The real purpose of the Minorite crusade against the eating of kosher meat by Christians emerged only rarely. It was part of an ambitious and much broader design to reinforce the natural barriers supposedly separating Christians from Jews in urban society, and to create yet further artificial barriers to replace the former where these had proved insufficient. The reason adduced in the Gubbio document to justify opposition to kosher slaughter ('so that an end shall be put to friendly concourse between Christians and Jews, in conversation as in eating') is only superficially surprising.[21] We find the same thinking in the words of fra Roberto Caracciolo da Lecce, who preached in Perugia in 1448: 'We particularly set our canon against the widespread dealings, converse, and company

[17] AC Spoleto, Rif., 44, fo. 57ᵛ (4 June 1468); AC Amelia, Rif., 41, fo. 190ᵛ (26 Mar. 1468); AC Gubbio, Rif., 51, fo. 84ᵛ (20 Mar. 1483); AC Spoleto, Rif., 53, fo. 479ʳ (13 May 1490).
[18] AC Spello, Con. e Rif., env. 1, prot. 3, fo. 16ᵛ (16 May 1473).
[19] AC Todi, Stat., 4, Add. 224, fo. 324ʳ (29 Mar. 1436).
[20] AC Amelia, Rif., 41, fo. 190ᵛ (26 Mar. 1468).
[21] AC Gubbio, Rif., 51, fo. 84ᵛ (20 Mar. 1483).

with Jews . . . which are today so prevalent and rife in almost all Italy that it is as though there were no prohibition against them at all.'[22]

Jewish reaction was particularly sharp when their diet was under threat. Their main concern was not the diminution of the pleasures of the table that a lack of meat would imply, but the threat to their health. Their most effective weapon was to claim that the municipal councils were violating the regulations of the charters they had signed, and to threaten to cease trading and leave town. As the Jews of Todi sensed in 1438, they had no alternative, 'because we cannot live in good health, being prohibited from buying meat'.[23] Generally speaking Jewish opposition proved effective, and once the emotion aroused by Minorite preaching had died down town councils showed no desire to exacerbate the arguments concerning kosher meat, knowing them to be utterly futile. Thus such decrees were often revoked after a few months, sometimes a few weeks.[24] The case of the Jews of Todi was unusual: they were obliged to live with the ruling for two-and-a-half years (the end of March 1436 to the beginning of October 1438) until it was abrogated following the intervention of Francesco Sforza, the city's ruler at the time.[25] Sometimes, to make their request more persuasive, Jews armed themselves with papal documents which stressed their right freely to avail themselves of slaughterers' services according to their own religious rules. When decrees against ritual slaughter were issued in Spoleto in the spring of 1468, the Jews had them revoked immediately by presenting the priors of the city with a bull, issued by Pius II on 18 July 1462, in which local governors were required 'to grant Jews all that was necessary for the observance of their particular religious regulations'.[26] But even when such measures were in force, with Jews expressly forbidden to sell meat to Christians, it seems that the authorities rarely policed their application or punished the transgressors.

[22] Cited in Toaff, *Ebrei a Perugia*, 66–7.

[23] AC Todi, Stat. 4, Add. 224, fo. 335ʳ (27 June 1438).

[24] The restrictions on Jewish ritual slaughter, put into force in Norcia from 18 Feb. 1442, were abrogated two months later, in Apr. 1442 (AC Norcia, Con. e Rif., 4, fos. 115ʳ, 135ᵛ–137ʳ). Those adopted by the authorities of Amelia on 26 Mar. 1468 were annulled on 7 Nov. of the same year (AC Amelia, Rif., 41, fos. 190ᵛ, 198ʳ). The measures applied at Spoleto on 13 Apr. 1451 lasted one month, and those issued by the priors of the same town at the end of May 1468 lasted less than two months (AC Spoleto, Rif., 36, fo. 205ᵛ; ibid. 44, fo. 57ᵛ).

[25] AC Todi, Stat., 4, Add. 224, fo. 324ʳ; ibid., Rif., 62, fo. 420ʳ. See also L. Leonij, 'Decreti del comune di Todi contro gli ebrei e giustizia loro resa da Francesco Sforza', *Archivio Storico Italiano*, 7/4 (1881), 25–8.

[26] AC Spoleto, Rif., 44, fo. 57ᵛ (4 June 1468).

This is borne out by the proceedings against the banker Mosè di Abramo, living at Gualdo Tadino, which were held in 1511 before the representative of the bishop of Norcia.[27] One of the many accusations against Mosè concerned the unlawful sale of kosher meat: he was said to have slaughtered animals for years in accordance with the Jewish rite, for his own consumption and that of his family. According to the ecclesiastical prosecutor, the residue, namely all the wethers, calves, and spring lambs not consumed directly, had been sold by Mosè to the town's Christians, unbeknown to them. This was in fact the charge to which judges and witnesses paid least attention during the course of the trial, and Mosè was finally acquitted of it.

A SLAUGHTERHOUSE IN THE HOME

Even if it took place in a Christian butcher's shop, ritual slaughter was performed by a Jewish slaughterer (*shohet*) who had taken a special examination, both theoretical and practical, and who had had a long apprenticeship, particularly in the technique of slaughtering the larger animals. It is therefore not surprising that the number of ritual slaughterers qualified to deal with oxen, wethers, and calves was by no means large, whereas many people were qualified to perform the relatively easy slaughter of poultry and other birds, which had far simpler rules and techniques. Indeed, we may assume that during the late Middle Ages every Jewish family included someone able to slaughter chickens, capons, and pigeons in the approved fashion. For instance, when in 1436 the Jews of Todi were forbidden to slaughter large animals, they continued to eat poultry, which they slaughtered in their own homes, each family seeing to its own needs.[28]

However, the 'professional' *shohet* had a special licence written in Hebrew, guaranteeing his qualifications and expertise and signed by the religious authorities. The following is the text of one such licence, granted in 1488 to Angelo di Gaio, a Jew from Spoleto:

Today the young Angelo di Gaio of Spoleto [Mordechai b. Izchaq Cohen], presented himself before us, the examiners, as expert and trained in the rules of ritual slaughter [*shehitah*], which he has studied and committed to memory as required. We have questioned him on the subject and he

---

[27] AS Perugia, Giud., Processus, env. 164, file 19 (5 Nov. 1511).
[28] AC Todi, Rif., 62, fo. 420ʳ (4 Oct. 1438).

answered yes where it was necessary to answer yes, and he answered no where it was necessary to answer no; he forbade what should be forbidden and permitted what should be permitted. Therefore, having seen that he was sufficiently prepared, we decided to grant him an unrestricted licence to perform ritual slaughter, both for his personal use and for the needs of other Jews. None the less this licence is conditional upon an apprenticeship, to be carried out under the guidance of a person expert in ritual slaughter. During his apprenticeship he shall ritually slaughter ten head of large cattle, bullocks, wethers, and calves, thirteen head of smaller animals, goats, and spring lambs, and thirteen others, including wildfowl and poultry, hens, capons, and pigeons. And this in order that his hand shall be exercised in the work of slaughter.[29]

A collection of theoretical notes on ritual slaughter, written around 1370 by the Umbrian Jew Guglielmo di Isacco (Benjamin b. Izchaq) da Narni, and on which local candidates for the *sheḥitah* examination were clearly examined, is preserved in a Hebrew manuscript in the Vatican.[30]

Some evidence concerning the activity of professional Jewish slaughterers in the slaughterhouses of Umbrian towns is provided by archival documents of the period. At the proceedings against Mosè di Abramo in 1511 one of the witnesses was the *shoḥet* Raffaele. He stated that he had been in the service of Mosè and his family for a long time and had ritually slaughtered many calves and spring lambs for the wealthy banker at the Christian butchers' shops belonging to Dominici and Franceschi at Gualdo.[31]

The wide dispersal of Jewish communities in late medieval and Renaissance Italy and the small number of Jewish families in any one place made it difficult for them to maintain their usual customs, and they sometimes had to compromise in order to survive. Butchery was an area requiring just such flexibility, as, where there was no one who could perform ritual slaughter, kosher meat was difficult to get hold of, and if they had no meat supply families were eventually forced to move on. Not surprisingly, therefore, women, and even children, were sometimes trained in ritual slaughter. The sight of a young Jewish boy struggling

[29] Heb. MS Casanatense H. IV. 13. 3147, fo. 14ᵛ, described in G. Sacerdote, *Catalogo dei codici ebraici della biblioteca Casanatense di Roma* (Florence, 1897), 500 n. 32. The same MS (fos. 15ʳ–16ʳ) contains transcriptions of three other 'slaughterer's licences' granted to Jews, presumably from Umbria and the Marches, in 1481–2.

[30] MS Urb. Heb. 31. This MS contains other writings concerning the rules for ritual slaughter, including some by the father of Guglielmo da Narni, Isacco, and Leone di Guglielmo (Jehudah b Binjamin Anaw 'de Urbe').

[31] AS Perugia, Giud., Processus, env. 164, file 19 (5 Nov. 1511).

with a hefty bullock weighing several hundred kilos cannot have been unusual in town butchers' shops at the time.

In 1545 a slaughterer's licence was granted to Giacobbe da Spoleto.[32] His apprenticeship involved the slaughter of four head of large cattle, five smaller animals, and six head of poultry and other birds. The document ended with an apparently surprising clause: 'none the less, until he attains his religious majority [at 13], he shall be authorized to slaughter only if assisted by an adult.' Young Giacobbe, barely 12 years old, was already being trained to slaughter wethers, calves, and spring lambs, and to handle an extremely sharp knife with a steady hand. At 13 he would be recognized as an expert and experienced slaughterer by the whole community.[33] Today we find the idea of a child taken from play and obliged to spend part of his time in the slaughterhouse, amid the blood and guts of the creatures he himself has butchered, extremely disturbing. But this activity was vital for his family and possibly also for the small Jewish community living in his town. Everyone depended upon his steady hand and expertise for their supply of kosher meat: he held their very survival in his hands. Our modern reaction is probably excessive and misguided. In the violent Italian town life of the time, where factions and quarrels fuelled positive bloodbaths daily, it is doubtful whether the sight of calves' or bullocks' blood in a butcher's shop could have retained the power seriously to alarm a child.

In addition, it is possible that ritual slaughter might sometimes have been performed by supposedly frail female hands. Elsewhere women's contribution to ritual slaughter, regarded as a male preserve, is unambiguously documented.[34] The regulations concerning *sheḥitah*

---

[32] MS Heb. Casanatense I. III. 11. 2972, fo. 151ʳ (described in Sacerdote, *Catalogo dei codici ebraici*, 493 n. 23). The MS includes four other certificates awarded to Jews of Spoleto, Fermo, and places in Umbria and the Marches in the first half of the 16th cent.

[33] In 1507 the rabbis of the Po communities attempted to put a brake on the custom, widespread among the Jews in Italy, of training children barely over 13 for ritual slaughter by issuing ordinances banning anyone under 18 from holding the licence of *sheḥitah*. It is extremely unlikely that this met with any success, since it ran counter to the needs of a large number of Jewish families living far from centres with a large and organized Jewish nucleus; see Bonfil, 'Aspects of Social and Spiritual Life', 71, 90–3. Half a century later, the study curriculum of a 12-year-old Jewish child still included an apprenticeship in ritual slaughter; see S. Asaf, *Sources for the History of Education among the Jewish People* (Heb.) (Tel Aviv, 1930), 114.

[34] Research into the reasons for the custom of training women as ritual slaughterers (whose extent among Italian Jewish families in the late medieval and Renaissance period is as yet unclear) has recently received wider attention: see C. Roth, *The Jews*

issued by the rulers of Perugia in 1439, which do not differentiate between male and female slaughterers, imply that the idea of a woman slaughterer was less surprising than it would be today. They actually begin with the warning that 'no Jew or Jewess, living in the city of Perugia, may in any way slaughter any beast . . . except in the said slaughterhouses of the Jews'.[35] Without wishing to ascribe too much importance to this passage, it is still clear that the need to obtain kosher meat at any cost led many Jewish families to justify the involvement of women and children in ritual slaughter.

The location of the slaughterhouses providing meat for Jews was usually decided by the authorities.[36] Often, to avoid shocking and inconveniencing the local Christian population, Jews were required to 'slaughter in their own houses', that is, to turn their ground floor into a slaughterhouse.[37] This measure, which hardly helped to make the Jewish presence in the town particularly welcome or pleasant, was imposed, for instance, on the Jews of Todi in 1436 and, following pressure from the Minorite friar Cherubino, on the Jews of Spoleto in 1451.[38] Here premises were chosen adjacent to the house of the de Pomis, doctors and bankers, on the so-called 'street of the Jews' near the

---

in the Renaissance (New York, 1965), 49, 52; Shulvass, *Jews in the World of the Renaissance*, 163, 166; R. Bonfil, 'The Historian's Perception of the Jews in the Italian Renaissance: Towards a Reappraisal', *Revue des études juives*, 143 (1984), 71–5. Such discussion strikes me as quite fruitless. Bonfil is undoubtedly right when he maintains that training young girls and women as ritual slaughterers was an attempt to provide a practical solution to problems posed by the dietary laws for a considerable number of Jewish families scattered over any number of small localities. It was thus a compromise and not an end in itself, as Roth and, to a lesser degree, Shulvass would have it. Furthermore it seems indisputable that the choice of such a compromise itself reflected the spirit of the times, which blithely countenanced giving women functions which were subsequently seen by both Jewish and Christian society as exclusive male preserves.

[35] AS Perugia, Con. e Rif., 75, fo. 72^r (22 June 1439).

[36] Sometimes Jews bought and ran butchers' shops in partnership with Christian butchers. At Sermoneta, for instance, towards the middle of the 15th cent., the wealthy merchant Abramo di Mosè ran a butcher's shop with an adjoining slaughterhouse, in the town square, in partnership with three Christian butchers. He also reared livestock and owned herds of buffalo and flocks of sheep; see Caciorgna, 'Presenza ebraica', 140–1, 149, 163–4, 167.

[37] At Parma in 1448 Jews were required to 'slaughter both small and large beasts in their houses'; see Simonsohn, 'Ebrei a Parma', 249. At Cesena in the same period Jews also slaughtered 'in their houses'; see Muzzarelli, *Ebrei e città d'Italia*, 151–3.

[38] AC Todi, Stat., 4, Add. 224, fo. 324^r (29 Mar. 1436); AC Spoleto, Rif., 36, fo. 205^v (13 Apr. 1451).

church of S. Gregorio della Sinagoga. But this decision on the part of
the rulers of Spoleto was soon to reveal itself in all its imprudence. In
1503 there were protests from the inhabitants of the streets around the
Jewish quarter, adjacent to the market square, because the Christian
butchers who prepared meat for the Jews habitually threw the entrails
and rejected portions into the street, so that the 'street of the Jews'
became impassable because of the stench, particularly in the hot summer
months:

> Those living near the butchers around the market square, at the end of the
> street commonly known as the street of the Jews, and also the artisans
> around the square, and other citizens frequenting the said street, declare
> that the inconvenience and stench of the slaughter carried out by the
> butchers is such in the premises around the said butchers' shops, that they
> can hold out no further, and that it is a disgrace to the whole city that such
> filth should run down the middle of one of the main streets of the said city.

The hapless citizens asked the commune to take urgent measures, and
above all to 'make new provisions so that henceforth no person should
disembowel or throw away rubbish, or guts or entrails, into the said
place or in any place surrounding the market square'. For its part, the
commune threatened to issue severe fines to anyone who continued to
use the 'street of the Jews' as a rubbish dump and, if the situation did
not improve, to take the 'ratio extrema' of closing down the 'macellum
strate Judeorum civitatis Spoleti'.[39]
   But the measures do not seem to have had the desired effect, and
some years later, in 1512, a group of the town's artisans, including
blacksmiths whose forges were near the fountain in the market square,
warned the authorities that 'the street of the Jews . . . is on the verge of
ruin', overrun as it was by mud, dung, and refuse from the kosher
butcher.[40] After this protest, the commune paid for the entire street to
be cleaned and repaved, but to no lasting avail. Entrails, guts, and other
refuse, flushed out by ever-plentiful drainwater, soon reigned supreme
once more. The street of the Jews, originally on the outskirts but subsequently, as Spoleto grew in size, near the centre of the town, a step away
from the market square, cannot have been a pleasant or edifying sight.
Nor can the heartfelt lowing of the luckless animals brought to the Jews'
butchers for slaughter have lessened the sense of dereliction; and
the authorities were bitterly to regret their improvident decision to

[39] AC Spoleto, Rif., 64, fos. 260ᵛ–262ᵛ (28 May 1503).
[40] Ibid. 70, fos. 285ʳ, 490ʳ (11 Feb. 1512).

order the Jews to open slaughterhouses in the ground floors of their houses. Years later, in 1552, the priors were still having to set aside a considerable sum to patch up and repave the 'street of the Jews', again in need of urgent repairs.[41]

Beef and mutton played a basic, indeed irreplaceable, role in the diet of the meat-eating Jew of this period. Forced for nearly three years to eat only poultry and wildfowl, the Jews of Todi were driven to despair, and by 1438 they were obliged to address an urgent protest to Francesco Sforza which was to prove highly convincing: 'We are no longer able to provide sustenance for ourselves or our families, because we have been forced to eat only poultry for too long.'[42] A long-enforced diet of salami made from goose and the insipid flesh of chickens, wildfowl, capons, and pigeons had made the Jews of Todi desperately crave good food and a more varied and appealing menu, including ossobuco, tripe, and rump-steak. Bon viveur that he was, the count of Cotignola could not but heed their pleas.

But we know little of the meat-eating habits of Jewish families during this period; such information as we do have is quite inadequate.[43] We know that in 1481, for instance, the merchant Samuele da Rieti had accumulated a debt of 30 florins at the butcher's shop belonging to Nicola Andrei on Piazza della Croce at Foligno,[44] but we cannot tell whether this was a typical situation. The figure corresponds to his family's annual meat consumption, which was thus clearly extremely high. It was broken down as follows: 882 *libbre* (291 kilos) of beef, 14 florins; 720 *libbre* (237 kilos) of sucking calf, 3 florins; 18 kids and spring lambs, 3 florins; 36 brace of pigeon, 4 florins; 10 brace of capon, 6

---

[41] Ibid., ser. 2, 11, fo. 177ʳ (18 Sept. 1552).

[42] AC Todi, Stat., 4, Add. 224, fos. 324ʳ (19 June 1436), 335ʳ (27 June 1438); ibid., Rif., 62, fo. 402ʳ (4 Oct. 1438). See also Leonij, 'Decreti del Comune di Todi', 25–8. In Sept. 1527, on the eve of the feast of Tabernacles (*Sukkot*), rabbi Azriel Diena sent a relative a present of a quarter of spring lamb, explaining that he preferred to give him that type of meat since chicken was not good for the health; see Y. Boksenboim (ed.) *Responsa of Rabbi Azriel Diena* (Heb.) (Tel Aviv, 1977), i. 321.

[43] Equally, there are not many studies on meat consumption generally in Italian society of the period. See amongst others A. M. Nada Patrone, *Il cibo del ricco ed il cibo del povero: Contributo alla storia qualitativa dell'alimentazione—l'area pedemontana negli ultimi secoli del Medio Evo* (Turin, 1981); M. S. Mazzi, 'Consumi alimentari e malattie nel basso Medioevo', *Archeologia medievale*, 8 (1981), 328–30; A. Cortonesi, 'Le spese in victualibus della Domus Helemosine Sancti Petri di Roma: Contributo alla storia del consumo alimentare in area romano-laziale fra XIII e XIV secolo', *Archeologia medievale*, 8 (1981), 220–4.

[44] AC Foligno, Not., Taddeo Angelelli, 11/5, fo. 89ʳ.

florins. Samuele's monthly meat consumption thus amounted to about 25 kilos of beef, 20 kilos of veal, one-and-a-half lambs, 6 pigeons, and a couple of capons.[45] It seems reasonable to assume that meat was served at Samuele's table at every lunch and dinner; but we do not know how typical he was of the habits, tastes, and above all the means, of other Jews of his city, and of the Italian Jewish communities of the time.[46] He may have been far more typical than we might tend to believe. Rabbi Israel Ashkenazi, who moved from Perugia to the Holy Land around 1520, regretted being forced to give up his daily meat-based dishes. 'We all find ourselves in difficulties', he wrote, 'because in Jerusalem we do not find meat every day, as we do in our home town.'[47]

VINES, WINES, AND 'GRAPES FOR HANGING'

The supply of wine posed Jews problems similar to those concerning meat. The age of spirits, destined to threaten and then supplant wine's primacy, was still far off. In medieval Italy wine was by far the most widely produced and consumed drink. It was present everywhere: at church, at synagogue, in the tavern and brothel, in the apothecary's shop, and at the bedside of the sick. It was drunk in large quantities at the rich man's table and at the open-air peasant dance. In many farmhouses, it was easier to obtain a cup of wine than a cup of water. Wine's social and socializing value was felt at all levels of society, making it a prime necessity.[48] So wine was inevitably found at the

[45] On the price of meat in Umbrian towns in the 14th and 15th cents. see also A. Sansi, *Storia del Comune di Spoleto dal secolo XII al XVII* (Foligno, 1884), ii. 132–3; P. L. Menichetti, *Le corporazioni delle arti e mestieri medioevali a Gubbio* (Città di Castello, 1980), 141–50.

[46] If it is true that eating meat only three times a week was regarded as a sign of poverty in medieval Italian society (see Montanari, *Campagne medioevali*, 166–7), it is probable that the amount eaten by Samuele da Rieti and his family was far more typical of Italian Jewish society at the time than we might at first think.

[47] See A. Yaari, *Letters from the Holy Land* (Heb.) (Tel Aviv, 1943), 166–8; Toaff, *Ebrei a Perugia*, 131–3.

[48] See Braudel, *Capitalism and Material Life*, 162–6. In what Braudel calls 'that particular Europe', namely as a producer and not just a consumer of wine, in which Italy undoubtedly played a leading role, it is eminently understandable that increasingly large tracts of land should have been given over to vine-growing. On the production and consumption of wine in medieval and Renaissance Italy, see e.g. A. Marescalchi and G. Dalmasso, *Storia della vite e del vino in Italia* (Casale Monferrato, 1931); Ch. De La Roncière, 'Le Vin et la vigne dans le contado de Florence au XIVème siècle', in *Le Vin: Production et consommation*, proceedings of the second con-

tables of the Italian Jews of the period, above all in such a great wine-producing and consuming area as Umbria, whose countryside is today still characterized by extensive vineyards.[49] As with meat, Jewish law laid down precise rules defining kosher wine. In practice these required that the grapes should be pressed only by Jews, who should also directly supervise the subsequent process of vinification, overseeing the various phases until the product was ready for consumption. None the less, unlike kosher meat, whose availability was regarded by Jewish families of the time as an essential precondition for their settling in any particular place, wine was seen as far less vital. If necessary, ordinary must and wine would be used, without excessive scandal, and a blind eye was turned to the fact that it was produced by Christian feet. Even in 1608 the famous Venetian rabbi Leon da Modena observed pragmatically that 'ever since I have been able to distinguish between my left hand and my right, I have known that from time immemorial our forefathers in Italy habitually drank ordinary wine'.[50]

---

ference of the Société des Historiens Médiévistes de L'Enseignement Public (Grenoble, 1971); M. C. Daviso di Charvensod, 'Coltivazione e reddito della vigna a Rivoli nel secolo XIV', *Bollettino storico bibliografico subalpino*, 3 (1950), 1–13; A. I. Pini, 'La viticoltura italiana nel Medioevo: Cultura della vite e consumo del vino a Bologna dal X al XV secolo', *Studi Medioevali*, ser. 3, no. 15 (1974), 795–884; M. Montanari, *L'alimentazione contadina nell'alto Medioevo* (Naples, 1979), 373–84; G. Papagno (ed.), *Il vino e l'uomo* (Florence, 1984); P. Larivaille, *La vita quotidiana in Italia ai tempi del Machiavelli* (Milan, 1984), 261–5. On the situation in France, another great wine-producing country, see R. Dion, *Histoire de la vigne et du vin en France des origines au XIXème siècle* (Paris, 1959); Heers, *L'Occident aux XIVème et XVème siècles*, 112, and *Le Vin: Production et consommation*.

[49] As yet there are no studies on the consumption of wine by Italian Jews in the Middle Ages and Renaissance. The various historical monographs on the Italian Jewish communities provide sporadic and insufficient information on the subject. On the production and consumption of wine and its by-products in Umbria in this period, see S. Nessi, 'La coltivazione della vite e la produzione del vino a Montefalco attraverso i secoli', *Spoletium*, 15 (1973), 31–8; Menichetti, *Le corporazioni delle arti*, 151–6; G. Mira, 'Contribuzione alla conoscenza dei consumi nell'età di mezzo: Il consumo di vino a Perugia', *Studi in memoria di P. M. Arcari* (Milan, 1978), 525–32.

[50] See Leon da Modena, *Letters* (Heb.), ed. Y. Boksenboim (Tel Aviv, 1984), 135–6. Rabbi Meir Katzenellenbogen of Padua (1482–1565), speaking on behalf of Jewish immigrants to Italy from the German communities, protested against the custom, widespread among the Jews of Modena, of drinking wine which they purchased from Christians at market; see J. L. Bato, 'L' immigrazione degli ebrei tedeschi in Italia dal Trecento al Cinquecento', in U. Nahon (ed. *Scritti in memoria di Sally Meyer* (Jerusalem, 1956), 25; Sh. Schwarzfuchs, 'I responsi di Rabbi Meir da Padova come fonte storica', in D. Carpi, A. Milano, and A. Rofé (eds.), *Scritti in memoria di Leone Carpi* (Jerusalem, 1967), 130. Like Italian Jews, Jews of the Franco-German

The habit of drinking ritually prepared wine does not seem to have been widespread among the Jews of the Umbrian communities of the period either. However, there were cases when they explicitly demanded this right from local authorities, and included a clause in their charters allowing them ritually to 'press the grapes'. This was the case at Norcia in 1432, and at Terni in 1456 and 1474.[51] In practice Jews were allowed to do the pressing directly in vats or tubs at the peasants' farms, or in cellars in the towns. They then bought as much must as they needed from the peasant or vineyard owner, and arranged to have it transported to their houses to ferment. We know that many Umbrian Jews owned vineyards, and in such cases the preparation of kosher wine for their own consumption was much simpler.

We have seen that kosher meat presented city butchers with the problem of disposing of the remains to a Christian clientèle. The unused remains of the must produced from grapes pressed by Jewish feet likewise presented peasants, vinedressers, and innkeepers with the problem as to whether it was permissible to trade in it and sell it off to Christian consumers. The problem concerned not only must, but also wine and its by-products, marc and the light wine produced by the blending of the last pressing of the marc. Usually, once Jews had completed the various processes of vinification according to their laws, the authorities required the peasant to throw away any remaining must and marc, and not sell them to Christians. The ruling laid down by the priors of Terni in 1456 is explicit on this matter:

---

communities, or originally from them, also bought must from Christians to make kosher wine. On the problems such customs posed in ensuring the wine was kosher, and the development of rabbinical legislation in this connection, see H. Soloveitchik, 'Can Halakhic Texts Talk History?', *Association of Jewish Studies Review*, 3 (1978), 153–96; R. Bonfil, 'A Proposal for the Foundation of a Rabbinic Academy in Southern Italy at the End of the Fifteenth Century' (Heb.), *Studies in Memory of Rabbi Isaac Nissim*, 4 (Jerusalem, 1985), 185–204.

[51] AC Norcia, Con.' e Rif., 4, fos. 135^v–137^r (18 Aug. 1432); AS Terni, Rif., 499, I, fo. 185^v (26 Dec. 1456); ibid. 503, III, fo. 84^v (30 Nov. 1474). Elsewhere too, in Italy, Jews enjoyed the right to make wine for their own use or to purchase it freely. For instance, the charter between the Jews and the commune of Reggio dated 30 July 1413 allowed them to 'take wine to Reggio for their use'; see Balletti, *Gli ebrei e gli Estensi*, 22. In 1408 the representatives of the Jewish community in Rome bought two vineyards from the convent of S. Maria in Aracoeli to provide the city's Jews with kosher wine; see J. C. Maire Vigueur, 'Les Juifs à Rome dans la seconde moitié du XIVème siècle', in S. Boesch Gajano (ed.), *Aspetti e problemi della presenza ebraica nell'Italia centrale-settentrionale (secoli XIV e XV)* (Rome, 1983), 23.

Any Christian selling a Jew a vat or tub of must or grapes shall be sentenced to a fine of 2 ducats for each vat or tub he may sell; but this measure shall be applied only where the latter, after the Jews have removed the must and light wine from the vat for their use, do not throw away the remainder of the marc, so as not to make subsequent use of it; Jews are free to press their grapes and to press the marc, but Christians may not make any use of this marc, must, or light wine; thus as soon as the Jews have concluded the various processes of vinification, the Christian sellers must throw away everything the Jews have not taken away for their own use, and shall be obliged to swear that they have indeed completed this operation, producing at least one trustworthy witness.[52]

In practice these regulations went largely unheeded. Once the peasant had been paid the full price for the must which Jews had pressed in his cellar, he can rarely have resisted the temptation to sell what remained, or consume it himself. After all, the grapes had been pressed in front of his own eyes, and the must in question was no different from the must he always used in his own vats and tubs. It is unlikely that religious considerations prevented him from drinking the wine, whether white or red.

Only rarely, and almost always under pressure from the Observant friars, did municipal authorities decide to take extreme measures and forbid Jews to press their own wine. In 1438, for instance, the authorities of Todi decreed that 'in the season of the wine harvest Jews should be forbidden to press the grapes, as they normally do, or to sell their wine directly or indirectly, either in the city of Todi or in the surrounding countryside . . . a fine of 10 *lire* should be paid by each Christian who allows Jews to press grapes in his cellar'.[53] In 1442 the priors of Norcia adopted the same measures, concerned as they appeared to be that 'wine pressed by Jews should not bring about the damnation of our souls'.[54] At Terni in 1444 the town authorities prohibited Jews from making kosher wine 'because they buy the grapes or wine in tubs, pollute it, then leave it to Christians'.[55] In 1468, after the founding of the local Monte di Pietà, the commune of Amelia, too, decided to forbid Jews to prepare wine 'according to their ancient custom'.[56] The measures envisaged in the decrees of Perugia of 1439 seem particularly

[52] AS Terni, Rif., 499, I, fo. 185ᵛ. See Ghinato, *Studi e documenti*, ii. 112, 141.
[53] AC Todi, Stat., 4, Add. 224, fo. 324ʳ (29 Mar. 1438).
[54] AC Norcia, Con. e Rif., 4, fo. 107ʳ (14 Feb. 1442).
[55] AS Terni, Rif., 497, fo. 69ʳ (11 Nov. 1444).
[56] AC Amelia, Rif., 41, fo. 190ᵛ (26 Mar. 1468).

severe, and are similar to those adopted elsewhere in Europe from the thirteenth century onwards. Regarded as 'untouchables' like lepers and prostitutes, Jews were also forbidden all manual contact with the food-stuffs, fruit, and vegetables laid out on market stalls, and especially with grapes for wine:[57]

No Jew or Jewess may purchase or cause to be purchased any quantity of must in the city or region of Perugia, unless they purchase the whole vatful of grapes and make all the wine from the said vat; and no Christian may sell the said vat of grapes unless they include the must in the sale; no Jew or Jewess . . . may in any circumstances sell, nor cause to be sold, nor give away, either overtly or covertly, any quantity of lasagne; these same Jews may not in any way touch any type of fruit unless they have purchased it first, excluding melons, garlic, onions, and walnuts, and all fruits with hard skins.[58]

These were futile attempts to create an artificial barrier between Jews and Christians in medieval society, while in daily practice their relations were marked by a familiarity and respect which friars and preachers considered excessive and harmful.[59] In general these attempts changed nothing, and barriers crumbled of their own accord, eroded by daily customs, with their natural and spontaneous power of persuasion. The measures taken to prevent Jews from pressing grapes were destined to meet the same fate, for the simple reason that no one was interested in their application. In 1442 in Norcia, for example, they were revoked

[57] On Jews regarded as 'untouchables' in the statutes of Avignon and Provence at the end of the 13th cent., contact with whom would bring about the deterioration and pollution of foodstuffs, see Grayzel, *The Church and the Jews*, 72–3; Kriegel, 'Un trait de psychologie sociale dans les pays méditerranéens du bas Moyen Âge'; Coulet, 'Juif intouchable et interdits alimentaires', 207–21; Rossiaud, *Medieval Prostitution*, 56–64.

[58] AS Perugia, Con. e Rif., 75, fo. 72ʳ (22 June 1439). See Fabretti, *Sulla condizione*, 38–42; Toaff, *Ebrei a Perugia*, 63–4. At an earlier date, in the ordinances issued on 10 Apr. 1432, the rulers of Perugia had already described as 'obscene and absurd' the fact that Jews 'observed particular habits and customs in their manner of eating and in buying must and wine'; see Fabretti, *Sulla condizione*, 29–30; Toaff, *Ebrei a Perugia*, 106.

[59] I agree with Rossiaud and Coulet that the Church intended these ordinances to encourage reaction against the laxity prevailing in relations between Christians and Jews in everyday life; see Rossiaud, *Medieval Prostitution*, 58; Coulet, 'Juif intouchable et interdits alimentaires', 207–21. Their conclusions may equally be applied to the social reality of Perugia and the other centres of Umbria in the 14th and 15th cents.

after two months, while at Amelia they were already a dead letter a few weeks after the beginning of the wine harvest.[60]

If they sometimes made their wine separately, Jews and Christians continued to drink it together. There is nothing surprising in the fact that the hot summer days of 1375 saw father Taddeo, the abbot of the monastery of S. Salvatore at Monte Acuto, unfailingly leading his monks to pay a call on Aleuccio di Salomone at Pian della Metula, in the green hills of Romeggio.[61] These visits were probably not entirely disinterested, because the Jewish owner of la Fratta usually offered the hot and thirsty monks at least one cup of his good red Trebbiano, not to mention the cool shade of his vines. According to father Taddeo, who was undoubtedly a connoisseur, it was the best wine in the district. Nor were the monks of S. Francesco at Assisi averse to sharing the table of their doctor, Sabbatuccio da Roma, to drink his 'old wine' together and, when called for, to buy the occasional barrel for the monastery's use. At Assisi it was well known that Sabbatuccio's Sangiovese and Vernaccia were truly outstanding, and a small 50-litre cask of this nectar was well worth the rather steep price of half a florin.[62] For their part Jews too appreciated the fine wine produced by the monks. In 1549 the merchant Guglielmo da Trevi and his wife Stella had the must of the renowned Sagrantino of Montefalco dispatched by the monks of the monastery of the Madonna delle Lacrime. The cart bearing the casks of the precious must was driven to Trevi by brother Apollonio himself.[63]

We possess a certain amount of significant information about the consumption of wine, must, and 'grapes for hanging' (grapes hung up in the kitchen after the wine harvest and destined for the table during the winter months) among the Jews of Umbria.[64] At the beginning of

---

[60] AC Norcia, Con. e Rif., 4, fos. 135ᵛ–137ʳ (15–18 Apr. 1442); AC Amelia, Rif., 41, fo. 198ʳ (7 Nov. 1468).

[61] AC Umbertide, Not., Giunta Loli da Montone, 258/26, fos. 13ᵛ, 64ʳ, 119ʳ.

[62] Archive of the Convent of S. Francesco, Assisi, Archivi Amministrativi, 372, fo. 1ʳ (20 May 1377). See Toaff, *Jews in Medieval Assisi*, 31.

[63] In Oct. 1549 Guglielmo and his wife were tried at Trevi for having imported must from Montefalco without paying tax. Guglielmo defended himself by maintaining that the friars had agreed to pay the town duty on his behalf (AC Trevi, Tre Chiavi, env. 16, reg. 238, fos. M–N).

[64] As far as the other regions of Italy are concerned, we have numerous documents concerning the purchase of must and wine by Jews; e.g. at Padua in 1404, at Sermoneta in 1442, at Bagnoregio in 1470. See Ciscato, *Ebrei in Padova*, 25; Caciorgna, 'Presenza ebraica', 161; Luzzatto and Tagliacozzo, 'Ebrei a Bagnoregio', 277. In the first half of the 16th cent. Jews from Iesi were engaged in the local wine trade; see G. Annibaldi, 'I banchi degli ebrei ed il Monte di Pietà di Iesi', *Picenum Seraphicum*, 9 (1972), 102, 105.

December 1342 Salamonetto di Vitale, acting on behalf of three Jewish families from Assisi, acquired 23 *some* of must from a peasant, to be used for their wine requirements during the following year. This was the equivalent of forty-six casks, with an overall capacity of 1,575.5 litres of must.[65] We may therefore deduce that the annual consumption of the three Assisi families was around 500 litres each. A similar quantity of wine was made by Salomone di Sabbatuccio, a Jew from Perugia who, around the mid-fourteenth century, had 8 *some* of must brought to him from the vines on the hills of S. Maria Rossa.[66] Abramo di Salomone, another Jew from Perugia, stocked up on red wine from the well-known cellars of la Fratta. In 1461 at least twelve casks of wine, equal to 6 *some*, arrived to grace his table at his house in the district of Porta S. Susanna.[67] The herbalist Benamato di Lazzaro regularly had a considerable quantity of wine, over 10 *some*, equal to about 700 litres, sent from the vineyards of Coccorano, on the hills separating the region of Perugia from the territories of Gubbio and Assisi. But it is probable that apart from being used for his annual household consumption, this wine was also largely used professionally in his shop.[68] At the end of the fourteenth century the carter Vitaluccio di Porta Sole in Perugia was ordering 6 *some* of wine and must each year, the equivalent of twelve casks, from the peasants of Valiano, who had their own vines along the road to Monteluce. The carter's annual consumption thus amounted to 400 litres.[69] The requirements of the family of Ventura di Isacco, a Jew from Spoleto, seem to have been higher still. On 4 February 1506 he ordered 5 *some* of must from a peasant of Morgnano, with the condition that they be delivered to him at the time of the following year's grape harvest, at the price of 2½ florins. One week later Ventura was acquiring a further '10 *some* of must for the use of the Jews, and 2 *some* of grapes for hanging' from an estate at Villa S. Croce, at an overall price of 6 florins. Here too must and grapes were to be delivered to him at the time of the harvest. The annual consumption of Ventura's family must therefore have

[65] Archive of the Confraternità di S. Stefano, Cathedral of S. Rufino, Assisi, documents of the notary Giovanni di Cecce, 38, fo. 8ᵛ (2 Dec. 1342). In Umbria as in the Marches the *soma* of wine, consisting of two casks, corresponded to 68.5 litres/kg.; see S. Anselmi (ed.), *Ancona e le Marche nel Cinquecento* (Ancona, 1982), 41.
[66] AS Perugia, Ospedale di S. Maria della Misericordia, Nicola di Pero da Porta Sole, contr. 8 (12 July 1345); ibid., Francesco di Egidio, contr. 9 (23 Feb. 1346).
[67] AS Perugia, Not., Giacomo di Lorenzo, 239, fo. 25ʳ (6 Mar. 1464).
[68] Ibid., Ospedale di S. Maria della Misericordia, Luca di Nicola, contr. 32 (4 June 1378) and 33 (21 Mar. 1381).
[69] Ibid., contr. 51 (15 Apr. 1394).

amounted to at least 15 *some*, equivalent to thirty casks holding 1,027.5 litres overall. Two *some* of 'grapes for hanging', equivalent to 137 kilos, were then added. Ventura may undoubtedly be considered something of a drinker, even by the generous standards of the time. In June 1461 Mosè di Abramo, a Jew from Terni, bought 9 *some* of must from a peasant of S. Brizio on three occasions, at an overall price of 3 florins. His family's annual consumption must therefore have been over 600 litres. In April 1492 another Jew from Spoleto, Aleuccio di Mosè, ordered 11 *some* of Trebbiano, Grechetto, and Moscatello, as well as must, from peasants from Castel Ritaldi. His family's needs are therefore to be estimated at about 750 litres a year.[70] It seems legitimate to consider these figures as indicative of the average consumption of wine by the Jews of Umbria during the late Middle Ages, so that we may deduce that each family drank between 1½ and 3 litres of wine a day.[71] In this too Jews do not seem to have differed from the rest of society, if we consider, for instance, that the individual level of wine consumption in medieval Bologna was at least double that of today, approaching 200 litres per person a year, that is, over half a litre of wine per person per day.[72] In Florence in the fifteenth century it seems that each inhabitant drank 300 litres a year, and in Siena and the surrounding region consumption was a little under 1½ litres per person per day.[73]

Clearly, wine had an important social function, acting as a comfort and release, often being drunk during leisure hours, and offering a form of escape that was widely sought after and enjoyed. But sometimes, and not only in relation to inns and taverns, it had less positive connotations, and was regarded, rightly or wrongly, as causing, or revealing, licentious, immoral, or heretical behaviour. Inevitably, Jews were not exempt from generalizations of this kind. Particularly when people wanted to accuse them of irreverent behaviour towards the Christian religion, it was convenient to portray Jews as hard-bitten drinkers, ever ready to

---

[70] AC Spoleto, Not., Giovan Battista alias Moscato, 110, fo. 28ᵛ; ibid., Moscato di Giovanni, 96, fo. 202ᵛ; ibid., Lorenzo di Liberato, 85, fo. 137ʳ; ibid., Angelo Parenzi, 136, fo. 70ʳ.

[71] Nor is there any reason to believe that Jews from other Italian cities drank less. For instance the cellars of the palazzo of the banker Abramo Sforno at Bologna in 1503 held 6,200 litres of wine, kept in barrels and other receptacles of various sizes; see Rinaldi, 'Un inventario di beni', 316, 324.

[72] See Pini, 'La viticoltura italiana', 873.

[73] See Ch. de la Roncière, 'Alimentation et ravitaillement à Florence au XIVᵉᵐᵉ siècle', *Archeologia medievale*, 8 (1981), 183–92; D. Balestracci, *La zappa e la retorica: Memorie familiari di un contadino toscano del Quattrocento* (Florence, 1984), 117–22.

over-indulge in alcohol and reveal themselves in all their arrogance. Several witnesses at the proceedings against Daniele da Bevagna and his brothers in 1485, for instance, were ready to swear to 'having seen at least four foreign Jews in the house of the accused on Good Friday, towards evening, playing games of chance and drinking wine, and making a fiendish racket'.[74] An innocent game of *scopa* and a cup among friends might conceal unforeseen dangers when the popular imagination was fed by suspicion and prejudice. Umbria also had a number of taverns run by Jews, who were official members of the tavern-keepers' guild. They served a motley clientèle, drawn from every social class, naturally not only Jewish. It would be idle to speculate whether the wine served there was entirely kosher. In 1381 a 'Jewish tavern-keeper' was running the 'Osteria del Campo' on the square of S. Maria degli Angeli in Assisi. It will come as no surprise to find the monks of the Confraternity of S. Stefano among its most regular clients, buying wine at 8 *denari* per *foglietta*.[75] In 1376 the commune of Trevi bought the wine it served on official occasions from the tavern of the Jewess Chiaruccia on via del Piano.[76] These cannot have been exceptional cases. In 1508 two Jews from Perugia, Vitale di Mosè and David di Giuseppe, were running a tavern and shop for the consumption and sale of wine in the vicolo della Salsa. We know that the two publicans were members of the city's tavern-keepers' guild, paying a registration fee of 10 florins a year.[77] The tavern della Salsa did not enjoy a good reputation in Perugia, and was regarded as a haunt for drunks, criminals, and gamblers. The authorities made daily visits to settle brawls and prevent their degenerating into something worse.[78] But such professional hazards, which were in any case largely to be expected, did not discourage the two tavern-keepers from exercising their trade in Perugia over many years.

---

[74] AC Bevagna, Not., Crescimbene di Pietro di Percivalle, 1539, fos. I–III (10 Apr. 1485).   [75] See Toaff, *Jews in Medieval Assisi*, 31.
[76] AC Trevi, Tre Chiavi, env. 4, reg. 34, fo. 49ʳ (7 Aug. 1376).
[77] AS Perugia, Not., Tolomeo di Niccolò, 403, fo. 33ʳ. Jews ran inns and taverns in other towns in Italy too, e.g. in Rome, Mantua, Pavia, and Piacenza; see Esposito, 'Ebrei a Roma nella seconda metà del Quattrocento', 72–5; Simonsohn, *Jews in the Duchy of Mantua*, 348–51; Motta, 'Ebrei in Como', 42–3.
[78] On 11 Aug. 1508 one of the two innkeepers, Vitale di Mosè, had set up a company, together with a foreigner from Verona, for the manufacture of playing-cards (AS Perugia, Not., Benedetto di Massarello, 541, fo. 140ʳ). Previously the vicolo della Salsa had housed the premises of the woolcarders; see A. Grohmann, *Città e territorio* (Perugia, 1981), i. 66–7.

Lastly, we should not underestimate the therapeutic use of wine in medieval Italy. Wine was used unstintingly by the doctors and surgeons of the time, in the preparation of many medicines and also as an antiseptic because of its alcoholic content. Official medical science was unanimous in extolling wine's therapeutic and curative virtues. We have already seen how Sabbatuccio di Manuele, the physician at Assisi at the end of the fourteenth century, was appreciated by his patients partly for the excellent quality of the wine that he produced and was not above selling. Sabbatuccio was the owner of extensive vineyards around Assisi, acquired with the proceeds of his medical skills, and he saw directly to his own needs as an expert vine-dresser and consumer.[79] But quite often his vines did not produce enough wine for his professional needs, and then the doctor was obliged to turn elsewhere. In 1381, for instance, Sabbatuccio bought 11 *some* of red Viglione wine (over 750 litres/kg.) from a peasant, to be delivered to him in several stages over a period of three years.[80] His son Gaio, a doctor at Assisi like his father and then official surgeon to the commune of Spello, was a heavy wine-drinker, and not above having his bills paid in must rather than in cash. In 1419, having successfully treated a peasant from Poggio Morico for knife wounds to his throat and neck, Gaio asked for payment in the form of 2 *some* of wine 'according to the Jewish custom', which the patient undertook to deliver at the time of the grape harvest.[81] Musetto di Guglielmo, medical officer at Perugia at the beginning of the fifteenth century, owned vineyards at Pastene in the suburbs at Porta S. Angelo, and produced wine for the needs of his own family and his profession. His name figures regularly among those citizens of Perugia who paid the wine tax to the commune's treasurer.[82] Years later the famous head physician of Perugia, Laudadio de Blanis, owned a fine estate with vines and olive-groves at Ponte di Oddo in the hills near Perugia. Its yield must have been particularly abundant, because in 1552 and 1553 he sold considerable quantities of wine to inhabitants of the city and surrounding countryside.[83]

[79] See Toaff, *Jews in Medieval Assisi*, 196–9.
[80] AC Assisi, Not., Francesco di Tomaso, A3, fo. 129[r] (3 June 1381).
[81] Ibid., Giovanni di Cecco Bevignate, B18, fo. 428[v] (10 May 1419).
[82] AS Perugia, Conservatori della moneta, 38, fos. 21[v], 27[r] (1416); ibid. 44, fos. 12[r] 25[r] (1417).
[83] On the physician Laudadio de Blanis, see Toaff, *Ebrei a Perugia*, 149–50, and the extensive bibliography, esp. pp. 158 and 161–2.

4

The House of Prayer

ESTABLISHING THE SYNAGOGUE

ONE of the main requests made by Jews to municipal and ecclesiastical authorities as soon as they settled in any one place was for permission to gather in prayer and hold their own religious services. Usually this was granted by the priors and bishop, who signed clauses in their charters with the Jews allowing them to 'establish the synagogue', that is, choose a house where they could worship and gather for prayer whenever they wished. Permission to establish a synagogue appears with minor variants in almost all the charters granted Jews by the communes of Umbria in the late Middle Ages and Renaissance. 'They may and shall be allowed to establish and gather in their synagogue whenever they shall deem fit' (Assisi 1457); 'the said Jews may say their office in the synagogue and perform their ceremonies as other Jews do' (Foligno 1456); 'Jews may have, and rent, a house in the city of Terni, in a seemly place, where they may establish and congregate in their synagogue and perform their ceremonies' (Terni 1474); 'the said Jews may say their office in the synagogue and perform their ceremonies as do other Jews' (Todi 1481).[1] Even when the Jewish presence in any given town was limited to one single family and it was therefore impossible to establish a synagogue in the official sense, Jews were still granted the right to choose a place where they could pray. In 1445, for instance, the doctor and banker Leone da Rieti, asked by the commune of Amelia to practise his twofold career in the town, made his agreement conditional upon being granted the right freely to perform Jewish ceremonies and observe other religious rules: 'I, magistro Leone, along with all my family, may follow and practise all the ceremonies and customs and offices which have always been practised among us Jews from time immemorial.'[2] On occasions when for incidental rea-

---

[1] AC Assisi, H, Rif. 14, fos. 111ʳ–112ᵛ (1 July 1457); AC Foligno, Rif., 30, fo. 94ᵛ (29 June 1456); AS Terni, Rif., 503, III, fos. 84ᵛ–88ʳ (30 Nov. 1474); AC Todi, Rif., 82, fos. 43ᵛ–49ᵛ (28 Feb. 1481).

[2] AC Amelia, Rif., 38, fo. 74ʳ (15 July 1445).

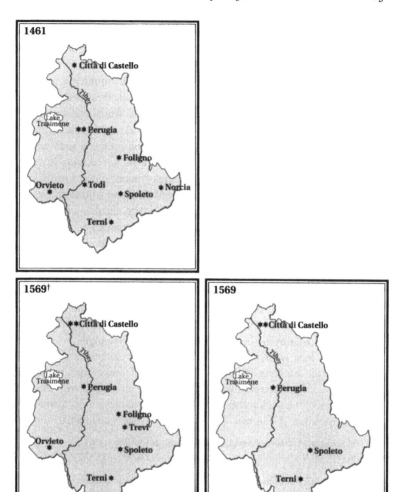

FIG. 4.1 Synagogues in Umbria (1461–1569)

sons, such as the holding of fairs, a number of Jews might spend a period of up to several weeks in places which had no significant Jewish presence, or where such a presence had died out, requests to the authorities
to establish a synagogue were also customary. In 1569, for instance, the

cloth merchant Dattilo di Signorello wrote to the priors of Foligno on behalf of all the Jewish merchants from Rome, Umbria, and the Marches who normally took part in the local summer fair, asking for 'a licence to establish the synagogue there for the period of the fair'.[3]

Once granted, this right was rarely revoked by the municipal authorities. Unlike the right to prepare kosher food, which frequently aroused suspicion and hostility in ecclesiastical circles and which was the object of restrictive local legislation, the Jews' right to their own house of prayer rarely seems to have been contested. I have found only one such case in fifteenth-century Umbria: in 1442 the commune of Norcia issued a series of directives intended to annul the privileges granted to the town's Jews in the charter signed with them ten years earlier. Among other things the Norcia authorities stated 'that the Jews of Norcia and the surrounding *contado* [countryside] should not be permitted to gather in their synagogue as they have been accustomed to do, thereby offending our faith'. The Jews' justifiable reaction was to threaten to break off their credit activities and leave the town. This had an almost immediate effect, and less than two months later the Norcia Jews' right to their own place of worship was fully re-established.[4] But I have found no other evidence that the ecclesiastical and municipal authorities in fifteenth-century Umbria tried to prevent Jews from establishing a synagogue.[5]

None the less, the right had its limits, and very precise ones at that. Above all, the building chosen as the house of prayer had to have a modest and simple exterior, so that it would not emulate even remotely the splendour of the churches, cathedrals, and basilicas which were the glory of the cities of Umbria. The more the synagogue blended in with

[3] AC Foligno, Memorie diverse, inventari, ind. 201 (2 Feb. 1569).

[4] AC Norcia, Con. e Rif., 4, fo. 115^r (18 Feb. 1442), fos. 135^v–137^r (15–18 Apr. 1442).

[5] In other cities of central and northern Italy bans were sometimes proclaimed, if infrequently. In 1487 the governors of Cesena protested because the synagogue was located in a central position, in front of the palace of the Podestà, and worship there disturbed the other citizens. They therefore proposed transferring it elsewhere. However, the decision does not seem to have been implemented before 1504, when the commune of Cesena won the support and approval of pope Julius II; see Muzzarelli, *Ebrei e città d'Italia*, 182–3. In 1492 the doge of Venice considered moving the synagogue at Ravenna, which was situated near the cathedral; see M. Maragi, 'La fondazione del Monte di Pietà di Ravenna e la situazione economico–sociale ravennate alla fine del secolo XV', *Studi Ravennati*, 17 (1966), 247; R. Segre, 'Gli ebrei a Ravenna nell'età veneziana', in D. Bolognesi (ed.), *Ravenna in età veneziana* (Ravenna, 1986), 168–9. In 1576 the commune of Lodi decided to move the local synagogue, which was bounded by three churches; see R. Segre, *Gli ebrei lombardi nell'età spagnola* (Turin, 1973), 75.

the surrounding houses, the more likely it was that its existence would be trouble-free and unchallenged. When the authorities had approved a Jewish community's choice of a place for its synagogue, the decision could not be altered. On no account could a synagogue be established on a different site: even in extreme cases such as war, epidemic, or, indeed, the collapse of the building, when other accommodation had to be found, the alternative was regarded as temporary, and the original synagogue was the only one fully authorized to serve the Jewish community. This applied even when the majority of a synagogue's members had moved to another part of town. Only rarely, when a Jewish community had grown especially big, would the bishop agree that it might open a second house of prayer. In Umbria only the Jewish communities of Perugia and Città di Castello were allowed to have second synagogues, and in both cases only for short periods. The Church's position on the Jewish right to a synagogue, with the relevant restrictions, was the same in Umbria as it was throughout Italy and the rest of Christian Europe in the Middle Ages.[6]

In 1465 the plague struck Città di Castello, causing many deaths, particularly in the neighbourhood of Porta S. Egidio, where the syna-gogue was situated in the house of the banker Isacco di Salomone and his brothers. The faithful were obliged to abandon this synagogue to avoid contagion, and the bishop agreed to the Jews' request that 'the Jews living in this city, wishing so far as possible to safeguard their health, beg that they may be granted a licence to celebrate their feasts and hold their ceremonies in the house of Bonaventura, situated in this city in the neighbourhood of Porta S. Maria'. But the bishop was careful to warn the Jews not to consider this arrangement permanent: 'for the Jews shall not be permitted to establish a new synagogue in the house of Bonaventura, nor shall this one replace the previous one; but the old synagogue shall retain the function it has had hitherto, so that when the epidemic ceases, the Jews of the city shall return to hold their ceremonies in the old syna-gogue.' To make his warning more convincing, the bishop threatened a fine of 200 florins, should it be disregarded.[7] Sometimes the ecclesiastical authorities granted such concessions in less urgent cases. In 1471 the

[6] On the Church's traditional position concerning Jews' right to establish a syna-gogue, see e.g. Grayzel, *The Church and the Jews*, 70–1; B. Blumenkranz, *Juifs et Chrétiens dans le monde occidental* (Paris–Hague, 1960), 309–15; V. Colorni, *Gli ebrei nel sistema del diritto comune fino alla prima emancipazione* (Milan, 1956), 47–8.

[7] Archivio Vescovile Città di Castello, vol. 7, fo. 55ᵛ (5 Oct. 1465). See Toaff, 'Ebrei a Città di Castello', 101–2.

deputy of the bishop of Assisi granted the French Jew Manuele di Giacobbe permission to conduct religious services in his own home, together with his father and other Jews. This permission was granted on the grounds that Manuele's old father was unable to leave his house to go and pray in the synagogue of Assisi, the only place in the town where, according to the privileges in their charter, Jews were allowed to conduct religious services.[8] In 1518 the deputy of the bishop of Spoleto authorized the repair of the outer wall of the synagogue, which was in danger of collapse and threatened neighbouring houses. However, to avoid any misunderstanding, he hastened to add that the restoration work 'was in no way to embellish the said synagogue'.[9]

Permission to establish a synagogue amounted at once to much less, and much more, than building a particular place of prayer: less in the sense that, in general, the choice of synagogue fell on a modest rented house whose exterior was not to be altered, so as not to attract attention, or one or more rooms made available to the community in the house of a rich and influential Jewish family; more, because these rooms, outwardly so unpretentious, did not serve simply for religious ceremonies and prayers, but often became the fulcrum of Jewish life, where Jews gathered to take decisions affecting the whole community.[10] Jews' minority status made it important for them to analyse and keep abreast of the legal and socio-economic structures within which they functioned as a group. In periods of emergency or danger it became necessary to hear the opinions and advice of the whole community before taking delicate decisions on its stance on a particular issue. The prayers of the Jews rose heavenwards from the synagogue, but often they sped their way towards the town hall or bishop's palace at the same time. These two paths were not mutually exclusive, but complementary, and could turn the workings of chance and fortune to the community's advantage. The synagogue was also used to discuss individual problems, to offer help, or sometimes sanction punishment. It was here that individual contributions to communal taxes were approved, and that elections to various community offices took place. The synagogue was thus more than a house of prayer:

---

[8] AC Assisi, Not., Nicola di Lorenzo, v9, file 2, fo. 72ᵛ (22 Sept. 1471). See Toaff, *Jews in Medieval Assisi*, 207–8.

[9] AC Spoleto, Not., Giovanni di Andrea Bancaroni, 68, fo. 274ʳ (22 Mar. 1518).

[10] On the multiple roles played by the synagogues of the Jewish communities of Italy and Europe at this period, see e.g. I. Abrahams, *Jewish Life in the Middle Ages* (New York, 1973), 1–34; Shulvass, *The Jews in the World of the Renaissance*, 74–6; R. Bonfil, 'La sinagoga in Italia come luogo di riunione e di preghiera', in A. Neppi Ventura (ed.), *Il centenario del Tempio Israelitico di Firenze* (Florence, 1985), 36–44.

it was the headquarters of the *Universitas Judaeorum*, the 'corporation' of the Jews, this being the term by which each organized Jewish community, whatever its size, was commonly designated in the documents of the period. Inevitably, the term 'synagogue' was increasingly used as a synonym for a Jewish community, for instance in the official acts of Perugia from the last part of the fifteenth century to the middle of the sixteenth. So it was the synagogue that acquired property and paid taxes, elected officials, paid homage to princes and bishops, and was expelled from and readmitted into civic life.

For Christians, therefore, the permission for Jews to 'establish and gather together in the synagogue' took on connotations which extended beyond the mere right to a place of prayer. In fact when Jews themselves wanted to refer to the place where their services were held they rarely used the word 'synagogue', preferring the term 'temple' or, more frequently, *scola* or *scole*. When, in 1473, fra Antonio da Macerata, prior of the Ospedale di S. Maria della Misericordia at Perugia, asked the representatives of the Jewish community if a sacrilegious theft had recently occurred in their synagogue, the Jews replied in the affirmative. They added that it had occurred at night, and that silver plate weighing eleven-and-a-half *libbre* had been removed from the synagogue, 'that is, from our temple'.[11] The term *scola* was commonly used by Jews to indicate their house of prayer at this period, and indeed almost up to the present day. The rabbi was therefore referred to as the *maestro di scola*, or simply *maestro*; this was the term applied to Servadio di Abramo da Bertinoro, the rabbi of Città di Castello in 1485, whom we have identified as the well-known Obadyah da Bertinoro, the author of a commentary on the Mishnah which became a classic.[12] The title *maestro di scola* was also given to the more humble figure of Bonaventura da Ferrara, the industrious rabbi of Perugia around the middle of the fifteenth century.[13]

LIFE AND DEATH IN THE *SCOLA*

As we have seen, at the approach of death many believers bethought themselves of their synagogue, and concern for the fate of their souls in the world to come loosened their purse-strings. Wills frequently

---

[11] AS Perugia, Not., Tolomeo di Niccolò, 76, fo. 688ʳ (30 Sept. 1473).
[12] Toaff, 'Ebrei a Città di Castello', 18–19.
[13] AS Perugia, Not., Giuliano di Piermatteo di Paolo, 154, fo. 830ʳ (15 Mar. 1467). In 15th-cent. Sicily, too, rabbis were known as *maestri di scuola*; see M. Gaudioso, *La comunità ebraica di Catania nei secoli XIV e XV* (Catania, 1974), 106, 118.

contained bequests for the purchase of sacred ornaments and ritual silver, and above all for the oil to be burned in the lamps of the houses of prayer for the souls of the deceased. A series of such bequests, included in the will of the merchant Mosè da Terni charts the locations of the synagogues of the Umbrian Jewish communities in the mid-fifteenth century.[14] The document provides evidence of the existence at this period of synagogues at Perugia, Spoleto, Todi, Terni, and Foligno. Further evidence enables us to add those of Città di Castello, Norcia, Orvieto, and possibly Assisi to the list, and also informs us that only at Perugia were there two houses of prayer serving the local Jewish community. Roughly a century later, in 1569, the list of synagogues in the Papal State which paid taxes to the Casa dei Catecumeni in Rome mentions the names of seven Umbrian towns (Città di Castello, Foligno, Orvieto, Perugia, Spoleto, Trevi, and Terni).[15] The note specifies that, while each of these centres had only one active synagogue, Città di Castello had two, one 'public' and the other 'private'. These eight synagogues paid the Casa dei Catecumeni the modest sum of 96 *scudi* a year, out of the 1,380 *scudi* which was the total annual contribution of the 115 synagogues taxed. The papal document implies that the number of synagogues in Umbria had not diminished much between the mid-fifteenth and mid-sixteenth centuries. This seems surprising, considering the downward turn taken by the fortunes of the Jews of the region in this period, which begins with the foundation of the Monte di Pietà and ends with their expulsion, on the orders of Pius V, in 1569. Furthermore, the existence of eight synagogues in Umbria is in sharp contrast with the demographic data we possess as to the size of the Jewish communities of the region, which diminished constantly as the sixteenth century progressed. But this is, as it were, an optical illusion: the demands of the Casa dei Catecumeni of Rome led assiduous papal officials to tax those Jewish communities where a synagogue had functioned in the past, but which had long been in drastic decline, or on the verge of complete extinction. Resuscitating them on paper was a calculated ploy to add a few *scudi* to the pious institution's meagre balance-sheet. We know for certain that the synagogues of Orvieto and Foligno had ceased to function at the beginning of the sixteenth century, and that there had never

---

[14] AC Spoleto, Not., Giovanni di Luca, 8, fo. 210ʳ (8 Dec. 1461).

[15] *All 'illustrissima Congregazione particolare deputata dalla Santità di Nostro Signore Pio PP. VI . . . per l'Università degli ebrei di Roma* (Rome, 1789), 22–3. First published for the Lazzarini, this document has been republished: M. Stern, *Urkundliche Beiträge über die Stellung der Päpste zu den Juden* (Kiel, 1893), 144–5.

been a real synagogue at Trevi. We have fairly precise information on the location of some of the Umbrian synagogues: the one at Spoleto was in the so-called 'street of the Jews', some dozen metres from the market square. It was situated in the house of the de Pomis family, who were doctors and bankers, and was flanked on one side by the church of S. Gregorio della Sinagoga and on the other by the palazzo of the noble family of the del Duomo.[16] At the beginning of the fifteenth century the synagogue at Città di Castello was in the district of Porta S. Egidio, by the house of the doctor Salomone di Bonaventura and his sons. The building, which housed Salomone's family and the adjoining synagogue, was owned by the friars of the monastery of S. Egidio, who had rented it to the Jews on a long lease.[17] Later, when the Jewish community grew in size, a second synagogue was opened in the district of Porta S. Maria.

The first synagogue at Perugia was situated in a palazzo on the old via Regale, later known as via Vecchia, which ran through the district of Porta S. Angelo, not far from the church of S. Donato.[18] Up to the middle of the fifteenth century the building belonged to the noble Perugian family of the Arcipreti. From 1448 to 1452 the Jewish community paid an annual rent of 7 florins to Agamennone Arcipreti, *cavaliere imperiale* (knight by the decree of the Emperor) and governor of the Città di Castello, for the use of the palazzo as a synagogue. In 1457 the Jews of Perugia rented another, adjacent, building, for 7 florins a year.[19] Some years later the two buildings were bought for 200 florins by the brothers Aleuccio and Angelo di Guglielmo, members of a rich and prominent family of Jewish bankers. The new owners embarked on a programme of restoration and enlargement, turning the buildings into a splendid residence befitting their own status as high-ranking financiers,[20] while at the same time guaranteeing the Jewish community free use of the premises where the synagogue had been for over half a century. In his will of 1471, Aleuccio also directed that at his death the whole palazzo was to pass to the Jewish community of Perugia, to be used as a permanent place of

---

[16] AC Spoleto, Not., Giovacchino di Giovanni, 106/I, fo. 435ʳ (27 Jan. 1501).

[17] AC Città di Castello, Not., Angelo di Battista di Angelo, 3, fo. 77ᵛ (21 Feb. 1465); ibid., fo. 81ʳ (1 Mar. 1465).

[18] On the location of the synagogue of Perugia, see Toaff, *Ebrei a Perugia*, 95–6; see also Fig. 8.1 below for a plan of the Jewish quarter in Perugia.

[19] AS Perugia, Not., Mariano di Luca di Nino, 115, fo. 130ᵛ (17 Apr. 1448); ibid., Giuliano di Piermatteo, 371, fo. 576ʳ (29 Dec. 1457). On the Arcipreti of Perugia see Grohmann, *Città e territorio*, i. 421–3.

[20] AS Perugia, Giud., Processus, file 4, bundle 38 (4 Dec. 1471).

worship.[21] But this was not to be, and in 1489 the property of the two
brothers was taken over by the banker Ventura di Abramo, who refused
to grant possession to the Jewish community. Only in 1490, after the representatives of Perugia's Jews had officially and unwillingly assigned him
full rights to the building, would the banker allow them use of the area
laid out as a synagogue. 'Having observed that the Jews of Perugia
acknowledge his rightful ownership of the house in the district of S.
Angelo, in the parish of S. Donato, Ventura di Abramo da Perugia grants
them and their families access to the said house to conduct their religious
services there, provided they behave well and respectably; this permission shall be valid for such time as the said Ventura shall feel it to be
opportune, and during this period he shall not be able to demand any rent
from the community of the Jews of Perugia.'[22] Not satisfied with this, a
year later Ventura was renting the building to a private individual to use
as his place of residence. But the contract specified that the rent did not
include 'the apartment where the synagogue is and where the Jews go to
scola, nor the entrance giving access to said *scola* or synagogue'.[23] On the
death of Ventura the building at last became the property of the Jewish
community, which was now reduced in numbers. But the life of the synagogue continued its stormy course: the inhabitants of the neighbouring
houses contested its boundaries and brought a lawsuit against the Jewish
community, involving it in a series of lengthy legal proceedings between
1522 and 1552.[24] The house on via Vecchia, 'known as the synagogue of
the Jews', was sold on 1 January 1571, a few months after the Jews'
expulsion from the city by special papal derogation. It was bought from
Giuseppe da Montagnana, the last Jew left living in Perugia, by the noble
family of Montesperelli, who paid the agreed price of 230 *scudi*.[25]
A second synagogue had functioned briefly in Perugia around the middle
of the fifteenth century, when the Jewish community was larger and more
active. It is referred to by the Spanish Jewess Ora di Giuseppe in her will
of 1457.[26] This synagogue was also located in the district of Porta S.

[21] AS Perugia, Guid., Processus, env. 215, file 3; ibid., env. 221, file 23 (1 Sept.
1522–18 Mar. 1523).
[22] AS Perugia, Not., Francesco di Jacopo, 223, fo. 123ᵛ (5 Mar. 1490).
[23] Ibid. 224, fo. 99ᵛ (4 Mar. 1491).
[24] AS Perugia, Giud., Processus, env. 215, file 3 (1–5 Sept. 1522); ibid., env. 221,
file 26 (18 Mar.–3 Apr. 1523); ibid., env. 508, file 8 (10–16 May 1551); ibid., env. 535,
file 36 (16–31 Oct. 1552).
[25] AS Perugia, Not., Ercolano Rossi, 1685, fo. 1ʳ (1 Jan. 1571). On the noble
Perugian family of the Montesperelli see Grohmann, *Città e territorio*, i. 522–3.
[26] AS Perugia, Not., Giovanni di Costante, 122, fos. 347ʳ–348ʳ (25 May–10 July
1457).

Angelo, in the parish of S. Donato, and opened on to via Oradina, an old street built in 1378, with the Pozzo Campana behind it. The *scola* on via Oradina had already ceased to function by the end of the fifteenth century, when the Jewish community of Perugia entered a period of crisis following the founding of the Monte di Pietà.

What did such synagogues look like, situated as they were inside private houses, and with façades identical to those of the surrounding buildings? We have no exact descriptions for the Umbrian area, but we can glean some idea from the synagogue functioning in Bologna in the palazzo of Abramo Sforno on via S. Stefano, mentioned briefly in an inventory of 1503. 'A chapel, or room for prayer with cloth of gold and silk brocade and silver lamps and chains, and lampshades and books left by various persons to the said chapel for the salvation of their souls.'[27] As we have seen, in Perugia and the other towns of Umbria the faithful made bequests to the synagogue, and gave presents, often for the salvation of the souls of the deceased. These might take the form of precious fabrics used to cover the Ark containing the *sifrei Torah*, the scrolls of parchment with the text of the Pentateuch for public reading in the synagogue, or ritual silver plate, or synagogue lamps. In her will of 1457 the Spanish Jewess Ora left the synagogue of Perugia books, silver plate, and sacred furnishings, including a curtain (*parokhet*) of blue silk with images of birds and a Hebrew inscription embroidered in gold and silver, two small silver lamp-chains, a seat upholstered in red brocade, and a scroll with the Pentateuch wrapped in blue linen with an elaborate mantle of white damask.[28] In 1389 a Jewess from Perugia, Nuccia di Salomone, presented the *scola* on via Vecchia with another *sefer Torah* for synagogue readings.[29]

Not surprisingly, the precious objects of worship sometimes attracted unwelcome attention. One September night in 1473 the entrance to the Perugia synagogue was forced open and much of the ritual silver plate was stolen, including 'seventeen silver chains weighing eleven-and-a-half *libbre*, according to the scales of the commune of Perugia, and an iron chain supporting the lamps needed for their divine services and sacrifices' (*sic*: the notary seems not to understand what the Jews actually did in the

[27] See Rinaldi, 'Un inventario di beni', 324. For a brief description of the 'synagogue and private oratory of the Jews of Forlì', situated near Porta Merlonia in 1466, see E. Rinaldi, 'Gli ebrei a Forlì nei secoli XIV e XV', *Atti e Memorie della R. Deputazione di Storia Patria per le Province di Romagna*, ser. 4, no. 10 (1920), 310–13.

[28] See Majarelli and Nicolini, *Monte dei Poveri di Perugia*, 218–22.

[29] AS Perugia, Not., Onofrio di Gilio, 27, fo. 17ʳ (7 May 1389).

synagogue). Some days later, the repentant thieves confessed their sacrilegious theft to the prior of the Ospedale di S. Maria della Misericordia,
and handed over the stolen goods;[30] the silver lamps and chains were
returned to their rightful owner and replaced in the rooms on via
Vecchia. But the peregrinations of the objects of worship were not yet
over. In 1493 a precious silver ciborium belonging to the Perugia synagogue was stolen, this time by Jewish thieves, who added insult to injury
by pawning it at the Monte di Pietà.[31] The Perugia Jews naturally hastened to redeem the object and return it to their place of worship. Finally,
at the end of the summer of 1567, crippled by debt and on the eve of their
enforced exodus from the city, the Jews of Perugia were forced to
abandon most of their objects of worship once and for all. Lamps and
silver chains weighing almost fifteen *libbre* 'according to the steelyard'
were handed over by the few Jews remaining in Perugia to the banker
Giuseppe da Montagnana, who was to go to Rome to pay the debts that
had built up with the Casa dei Catecumeni.[32]

As we have seen, the synagogue was used for all the general and
municipal business of the Jewish community. The Jews of Perugia, for
example, gathered in the synagogue on via Vecchia to discuss members'
shares in the communal taxes on 28 October 1457, in the presence of the
bishop's nunzio. On 18 April 1458 the same synagogue was the scene of
a general meeting to elect the community's representatives in negotiations with the commune of Perugia to draft the clauses of a new charter.
It was here, in the winter of 1461, that the community leaders discussed
the resources of its individual members in relation to the relevant taxes
and contributions. In April 1567 the community assembled once more to
discuss the sale of their cemetery to the nuns of the Beata Colomba.[33]
The rabbinical court and court of arbitration of the Jewish community
also had their permanent headquarters in the synagogue premises, and it
was here that members were summoned to settle the various controver-
sies arising among them. It seems that the rabbinical court of Perugia
had jurisdiction over Jews living in the other Umbrian centres, and
that the appointment of its judges required ratification by the papal

[30] AS Perugia, Not., Tolomeo di Niccolò, 76, fo. 688ʳ (30 Sept. 1473).
[31] Ibid., Francesco di Jacopo, 227, fo. 218ʳ (19 June 1493).
[32] Ibid., Collegio del Cambio, various papers, atti giud., cat. 5, env. 140, fo. 16ʳ (21 Aug. 1567).
[33] Ibid., Not., Tomaso di Antonio, 391, fo. 138ʳ (28 Oct. 1457); ibid. fo. 190ʳ (18 Apr. 1458), fo. 404ʳ (20 Jan. 1461), and fo. 457ʳ (22 Apr. 1461); ibid., Collegio del Cambio, atti giud., cat. 5, env. 140, fo. 8ʳ (10 Apr. 1567).

governor.[34] Half-way through the fifteenth century the three members of the rabbinical court of Perugia, presided over by the *maestro di scola*, were referred to in the documents as 'judges and syndics of the synagogue of the Jews of the city of Perugia, under the decree of the governor of Umbria, and their court sits in the synagogue'. In 1459, for instance, the doctor and banker from Assisi, Bonaiuto da Tivoli, had threatened to go to the Perugian magistrates to ask them to arrest a Jew who had fled the city owing him money; this delicate matter, which had implications that were unpleasant for the entire community, was submitted to the arbitration of the judges of the rabbinical court of Perugia. They ruled that Bonaiuto should be guaranteed repayment of the debt by two Jews from Assisi, and should therefore withdraw his denunciation, allowing his debtor to return to the city.[35]

The conflicts endemic within the Jewish community tended to come to a head in the synagogue, often with surprising violence. The meeting-place became a place of confrontation; the house of prayer offered an opportunity to express personal protest against injustices, real or imagined, and to give vent to all manner of frustrations. These were often exacerbated by the oligarchic structure of the community, whose life was linked to the conduct of the bankers, with their position of marked privilege in relation to other Jews.[36] Conflicts and grudges of a social, economic, or even purely personal nature within a Jewish society that appeared to be more or less homogeneous when considered in terms of its relationships with the surrounding society, would then reveal themselves in all their virulence. Interestingly, two of the three murders committed in this period by Umbrian Jews took place within the synagogue's four walls. Similar examples are documented elsewhere in Italy, implying that this phenomenon was not exceptional; and I believe it deserves more attention than it has so far received.[37] In 1508 the life of the Jewish com-

---

[34] On the activities of the court of Perugia in the 15th cent. see Toaff, *Ebrei a Perugia*, 99–100; id., *Jews in Medieval Assisi*, 75. On the prerogatives of the rabbinical courts and courts of arbitration within the Jewish communities in the Renaissance, see esp. R. Bonfil, *Rabbis and Jewish Communities in Renaissance Italy*, trans. Jonathan Chipman (London, 1993), 207–69.

[35] AS Perugia, Not., Tomaso di Antonio, 391, fo. 284ᵛ (17 Sept. 1459).

[36] See Bonfil, 'La sinagoga in Italia', 38.

[37] Let us consider some incidents that occurred in Iesi by way of random example. In 1532 a brawl involving four Jews, three men and a woman, took place in the local synagogue, after which two of the protagonists were left lying wounded on the ground. On 16 Nov. 1538 the banker Mosè Vivanti insulted a Jewish beggar in the synagogue: the beggar was a refugee from Sicily, and Mosè's terms of insult included '*marrano* [traitor, pig], blockhead, and down-and-out'; he then thrashed him and

munity of Spoleto was disrupted by the death of Eva, a young woman
killed by her husband on the synagogue premises. Many of the meetings
which the Jews of the city subsequently held to discuss what to do about
Eva's under-age daughter took place at the scene of the crime, the synagogue in the house of the de Pomis. These sessions were attended by a
notary and the civil court judge of Spoleto, 'who was seated at a bench
within the said synagogue'.[38] In 1487 Angelo di Guglielmo, one of the
richest Jews of Perugia, met his death in the synagogue on via Vecchia at
the hands of Deodato di Mosè, a pathetic figure who had previously eked
out a living as a dancing-master. The killer was arrested, sentenced to
payment of a fine which reduced him to utter penury, and banished from
the city. He returned to Perugia two years later to ask forgiveness of
Frescarosa, the victim's daughter, who had moved to Fermo in the mean
time. He paid dearly for her pardon, as its conditions included lifelong
excommunication from the Jewish community, and he was forced to sign
a solemn pledge swearing that 'for the rest of my life I shall not go anywhere near the town of Fermo and shall not enter the *scola*, that is, the
synagogue of the Jews of Perugia, where religious services are currently
celebrated, because I have committed homicide in that house; furthermore, for a period of one year I shall not go down nor cross the public
street in the parish of S. Angelo, known as via Vecchia, by which you

---

drove him from the house of prayer. Not satisfied with this, he had him arrested and
fined. On 28 Aug. 1540 six Jews 'of lowly extraction' attacked the doctor Leone da
Montolmo with fists and sticks while he was at prayer in the synagogue, inflicting various injuries. On 14 Oct. 1542 a porter known as David tried to stab the same Leone
while he was in the synagogue, but he was arrested, imprisoned, and sentenced to the
strappado; see G. Annibaldi, 'I banchi degli ebrei', 102–3. Similar events were not
infrequent elsewhere. At Pisa in 1561 a noisy and violent scuffle broke out involving
various Jews at the door of the synagogue after the service; see Luzzatti, *La casa dell'e-
breo*, 135. The phenomenon of violence in the synagogue was probably not infrequent
outside Italy either: the ordinances of Valladolid of 1432 severely punished anyone
who had been involved in violent and bloody brawls within the synagogue. Huge fines
were payable by any Jew in the place of worship 'who might attempt to strike his companion in the face either with his fists or with a buffeting, or pull the hair of his head
or beard or take out any offensive weapon to strike him, or to strike him bodily with
his hand . . . or use a knife or stone or any other weapon that might kill'; see
Finkelstein, *Jewish Self-Government*, 355–6; Moreno Koch, 'The Taqqanot of
Valladolid', 90–7. At this time churches, too, were frequently the setting for shows of
violence and vicious fighting. As Bonazzi observes, 'very often priests found themselves having to reconsecrate the profaned churches with elaborate rites, because if
they did not skirmish in the town square, such roughnecks would do so in church'; see
L. Bonazzi, *Storia di Perugia* (Città di Castello, 1960), ii. 271–2.

[38] AC Spoleto, Not., Pietro di Giovanni, 91, fos. 60ʳ, 148ʳ, 264ᵛ (21 Oct. 1516).

enter the synagogue, that is, the *scola* of the Jews'.[39] Were he to violate this oath, Deodato was to be sentenced to payment of a fine of 100 florins. It seems clear that the rabbinical court of Perugia, or one of the *maestri di scola*, must previously have pronounced an excommunication in connection with the former dancing-master.[40] Indeed it seems that the heads of the synagogue also used such bans to punish far less serious crimes. In 1508 the administrators of the Jews of Perugia accused Dattilo di Salomone, the cemetery-keeper, of having unlawfully taken fruit from the fields adjoining the burial-ground, which also belonged to the Jewish community. The court of arbitration sentenced him to hand over a certain amount of corn to the administrators. At the same time the *maestro di scola* Giacobbe di Vitale assured Dattilo 'that he had never excommunicated either him or any other Jews from their synagogue, or from other divine offices of the Jews'.[41]

A TIME FOR PRAYER AND A TIME FOR WORK

For the Jewish banker and merchant, as for his Christian counterpart, religious time and professional time moved at different rates. As Jacques Le Goff rightly observes with regard to Christian merchants, the time in which a Jew worked in his chosen profession was not the time in which he lived religiously.[42] There were superficial links: the banker or merchant drew on the income from his business to supply the alms which would ensure him an easier passage to the world to come; in his home, where he had often established the community's synagogue, the banker also prayed to God for the success of the business he ran on the ground floor. But generally work and religion were kept separate. This division between religious observance, or God's time, and profit, or secular time, was not born of hypocrisy: in the mind of the Jewish merchant and banker, the two moved along completely different paths and within different contexts; I do not share the view that synagogue time was secular time, essentially undistinguishable from professional time.[43] To take just a few examples: on 16 March 1417, after having bought a mattress and

---

[39] AS Perugia, Francesco di Jacopo, 222, fos. 209ᵛ–210ʳ (22 Apr. 1489).

[40] On the institution of excommunication (*herem*) among Jewish communities at this period see Bonfil, *Rabbis and Jewish Communities in Renaissance Italy*, 65–82.

[41] AS Perugia, Not., Ranaldo di Bartolomeo, 565, fos. 278ʳ–279ᵛ (14 Oct. 1508).

[42] See J. Le Goff, 'Merchant's Time and Church's Time in the Middle Ages', in his *Time, Work and Culture in the Middle Ages* (London, 1980), 29–42.

[43] See Bonfil, 'La sinagoga in Italia', 38–9.

blanket from the Jew Deodato, a Christian from Perugia went to the merchant's house to pay for his purchases. But as it was Saturday, Deodato's shop was shut and he was celebrating his rest day at home. None the less, payment took place and the Christian noted that 'it was their feast day, when they do not handle money; he was in his aforesaid house, so he had me put two florin coins in a small copper box with a lid which was standing on a shelf'.[44] On 5 November 1511 the banker Mosè di Abramo, living in Gualdo, was put on trial for, among other things, having accepted a silver paten belonging to the church of S. Maria di Crocicchio as a loan pledge. Pandolfo, the Christian who had handed the pledge over to the banker, told the judges that he had gone to Mosè's house because his bank was closed, as it was Saturday, and that he had found the banker resting in bed. According to the Christian's deposition, 'the said Pandolfo said: "Mosè, I want you to lend me a florin on this paten." Whereupon Mosè said he could not do so (because it was his day of rest) . . . And the said Pandolfo, because of the trust he had in the said Mosè, opened a strong-box which was by the bed, and he himself took out a florin and put the said paten in the said strong-box, and went his way with God.'[45] Whereas God's time, the Sabbath, was essentially static, like Mosè da Gualdo stretched out upon his bed, professional time continued to flow, and the money for the loan and its interest found its way into the 'small copper box' and the 'strong-box by the bed'. Religious observance did indeed forbid both Mosè and Deodato to handle money on a Saturday, but what we see here is neither hypocrisy nor inconsistency. In the psychology of these Jews, the two dimensions of their existence, the religious and the professional, coexisted virtually without coinciding, and certainly without clashing. The Jewish merchant and banker of this period, like his Christian counterpart, was as yet untroubled by the need to seek a conscious fusion of the two realms through consistent behaviour. We should also note that the evidence given by the two Christians reveals a natural respect for Jewish religious observance, free as it is from any touch of irony or contempt concerning a mysterious and alien religion.

For their part, Jews sought to incorporate their right to observe Jewish religious precepts into the clauses of the charters they signed with the governors of the communes. Indeed all charters, even the oldest, from

---

[44] AS Perugia, Not., Niccolò di Bartolomeo, 77, fo. 1ʳ. See also R. Abbondanza, *Il notariato a Perugia* (Perugia, 1973), 296; M. Luzzati, 'Ebrei in Umbria', *Annali della Scuola Normale di Pisa, Classe di Lettere*, 10 (1980), 1865–6.

[45] AS Perugia, Giud., Processus, env. 164, file 19.

that of Todi in 1289 to that of Gubbio in 1387, allowed Jews to close their banks on Saturdays and Jewish festivals and not to be summoned to court on such days.[46] On 21 January 1390 the Jews of Città di Castello formulated the following requests as conditional for the ratification of the charter which 'the priors were proposing to sign with them: 'Above all, for the praise, glorification, and veneration of almighty God and the observance of the law given to them by the prophet Moses, the Jews ask that it shall be agreed and established that neither they, nor their sons or family shall for any reason be obliged against their will by the authorities of the said commune, to give or arrange loans on Saturdays and other feast-days.'[47] Jews ensured that the municipal authorities did not fail to enforce this agreement. Summoned in 1455 before the civil judge of Spoleto to answer the charge of falsifying an official document, two Jews from Amelia rejected the summons to appear: 'We shall not present ourselves [they explained] because today is Saturday, a holiday for Jews, and on that day we cannot legally defend ourselves.'[48] On 31 May 1551 a case began brought by the Jews of Perugia against the Christian owners of a building whose drain emptied sewage into the synagogue garden. Here too the community representatives refused to appear before the judge, because the day in question was the Jewish festival of Pentecost (Shavuot).[49] Their defence was accepted by the court without objection. The documents confirm that Jews almost always observed their feast-days. We know, for example, that for the autumn feast of Tabernacles the Jews of Perugia had the palm branches and citrus fruits needed for their celebrations brought by mule from Florence.[50]

[46] See L. Rossi, 'Ebrei in Todi nel secolo XIII', *Bollettino della Deputazione di Storia Patria per l'Umbria*, 67 (1970), 31–71; A. Toaff, 'Gli ebrei a Gubbio nel Trecento', *Bollettino della Deputazione della Storia Patria per l'Umbria*, 78 (1981), 153–92.

[47] See Toaff, 'Ebrei a Città di Castello', 41.

[48] AC Spoleto, Not., Giovanni di Luca, A, fo. 84ʳ (11 Jan. 1455).

[49] AS Perugia, Giud., Processus, env. 509, file 8.

[50] Ibid., Not., Mariano di Luca di Nino, 114, fo. 171ᵛ (18 Sept. 1446). Many Jewish communities in Italy and central Europe obtained the palm branches (*lulavim*) and citrons (*etrogim*) needed for the celebration of the feast of Tabernacles from Sanremo. The 1435 Sanremo statutes made provision for the sale of citrons and palms to Jews, who had the right to choose those still on the trees, in accordance with their ritual requirements; see R. Urbani and G. Zazzu, *Ebrei a Genova* (Genoa, 1984), 22. At the end of the summer of 1422 the Jews of Rome imported citrons and palm branches for the feast of *sukkot* from the Ligurian riviera; see M. L. Lombardo, *La dogana minuta a Roma nel primo Quattrocento* (Rome, 1983), 89–90, 94–5.

5

Outcasts from Society

VAGRANTS, BEGGARS, AND THE IMPOVERISHED

IF it is true that the entire Jewish population was the object of more or less violent discrimination in medieval Italian society, it is also true that Jewish society itself rejected or excluded some of its members, with a logic similar to that at work in Christian circles. We can distinguish at least three levels of marginalization: that of the Jewish community as a whole, as a religious minority; that of outcasts from Jewish society, consisting mainly of Jews who threatened the established order; and that of those individuals banished from all society, Jewish and Christian, because of their deviant behaviour.[1]

At the first level, Jews were legally marginals in medieval Italian society, even if the process of exclusion was not constant, and indeed not always clearly discernible during the early medieval period. I believe that Raffaello Morghen is basically correct when he says:

Jewish civilization in the Middle Ages did not exist separately or removed from contemporary Christian or Muslim society; it occupied its own area of traditional spirituality and thought, but not simply as a world closed in on itself, as in the modern age, without influence, contributions or exchanges with other worlds. It was identified with the history of a people and a religion which was accorded a clearly defined legal and ethical status and treated, if not on a par with other peoples or faiths, at least with broad understanding and tolerance.[2]

The first signs of real exclusion are found, at least in Italy, after the middle of the fifteenth century, just before the founding of the first Monti di Pietà. As we shall see, it was only in the last quarter of the century that the process of exclusion became determined and thorough-

---

[1] On marginalized people in medieval society, including Jews, see M. de Combarieu *et al.*, *Exclus et systèmes d'exclusion dans la littérature et la civilisation médiéval* (Aix-en-Provence, 1978); id. (ed.), *Les Marginaux et les exclus dans l'histoire* (Paris, 1979); J.-C. Schmitt, 'L'Histoire des marginaux', in J. Le Goff (ed.), *La Nouvelle Histoire* (Paris, 1978), 257–87; J. Le Goff, *L'Imaginaire médiéval* (Paris, 1981), 163–72.

[2] See R. Morghen, *Medioevo cristiano* (Bari, 1974), 146–7.

going. The almost universal obligation to wear a distinctive sign, like lepers, heretics, and prostitutes; the proliferation of accusations of ritual murder and defamation of the Christian religion; and reiterated attempts by municipal governments to force Jews to live in a particular neighbourhood (the precursor of the ghetto) all point to an irreversible strengthening of this tendency. At first characterized by phases of exclusion alternating with phases of reintegration, the exclusion of Jews gradually turned into a relentless process.[3] Marginalization became a permanent condition, and Jews were to be considered along with other irredeemable outcasts, marked physically and psychologically by God: inveterate rebels, heretics and criminals, witches and gypsies.

The second level of marginality concerns those excluded within Jewish society itself.[4] Essentially, the purpose of the exclusion was to bolster the Jewish social order, embodied by the ruling class of bankers and rich merchants, and to reject individuals and groups regarded as potentially dangerous for the community's socio-economic and religious structures. The category of the excluded and marginalized within Jewish society included primarily the poor and beggars, the mad and sick, and converts to Christianity, particularly if they were poor. Impoverished bankers, bankrupt merchants, and others who had come down in the world also belonged to this category, as did foreign Jews and exiles with no fixed abode. Their very presence constituted a threat to the established order, a potential rallying-point for opposition, and a perennial source of insecurity and disquiet for the ruling class. As Jacques Le Goff says, referring to medieval society as a whole, Jewish society too was a great generator of outcasts.[5]

Given the scarcity of sources deigning to turn their attention to the large group of have-nots, we do not really know what proportion of the Jewish community owned little or nothing. But if we do not know its size, we can unhesitatingly say that the influence of this group on the life of the community was minimal or non-existent. In his dictionary *Tsemah David* the Spoleto doctor David de Pomis does not mince words concerning his distaste for vagrants and beggars, but he is more warmly disposed towards those who have lost status, the 'shamefaced' poor: 'Vagrants are called street-corner men [*yoshevei keranot*] because they are continually sitting at street corners, doing nothing but gossiping . . . then

[3] See Le Goff, *L'Imaginaire médiéval*, 166.
[4] There are as yet no adequate studies of marginalization in Jewish society, either in Italy or in other countries with sizeable Jewish communities in the Middle Ages.
[5] *L'Imaginaire médiéval*, 169.

there are those who are persistently deprived of certain of their needs, as often happens to the shamefaced poor, those who have been rich in the past, but are not bold enough to ask others for what they need; these latter are worthy of compassion, but not so those who go a-begging . . .'[6] The wills of rich Jews were often generous with charity for beggars and poor spinsters, revealing an awareness that money, after ensuring them a good life, could also help towards a good death by easing, or indeed forcing open, the gates of Paradise. Here the paupers are anonymous, flocking around the tombs of the rich on anniversaries, praying and singing psalms, hands outstretched for the alms left by their generosity, or patiently awaiting the opening of the 'poor box' fixed to the synagogue wall, used by the faithful mainly to dispose of their inconvenient small change before Sabbaths and Jewish holidays. The documents of this period offer few descriptions of these poor people, who sometimes included disabled beggars, and the infirm, blind, deaf, or maimed.[7] But one such description can be found in the deposition made by several Jews before the civil judge of Spoleto in 1469, where the condition of Mosè and Chiaruccia, two of the city's paupers, is described with realism and scant compassion. 'I have seen Mosè sick with a quantity of ills', runs one deposition; 'he is poor and deaf, so that we have to shout into his ear if he is to hear us. This unfortunate man has eight persons in his charge, including children and grandchildren, and has even been forced to sell his house at Beroide. Furthermore all the Jews of the city can testify that Mosè is sick, and very deaf and poverty-stricken.' The description of Chiaruccia's state, in another Jew's deposition to the judge, is equally stark and unflinching: 'Everyone knows that Chiaruccia is a decrepit old woman in her dotage, weak and hunchbacked. All the Jews of Spoleto who see her wandering, hunched, through the streets of the town, agree that she is a decrepit old woman, afflicted by numerous infirmities and extremely poor.'[8] A man called Guglielmo, found stealing figs from

---

[6] *Zemach David* (Venice, 1587), 200[b], 208[a].

[7] Of the many studies of pauperism and vagrancy in medieval society, see e.g. M. Mollat, *The Poor in the Middle Ages* (London, 1986); B. Pullan, 'Poveri, mendicanti e vagabondi', *Storia d'Italia*, i. *I marginali* (Turin, 1978), 981–1047; G. Politi, M. Rosa, and F. Della Paruta (eds.), *Timore e carità: I poveri nell'Italia moderna*, proceedings of a conference on pauperism and social security in the old Italian states, held at Cremona 28–30 Mar. 1980 (Cremona, 1982); P. Camporesi, *Il libro dei vagabondi* (Turin, 1980). See also Heers, *L'Occident aux XIVème et XVème siècles*, 293–305, 356–9.

[8] The depositions were made on 4 Aug. 1469 by Angelo di Abramo da Recanati and Manuele di Abramo da Orvieto; AC Spoleto, Not., Giovanni di Luca, 11b, fos. 116[r]–117[v].

someone else's field in 1463, and brought to trial and banished from Spoleto, belonged to this same world of pauperdom.[9]

Beggars and paupers often saw conversion to Christianity as the solution to many of their problems. Alms, hand-outs, and sometimes the prospect of regular employment lured them towards the baptismal font, but for most life was not radically altered in the long term. If they had been elbowed to the margins of Jewish society by their poverty, they essentially remained marginal in Christian society after their conversion. Benigno was a young beggar reduced to poverty after the death of his father, Ventura di Sabato, a Jewish tailor from Spoleto; on 28 April 1456 he was baptized Giovanni and taken on as a domestic at the Palazzo dei Priori.[10] In 1500 a poor and sick converted Jew from Assisi, who had taken on the name Menico, was employed as a municipal messenger by the city's priors.[11] In 1554 a deaf-mute beggar from Spoleto converted to Christianity and was taken on as the priors' bellringer. For the next forty years Angelo, 'a deaf and dumb Jew who had become a Christian', was to continue to mark the passing of the hours by ringing the bells of the tower of the Palazzo dei Priori.[12] Locked in silence, he was to retain the hallmarks of isolation and exclusion until his dying day.

The other group included in the category of marginals within the Jewish community was that of the *déclassé*: bankers who had fallen on hard times and merchants who had descended the slippery slope towards poverty. They could rarely count on the help and solidarity of the community. Once ill fortune had struck, depriving them definitively of the economic power that had previously sustained them and thrust them towards the apex of society, these Jews found themselves irremediably in the hopeless world of the excluded and outcast. In the Middle Ages, fortunes might veer suddenly and frequently. The careers of bankers and merchants offered plenty of scope for sudden reversals: rash investments, family troubles, wars and looting, falls from favour with governors, persecution, expulsion, and trouble with the law.

In Spoleto in April 1390 a popular revolt broke out against the nobles in the government. Bands of Ghibellines, hill-dwellers, and shepherds

[9] AC Spoleto, Registri Camera Apostolica, 1463, fo. 16ʳ (3 Oct. 1463).

[10] AC Spoleto, Camerario, Uscite, 1456, fos. 27ʳ, 44ᵛ; ibid., Uscite, 1457, fos. 35ᵛ, 53ᵛ, 62ʳ; ibid., Uscite, 1458, fo. 81ʳ.

[11] AC Assisi, Not., Girolamo di Giovanni da Portella, X7, file 7, fo. 23ʳ (7 Jan. 1500); ibid., Simone Paolozzi, N20, fo. 172ʳ (27 Nov. 1512).

[12] Angelo is documented as bellringer to the commune, with a salary of 2 florins a month, from 28 Dec. 1554 (AC Spoleto, Camerario, Entrate e Uscite, 1554, III, fo. 65ᵛ) until 24 Apr. 1590 (ibid., 1590, I, fos. 8ʳ, 14ᵛ).

came down from the Valnerina, Vallinarca, and Monteleone to give vent to their anger, robbing, looting, and putting the town to fire and sword. Their preferred targets were the richer citizens, including Jewish bankers. At the end of those days of revolt the chronicler Parruccio Zambolini, deeply alarmed, noted the long list of rich who had been made poor: they included

maestro Vitale, a Jew, and certain other Jews (I cannot mention them all), who were robbed of part or all of their possessions . . . and those who were robbed were not all followers of the nobles who were robbed, but some had too many possessions and lived immoderately. Messrs Vitale, Salomone, Sabbatucciu, Liucciu, and Pennuza, all Jews, were grievously robbed . . . The property of certain people of Spoleto was stolen and squandered by many mountain castellans and other outsiders, and robbery on such a scale had never been known before in Spoleto at any time or by any means.[13]

When Spoleto was looted by the mercenary troops of Niccolò Piccinino in 1441, the banker Ventura di Sabato complained to the priors of the city that he had been robbed of everything, informing them that lack of means would therefore prevent him from continuing in the money trade. 'In the great looting recently experienced by the town of Spoleto'—the Jew continued—'I was taken prisoner and robbed of everything so cruelly, that I can no longer continue to lend money as I did in the past.'[14] Often at this juncture the penniless banker saw his position plummet within the Jewish community as well. As though his misfortune were the indelible sign of divine wrath, the impoverished man might now see his many enemies dating from the time of his prosperity joined in their contempt and indifference by those who had previously stood alongside him and shared the advantages of his privileged economic condition.[15] Salomone, a Jew from Spoleto who belonged to a long-established family of the city's bankers and who was now plunged into the world of poverty, complained roundly to the priors in 1510 that he had been cold-shouldered by the

---

[13] See Parruccio Zambolini, 'Annali de Spuliti', in A. Sansi (ed.), *Documenti storici inediti* (Foligno, 1879), 122–6.

[14] AC Spoleto, Rif., 28, fo. 12ᵛ (29 Jan. 1441).

[15] Bonfil has recently reached quite different conclusions concerning Jewish society's attitude towards the *déclassés*: he sees it as permeated 'by the ethical and prescriptive principle of the duty of solidarity'. This view appears somewhat unfounded and apologistic in the light of his own admission in this same work: 'in the Jewish social élite, where everyone is more or less closely related to everyone else . . . the link of kinship seems to offer a dubious guarantee of solidarity in case of need'; see R. Bonfil, 'Una enciclopedia di sapere sociale', *Rivista di storia della filosofia*, 1 (1985), 127–30.

Jewish community, excluded from the privileges and rights assured in the charter, deprived of all protection and help, and abandoned to his fate in a state of vulnerability and great disadvantage. 'Indeed', explained Salomone in his doleful indictment, 'though I have fallen into poverty not through any fault of my own, but rather through adverse fortune, the other Jews of this city, regarding me as a ruined man, and impoverished, have had certain clauses confirmed, in which they have not named me, nor made any mention of me whatsoever, it seeming to them perhaps that, since I have fallen into pauperdom, no mention at all need be made of me.'[16] Marginalized by his own community, to which he still felt he belonged as of right, even if he was now among the ranks of the poor and dispossessed, Salomone sensed that society hoped to relegate him to oblivion, to erase him from history, because it now considered him useless and worthless. His image now had inconvenient implications, disruptive of the Jewish social order and, as such, to be mercilessly expunged.

DELINQUENTS AND CRIMINALS

The third, and most typical, category of the excluded was made up of criminals and delinquents (murderers, kidnappers, thieves) whose marginalization was independent of whether they were Jews or Christians. Research based mainly on the legal registers of Perugia and other Umbrian communes from 1320 to around 1520 has produced material enabling us to examine formal accusations concerning 190 offences by Jews during this period.[17] Unsurprisingly, given the particular socio-economic and professional position of much of the Jewish population, a good 69 cases, or 36 per cent of the total, are linked to violations of the rules for moneylending, petty theft, fraud, and swindling. It is, however, surprising to note that 28 per cent of the accusations under consideration, or 53 cases in all, could be categorized as cases of aggression, violence, and insult. Victims were both Jews and Christians, with a marked prevalence of the former, a telling sign of tensions and conflicts within the Jewish community. If 20 per cent of the Jews who had brushes with the law appeared before the judges charged with having attacked, struck, or insulted other Jews, the relative prevalence of the phenomenon justifies further examination of the documents: this might at least provide some understanding of the social conflicts, or

[16] AC Spoleto, Rif., 69, fo. 782ʳ (24 Nov. 1510).
[17] The documents concerning this sample, either transcribed or summarized, are reprinted in my *Jews in Umbria*.

TABLE 5.1   Criminal charges against Jews in Umbria

	Perugia		Other Centres		All Umbria	
	1320–1520	Of which after 1450	1320–1520	Of which after 1450	Total	%
Murders	1	(1)	2		3	1.5
Attempted murders	4	—	1	(1)	5	2.5
Kidnappings	1	—	—	—	1	0.5
Sexual offences	4	(2)	5	(2)	9	5.0
Aggression, violence, Insults:						
against Christians	11	—	5	—	16 ⎫ 53	28.0
against Jews	26	(23)	11	(12)	37 ⎭	
Theft, fraud, swindling	12	(6)	13	(5)	25 ⎫	
Violation of rules for moneylending	23	(18)	21	(13)	44 ⎭ 69	36.0
Games of chance	11	(5)	5	(3)	16	8.5
Defamation of Christian religion	8	(2)	13	(9)	21	11.0
Other offences	2	—	11	(3)	13	7.0
TOTAL	103	(57)	87	(48)	190	100.0

religious and family frictions, underlying these incidents, even if it does not enable us to reconstruct them in their entirety. Furthermore, an interpretation of these court documents is of great interest for the recreation of the climate of Jewish daily life in Italian society of the late Middle Ages. I shall look at several examples, including some cases of aggression and violence, where the protagonists were Jews and Christians.

In the summer of 1469 Gabriele di Musetto, a Jewish jobbing agricultural labourer from Castel delle Forme near Perugia, beat up his employer, a peasant from Castell'Olmeto, dispatching him to hospital.[18] Gabriele had already fallen foul of the law and spent some time in prison several years earlier, having been found guilty of rape and violence.[19] This hot-tempered Jewish labourer clearly belonged to the world of the anti-social and the vagrant, whose belligerent and disruptive behaviour placed them outside the established order. But possibly Gabriele was not

[18] AS Perugia, Giud., Sentenze del Podestà, 1468–9, fo. 28ᵛ (19 June 1469).
[19] Ibid. 1462, fo. 11ᵛ (9 Feb. 1462).

an out-and-out criminal, any more than Isacco di Lazzaro, a shopkeeper, and Travaglino, a soldier, who got into a noisy brawl in March 1480, insulting and threatening each other in the market square in Spoleto.[20] Their fight was vividly described in the witnesses' testimony: 'And Isacco uttered the following threatening words to the bristling Travaglino: "I'll kick your arse!" And Travaglino retorted: "I'll have your guts yet!" And Isacco said: "I'll fillet you alive!" Then Travaglino began to bawl: "I'll thrash you to within an inch of your life!" and Isacco retorted: "You'll get a good few inches of my knife in your chest!" ' Intent as they were on stepping up their ringing mutual threats, both the Jewish shopkeeper and the Christian soldier steered clear of any inflammatory reference to their respective religions. The gesture and the scurrilous phrase still reigned supreme in Spoleto market-place, despite preachers' efforts to single out the mere condition of Jewishness as a basis for insult.[21]

Now let us look at the numerous acts of violence where Jews fought, or were attacked by, other Jews, In November 1365 Matassia di Sabbatuccio da Perugia, one of the chief Italian bankers of the period, was attacked and violently beaten by two other Jews while he was walking down the street leading to the church of S. Lorenzo Maggiore.[22] Here is the notary's precise, indeed pedantic, description of the thrashing meted out to the powerful banker.

In the month of November last, the aforesaid Dattiluccio and Abramuccio, his son, seized by anger and a fit of violence, roughly insulted and attacked the said Matassia. Abramuccio gave him three backhanders to the face, causing blood to spurt from his mouth. Then he grabbed him by the hair and knocked his hat from his head, punching him twice in the neck. Eager for more, he scratched him on the neck and face, causing wounds from which the blood flowed copiously. Finally, after Abramuccio had struck Matassia at least four more times on the face and body, his father Dattiluccio also approached the victim and, after knocking the hat once more from his head (for he had succeeded in putting it on again in the mean time), he gave him a violent blow to the stomach.

---

[20] AC Spoleto, Not., Giuliano da Monte Publico, 137/II, fo. 61^r (30 July 1480).
[21] On the language of the marginalized in Italy see E. Ferrero, *I gerghi della malavita dal Cinquecento a oggi* (Milan, 1972). On the history of the relationship between the insult and the world-view and value-systems of Renaissance and modern Italy, see P. Burke, *The Historical Anthropology of Early Modern Italy: Essays on Perception and Communication* (Cambridge, 1987), 118–38.
[22] AS Perugia, Giud., Miscellanea Historica, MS 30 (24 Dec. 1365).

Matassia was left unconscious at the roadside, but his two assailants (concerning whom the documents of the period give no more details) were promptly arrested by the municipal police. Payment of the considerable fine of 35 florins brought with it the rich banker's pardon and freedom from prison, but it probably did not save them from expulsion from Perugia. In March 1412 the Jewish carter Deodato attacked and knifed the banker Dattilo di Salomone in the house of the Perugian doctor Salomone, in the district of Porta S. Pietro. The violent scuffle between the two Jews, which almost ended in tragedy, was preceded by a graphic exchange of insults and abuse.[23] In November 1455 the Assisi banker Angelo da Ferrara confronted Dattilo the mattress-maker outside the church of S. Cristoforo; after calling him a brazen liar ('You're lying through your teeth!'), he attempted to hit him with a stone. The unfortunate mattress-maker beat a speedy retreat. But the following day he was less lucky: Angelo's brother Manuele surprised him on the same spot and gave him a punching so severe that he needed treatment in hospital.[24] The brutal Angelo da Ferrara got off with the payment of a light fine, plus expenses for his victim's medical attention, but he was to end up in prison in Perugia shortly afterwards for having swindled Braccio Baglioni, lord of the city.[25] One April morning in 1480 the banker Mosè di Ventura was crossing the main square in Spoleto when he was suddenly set upon with kicks and punches by two other Jews, Musetto and Isaia, his son, fair traders by profession. Despite his speedy reaction Mosè ended up unconscious and bleeding on the ground. Witnesses to this violent brawl recalled that before hurling himself upon his victim, Musetto had addressed to him the following sybilline accusation: 'You caused two of my children to die of the plague by having them driven out of Recanati.'[26] In March 1490 Ventura di Abramo, an influential Jewish banker from Perugia, was attacked and thrashed until he bled by the tailor Elia di Vitale and his brother Angelo, an itinerant pedlar. The two Perugian Jews were brought to trial and sentenced to a fine of 18½ florins, half to be paid to the Apostolic Camera and half to Ventura.[27] The banker voluntarily renounced the right, shrewdly granted by the judge, to return his assailants' punches in kind. In September 1461 the itinerant Isaia di Abramo, slapped by the Perugian rabbi Elia di Bonaventura, also

[23] AS Perugia, Not., Cola di Bartolino, 23, fo. 4ʳ (10 Mar. 1412).
[24] AC Assisi, G, Libri mallefitiorum, portfolio 1 (1455–6), fos. 1ᵛ–2ᵛ. See Toaff, *Jews in Medieval Assisi*, 209–11.
[25] AS Perugia, Not., Ludovico di Cristoforo, 162, fo. 130ʳ (27 Feb. 1457).
[26] AC Spoleto, Not., Giuliano da Monte Publico, 137/II, fo. 62ʳ (2 Apr. 1480).
[27] AS Perugia, Not., Francesco di Giacomo, 223, fo. 134ʳ (10 Mar. 1490).

renounced his right publicly to return the blow: 'Isaia di Abramo renounces the right to repay a slap' (the text uses a vivid dialectal term, *sleppa*) 'to maestro Elia di Bonaventura here present, a right which he is entitled to by the statutes, for he has no intention of returning the slap, for all said maestro Elia would have deserved it.'[28] In May 1493 seven Jews from Perugia—pedlars, tailors, and cloth merchants—were arrested for taking part in a violent affray, after which many of the participants required medical treatment. But fines failed to calm down their seething violence, and in the following years the same Jews were arrested several times on the same charge.[29] Often denunciations leading Jews to the dock were maliciously instigated by other Jews. The son of Mosè di Ventura da Spoleto was denounced to the judge of the Podestà in April 1480 for an amorous intrigue with a Christian woman. This is how the young man's father was informed, to his surprise, by the pimp Filippino, that his son had been denounced by another Jew of the same city: 'And Mosiè said to the said Filippino: "My son has been accused of having dealings with a girl from Lombardy." And Filippino said to Mosiè: "Do you know who accused him?". And the said Mosiè said: "It was Ioanni and Iaco Antonio; but who do you think it was who accused him?" And Filippino said to Mosiè: "I have heard that it was Raffael de Rimino." '[30]

Not surprisingly, some of the protagonists in these scuffles, whether aggressors or victims, were converted Jews. The Jewish community's rancour and resentment towards those who had accepted baptism, on the one hand, and the converts' fervour on the other, sometimes carried disagreement to the level of physical skirmish. Vitale was the medical officer for Spoleto at the end of the fourteenth century and an eminent figure in the local Jewish community. The elder of his two sons, Guglielmo, who had followed in the footsteps of his father, had moved to Trevi in 1380, accepting the post of medical officer offered him by the commune there.[31] His two

---

[28] Ibid., Tomaso di Antonio, 391, fo. 505ᵛ (23 Sept. 1461).

[29] The brawl on 17 May 1493 involved Tobia di Isacco da Rimini, his son Isacco, and the five sons of Mosè da Perugia: Elia, Giacobbe, Deodato, Giuseppe, and Vita (AS Perugia, Not., Francesco di Giacomo, 227, fo. 183ʳ). One week earlier this same Tobia had insulted and struck the banker Ventura di Abramo (AS Perugia, Not., Francesco di Giacomo, 227, fo. 173ʳ). Isacco di Tobia and Elia di Mosè were again involved in an affray, together with Giacobbe di Vitale and Manuele di Giacobbe da Viterbo, in Feb. 1501 (AS Perugia, Not., Mariano di Petruccio, 600, fo. 23ᵛ). In Aug. 1502 the brothers Giacobbe and Elia di Mosè, on the one hand, and Isacco di Tobia on the other, were once again striking and insulting one another (AS Perugia, Not., Gianfrancesco di Pietro, 551, fo. 459ᵛ).

[30] AC Spoleto, Not., Giuliano da Monte Publico, 137/ii, fo. 57ʳ (30 Apr. 1480).

[31] AC Trevi, Tre Chiavi, env. 4, reg. 35, fo. 235 (27 May 1380); ibid., env. 5, reg. 41, fo. 48ᵛ (14 Sept. 1393), ibid., fo. 103ᵛ (25 Aug. 1394) and fo. 132ʳ (29 Apr. 1395).

daughters had stayed in Spoleto in the house of their grandfather who, under pressure of work, had virtually entrusted them to the care of the other, younger, brother, a pharmacist. In June 1394 this younger brother made a sensational conversion, taking on the name Battista.[32] One month later, one of Guglielmo's daughters, Morbidella, followed in her uncle's footsteps.[33] A few years later her sister, too, had herself baptized.[34] Guglielmo, who had remained a Jew, can scarcely have failed to blame his brother for the conversion of his two daughters, and must have borne him some ill will in this connection. So when Battista went to see him in Trevi in the summer of 1395, the meeting soon degenerated into a violent free-for-all, with the neophyte apparently having the worst of it. Interestingly enough, however, concerned as they were not to provoke their medical officer, whose services they continued to enjoy, the priors of the town intervened in the dispute, taking his side and dispatching the zealous Battista.[35] In April 1496 the chief Jewish banker of Foligno, Angelo da Camerino, was attacked and beaten in the Piazza della Croce by the convert Giovanni Francesco, who had been living as a Jew in Spoleto until a few months previously under the name Aleuccio. Now that he had been baptized, he was hoping to leave his home town and move permanently to Foligno.[36] The root of the trouble may have been Giovanni's suspicion that the influential banker was hatching some plot to scuttle his project, exploiting the support he enjoyed in the Palazzo dei Priori.

But it would be unfair to apply the term delinquent to the lesser figures (small traders, pedlars, tailors, innkeepers, carters, mattress-makers) who appear in these violent scuffles, and who used their fists, perhaps somewhat too freely, to obtain rough justice when they felt they had no other resort. At most they could be regarded as pointers to the fact that life within late-medieval Jewish communities ran less smoothly than the official documents imply. However, the fragmentary nature of the evidence concerning these disagreements does not allow us to build up a reliable or complete picture of the complex internal social and economic reality of these communities, but only to sense it obscurely. Even the murders committed by Jews in Umbria at this period cannot reliably be imputed to hardened criminals. In one case, in Spoleto in 1508, as we have seen in Chapter 1, murder was the outcome, possibly unpremedi-

---

[32] AC Spoleto, Rif., 12, fo. 75[r] (8 June 1394).
[33] Ibid., fo. 87[r] (1 July 1394), fo. 96[r] (24 July 1394), fo. 109[r] (11 Nov. 1394).
[34] Ibid. 24, fo. 393[r] (11 Oct. 1416).
[35] AC Trevi, Tre Chiavi, env. 5, reg. 41, fo. 140[v] (1 Aug. 1395).
[36] AC Foligno, Not., Taddeo Angelelli, 16, fo. 344[v] (22 Apr. 1496).

tated, of a dispute between a husband and wife.[37] At Perugia in 1487, the murder of the most influential banker in the town by a poor dancing-master was the tragic conclusion to one of the many violent disputes we have already discussed, where the most usual weapons were hands and feet.[38] We do not know the details of a third murder, committed by a Jew at Terni in 1514, except that the murderer was released from prison on payment of a fine of 100 ducats and was banished from the city.[39]

Abramo di Ventura da Roma, on the other hand, was a professional criminal; he lived in Perugia, and his misdeeds recur in the documents of the Podestà's court cases throughout the 1430s.[40] Here Abramo emerges as the brains behind a criminal association numbering, in the spirit of the times, both Jews and Christians among its members, and specializing in kidnapping for purposes of extortion. Abramo had recruited his workforce from the various Umbrian cities, drawing on a vast fraternity of criminals, crooks, and vagrants. The gang consisted of one Bartolomeo da Bologna, whom the documents describe as a 'turncoat, a vagrant, an individual of very low social standing, of the basest reputation and behaviour, a thief and kidnapper', and undoubtedly a hardened criminal; a shepherd from Castel S. Urbano near Narni, Pietro da Como; and a beggar from Perugia, Paganino da Milano. The gang specialized in kidnapping the children of bankers and rich Jewish merchants, and was active in Umbria and central Tuscany, between Arezzo and Siena. Abramo provided his accomplices with the necessary information concerning the movements of the victims and the economic standing of whoever was to be asked to pay the ransom. He often took direct action to expedite the various phases of the kidnapping, exploiting the trust extended to him by Jewish families in the region. In the summer of 1433 Abramo mobilized his gang to kidnap the son of the banker Salomone da Arezzo, Guglielmo, a child of 11.[41] Lured to Siena while returning from a seaside holiday, Guglielmo was kidnapped by Bartolomeo and taken on

---

[37] AC Spoleto, Not., Pietro di Giovanni, 91, fo. 264 (14 Oct. 1508).

[38] AS Perugia, Not., Francesco di Giacomo, 222, fo. 209ᵛ (22 Apr. 1489).

[39] AS Terni, Rif., 511, I, fo. 20ᵛ (31 May 1514). See Bonazzi, *Storia di Perugia*, i. 440–2, on the punishments established in the city statutes for the various crimes: 'crimes such as homicide in brawls or vendettas, rape, abduction of young girls and nuns, woundings, blows, and insults carried pecuniary penalties, varying according to the nature of the crime'.

[40] AS Perugia, Giud., Sentenze del Podestà, MS file 111 (1433–4), fos. 59ʳ–60ᵛ.

[41] Young Guglielmo was the son of Salomone di Aleuccio, a banker at Arezzo in the first half of the 15th cent., and brother of Aleuccio di Salomone, a doctor in Florence; see Cassuto, *Ebrei a Firenze*, 34–5.

horseback to Perugia, where he was hidden in a hovel on via Peretola, on the outskirts of the city. The gang asked the child's father for a ransom of 2,000 ducats, an enormous sum, most of which was to go to Abramo. However, probably as a result of a tip-off, the Podestà's guards located the house where the young victim was being held prisoner; they freed Guglielmo and arrested his gaoler, Bartolomeo. Apparently the other members of the gang, and their leader, managed to make their escape from Perugia before the police could lay their hands on them. On 7 June 1434 the Podestà of Perugia, Simone Monteboni da Firenze, brought Bartolomeo da Bologna to trial and sentenced him to death. A few days later the condemned man was hanged publicly in the city square, but we know nothing of the fate that befell his accomplices and, in particular, Abramo, who had recruited and organized the kidnappers.

In the winter of 1317 Sabato di Abramo and three other Jews from Perugia were accused of the attempted murder of several local citizens ('spurred on by the spirit of the devil, in a cruel and premeditated fashion, they gave their victims poisoned dates, with the intention of killing them').[42] Brought to trial before the *capitano del popolo*, the Jews were acquitted. A few years later, in 1320, Sabato was murdered in mysterious circumstances. On that occasion, according to Bartolo da Sassoferrato, the municipality had offered a large cash prize to anyone giving information leading to the capture of the guilty parties. When a certain Fornarolo had named the murderers and claimed the reward, he had been arrested as an accomplice to the crime.[43] It is quite possible that Sabato's murder was an act of vendetta, linked to the earlier accusation of poisoning which he had somehow managed to evade.

GAMBLING DENS AND GAMES OF CHANCE

Games of chance occupy an important place in offences committed by the Jews of Umbria in this period. Of the 190 charges against them registered from 1320 to 1520, 16 cases, or 8.5 per cent of the total, are concerned with gambling. This comes as no surprise, since gambling was a widespread vice in medieval society, vainly and frequently inveighed

[42] AS Perugia, Giud., Sentenze del Capitano del Popolo, 125, fo. 230ᵛ. See J. P. Grundman, *The 'Popolo' at Perugia (1139–1309)* (St Louis, Miss., 1974), 522.

[43] Bartolus a Saxoferrato, *Omnia quae extant opera* (Venice, 1603), vol. ii, fo. 43ᵛ (Comm. in D. 12.5.4.4.); P. Pellini, *Dell' Historia di Perugia* (Venice, 1664), i. 441–3; Toaff, 'Ebrei a Perugia', 22–3, 47–9.

against by preaching friars in town squares and by rabbis in the synagogues. In particular, a passion for dice and cards raged among Italian
Jews, unaffected by the efforts of the religious authorities to discourage
them, and indeed persisting throughout the following centuries. The lure
of risk-taking and the mirage of speedy gains lay at the root of the irre-
sistible fascination of the figures of the tarot and the numbers on the dice,
a fascination exerted upon rich and poor, educated and uneducated
alike.[44] In Jewish society gambling struck blindly, drawing its victims
indiscriminately from among beggars, bankers, and merchants. Sometimes even rabbis succumbed.

The congress of Jewish communities of Roman origin which met in
Forlì in 1418 thus felt obliged to take measures concerning games of
chance and tried, in accordance with the precepts of Minorite preaching,
to put a brake on the vice, by now rampant in Jewish society.[45] But we
may well doubt the effectiveness of the swingeing punishments devised
for those contravening these measures. Where the municipal statutes
and sumptuary laws promoted by the Observant friars had failed and
continued to fail, it is unlikely that rabbinical deliberations and prohibitions would be met by greater success. In reality, cards and dice continued to play a key role in the leisure activities of Italian Jews during the
Middle Ages and Renaissance. At the congress of Forlì the Jews of the
Roman communities were told 'not to give house-room to schools of
players of games of chance, whether Jewish or Christian'. Furthermore,
'no Jew living in the aforementioned communes, walled towns, or villages
should venture to play games of chance with cards or dice, even indirectly, with other Jews or Christians in his own home or those of others'. The
penalty for infringement of these rulings was a ducat, to be paid into the
coffers of the commune to which the offender belonged. At about the
same time S. Bernardino da Siena, preaching at Perugia in the autumn of
1425, had also taken up the cudgels against games of chance, with some
apparent success.[46] The bonfires of cards and dice, and the new bans
incorporated into the statutes which bear his name, had made a deep
impression, but ultimately they too were to prove utterly ineffective. As

---

[44] See C. Ferrai, 'Gergo e frodi in giocatori d'azzardo', *Archivio di psichiatria, scienze penali e antropologia criminale*, 19 (1898), 118–53; E. Altavilla, *I giochi d'azzardo*
(Milan, 1963). On gambling among Jews, see e.g. Abrahams, *Jewish Life in the Middle
Ages*, 388–98; Roth, *Jews in the Renaissance*, 26–7; Colorni, *Legge ebraica*, 221–2; L.
Landsman, 'Jewish Attitudes Towards Gambling', *Jewish Quarterly Review*, 57
(1967), 298–318, and 58 (1968), 34–62.
[45] See Finkelstein, *Jewish Self-Government*, 284.
[46] See A. Fantozzi, 'Documenta Perusina de S. Bernardino Senensi', 108–29.

the chronicler Antonio dei Veghi wrote: 'On this day, 25 September 1425, Bernardino gave a sermon speaking out against women dancing in the *striscio* [low-necked dress] and wearing the *balzo* [wig], or other people's hair; and his fine speaking struck home so powerfully that after a couple of weeks the women sent their baubles to him at San Francesco, as did the men their boards, dice, and cards; and in the month of October he had everything burnt in the square, between the Fountain and the Bishop's Palace.'[47] At Spello on 5 March 1469, following the preaching of the Minorite Francesco Coppoli (which was to lead to the founding of the local Monte di Pietà), the priors' council introduced an unusual measure concerning games of chance: any Jew living in the town found playing cards or dice in the Palazzo del Podestà would be arrested and punished with a severe fine.[48] Clearly even the austere premises of public buildings were not safe from the passion for gambling, and municipal functionaries, too, were probably often involved. Once again it was the preaching of another well-known Minorite friar, Bernardino da Feltre, which led the governors of Perugia to issue a proclamation on 1 June 1486 forbidding Jews to manufacture cards and dice for games of chance, on pain of physical and fiscal punishment. Cards, dice, and the instruments for their manufacture were to be handed over forthwith to municipal officials to be destroyed. 'All Jews making cards or dice and any instruments for gambling forbidden by the statutes, or owning the aforesaid or causing them to be made, must deliver up all moulds and all other instruments for making cards, dice, and any games forbidden by the statutes to the aforesaid magnificent Priors, on pain of a fine of 10 ducats and four strappados.'[49]

Bans and punishments seem to have served only to give the ubiquitous passion for gambling the added spice of the illicit. In May 1431 Donna di Dattilo, a Jewish woman from Perugia, did not scruple to give her young nephew, Abramo di Vitaluccio da Montefalco, various books with instructions for games of cards and dice.[50] After all, a knowledge of *basset*, *faro*, *tre sette*, *lansquenet*, and *pariglia* were part and parcel of the practical education and experience of any young man of the time. Jews arrested and fined for tempting fate with dice or tarots are found almost every-where in Umbria in the fifteenth century. At Spoleto in 1439 Isacco di

[47] See Antonio dei Veghi, 'Diario', in A. Fabretti (ed.), *Cronache della città di Perugia* (Turin, 1888), ii. 5–7. See also Toaff, *Ebrei a Perugia*, 80–2.
[48] AC Spello, Con. e Rif., env. 2, prot. 4, fo. 31ᵛ.
[49] AS Perugia, Editti e Bandi, 2, fo. 18ʳ. See Toaff, *Ebrei a Perugia*, 286–90.
[50] AS Perugia, Not., Mariano di Luca di Nino, 10, fo. 38ʳ (8 May 1431).

Elia, a pedlar, and Aleuccio, a carter, were caught playing *tre sette* and sentenced to a fine of 15 *soldi*.[51] A higher fine was paid by the banker Dattilo di Manuele da Assisi, charged with having played dice several times in the spring of 1463 at the house, on the town square, of a notary from Perugia, ser Domenico di ser Tribolo.[52]

Bernardino da Feltre's 1486 statutes made explicit reference to the Jews of Perugia as manufacturers of cards and dice for games of chance. Here at least the friar does not seem to have overstated the situation, carried away by his habitual animosity towards the Jews. Other sources clearly point to the part played, for example, by the Jews of Siena and Florence in the making of dice and playing-cards.[53] Nor is there any lack of evidence from Umbria. In May 1490 the guards of the governor of Spoleto arrested Aleuccio di Mosè da Terni and Ventura di Deodato, managers of a popular gambling-den in vaita Petrenga. A police search of their place of residence led to the discovery of moulds and instruments for the manufacture of cards, dice, and other paraphernalia needed for games of chance. Detained in the Palazzo del Podestà, in order to obtain their provisional freedom the two Jews solemnly promised the judges 'that they, their children and their families, would never again, during their entire lives, make or sell playing-cards, nor harbour the moulds needed for the making of cards or dice, on pain of a fine of 100 ducats'.[54]

Gambling was rife all over Perugia, but particularly in the notorious vicolo della Salsa, in whose taverns and brothels local and foreign low-life eagerly forgathered. This fetid meeting-place for vagrants, pimps, foot-pads, and prostitutes, where the world of poverty often coincided with that of crime, where mercenaries sought wine, adventure, and revelry until the small hours, was also the natural habitat of certain Jews, along-side other outcasts and rejects. Jews also ran gambling-dens and taverns on this cramped street (home, during the day, to the vile-smelling work-shops of the wool-carders); and here, after sundown, a jaded night-life came into being, where the city's pent-up violence might find some release. Here, one August night in 1462, the Podestà's guards swooped upon Musetto da Bevagna's house, which he had turned into a well-

[51] AC Spoleto, Camerario, entrata 1439, fo. 8ᵛ (18 Aug. 1439).

[52] AS Perugia, Giud., Sentenze del Podestà, n. 13, orig. A, fo. 39ʳ (18 May 1463).

[53] In 1527 two Jews were arrested at Florence charged with having manufactured playing-cards. The following year another Jew from Florence was arrested for having imported cards and dice to Siena; see Roth, *Jews in the Renaissance*, 27.

[54] AC Spello, Not., Moscato di Giovanni, 95, fo. 22ʳ (3–4 May 1490).

equipped gambling-den. They arrested the manager together with two regulars, Bonaiuto da Sarteano and Samuel, known as 'the Frenchman', caught red-handed playing a game of chance revealingly known as 'the condemned woman'. Apparently Musetto's gambling-den had opened in the spring of that year and had been in business consistently, and successfully, almost every day for over four months. The manager was sentenced by the Podestà to a steep fine of 200 *lire*, while the players got off with a tenth of that sum.[55] But in vicolo della Salsa gaming continued unabated even after this establishment was closed down. The venue was now the tavern run by Vitale di Mosè, where hardened gamblers, both Jews and Christians, were sure of finding not only a jug of Trebbiano, but also dice for *zara* and tarot cards. In 1508 the innkeeper Vitale had entered into official partnership with a skilled old Christian artisan from Verona; the Jew had entrusted those expert hands with the making of the cards and dice lying ready each evening on the tables of the tavern of la Salsa, for the delectation of its regular clientèle, drawn from the local and less local underworld.[56]

As we have seen, the passion for games of chance was not restricted to the world of poverty or crime, nor indeed to the lower social ranks. Rich and noble families often lived in fear of 'being undone' by gambling debts accumulated in secret by some of their most eminent members. An ill-fated game of *tre sette* could cause property to change hands in castle or turreted palazzo—it could cause vineyards, olive-groves, and other landed property to pass from one owner to another, and send the earnings from the sale of a large consignment of valuable cloth or foreign leather up in smoke within minutes. For a financier, gambling losses sometimes led to bankruptcy, while an unfortunate combination of dice might mean the instant loss, for a doctor, of a whole year's bills. In 1548, for instance, the well-known and wealthy medical officer of Perugia, Laudadio de Blanis, thought nothing of hauling up his own four sons, Angelo, Salvatore, David, and Giacobbe, before a notary and making them solemnly promise to give up games of chance, on pain of losing the huge paternal fortune awaiting them (and which itself was in danger of being dissipated). To avoid being accused of excessive severity, Laudadio

[55] AS Perugia, Giud., Sentenze del Podestà, orig. E, fo. 25^r (26 Aug. 1462).

[56] Ibid., Not., Tolomeo di Niccolò, 403, fo. 33^r (4 Apr. 1506); ibid., Benedetto di Massarello, 541, fo. 140^r (11 Aug. 1508). People also played games of chance in the Jewish Osteria del Falcone at Pavia, and in a tavern run by Jews in Piacenza in 1478–9, but Christian participation was prohibited by the authorities; see Motta, 'Ebrei a Como', 42–3.

allowed his sons to play cards provided the stake did not exceed the value of one lunch or dinner.[57] Here the doctor, and many like him, was less concerned with upholding common morality or religious precepts or stamping out vice than with effectively safeguarding his inheritance from the ruinous threat posed by games of chance.

[57] AS Perugia, Not., Teseo di Antonio Baldella, 965, fo. 267ʳ (25 June 1548). G. Fantaguzzi, in his Cesena chronicle for the year 1480, recalls that the real and personal estate of the bankers Gaio and Salomone, estimated at more than 12,000 ducats, was entirely squandered by their sons' gambling; Muzzarelli, *Ebrei e città d'Italia*, 193–4.

6

Witchcraft, Black Magic, and Ritual Murder

ACCUSATIONS AGAINST THE JEWS

IF we look at the actions brought against the Jews of Perugia and Umbria and the crimes of which they were accused in the period between 1320 and 1520 (see Table 5.1), we can see that 55 per cent of these accusations (105 out of a total of the 190 found), were concentrated in the second half of the fifteenth century, in the years immediately preceding and above all in those following the setting up of the first Monti di Pietà. In this half-century, marked by the extensive and virulent anti-Jewish polemics of the preaching friars in all the Umbrian cities, Jews were frequently brought to trial accused of having violated the rules governing the practice of moneylending, or of having continued to extend credit after this activity had been declared illegal by the local authorities. But there was also an increase in more insidious and threatening accusations, in particular of all manner of defamation of the Christian religion. Jews had previously been accused and found guilty of disrespectful behaviour towards Christianity: in February 1323, for instance, a Jew from Visso in the upper Valnerina was sentenced for having performed irreverent acts in connection with the cross.[1] During the same period Abramo from Gualdo Cattaneo in the duchy of Spoleto, whom I have already had cause to mention (pp. 10–11), was the protagonist in a series of more sensational and bizarre events. He belonged by right to the world of the marginalized, not just because he was a Jew, but above all by virtue of his deviant behaviour, his systematic protests, and his provocative attitude towards the established order. His vicious jeering and vulgar mockery of the political and religious symbols of Christian society, and his unbridled sexual practices, including adultery and homosexuality, made Abramo an asocial being by vocation and choice; the fact that he was a Jew was neither here nor there. Within the brief span of one-and-a-half years, he

---

[1] AV, Camera Apostolica, Registri del Ducato di Spoleto, Entrate e Uscite, 25, fo. 133ᵛ (7 Feb. 1323). See Fumi, 'I registri del Ducato di Spoleto', 5: 164.

was tried and sentenced four times for offences against the pope and the Christian religion, and for having adulterous and homosexual relations. The scandalized peasants of Montefalco reported that Abramo habitually burst into the churches of the region during Sunday mass, completely naked and wearing a bishop's mitre pulled down over his eyes, sowing confusion among the faithful.[2]

It was particularly in the last part of the fifteenth century, in the years following the founding of the Perugia Monte di Pietà in 1462, that accusations against Jews of witchcraft, ritual assassination, and black magic became a positive obsession in Umbria, as in the rest of the peninsula. In 1471 the Sienese Antonio Bettini, bishop of Foligno, stirred by the preaching of fra Fortunato Coppoli of Perugia, cast caution to the winds and used unrestrainedly alarmist imagery when talking of the Jews: 'The Jews of this city and diocese open their famished jaws like slavering dogs, not just to gobble up the possessions of the poor, but actually to drink their blood, sucking it from their veins.'[3] Preaching during Lent in the cathedral of S. Maria at Spoleto in 1491, Andrea da Faenza, an associate of Bernardino da Feltre, used equally venomous language to describe the Jews, whom he called 'treacherous, rabid and mercenary, usurping the Christians' goods and sucking their blood'.[4] The 'Recipe for Grace, or Stone of St Paul', a strange printed document written by the Pauline Giovan Pietro da Camerino, dates from the end of the fifteenth century. It celebrates the extraordinary therapeutic virtues of the 'stone of St Paul', a kind of white clay from the cave of St Paul in Malta. When ground up and swallowed in small quantities of wine or water, this was said to ward off snake-bite and rabies, neutralize the effects of poisonous mushrooms, and act as protection against sorcery, spells, and witchcraft. Its properties were also effective for animals, with the sole exception—as the reader is warned—of dogs, pigs, and Jews. 'Those who have this grace should know that, apart from the said poisons, they are safe from spells, potions, sorcery, and charms . . . it can help every baptized person bitten by venomous animals, if they are given a little of the said stone to

[2] AV, as n. 1 above, 21, fo. 124ᵛ (15 Sept. 1322) and fo. 126ʳ (11 Oct. 1322); ibid. 22, fo. 136ʳ (13 Mar. 1323) and fo. 153ᵛ (6 Nov. 1323). See Fumi, 'I registri del Ducato di Spoleto', 4: 141, 144; 5: 142; Reydellet-Guthinger, *L'Administration pontificale*, 73. On the subject of provocative marginal figures, to which group Abramo da Gualdo Cattaneo belonged, see Schmitt, 'L'Histoire des marginaux', 280–2.
[3] AC Foligno, Rif., 26, enc. with fo. 16. See Messini, *Origini e i primordi del Monte di Pietà*, 15.
[4] AC Spoleto, Rif., 54, fo. 27ʳ (22 Mar. 1491). See M. Sensi, *Vita di pietà e vita civile in un altopiano tra Umbria e Marche (secc. XI–XVII)* (Rome, 1984), 107–9, 155.

drink in water or in wine; and with its said grace it may help any animal, with the exception of dogs, pigs, and Jews.'[5]

In the grim bestiary of Observant preaching, obsessed as it was by usury, the Jews were 'ravening wolves' (Bernardino da Siena), 'rabid, thirsting dogs' (Fortunato Coppoli), 'rabid curs' (Andrea da Faenza), 'foxes and servants of the devil' (Cherubino da Spoleto), 'gluttonous dogs . . . with famished, insatiable jaws' (Fortunato Coppoli), 'like ravening she-bears' (Fortunato Coppoli). Giovan Pietro's 'Recipe for Grace' compares them to dogs and pigs. In Chiavasso's 1474 statutes, which echo themes and expressions from the preaching of Antonio da Cremona, Jews are guilty 'of oppression, violence, usury, fraud, evil practices, heresies, conspiracy, false images . . . and an infinity of foul deeds and diabolical operations, more than the serpent is full of venom'.[6] It is true that the belligerent friars also heaped their contemptuous and graphic insults upon secular sinners and the peasant world, for which they harboured an innate and incurable antipathy, but this was scant consolation for the Jews.[7] Their activity was said to corrupt the economic life of the city, while their very presence constituted a threat to the Christian's moral health. Fortunato Coppoli referred to them from the pulpit as murderous parasites upon society, 'devouring poor Christians, as rust does iron'.[8] More seriously, these rapacious wolves and rabid dogs, accomplices of the devil and 'full of infinite filth', thirsted after Christian blood and went around in search of this gruesome beverage. Coppoli put his terrorized audience constantly on their guard, explaining that 'Jews are truly like rabid, thirsty curs, they have sucked our blood

[5] The text of the 'Ricetta della Grazia o Pietra di San Paolo, composta da maestro Giovan Pietro' is reproduced in its entirety in M. Sensi, *Vita di pietà*, 350–1, where he rightly observes that this popular medical text 'echoes the heated tones of the anti-Jewish crusade in fifteenth-century itinerant preaching'. In the last part of the 15th cent. such topics had a broad popular appeal throughout Italy, and the 'Ricetta' is a typical example.

[6] Quoted in R. Segre, 'Bernardino da Feltre, i Monti di Pietà e i banchi ebraici', *Rivista Storica Italiana*, 40 (1978), 829.

[7] Like many Minorite preachers, Bernardino da Feltre did not conceal his deep contempt for peasants and country-dwellers, seeing them as rank and ignorant; see Segre, 'Bernardino da Feltre', 832. A loathing of the peasant world—rough, fetid, a prey to instinct and hotbed of rampant sexual licence—is reflected in 14th- and 15th-cent. Italian writing: see Ch. Bec, 'La figura del contadino nella novellistica toscana del secondo Trecento e del primo Quattrocento', in id., *Cultura e società a Firenze nell'età della Rinascenza* (Rome, 1981), 79–103; Nigro, *Le brache di S. Griffone*, 76–80.

[8] This was one of the themes of the sermons by Fortunato Coppoli at Assisi in the period immediately preceding the founding of the Monte di Pietà (1469). See Toaff, *Jews in Medieval Assisi*, 61.

and suck it still', and referring to them as 'the vilest enemies of the
Christian faith, like madly rabid dogs athirst for Christian blood, convinced that they are committing a great action in satiating themselves
with it . . . devoured by the cruellest rage'.[9] His words have echoes of
Bernardino da Siena's hysterical preaching against usury: 'Ravenous
curs, gluttonous misers, carnivores besmirched by the dung of this
deceiving world, daily you go in pursuit of usury . . . you drink the blood
of the poor . . . like sentinels of the devil'; 'O usurer, what have you done?
O blasphemer, o deceiver of men, o bloodsucker of the poor, o disem-
boweller of widows and little children'.[10] Influenced by Bernardino,
Jacopo della Marca was equally enraged: 'Woman, press the sleeve of the
usurer's wife, and you will see blood spurt forth.'[11] For Bernardino da
Feltre there was no doubting that 'Jews drink the blood of Christians and
take it into themselves.'[12] At the end of the fifteenth century, in an antisemitic pamphlet, Pietro Bruti of Vicenza states explicitly that ritual
murder and the shedding of Christian blood are the literal and symbolic
equivalent of what Jews do every day, bleeding Christians white through
usury.[13] Nor were inquisitors long in reaping the harvest sown by the
Observant friars: suspected iconoclasts, witches, sorcerers, devotees of
black magic, and diabolical and murderous rites were discovered everywhere.[14] Often, however, and fortunately for the accused, no precise
proof or convincing evidence would materialize.

[9] Fortunato Coppoli used such expressions in the introduction to the 1472 statute
of the Monte di Pietà of Cortona; see G. Mancini, *Cortona nel Medioevo* (Florence,
1897), 81; he did so again for the 1470 statute for the Monte di Pietà of Amelia; see A.
Ghinato, 'Fondazione e statuti del Monte di Pietà di Amelia', *Archivum Franciscanum
Historicum*, 48 (1955), 367.

[10] See Bernardino da Siena, *Le prediche volgari*, ed. P. Bargellini (Milan–Rome,
1936), iv. 103.

[11] The sentence is taken from the *Sermo de usurariis* by Jacopo della Marca, cited
in Nigro, *Le brache di S. Griffone*, 33–5.

[12] Quoted in Muzzarelli, *Ebrei e città d'Italia*, 171, in the paraphrase by the Cesena
chronicler Giuliano Fantaguzzi.

[13] Pietro Bruti, *Victoria adversus Judaeos* (Mantua, 1489), fo. 4ᵇ. See G. Fioravanti,
'Aspetti della polemica antigiudaica nell'Italia del Quattrocento', in Paolo Sacchi (ed.),
Atti del secondo convengno dell'Associazione Italiana per lo studio del Giudaismo, confer-
ence held at Idice, Bologna, 4–5 Nov. 1981 (Rome, 1983), 49–50; id., 'Polemiche
antigiudaiche nell'Italia del Quattrocento: Un tentativo di interpretazione globale',
Quaderni Storici, 22/64 (1987), 33.

[14] On witches in western Europe see especially J. C. Baroja, *The World of the
Witches* (London, 1964); M. Douglas (ed.), *Witchcraft* (London, 1970), and looking
only at France in the period following the one discussed here, R. R. Mandrou,
Magistrats et sorciers en France au XVIᵉᵐᵉ siècle (Paris, 1968). Excellent studies on the
subject in Italy include E. Battisti, *L'antirinascimento* (Milan, 1962); and, with

The pedlar Abramo da Camerino had been licensed to wheel his hand-cart, selling rags and second-hand clothes, through the small Sunday market of S. Maria delle Lacrime at Trevi since 1475. In March 1477 he was arrested on a charge of having 'overlooked' a local peasant woman, Speranza da S. Lorenzo. Although Abramo's innocence was proven, and he was released from prison, he was none the less deprived of the right to citizenship previously granted him, and banished from Trevi.[15] In July 1480 the shopkeeper Elia di maestro Zucchero da Foligno was imprisoned in the fortress at Spoleto for having cast spells on a local citizen. Here, too, lack of evidence led to his release. But awaiting him outside the prison gates was his supposed victim with a group of friends, who attacked him, beat him till the blood flowed, and left him unconscious on the ground.[16] Gabriele, Prospero, and Eliseo, the sons of the wealthy Città di Castello banker Angelo da Orvieto, were imprisoned in January 1498 charged with a serious offence against the Christian religion. This crisis united the city's entire Jewish community, who intervened in defence of the accused, vouching for their innocence. But the three young men were released only after their family had paid the huge fine of 1,500 ducats, probably with contributions from other Jews of Città di Castello.[17]

In medieval Italy fear of witches generated a constant sense of danger threatening the economic, physical, and spiritual well-being of the whole community. They exerted a specially deep and ambiguous fascination in

---

G. Battisti, *La civiltà delle streghe* (Milan, 1964); G. Bonomo, *Caccia alle streghe: La credenza nelle streghe dal sec. XIII al XIX con particolare riferimento all'Italia* (Palermo, 1959), as well as the important studies by C. Ginzburg, 'Stregoneria e pietà popolare: Note a proposito di un processo modenese del 1519', *Annali della Scuola Normale di Pisa*, 30 (1961), 269–87; id., *The Night Battles: Witchcraft and Agrarian Cults* (London, 1983). On witchcraft and the Jews, in Italy and elsewhere, see J. Trachtenberg, *The Devil and the Jews: The Medieval Conception of the Jew and his Relation to Modern Antisemitism* (New Haven, Conn., 1943); Roth, *Jews in the Renaissance*, 59–63.

[15] AC Trevi, Tre Chiavi, env. 9, reg. 141, fos. 30^r, 105^r, 123^v, 161^v (30 Mar. 1477–19 Apr. 1478). A similar case was attested in 1476 at Novara, where two local Jews were arrested on a charge of having cast a spell on a young woman named Caterina who had recently converted to Christianity. The alleged sorcerers were subsequently freed, since the charge went unproven; see Simonsohn, *Jews in the Duchy of Milan*, i. 653; L. Fumi, 'L'Inquisizione Romana e lo Stato di Milano', *Archivio Storico Lombardo*, 37 (1910), 303; Antoniazzi Villa, *Un processo contro gli ebrei*, 56.

[16] AC Spoleto, Not., Giuliano da Monte Publico, 137/II, fos. 52^v, 73^v (22 July 1480).

[17] AC Città di Castello, Not., Marco Feriani, 2, fo. 100^v; Prov., 1498, fo. 45^v. See Toaff, 'Ebrei a Città di Castello', 20–1.

the small agricultural and mountain communities scattered all over Umbria. In the popular imagination, by virtue of making a pact with the devil and riding roughshod over Christian religious precepts, witches could kidnap and kill children, make men impotent with potions and spells, cause storm and drought, and unleash the plague and other horrendous epidemics. Burckhardt recalls that in the Italy of the late Middle Ages, the duchy of Spoleto, particularly the mountainous area between Norcia and Nocera, was universally regarded as 'the centre of all witchcraft and spells'.[18] But in fact all Umbria, from the lower valley of the Nera to the gates of Narni, Terni, and up to Perugia, was regarded as the favoured haunt of sorcerers and witches. Bartolo da Sassoferrato records the trial of a witch from Orte between 1331 and 1342, during the course of which the woman was accused of having performed offensive acts in relation to the cross, and of having bewitched various children, bringing about their death.[19] Punishment for witchcraft was often bizarre and laden with symbolism. In March 1445, for instance, Santuccia, a peasant woman from the mountains between Assisi and Norcera who was accused of soothsaying and sorcery, went to the stake in the Campo della Battaglia. Accompanied by a macabre and motley procession, the old woman rode to her death seated backwards on a donkey, wearing a mitre held up by two figures of devils.[20] Vilification of the Christian religion, together with magic and ritual murder, were the most frequent accusations made against witches, as against Jews; and these alleged crimes dogged their image in the popular imagination, fed as it was by the fanatical and self-interested preaching of the Minorites. Hunting Jewish witches was a self-evidently tautologous exercise—simply being Jewish laid one open to accusations of witchcraft—but this did not mean that their uselessness was always quite so clear to those performing or promoting them.

In October 1462 the Jewess Bellaflora, wife of Musetto da Bevagna, 'a witch, a caster of spells, and an invoker of evil spirits', appeared before the *capitano del popolo* of Perugia. Her accusers claimed to have seen her acting suspiciously one August night while approaching the fountain of Piantarosa, in the district of Porta S. Pietro in Perugia. Their deposition continues: 'Bellaflora lifted a jar she had with her and began to draw

---

[18] See J. Burckhardt, *The Civilization of the Renaissance in Italy* (London, 1928), 526–7.
[19] Quoted by A. di Nola in *Enciclopedia delle Religioni*, v (Florence, 1973), col. 1430, s.v. 'Stregoneria'.
[20] See Bonazzi, *Storia di Perugia*, ii. 526–7.

water from the fountain; then she raised the jar skywards and cast a spell upon the water, uttering diabolical words while she poured it into her lap. The Jewish witch performed the spell three times in this fashion before withdrawing from the fountain, thus offending morality and the Christian religion.' At the end of the inquiry, after considering the various depositions, the court of Perugia took note of the flimsiness of the charges against the woman and acquitted her.[21] But in all likelihood, even after her acquittal, people continued to regard Bellaflora as 'the witch of Piantarosa' who had bewitched the Perugia fountain. This was by no means the first case in which a Jew had been accused of polluting well-water or poisoning fountains.[22] The suspicion that Jews might want to poison the Christian community would also explain a ruling in the 1371 Narni statutes which states that 'no Jew, whether man or woman, may live near the fountains and aqueduct of Narni, that is, at a distance of less than twenty-five feet from the same'. This ruling may well conceal a desire to prevent Jews coming into contact with the city's drinking-water.[23]

The charges of iconoclasm and of the 'scraping off' of sacred images were also sometimes brought against the Jews of the Umbrian communities.[24] Such removal of images was quite common in Italy at this period, as exemplified in the famous case of the banker Daniele da Norsa at Mantua: accused of having obliterated the image of a Virgin and Child from the outside wall of the house he had bought, he was obliged to make good the blasphemous gesture by financing the building of a church dedicated to the Virgin. It was on this occasion that Andrea Mantegna painted his famous *Madonna della Vittoria*, now in the Louvre, and an anonymous artist completed a second panel, the so-called *Madonna of the*

[21] AS Perugia, Giud., Sentenze del Capitano del Popolo, orig. A (27 Oct. 1462), fo. 15ʳ. See Toaff, *Ebrei a Perugia*, 93–4.

[22] Talking of the fearful epidemic of 1348 known as the Black Death, popularly imagined to have been spread by Jews, the Spanish chronicler Shelomh Ibn Verga relates: 'The accusers testify to having seen Jews approaching the water courses at dead of night and throwing in some nameless substance, and while so doing, uttering incomprehensible formulas'; see Shelomh Ibn Verga, *Shevet Yehudah* (Heb.), ed. A. Shochat (Jerusalem, 1947), 71. On the accusations that Jews poisoned wells and fountains, see also Grayzel, *The Church and the Jews*, 74, and Dito, *La storia calabrese*, 271, which cites the suspicion that Jews poisoned fountains with a 'specially prepared powder', and caused the plague that raged there in 1422.

[23] AC Narni, Stat., 1371, I. xxv. See also *Statuta Illustrissimae Civitatis Narniae* (Narni, 1716), 27.

[24] On cases of iconoclasm involving some of the most famous Jewish families in the second half of the 14th cent., see the excellent study by M. Luzzati, 'Ebrei, chiesa locale, principi e popolo: Due episodi di distruzione di immagini sacre alla fine del Quattrocento', *Quaderni Storici*, 22/54 (1983), 847–77.

Jews, now in the church of S. Andrea in Mantua, in which Daniele da Norsa and his family are portrayed with the yellow badge on their garments, to differentiate them from members of the Christian community.[25]

In February 1471 Samuele di Consiglio, a banker at Gubbio, bought a house in the district of S. Pietro, on whose outer wall was a painting by Jacopo Bedi, *Virgin with Child, St Antony Abbot and St Ubaldo Bishop*. In view of his intention to remove the painting from the walls of his house, Samuele consulted the deputy of the bishop of Gubbio, Angelo Cerreti da Camerino, whose decision was upheld by the Dominican preacher Lazzaro Berti da Gubbio. Permission was given for the image to be scraped off, provided that Samuele commissioned a similar painting, at his own expense, to be executed by Jacopo Bedi and placed in the oratory of the recently built Fraternità dei Bianchi, or in some other suitable place chosen by the notary Antonio di Niccolò, charged with drawing up the contract between client and artist.[26] No trace of the

[25] Of the extensive bibliography on the case of Daniele da Norsa see esp. A. Portioli, 'La Chiesa e la Madonna della Vittoria', *Atti e Memorie dell'Accademia Virgiliana di Mantova*, 10 (1884), 60–2; id., 'La Chiesa e la Madonna della Vittoria di Mantegna a Mantova', *Archivio Storico Lombardo*, 10 (1883), 447–73; A. Luzio, 'La Madonna della Vittoria di Mantegna', *Emporium*, 10 (1899), 359; J. Lauts, *Die 'Madonna della Vittoria'* (Stuttgart, 1960), 12–14; P. Norsa, *Una famiglia di banchieri*; S. Settis, 'Artisti e committenti fra Quattrocento e Cinquecento', *Storia d'Italia*, iv. *Intellettuali e potere* (Turin, 1981), 712–22; Luzzati, 'Ebrei, chiesa locale', 847–8, 856–7. Elsewhere in Italy too, e.g. in the duchy of Milan, there were numerous cases of Jews being accused of having damaged sacred Christian images, some of which ended tragically: at Lodi in 1456, at Monza in 1470, and at Pavia in 1471; see Simonsohn, *Jews in the Duchy of Milan*, i. 199–200, 518–19, 552–4; Antoniazzi Villa, *Un processo contro gli ebrei*, 56. In 1488 the duke of Milan, Gian Galeazzo Sforza, brought an action against forty or so Jews living in his dominions, accusing them of using books containing expressions offensive to Christianity. Almost all the accused were asked whether they had profaned sacred Christian images or whether they had created such images with the aim of destroying them; see Antoniazzi Villa, *Un processo contro gli ebrei*, 56, 82–189. One such charge was levelled in Pisa against the well-known banking family da Pisa; see Luzzati, 'Ebrei, chiesa locale', 849–56. Other real or alleged episodes concerning the destruction of sacred images by Jews were reported at Florence in 1493: see Cassuto, *Ebrei a Firenze*, 64–5; at Reggio Emilia in 1539: see M. Ferretti, 'Ai margini di Dosso', *Ricerche di storia dell'Arte*, 17 (1982), 71; and at Venice around 1550: see B. Pullan, *Rich and Poor in Renaissance Venice* (Oxford, 1971), 131. In Piedmont in 1441, the Jews of Savigliano were accused of having made unleavened bread for Passover on which they had contemptuously stamped the image of Christ; in 1444 a Jew from Vigone was brought to trial for having profaned a crucifix; see Segre, *Jews in Piedmont*, i. 146–7, 171.

[26] AC Gubbio, Not., Antonio di Niccolò, 86, fo. 157ʳ (26 Feb. 1471); see M. Gualandi, *Memorie originali riguardanti le belle arti*, ser. 4 (Bologna, 1843), 51–3.

painting in question now remains in the oratory of the Fraternità dei Bianchi, which a passage in the *Cronaca di ser Guerriero da Gubbio* enables us to identify as the room beneath the Chiesa dei Bianchi at Gubbio, which has frescoes depicting the story of the Passion. Furthermore, since the walls of the oratory were entirely decorated with frescoes on a different subject (now partly destroyed) painted more or less during Bedi's time, it is reasonable to suppose that the mural painting mentioned in the document may never have been painted there at all. None the less, I do not share the view that the painting has been destroyed.[27] There is only one remaining signed painting by Jacopo Bedi, the *Stories of St Sebastian* in the Panfili chapel in the cemetery of S. Secondo near Gubbio. The frescoes are signed IACOPUS and dated 1458.[28] A stylistic comparison between this work and the frescoes in the penultimate chapel on the right (now largely destroyed) in the cathedral at Gubbio makes it possible to attribute this latter work to Jacopo Bedi. Among the subjects which appear in the chapel is a Virgin and Child with angels, S. Ubaldo, and another saint, now destroyed, but who in all likelihood was St Antony Abbot. This painting might therefore be the one commissioned by Samuele from Jacopo to make good his iconoclastic act. The fact that it is in the cathedral and not in the Fraternità dei Bianchi may be explained by the fact that the notary, Antonio di Niccolò, was left free to choose the place where Bedi should paint the work.

We also have information concerning another act of iconoclasm, which took place at Montefalco in 1511. It was imputed to a Jew of Montefalco, Bonaiuto da Spello, who was tried before Baroncello, the lord of the city, for having 'scraped off' an image of St Nicholas from the outside wall of the monastery of S. Maria Maddalena at Montefalco. Bonaiuto was acquitted for lack of evidence, after the bishop of Spoleto himself, Francesco Eroli, had interceded in his favour.[29]

In the second half of the fifteenth century several Umbrian Jews were also tried for false conversion, though such trials were not as frequent or as serious as those investigated by the Inquisition during the following century. The Jewish group involved was the one which had left the Iberian peninsula at the end of the fourteenth century, after the wave of

[27] See Luzzati, 'Ebrei, chiesa locale', 858–9.
[28] See U. Gnoli, *Pittori e miniatori nell'Umbria* (Spoleto, 1923), s.v. 'Jacopo Bedi'; M. Tabarrini, *L'Umbria si racconta: Dizionario* (Foligno, 1982), i. 148, s.v. 'Bedi, Giacomo'.
[29] AC Spello, Not., env. 13, Giovanni Felice Morichelli, 2, fo. 31ʳ (6 Dec. 1511: processo a Bonaiuto di Manuele da Spello).

bloody persecutions that began around 1391 and which culminated after the famous disputation of Tortosa (1413–14),[30] followed by the baptism, whether voluntary or enforced, of most of Spain's Jewish population. Spanish Jews had taken refuge in Italy, in the Papal State, in Rome and Ancona, in Florence under Medici rule, and in the duchy of Mantua.[31] A group of Spanish and Portuguese Jews had moved to Perugia, one of the foremost among them being the family of Mosè di Spagna. These families were usually wealthy, and they took up residence in the district of Porta S. Pietro near the two synagogues of Perugia, opening their banks and shops on via Vecchia.[32] Mosè, who had arrived in Perugia with his sister, three sons, and three daughters, opened an expensive clothes-shop in this district around 1450. His misfortunes began in the winter of 1461, when another Jew, Samuele di Emanuele, accused him of false conversion and heresy before the Apostolic Camera in Rome. The Jewish informer stated that Mosè had had himself baptized about forty years earlier in Spain, but that during the subsequent period he had decided to revert to the Jewish religion. To avoid the danger of being sent to the stake, Mosè had moved to Italy, taking up residence at Perugia, where he had lived as a devout Jew. The pope, Pius II Piccolomini, promptly charged the governor of Perugia, Ermolao Barbaro, bishop of Verona, to look into the case and to mete out fitting punishment for 'this grave contempt for the holy sacrament of baptism and the Christian faith, as well as the insufferable affront to almighty God and our Lord and saviour Jesus Christ'. The trial of Mosè di Spagna, 'despiser and vilifier of holy baptism, who had reverted to the laws and rites of Judaism, in which he persists to this day, causing an insufferable insult to the Christian religion', took place in the summer of the same year before the Podestà of Perugia, Giovanni da Balbiano. During the trial Mosè swore that he had never abandoned the Jewish faith, never having been baptized, and produced various pieces of evidence in his favour, thereby gaining

[30] On the 1391 persecutions in Spain see generally Y. Baer, *A History of the Jews in Christian Spain* (Philadelphia, Pa., 1961), ii. 95–169 and its extensive bibliography.
[31] We find Jewish refugees from the Iberian peninsula in Rome from 1405: see G. Marini, *Degli Archiatri Pontifici* (Rome, 1784), i. 293; at Ancona from 1422: see *All'Illustrissima Congregazione*, republished as Stern, *Urkundliche Beiträge*, 36 and C. Rosenberg, *Alcuni cenni bibliografici di rabbini e letterati della comunità israelitica di Ancona* (Ancona, 1932), xxiii–xxv; at Mantua in 1431: see Colorni, *Legge ebraica*, 367–8; and in Florence in 1446: see Cassuto, *Ebrei a Firenze*, 40.
[32] See Majarelli and Nicolini, *Il Monte dei Poveri di Perugia*, 218–22; Toaff, *Ebrei a Perugia*, 74–7.

absolution from the charge of heresy, which could have taken him to the stake.[33]

CHARGES OF RITUAL MURDER

The most serious charge made against Jews in the last part of the fifteenth century was that of ritual murder.[34] The case at Trento, prompted in 1475 by the dire preachings of Bernardino da Feltre, was to lead to the bloody extinction of the local Jewish community and to the subsequent beatification of the young Simonino, the alleged martyr.[35] Both in Italy and in the rest of Europe, the myth concerning the gruesome Jewish ritual of killing a Christian child over Easter had its apostles and its proselytes, who acted with varying degrees of cunning and good faith. In his *Sermones Quadragesimales* fra Roberto Caracciolo made routine mention of 'how the Jews . . . each year, in Holy Week, would secretly take Christians to certain hidden places to torture and kill them . . . and even in our own day the Jews of Trento martyred a young boy, the blessed Simon, of whom many praiseworthy things are said'.[36] In the decade 1475–85, actions against Jews accused of ritual murder mushroomed virtually everywhere, and inevitably the figure of Martino Tomitano, the famous friar from Feltre, a mettlesome champion of the Monte di Pietà, was almost always involved.[37] There is evidence of a

---

[33] AS Perugia, Diplom., MS 263 (reg. Belforti, II, 27 May 1461); ibid., Giud., Sentenze del Podestà, orig. A, fo. 62ʳ (20 July 1461). See Toaff, *Ebrei a Perugia*, 290–4.

[34] On the charge of ritual murder in general, see e.g. G. A. Zaviziano, *Un raggio di luce: La persecuzione degli ebrei nella storia* (Corfu, 1891); V. Manzini, *La superstizione omicida e i sacrifici umani* (Turin, 1925).

[35] Among recent studies of the case of the blessed Simone da Trento see G. Volli, 'I Processi Tridentini e il culto del beato Simone da Trento', *Il Ponte*, 19 (1963), 1396–1408; id., 'Contributo alla storia dei Processi Tridentini del 1475', *La Rassegna Mensile di Israel*, 31 (1965), 570–8; W. P. Eckert, 'Il beato Simonino negli atti del processo di Trento contro gli ebrei', *Studi Trentini di Scienze Storiche*, 44 (1965), 193–221.

[36] Quoted in M. Semeraro, 'Fra Roberto Caracciolo e gli ebrei', in C. Colafemmina (ed.), *Studi Storici* (Bari, 1974), 57.

[37] Scholars have also considered the case of the blessed Lorenzino da Valrovina, the alleged victim of the Jews of Bassano in 1485; see G. Chiuppani, *Gli ebrei a Bassano* (Bassano, 1907), 72–81; G. Volli, 'Il beato Lorenzino da Marostica presunta vittima d'un omicidio rituale', *La Rassegna Mensile di Israel*, 34 (1968), 513–26, 564–9. In the duchy of Milan accusations of ritual murder were made in Pavia in 1467 and at Arena Po in 1479; see Simonsohn, *Jews in the Duchy of Milan*, i. 658–9, ii. 688, 702, 772–8; Antoniazzi Villa, *Un processo contro gli ebrei*, 56. In 1441, and twice in 1458, the Jews of Chambéry were charged with the ritual murder of local Christian children; see Segre, *Jews in Piedmont*, i. 147–8, 286. In 1463 the Jews of Volterra were accused of

typical case of supposed attempted ritual murder at Bevagna in 1485.
Here we find a rehash of all the usual elements of what emerges as a
positive collective psychosis, cunningly fuelled by those who saw the
emergence of the Monte di Pietà as an opportunity to oppose the very
existence of Jews within Christian society, itself regarded as having been
all too tolerant of the Jewish presence hitherto.

In the second half of the fifteenth century Bevagna was home to two or
three Jewish families in all, nor does it seem that a greater number had
ever previously lived there. The largest and most important was that of
Abramo da Perugia. The son of Isacco di maestro Musetto, Abramo had
been born in Perugia in 1424 of an unremarkable family; here, in 1449,
he married Rosa di Giacobbe, a girl from Bevagna who brought him a
modest dowry of 100 florins.[38] She bore him five sons, Bonaventura,
Daniele, Gabriele, Michele, and Giacobbe, and two daughters, Graziosa
and Stella. In the years immediately following his marriage, Abramo
moved to Bevagna, his wife's home town, and here he gradually built up
his fortune. He opened a bank specializing in loans secured on pledges
and landed property, usually for small sums that rarely exceeded 50
florins, and basically serving the needs of the townspeople and those in
the surrounding countryside. The commune made use of Abramo for
loans at reduced rates, often to pay the modest salary of the Podestà.[39]
Abramo's relations with the town's governors were thus close and
cordial, as apparently they also were with the local clergy, and in
particular with the canons of the church of S. Maria in Laurenzia, who
frequently made use of his bank when the need arose.[40] Thus it was not
surprising that the parish priest, don Melchiorre, should have been a
constant visitor to the house of his close friend, to drink a glass of good
Trebbiano with him under the pergola looking out over the vines and

---

having crucified a Christian; see M. Luzzati's introduction to *Ebrei e Cristiani
nell'Italia medioevale e moderna: Conversioni, scambi, contrasti*, proceedings of a conference held at S. Miniato, Pisa, 4–6 Nov. 1986 (Rome, 1988), 9–17. For an updated
biography of Bernardino da Feltre see V. Meneghin, *Bernardino da Feltre e i Monti di
Pietà* (Vicenza, 1974); his thesis, which minimizes the strongly antisemitic tendencies
of Bernardino's preaching, is refuted by R. Segre, 'Bernardino da Feltre, i Monti di
Pietà e i banchi ebraici', *Rivista Storica Italiana*, 40 (1978), 818–33.

[38] AS Perugia, Not., Mariano di Luca di Nino, 116, fo. 36ᵛ (10 June 1449).

[39] e.g. in 1466 Abramo had paid the salary of the Podestà Antonio Pierneri on
behalf of the commune of Bevagna: AC Bevagna, Con. e Rif., 130, reg. 1, fo. 8ʳ; ibid.,
Not., Bartolomeo di Gaspare, 1521, fo. 167ᵛ; ibid., Not., Gaspare di Angelo, 1523/II,
fo. 71ᵛ.

[40] Ibid., Not., Bartolomeo di Gaspare, 1521, fos. 6ᵛ–7ʳ.

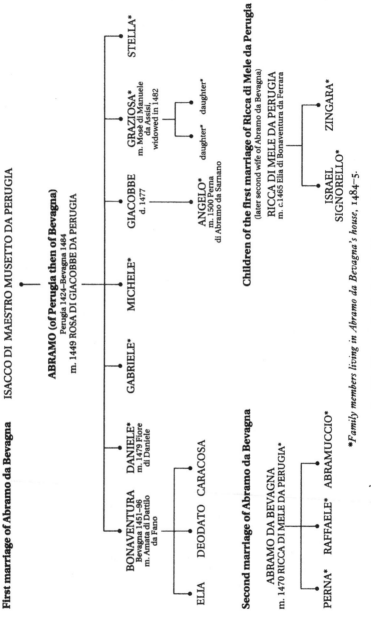

FIG. 6.1 The Bevagna family (15th–16th centuries)

olive-groves of the green hills outside the city walls and castle keep, on cool, clear spring days when no mist rose from the rivers Clitunno and Topino.

Abramo's business was beginning to prosper, and his activities now extended beyond the walls of Bevagna, if often unofficially: to Spello and to Spoleto, where he had securities in the bank of Ventura di Isacco, and to Foligno, where he had shares in the activities of the bank of Musetto di Angelo da Camerino, the town's chief Jewish financier.[41] In April 1464 Abramo had been fined by the Apostolic Camera for having continued to lend money illegally at Perugia, after the founding of the Monte di Pietà had led to the enforced closure of the Jewish banks.[42] The bank at Bevagna, too—the first and at that time the only one to have an official arrangement with the commune—had considerably increased the volume of its business and was attracting deposits and investments from the main Jewish financiers of Perugia and Foligno.[43] In 1465 Abramo di Isacco da Bevagna, as he was now known, having dropped any reference to Perugia, became a partner in the important Assisi bank of Giacobbe di Elia di Francia. He was subsequently to become its sole owner, entrusting its management to his first-born son, Bonaventura.[44] Finally, on 22 June 1481, Abramo obtained a loan charter for Amelia too and opened a third bank there, which he placed under the management of his son-in-law, Mosè di Manuele da Assisi, the husband of his daughter Graziosa.[45]

At the same time Abramo was consolidating his position in his adopted town, building himself a suitably imposing house there. In the winter of 1473 the banker Ventura di Abramo da Perugia sold him an elegant villa, surrounded by a garden with a well, in the vaita S. Angelo, on via Vecchia in Bevagna, at a price of 225 florins. The new owner

---

[41] AC Spello, Not., env. 7, Pier Tommaso Morichelli, 9, fo. 30ʳ; AC Bevagna, Not., Petruccio di Gaspare, 1524, fo. 68ᵛ; AC Foligno, Not., Taddeo Angelelli, 14/5, fo. 266ʳ.

[42] AS Perugia, Not., Tancio di Niccolò, 266, fo. 113ᵛ (9 Apr. 1464).

[43] Depositors in the bank of Abramo da Bevagna included the banker Ventura di Abramo da Perugia, Angelo di Musetto da Camerino, living in Foligno, and Aronne di maestro Zucchero da Foligno: AC Bevagna, Not., Bartolomeo di Gaspare, 1521, fo. 223ᵛ; ibid., Gaspare di Angelo, 1520, fo. 150ᵛ; AC Foligno, Not., Taddeo Angelelli, 15/2, fo. 46ʳ (3 Jan. 1498).

[44] AC Assisi, H, Rif., 9. fo. 8ʳ (28 Feb. 1465); ibid., 18, fo. 341ᵛ; ibid., Not., Ludovico di Giovanni di Angelo, vol. ii, s24, fo. 57ᵛ. See also Toaff, *Jews in Medieval Assisi*, 56, 65–6, 163–4, 171.

[45] AC Amelia, Rif., 47, fos. 368ᵛ–373ʳ (22 June 1481); AC Bevagna, Not., Crescimbene di Pietro di Percivalle, 1538, fo. 34ᵛ.

immediately invested a further 45 florins in his purchase, ordering various improvements and extensions to the building. Some years later his sons further enlarged the big family house, adding two adjacent buildings acquired for the price of another 110 florins.[46] Abramo's love for his 'manor house' was deep and uncompromising. He wanted it to be in a permanent state of readiness to accommodate his children and relatives, with their respective families, and in his will Abramo firmly forbade his heirs to sell it or in any way transfer its ownership, even in part.[47] If one of his sons ever needed money and might therefore want to sell the house, the others were to pledge themselves to buy him out, but always keeping the building, each contributing to pay him his share, fixed at 60 florins for each heir.

At the beginning of the 1480s, Abramo da Bevagna could certainly have been described as comfortably off. He was the owner of three banks, operating with exclusive arrangements at Bevagna, Assisi, and Amelia, and he had securities and investments at Spoleto, Foligno, and Perugia. Between them, his banks and partnerships meant that Abramo had investments which must have oscillated in value between 2,500 and 3,000 florins overall. Bearing in mind his own statement in his will, after taxes and running costs, this sum yielded a net profit of between 12 and 16 per cent per annum, and thus we may assess his overall income from his banks at between 300 and 500 florins a year. He also owned an elegant house at Foligno, with an adjoining shop and a storeroom on the ground floor on the central Piazza della Croce, near the cattle-market. This building, valued at about 350 florins, was rented to the family of Angelo di Musetto da Camerino, the main Jewish banker of Foligno, who paid an annual rent of 12 florins.[48] At Bevagna Abramo also intermittently traded in wheat, barley, and wine, and owned a large number of cattle, leased to local peasants.[49] Apart from the house in the district of S.

---

[46] AC Bevagna, Not., Bartolomeo di Gaspare, 1521, fo. 223ᵛ; AS Perugia, Not., Francesco di Giacomo, 221, fo. 170ᵛ; AC Bevagna, Not., Giacomo Lucangeli, 1529, fo. 6ʳ; ibid., Bartolomeo di Gaspare, 1519, fo. 239ʳ.

[47] Abramo's will, drawn up on 7 Mar. 1484, gives us precise information about the make-up of his family (AC Bevagna, Not., Gaspare di Angelo, 1523, fos. 47ᵛ–49ᵛ).

[48] AC Foligno, Not., Taddeo Angelelli 9/10, fo. 104ʳ (10 Apr. 1486); ibid. 12/10, fo. 176ᵛ; ibid. 15/2, fo. 46ʳ.

[49] AC Bevagna, Not., Bartolomeo di Gaspare, 1521, fo. 166ᵛ; ibid., Crescimbene di Pietro di Percivalle, 1536, fo. 146ᵛ, and 1543, fo. 94ʳ; ibid., Pernicola Ciccarelli, 1559, fo. 43ʳ; ibid., Giacomo Lucangeli, 1529, fo. 121ʳ; ibid., Gaspare di Angelo, 1520, fo. 143ᵛ, and 1523, fo. 68ʳ; ibid., Bernardino di Giacomo, 1528, fo. 141ᵛ; ibid., Crescimbene di Pietro di Percivalle, 1543, fo. 99ᵛ; ibid., Giacomo Lucangeli, 1530, fo. 4ᵛ.

Angelo, he also owned much arable land and pasture, and vines and olive-groves in the *contado*, at Arquata, Torre del Colle, Pretalata, Cerqueto, and Pantani. Abramo was thus a rich and virtually self-made man. But life had not always dealt him a kind hand. His son Giacobbe had died tragically in 1477, together with his young wife, leaving a very young son, Angelo, whom his grandfather had had to care for in his house in Bevagna. In 1482 his son-in-law, Mosè da Assisi, who ran the bank at Amelia, suddenly died, and Abramo unhesitatingly took his widowed daughter and her two baby daughters back into his house.[50] His wife, Rosa di Giacobbe, who had borne him seven children, died around 1468; two years later, at the age of 46, Abramo married a widow from Perugia, Ricca, the daughter of Mele di maestro Bonaventura. Together with a dowry of 200 ducats, his second wife also brought him two children from her first marriage to Elia di maestro Bonaventura da Ferrara, a Jew from Perugia: Israel, known as Signorello, and Zingara. Once again the generous Abramo immediately took in the two children, treating them as though they were his own. For her part, Ricca bore him three more children, Perna, Raffaele, and Abramuccio.[51]

When Abramo, now 60 years old, called the notary Gaspare di Angelo to draft his will on 7 March 1484, the house on via Vecchia must have been full of life.[52] Apart from the servants, Abramo himself, and his wife Ricca, fourteen other relatives were living there: Abramo's son Daniele, now grown up, with his wife Fiore, whom he had married in 1479;[53] two of Abramo's other sons by his first marriage, Gabriele and Michele, still under 25, and Signorello and Zingara, Ricca's children by her first husband; Graziosa, Abramo's widowed daughter, with her two small girls, and Stella, Abramo's youngest daughter by his first wife; and last-ly, perhaps playing in the garden, were four children, Perna, Raffaele, and Abramuccio, the banker's three children by his second wife, all born after 1470, and Angelo, Abramo's grandson.[54] In his will the old banker left an equal sum to all the children of both his marriages, as well as to his

---

[50] This information is taken from the will of Abramo di Isacco da Bevagna dated 7 Mar. 1484.   [51] Ibid.

[52] AC Bevagna, Not., Gaspare di Angelo, vol. 1523, fos. 47ᵛ–49ᵛ.

[53] In the *confessio dotis* of 3 Nov. 1479 Fiore di Daniele brought her husband Daniele di Abramo da Bevagna a dowry of 107½ florins (AC Bevagna, Not., Bartolomeo di Gaspare, 1521, fo. 330ʳ).

[54] The family of Abramo di Bevagna is a typical example of what historians and sociologists, when talking of the Italian noble and mercantile society of the time, call the 'multiple patriarchal family', where property is collective and undivided, and all

grandson Angelo, while each of his three daughters received a dowry of 200 florins. His wife Ricca was named usufructuary and administrator of his possessions, as long as she did not remarry, while the wardship of the under-age children, his sons and grandsons, was entrusted until their majority to his first-born son Bonaventura. Bonaventura was the only member of the family not living at Bevagna, since his father had appointed him manager of the family's most important bank at Assisi, a post which required his constant presence on the spot.[55] However, Bonaventura visited the house in Bevagna to see his family far more frequently than religious feasts and business meetings required. On such occasions he was accompanied by his wife, Amata di Dattilo da Fano, and his three children, Elia, Deodato, and Caracosa, glad of the opportunity for a trip to Bevagna to see their grandfather and to play in the garden with their uncles and young cousins.[56]

Some months later, between May and September 1484, Abramo died, presumably well pleased with his lifetime's financial achievements and the large family who surrounded him in his beloved house at Bevagna. But his last meetings with Bonaventura had not been reassuring.[57] At Assisi the Minorite friars were intensifying their campaign against Jewish moneylending, and chalking up significant political successes.[58] Not that business was going badly; indeed the usual clientèle remained faithful to their bank, and even those who blustered and protested in the streets or in the *palazzo del commune*, including priests and friars themselves,

---

the children live together in the same house as their parents. 'The heads of the families felt that it was more becoming, more honourable, for all the members of the family to be lodged together in one single building; and this building thus gradually became the symbol of the family, of its power and its cohesion'; see J. C. Davis, *The Decline of the Venetian Nobility as a Ruling Class* (Baltimore, Md., 1962), 70–3. See also the more recent work by Barbagli, *Sotto lo stesso tetto*, 34, 42, 141–4, 161, 189–96, 240.

[55] See Toaff, *Jews in Medieval Assisi*, 65–6, 171.

[56] Details of the composition of Bonaventura di Abramo's family are to be found in AC Bevagna, Not., Gaspare di Angelo, 1523 II, fos. 139ʳ–140ʳ (28 Dec. 1496).

[57] The last document in which Abramo di Isacco da Bevagna appears as still active in banking dates from 8 Apr. 1484 (AC Bevagna, Not., Crescimbene di Pietro di Percivalle, 1538, fo. 41ʳ). His sons Daniele and Gabriele seem already to have replaced him in running the Bevagna bank by the beginning of the following November (ibid., Gaspare di Angelo, 1523, fo. 65ᵛ; ibid., Crescimbene di Pietro di Percivalle, 1538, fo. 57ᵛ).

[58] On this, and the following, concerning the events which were to lead to the extinction of the Jewish community in Assisi in 1485 after the preaching of Bernardino da Feltre, see esp. Toaff, *Jews in Medieval Assisi*, 57–71, 163–73.

ultimately went to the bank, pledge in hand, to ask for money. But men of experience such as Abramo, who could scent danger, knew that trouble was brewing. Elia di Manuele di Francia, the Jewish medical officer of Assisi, universally respected in his profession and enjoying the favour and protection of Sixtus IV himself, had been shamefully driven from the commune, unable to withstand the pressure of the Minorites, Antonio da Vercelli and Fortunato Coppoli da Perugia, who had mounted a violent anti-Jewish campaign in the town, ostensibly to protect the recently established Monte di Pietà. There had been a proliferation of baptisms among the depleted Jewish group in Assisi, a sure sign of which way the wind was blowing and of what the future might hold. These worries left their mark on Abramo's will: leaving a sum of money to his home town, he explained the motives behind his generosity as follows: 'I make this bequest mindful of the many benefits which I the testator have received from the commune of Bevagna, and in the hope that these benefits may be renewed in the future and trans-ferred, after my death, to my sons.'[59] This was a prudent, if naïve, way of staking a claim on the future, of trying to ensure that his family would continue to enjoy a security which recent events had seemed to threaten. But he could not sway the future, and Abramo was to be spared the grief, worry, and tragedy which his children were to confront.

At the beginning of 1485 Bernardino da Feltre arrived in Umbria to complete a plan—originally formulated by his fellow-preachers—to close down the Jewish banks by consolidating the recently established Monti di Pietà and putting an end to the presence of Jewish communities in the region. The mere name Bernardino struck terror among the Jews, associated as it was with the recent memory of events at Trento, the accusation of the ritual murder of young Simonino, and the deaths of its alleged perpetrators. His preaching in the squares of Umbria began at Perugia and continued at Gubbio, with considerable success.[60] At Gubbio, at his request, the guild consuls denounced the charter signed with the Jews, giving them no alternative but to leave the city. At Perugia, where Jewish banks had long ceased to operate officially, Bernardino had succeeded in having severe restrictive measures applied in connection with local Jews, including the obligatory wearing of the distinctive yellow badge on their clothing. A wave of conversions within the alarmed Jewish community followed Bernardino's fanatical

---

[59] AC Bevagna, Not., Gaspare di Angelo, 1523, fos. 47ᵛ–49ᵛ.

[60] See C. Roth in *Encyclopedia Judaica*, iv (Jerusalem, 1971), 672, s.v. 'Bernardino da Feltre'.

preaching.[61] His fervid sermons at Assisi at the beginning of the summer of 1485 were to lead to the closing down of Bonaventura's bank and to a definitive Jewish exodus from the city.[62] Two years later, writing to the priors of Assisi, Bernardino recalled the efficacy of these anti-Jewish sermons with ill-concealed glee: 'Coming here from Gubbio I preached two sermons against Jewish usury and in favour of the Monte di Pietà, and by the grace of God I was inspired to deliver some that were so effective, that thenceforth the Jew was to be forbidden from lending money in perpetuity, nor were all his malicious wiles of any service to him.' Bernardino warmly congratulated the governors of Assisi for having prudently decided, for the love of Jesus and the salvation of their souls, 'to have done with usury and with Jews'.[63]

The charge of attempted ritual murder over the Easter period which was brought against Abramo's sons should be seen in this context. They had been denounced by the alleged victim, Pietro Antoniuccio, a child from a family of poor peasants from Bevagna. Antoniuccio reported that on Good Friday he had been lured to the house of the Jews, in the district of S. Angelo, by Zingara, Ricca's daughter. Here Daniele and his brothers had stripped him of his clothes, and, after having whipped and wounded him on the hands and feet with a sharpened rod, they had allegedly crucified him on a wooden cross, gathering his blood in special receptacles. The child did not explain how he had managed to escape from his place of torture so as to inform the whole town of the terrible crime the Jews had attempted to commit. In the days that followed fra Battista da Terni, the inquisitor of the province of S. Francesco, arrived at Bevagna to investigate the matter and severely punish those responsible. The inquest was carried out between 10 April and 10 June, with the interrogation of fifteen or so witnesses, including the relatives of Pietro Antoniuccio.[64] The child's father, Liberatore Allevoli, stated that he had

[61] See Toaff, *Ebrei a Perugia*, 80–1, 115; Majarelli and Nicolini, *Il Monte dei Poveri*, 94–7.

[62] AC Assisi, H, Rif., 9, fo. 32ʳ (14 Aug. 1485). See Toaff, *Jews in Medieval Assisi*, 65–71, 172.

[63] Bernardino da Feltre's letter to the priors of Assisi, dated 7 Oct. 1487, is published in A. Cristofani, *Le Storie di Assisi* (Venice, 1959), 457–8, and Toaff, *Jews in Medieval Assisi*, 173.

[64] AC Bevagna, Not., Gaspare di Pietro di Percivalle, 1539, fos. I–III. I was fortunate enough to rediscover the records of the inquisitor friars on a sheet used as a cover for record-book no. 1539 of the notary Gaspare di Pietro di Percivalle, in the civic archive at Bevagna. In order to read the contents, I had to loosen the binding of the protocol, freeing the parchment cover from the rest of the volume. The reconstruction of the text, which was partly damaged, crossed out, and full of gaps, was made

been out of town that day gaining indulgences, and that he had learned of the event on his return to Bevagna. The evidence given by the other witnesses was also based on the alleged victim's version. The one exception was the deposition of Allegrezza, the boy's mother, whom her son had caused to be arrested and held in the prisons of the Palazzo del Podestà, as the Jews' suspected accomplice. At the beginning of her interrogation, the woman turned to her son, begging him to explain his strange behaviour. 'Why have you brought me here to meet my downfall?' she asked him, to receive the enigmatic reply: 'I was afraid that you would do me harm; it is true that they bound me by my right hand and whipped me and placed me upon the cross, and pierced my hand with a sharp stick, a stick like a lance.' Donna Allegrezza's deposition provided many clues which might have led the inquisitors to reconstruct the facts somewhat differently: she stated that she had formerly contracted a loan with Daniele and his brothers, on surety of a pledge consisting of a blanket, a pair of sheets, three napkins, and a cotton cover. Subsequently Allegrezza had redeemed her pledges, assuring the banker that she would repay the loan, with the relative interest, within a few days. But for some reason she had not kept her promise, apparently provoking a variety of reactions among Abramo's sons. Daniele was said to have asked the woman to send her son to his house with the money on Good Friday, threatening to denounce her should she fail to do so. Furthermore, according to Allegrezza, on meeting her by chance in the street, Daniele's brother Gabriele had insulted and abused her. None the less, on the day when Pietro Antoniuccio claimed he had been crucified by the Jews, she was not in town, having gone to Montefalco to hear the preaching of a certain friar. Other depositions, whose content was totally irrelevant to ascertaining the facts of the case, were clearly a blatant attempt to convince the inquiry of the Jews' potential guilt. For example, Lorenzo, the medical officer for Bevagna, reported that he had been called to Daniele's house to tend to a broken limb sustained by a member of his family, and that he had found twenty-five Jews from Bevagna and elsewhere making merry. Four further witnesses confirmed the doctor's evidence and reported having seen numerous foreign Jews on Good Friday in the house on via Vecchia, drinking wine, playing cards, and making a fiendish din. The real explanation—that Abramo da Bevagna's

---

possible thanks to the help of Marta Gaburri from Bevagna, and the expert advice of my friend Giocondo Ricciarelli of Perugia, sadly now deceased. The protocol of fra Battista da Terni's inquiry, dated 10 Apr.–10 June 1485, is published in its entirety in my *Jews in Umbria*, iii. 995-9.

family were quite simply celebrating the traditional Passover meal, to which many outside guests had been invited, as was the custom—was just not taken into consideration, either by the zealous witnesses or by the inquisition.[65]

As the hearing proceeded, several people expressed the fear that the Jews, alarmed about the possible outcome of the case, and the likely closure of their bank, might try to smuggle the pledges in their possession out of town, clandestinely transferring their goods elsewhere. One of the Jews' neighbours, who was in the habit of rising early to work in his garden, stated: 'At dawn on Monday 16 May [1485], I saw a foreign Jew coming furtively out of Daniele's house with a heavy bundle; mounting his horse, he galloped away down a secret road running along the walls, leaving Bevagna by the Porta S. Giovanni.' In the view of the inquisitor, this was enough to have the Jews severely punished, whether or not they were guilty of having tried to crucify the young Pietro Antoniuccio. On 10 June 1485 fra Battista da Terni ordered Andrea di Filippo Leri da Assisi, the Podestà of Bevagna, to hand over the brothers Daniele, Gabriele, and Signorello to be detained by him in the convent of S. Francesco until sentence was passed. The inquisitor threatened the Podestà with excommunication if he refused. At the end of the following July the banker Raphael di Isacco de Pomis, the brothers' lawyer, arrived in Bevagna from Spoleto, bringing the Podestà two letters from the apostolic magistrate interceding in favour of the accused and asking that they be heard in an impartial manner respectful of the law.[66] We do not know how instrumental these letters were in mitigating the sentence passed on the Jews; at all events it could not be described as lenient. Daniele, Gabriele, and Signorello were banished from Bevagna and the family was fined 200 ducats.

Meanwhile, Abramo's eldest son, Bonaventura, had returned to Abramo's house at Bevagna with his family; as we have seen, after Bernardino da Feltre's preaching, Bonaventura had been obliged to discontinue his activities at Assisi, and close down the local bank.

[65] In 1485 Good Friday fell on 1 Apr. In the corresponding Jewish year (5245) Passover fell on Thursday 31 Mar. So on the evening of Good Friday the Jews of Bevagna, like all others, were celebrating the second day of the feast of Pesach with the traditional supper (*seder*), during which the guests recite and sing from the ritual book of the *Haggadah* in memory of the Jews' exodus from Egypt. Traditionally, every guest must drink at least four glasses of wine during this meal. On the meaning of Pesach, *seder*, and the *Haggadah*, see E. D. Goldschmidt (ed.), *The Passover Haggadah: Its Source and History* (Jerusalem, 1969).

[66] AC Bevagna, Not., Gaspare di Angelo, 1523, fo. 90[r] (22 July 1485).

Bonaventura now took on the wardship of the under-age children still living in the villa in S. Angelo, and from October 1485 he became responsible for the affairs of the whole family.[67] Meanwhile his brother Gabriele, banished from Bevagna, had moved to Amelia, where he supervised the activities of the other remaining family bank in person until the summer of 1490, when he was granted permission to return to his home town.[68] It was probably now that he came into possession of the valuable legacy of Hebrew manuscripts which Abramo had left him, and which he had not been able to take with him in his exile to Amelia.[69] But the misfortunes of the family of Abramo da Bevagna were not yet over. In 1496 Bonaventura died suddenly: he was not yet 45, and left a wife and three young children.[70] More seriously, however, the family had lost the head which had guided it wisely for so long. The weight of this responsibility now fell upon the shoulders of the young Gabriele, still inexperienced and unequal to the task of replacing his brother at the helm of the family firm. Crisis soon struck on all fronts. The bank at Amelia was going through lean times, and periodic financial difficulties led to its definitive closure in 1507.[71] Neither were the affairs of the bank at Bevagna going as well as they had done in the past. Bonaventura's death caused many Jewish financiers who had invested large sums in his business to withdraw their deposits. Significantly enough, in April 1498 Angelo di Musetto da Camerino, the main Jewish banker of Foligno, who for many years had had interests in the bank of Abramo da Bevagna, now asked Gabriele to return a deposit of 150 florins, as well as 171 ducats, the dowry of Amata da Fano, Bonaventura's widow, whose interests were

[67] In 1486 Bonaventura figures in the documents as 'heir to said Abramo da Bevagna, guardian and administrator of his estate and factor of the house of his other brothers, namely Daniele, Gabriele, and Michele and of his half-brother Abramuccio and nephew Angelo' (AC Bevagna, Not., Crescimbene di Pietro di Percivalle, 1539, fo. 59ᵛ).

[68] From Oct. 1485 we find Gabriele di Bevagna at Amelia, where he was managing the affairs of the family bank, with Gabriele d'Elia da Perugia as its factor (AC Amelia, Rif., 49, fos. 51ʳ, 84ʳ). His name appears again in the documents of Bevagna from 7 July 1490. On that occasion, together with Bonaventura, he received power of attorney for the other brothers Daniele and Michele (AC Bevagna, Not., Crescimbene di Pietro di Percivalle, 1541, fos. 19ᵛ, 43ʳ.

[69] N. Allony has published the list of Hebrew books, from MS Heb. Vaticano 465, inherited in 1465 by Gabriele, son of Abramo da Bevagna (though the date should actually be amended to 1495: in 1465 Abramo was still alive, and Gabriele was a child of 2); see N. Allony, 'Old Booklists in the Vatican Library' (Heb.), *Areshet*, 4 (1966), 213–14.

[70] AC Bevagna, Not., Gaspare di Angelo, 1523/II, fos. 139ʳ–140ʳ (28 Dec. 1496).

[71] AC Amelia, Rif., 60, fos. 437ᵛ, 439ᵛ, 442ʳ, 451ᵛ; ibid., 61, fo. 83ʳ.

represented by Angelo. Unable to scrape the sum together, Gabriele was forced to sell Angelo da Camerino the large house, with the adjoining shop and storehouse, on Piazza della Croce, which he had rented for years from Abramo da Bevagna's family.[72]

One of the last events to gladden the life of the house on via Vecchia, now largely empty, was the marriage of the young Angelo, the orphan son of Giacobbe, the only one of Abramo's sons to have died while Abramo was still alive. On 29 October 1500 the villa was decked out for his marriage to Perna di Abramo da Sarnano, a girl from the Marches who brought him a modest dowry of 110 florins. Gabriele spared no expense on that occasion: possibly in an attempt to forget the recent tragedies which had befallen the family, he organized a princely banquet costing 24 florins, undoubtedly a considerable sum if seen in relation to the dowry Giacotte's wife brought him.[73]

Some years later new storm-clouds were gathering over the few Jews still living with Gabriele in the family house in Bevagna. At the end of February 1504 Cerbone, a 'simpleton' in the care of the Ospedale di S. Maria dei Laici, spoke publicly of a horrendous experience said to have befallen him on the night of Carnival Friday, when a host of evil spirits had attacked him in his bed, subjecting him to atrocious tortures. The inquisitor of the province of S. Francesco, fra Galeotto, immediately came to Bevagna to gather first-hand evidence of the details of Cerbone's diabolical vision.[74] In his sworn deposition to the inquisitor dated 28 February 1504, the beggar stated that on the night of the previous Friday, while he was in his bed at the hospice, two fiends had appeared to him, asking him to join their company. The spirits had reacted to his outraged refusal by passing a burning branch across his face, causing him to cry out and writhe in pain. The friar in attendance had come running at the poor tramp's desperate cries, and been beseeched to free him from the fiends who sought to burn him. Invoking the name of God, the friar had begun to whip Cerbone in a desperate attempt to rout the devil who had taken possession of him, and his success was as speedy as it was unexpected. The following day Cerbone had gone begging through the streets of Bevagna, as was his custom, eagerly telling the passers-by of his awesome adventure, and further embellishing it with one significant detail:

[72] AC Foligno, Not., Taddeo Angelelli, 14/5, fos. 259ʳ, 284ʳ (27 Apr. 1498).
[73] AC Bevagna, Not., Gaspare di Angelo, 1523/II, fo. 278ʳ.
[74] Ibid., Pietro Crescimbene di Percivalle, 1544, fos. 73ᵛ–74ᵛ (28 Feb. 1504). The text of the Franciscan inquiry into the matter denounced by Cerbone is published in Toaff, *Jews of Umbria*, iii. 1116–18.

without a shadow of doubt, he had recognized the fiends who had assailed him as several of the Jews living in the city. News spread like wildfire throughout Bevagna that once again Gabriele and his brothers had been responsible for a horrendous crime against the Christian religion, and anti-Jewish wrath mounted steadily. Cerbone concluded his deposition to the inquisitor by promising to travel to the shrines of St James of Galicia and Our Lady of Loreto on a pilgrimage of expiation and thanks for the perils averted.[75]

But fra Galeotto was apparently not convinced by the beggar's account and scrupulously continued his inquiries, also questioning two vagrants who had been sleeping in his room at the hospice of S. Maria dei Laici, as well as the friar in attendance. The inquisitor asked them whether it was possible that the Jews could have managed to gain entry into the hospice that night. The reply was negative since, as the witnesses stressed, the main door had remained closed until dawn and the lock did not appear to have been forced. At this point Cerbone collapsed and was forced to admit that he had invented virtually the whole story: he admitted that he had never been to the Jews' house at Bevagna and that he had falsely accused them. The idea of this false charge had come to him the morning after his vision of the fiends, when he had discovered the stigmata on his arms and hands, as though he had been pierced by nails or daggers. The memory of the alleged crucifixion of the young Pietro Antoniuccio on Good Friday twenty years earlier in the house of the Jews in vaita S. Angelo still lived on at Bevagna, and it was therefore not surprising that an enterprising vagrant such as Cerbone should be tempted to revive it to his own advantage, casting himself, over-enthusiastically perhaps, in the part of victim.

This was the second time within a few years that Abramo da Bevagna'a family had found itself facing an accusation of such gravity. This time, fortunately for them, they got off lightly. But in the mean time it was becoming increasingly problematic for Gabriele and his brothers to stay on at Bevagna. Their financial situation was far from stable. The bank at Assisi had closed down in 1485, and the one at Amelia in 1507, though Gabriele continued to manage the family's last remaining bank at Bevagna until the summer of 1512; but at that point he found it impossible to continue, and he gave up.[76] A few months later the large house

[75] On the identification of the old district of Bevagna, and its streets, institutions, and churches, some of which are mentioned in this chapter, see G Bragazzi, *La rosa dell'Umbria* (Foligno, 1864) 249–84.
[76] Gabriele di Abramo da Bevagna had the charter for the Amelia bank confirmed

on via Vecchia, with the garden and the well—the house that old Abramo had proudly considered the symbol of his economic success and the outward sign of his hard-earned but fruitful financial integration into the town's social life—was becoming overrun with nettles and undergrowth, awaiting new owners who were prepared to shut their minds to the events that were rumoured to have occurred in those rooms.

I have looked at the fortunes of the family of Abramo da Bevagna at some length because the considerable documentation concerning it allows us to use it as a paradigm from which to reconstruct the mood of the years which followed the foundation of the first Monti di Pietà in Umbria. It was a period characterized by a general shift in attitude towards the Jews, by the way in which Minorite preachers took the lead in challenging the economic and physical presence of Jews within Christian society, and by the Jews' own desperate efforts to resist this irreversible process, which was to be completed during the following century.

---

on 15 June 1502 for a period of twenty years (AC Amelia, Rif., 58, fos. 71^v–72^r, 83^v, 95^v; ibid., 59, fos. 11^r–12^v). However, the bank immediately entered a period of crisis in the following years, mainly because vast sums lent to the commune were not repaid. On 13 May 1507 Gabriele's charter was revoked unilaterally by the Consiglio Generale del Popolo di Amelia, and the following Nov. the bank ceased business (AC Amelia, Rif., 60, fos. 437^v, 442^r, 451^v; ibid., 61, fo. 83^r). The last document found concerning the activity of Gabriele's bank at Bevagna dates from 9 Mar. 1512. On 24 May of that year Gabriele was making arrangements for the sale of his family's landed property in the *contado* (AC Bevagna, Not., Crescimbene di Pietro di Percivalle, 1545, fos. 193^v, 198^v). In the following years the citizens of Bevagna used the bank of Angelo di Vitale da Camerino, at Trevi, which was still one of the most important Jewish banks in Umbria (AC Bevagna, Con. e Rif., folder 8C 7, fos. 24^r, 38^v, 45^r, 107^r).

7

Converts and Apostates

TRENDS IN CONVERSION

As we have seen, the Jews of late medieval Italy were dispersed throughout hundreds of small and isolated communities, immersed in a Christian society whose power of attraction could make itself felt well in excess of an already crushing numerical superiority; this inevitably left their numbers exposed to depletion by conversion and baptism.[1] Naturally enough, this tendency was more pronounced at times of crisis, when friction between Christian society and the Jewish minority was exacerbated by the enforcement of oppressive measures such as expulsion. The erosion of the spirit of tolerance and peaceful coexistence with which a Jewish group had been accepted in any one place was usually a gradual process. When, as sometimes happened, it culminated in open hostility, some Jews chose baptism in preference to discrimination or exile, and conversions assumed proportions great enough to cripple the Jewish community as a whole and to cast a shadow across its future. The phenomenon of conversion and baptism in the Italian cities of the late Middle Ages has not as yet been the object of any quantitative research which would enable us to measure its impact on the Jewish community with any accuracy, and it is not therefore possible to verify its demographic effect or to correlate it, in quantitative terms, with other significant influences on Italian Jewry in the fourteenth and fifteenth centuries. Any conclusions as to overall trends must thus often be limited to the level of general impressions and theories usually based on interpretation of historical texts. Scholars are virtually unanimous in agreeing that the number of baptisms within Italian Jewry (and especially of those Jews living in the Papal State) rose sharply during the Counter-Reformation,

This chapter is a slightly modified version of the paper I presented at the international conference Ebrei e Cristiani nell'Italia Medioevale e Moderna: Conversioni, Scambi, Contrasti held at San Miniato, Pisa, 4–6 Nov. 1986. The paper was entitled 'Conversioni al cristianesimo in Italia nel Quattrocento, movimenti e tendenze: Il caso dell'Umbria'.

[1] See R. Bonfil, 'Jewish Emigration to Italy in the Late Middle Ages', 152.

as a result of the Church's increasingly intense policy of conversion and the antisemitic measures taken by the popes from the middle of the sixteenth century onwards. The period running from the 1542 bull *Cupientes iudaeos* (with which Paul III reinforced the measures encouraging Jewish baptism) to the 1555 *Cum nimis absurdum* (in which Paul IV gave an aggressive fillip to the Church's anti-Jewish policy), down to Pius V's bull *Hebraeorum gens* of 1569 (ordering the expulsion of the Jews from papal territory), undoubtedly witnessed a large number of baptisms within an increasingly disoriented and alarmed Jewish population.[2] The demographers Roberto Bachi and Sergio DellaPergola have recently suggested an average figure of 2.3 per thousand per annum for the number of conversions among Roman Jews in the period between 1542 and 1563.[3] Their estimates are based essentially on the data which Attilio Milano extracted from the registers of the Casa dei Catecumeni in Rome, and they may in fact be underestimates.[4] Certain it is that in the other cities in the Papal State, where numerous small Jewish communities were living in trepidation on the eve of their definitive departure, the average level of conversions must have been much higher. Writing of the application of the anti-Jewish measures in the Church's lands envisaged by Paul IV's *Cum nimis absurdum*, the chronicler Beniamin Nehemia b. Elnatan da Civitanova observed in a worried tone:

The Jews of Campania, Umbria, and the Duchy of Spoleto are already suffering their consequences . . . as are those of Benevento in the Kingdom of Naples. For the papal delegates subject them to exorbitant taxation and huge fines, reducing them to the most utter poverty, leaving them nothing to live

[2] On the Church's proselytizing policy during this period, see K. R. Stow, *Catholic Thought and Papal Jewry Policy, 1555–1593* (New York, 1977); id., *Taxation, Community and State: The Jews and the Fiscal Foundations of the Early Papal State* (Stuttgart, 1982); B. Pullan, *The Jews of Europe and the Inquisition of Venice, 1550–1670* (Oxford, 1983), 251–3; J. I. Israel, *European Jewry in the Age of Mercantilism, 1550–1750* (Oxford, 1985), 17–22.
[3] 'Did Characteristics of Pre-Emancipation Italian Jewry Deviate from a General Demographic Paradigm for Jewish Traditional Communities?', in V. O. Schmelz and S. DellaPergola (eds.), *Contemporary Jewry: Essays in Honour of Moshe Davis* (Jerusalem, 1984), 165. On conversion to Christianity as a factor in the transformation of the Jewish people during the course of its history see DellaPergola, *La trasformazione demografica della diaspora ebraica*, 69–74.
[4] See Milano, *Il ghetto di Roma*, 283–306; id., 'Battesimi di ebrei a Roma dal Cinquecento all'Ottocento', in D. Carpi, A. Milano, and U. Nahon (eds.), *Scritti in memoria di Enzo Sereni* (Jerusalem, 1970), 133–67. On Jewish baptisms in Rome during the ghetto period see also E. Natali, *Il ghetto di Roma* (Rome, 1887), 233–54.

off. So that many choose the way of baptism, fearing that they can no longer resist persecution. This has happened at Morrovalle, a small village in the Marches, where seventeen Jews were baptized all at one time, while the rest preferred to flee, seeking safety elsewhere. Today there is not one single Jew in that place. But elsewhere too, during these days, Jews are having themselves baptized the length and breadth of the state, and it could be said that there is no town without its Jewish converts.[5]

None the less, and without wishing to underestimate the extent of the phenomenon of conversion within the Jewish community during the Counter-Reformation, I believe that it may have been even more prevalent in earlier periods. I have studied conversions to Christianity among the Jews of Umbria through a systematic examination of late medieval archival material. Examination of the books of the Riformanze of the various communes, and of administrative protocols which contain resolutions on the baptism of Jews and the charitable donations to be granted them, has enabled me to reconstruct the trend of conversion to Christianity among this Jewish population from the end of the fourteenth century until the middle of the sixteenth with a certain degree of accuracy.[6] Some of the information that has emerged is surprising, and calls for further study; it might prove to be of great significance if confirmed by the results of comparable research into the other Jewish communities of central Italy during the same period. Between 1386 and 1445 the annual average of Jewish conversions to Christianity in Umbrian towns varied between 0.5 and 1.2 per 1,000, and then rose to 2.8 per 1,000 during the years 1446–65. The average then climbed steeply, reaching exceptional annual rates of 8.5 per 1,000 in the period 1466–85. It fell again to 2 per 1,000 in the years 1486–1505, then rose constantly as the sixteenth century progressed: to 4.2 per 1,000 in 1506–25, and to 6 per 1,000 in 1526–45.

[5] Beniamin Nehemia b. Elnatan da Civitanova, 'Chronicle of Pope Paul IV' (Heb.), in I. Sonne (ed.), *From Paul IV to Pius V* (Jerusalem, 1954), 28–9.

[6] I have reconstructed the average size of the Jewish community in the periods under consideration using the census data of the various Umbrian communes. In making this calculation I took account of the number of baptisms and referred these back to the native population. For emigration, I assumed a linear development in the periods running between one census and the next. Thus, I calculated the annual average number of baptisms for each of the twenty-year periods considered, and related this to the size of the Jewish population in each period to give the rates of conversion shown in the graph. I would like to thank my friend the demographer Sergio DellaPergola for his invaluable help in the elaboration of the data referred to above. The documents concerning the trend of conversions to Christianity within the Jewish population of Umbria appear in full or in summary in my volumes *Jews in Umbria*.

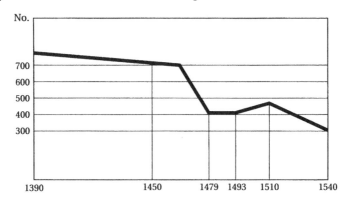

FIG. 7.1 The Jewish population of Umbria (1390–1540)

The phenomenon of conversion therefore seems to have had a minimal demographic impact on the Jewish communities of Umbria until the middle of the fifteenth century; and the rise in the number of baptisms in the sixteenth century, as Church policy made itself increasingly heavily felt in the towns of Umbria, may seem only to be expected. But the data relating to the period 1466–85 are surprising, and to some degree problematic. During those years more than 100 Jews were baptized in Umbria, while the Jewish population of the region—about 700

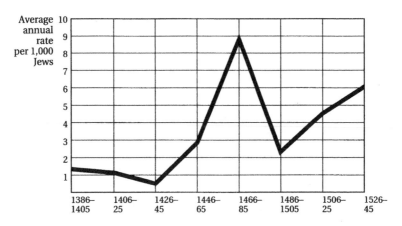

FIG. 7.2 Annual rate of conversion to Christianity among the Jewish population of Umbria (1386–1545)

individuals around the middle of the fifteenth century—had dropped to about 400 by 1480–6. We can therefore calculate that between 1465 and 1485 almost 40 per cent of Umbrian Jews abandoned their communities, with a large proportion choosing the way of conversion. Here the phenomenon emerges as very widespread, producing demographic effects that were to be decisive in both the short and long term.

An examination of the factors influencing the life of the Jewish communities of Umbria during this period reveals the reasons for this crisis, and the huge increase in conversions which was its obvious outcome. The period beginning with the founding of the first Monte di Pietà in Perugia, followed by their proliferation elsewhere fostered by Minorite preaching in almost every Umbrian city, saw the enforced closure of many Jewish banks, particularly in the smaller centres. The extent and impact of these closures is often underestimated by those who prefer to emphasize the continued activity of Jewish banks in many towns, even after a Monte di Pietà had been established.[7] But there is no doubt that, preceded and followed as they were by the fanatical and aggressive antisemitic preaching of the Minorites and Augustinians, which often took on proselytizing overtones, they ultimately brought about the extinction of many Jewish communities. Bernardino da Feltre's visits to the towns of Umbria on various occasions in 1485 and 1488, for example, set in motion a positive wave of conversions.[8] In general, when relations between Christian majority and Jewish minority had been irretrievably damaged by the destabilizing and aggressive activities of the Minorites, the intellectually and spiritually well prepared ranks of the Augustinians would step in to exploit the crisis in the Jewish community to its utmost. From the middle of the fifteenth century Jewish conversions to Christianity in the communes of Umbria (and possibly elsewhere too) seem largely linked to the preaching or direct intervention of Augustinians such as Alessandro da Sassoferrato, Michele da Perugia, and Alessandro da Ancona at Perugia, and Giovanni da Pontremoli at Spoleto. Their proselytizing activities were more consistent than those of the Minorites, and undoubtedly more effective.

At Spello, where the founding of the Monte di Pietà in 1469 had promptly led to the contemporaneous closing of the moneylending

[7] See esp. Poliakov, *Jewish Bankers and the Holy See*, 150–9.
[8] AS Perugia, Con. e Rif., 82, fos. 121ᵛ–122ʳ (26 Mar. 1467); ibid., 103, fo. 51ʳ; ibid., 108, fo. 7ᵛ (15 Apr. 1467); ibid., Not., Giacomo di Pietro, 1467, fo. 1ʳ; AC Spoleto, Rif., 11, fos. 172ʳ, 295ʳ (24 May 1474). See also Fabretti, *Sulla condizione degli ebrei in Perugia*, 43–5; Toaff, *Ebrei a Perugia*, 298–300.

banks, the Jewish presence was virtually extinguished one year later.[9] The last documents in the municipal registers concerning the town's Jews report the baptism of whole families, to whom the priors granted charity and citizenship.[10] At Assisi the Monte di Pietà had been established in the summer of 1468. There followed a period of great tension between the Christian population and the local Jews, fuelled by Franciscan preaching and culminating in 1485 with the visit of Bernardino da Feltre.[11] There can be no doubting the efficacy of his preaching at Assisi if, as he himself said, two sermons sufficed to induce the priors to drive the Jews from the city once and for all.[12] Here too the last documents referring to the presence of Jews in Assisi record many baptisms and charitable donations.[13] At Gubbio in the same year, 1485, Bernardino da Feltre's preaching led to the termination of the charter signed between Jews and commune, and to their expulsion from the town.[14] At the same time, as we have seen (pp. 136 ff.) an accusation of ritual murder was threatening the security of the Jews of Bevagna.[15]

At Perugia, the main Jewish centre of the region, conversions to Christianity appear to be particularly concentrated in the years 1467 to 1474. Writing on the subject a few years ago, I noted that during these years the local Jewish community's state of distrust, insecurity, and confusion enabled the friars' proselytizing preaching to reap considerable rewards.[16] My subsequent tracing of much documentary material on the subject has not merely confirmed this observation, but has shown that it was even more extensive than previously believed. It is now clear that in the years preceding Bernardino da Feltre's preaching at Perugia, which took place on several occasions in 1485 and during the following three

---

[9] See P. Fabbri, 'Il Monte della Pietà a Spello', *Bollettino della Deputazione di Storia Patria per l'Umbria*, 14 (1908), 161–92.

[10] AC Spello, Con. e Rif., env. 2, prot. 4, fos. 86ᵛ (22–3 Apr. 1470), 88ʳ–88ᵛ; ibid., Not., Domenico di Bartolomeo Micinelli, 2, fo. 147ʳ, and 3, fo. 172ʳ.

[11] Toaff, *Jews in Medieval Assisi*, 57–71.

[12] See A. Cristofani, *Le Storie di Assisi*, 457–8; Toaff, *Jews in Medieval Assisi*, 173.

[13] AC Assisi, H, Rif., 18, fos., 337ᵛ–339ᵛ; ibid., P. Bollettari, 5, fo. 64ᵛ; ibid., Not., Girolamo di Giovanni da Portella, x7, file 7, fo. 23ʳ (7 Jan. 1500); ibid., Simone Paolozzi, N20, fo. 172ʳ (27 Nov. 1512); ibid., Silvio Allegretti, R13, fo. 306ᵛ (5 Jan. 1525).

[14] AC Gubbio, Rif., 31, fos. 132ʳ⁻ᵛ, 135ʳ (26 Jan.–5 Feb. 1485). On the preaching of Bernardino da Feltre at Gubbio and the expulsion of the city's Jews see also C. Roth in *Encyclopedia Judaica*, iv (Jerusalem, 1971), 672, s.v. 'Bernardino da Feltre'.

[15] See pp. 136–8 above.

[16] See Toaff, *Ebrei a Perugia*, 72–84.

years, about a third of the Jews of the city converted, while many others
were obliged to emigrate.[17] The break in the history of the Jews of
Perugia is so definitive that after 1485 the documents refer to them as
'survivors of the former Jews living in the city of Perugia'.[18] The implications of this definition are all too clear, and they confirm the gravity of
the crisis which had so severely reduced the city's Jewish population.

During those years the phenomenon of conversion was so widespread
that professional swindlers disguised themselves as Jews seeking baptism,
in order fraudulently to obtain benefits and charity from the naïve and
credulous. To increase their gains, they would have themselves baptized
in several places, accompanying the ceremony with edifying stories
whose aim was to move the Christians to loosen their purse-strings. In
his *Speculum cerretanorum*, a lively enquiry into the low life of the time,
Teseo Pini refers to these fraudsters as *Iucchi*, and describes their misdeeds as follows:

Of the Iucchi, or several times baptized. They are so called because they cunningly receive baptism several times over, delighting in holy water no less
than the drunkard in wine and the duck in water. They pretend to be Jews
who have become enriched by usury; but after terrible visions and prodigious
and incredible miracles inspired by God, they tell how, like the Apostles,
they left everything they had, to follow Christ in poverty. They have themselves baptized anew in every city they come to, and then, in addition to what
is given them by their sponsors, they go fishing for the possessions and
money of others, which are promptly handed over to them by the faithful,
and thus they filch rich pickings.[19]

We know little about Pini's life, except that he wrote the *Speculum*
around 1485, and dedicated it to his patron, Bishop Girolamo Santucci,
for whom he acted as deputy for many years. But we do know that
Santucci, whose father Agostino di Stefano had been professor of

[17] On Bernardino da Feltre's preaching at Perugia see L. Wadding, *Annales
Minorum*, xiv. *1472–91* (Ad Claras Aquas, 1933), 456–9, 468, 472–4, 518–20; E.
Casolini, *Bernardino da Feltre: Il martello degli eretici* (Milan, 1939), 219–21; O.
Marinelli, *La compagnia di S. Tommaso d'Aquino a Perugia* (Rome, 1960), 19, 62.

[18] AS Perugia, Not., Rinaldo di Bartolomeo, 565, fos. 278ʳ, 279ᵛ (3 Nov. 1508).

[19] Camporesi, *Il libro dei vagabondi*, cvi, cxiii, clvi–clvii, 44–5, 140–1. The
Speculum cerretanorum by Teseo Pini, written *c.*1485, remained in MS for about a century, and was then discovered, adapted, and modernized by the Dominican Giacinto
Nobili, who printed it under the pseudonym Raffaele Frianoro. The first printed edn.
of Pini's treatise was published at Viterbo in 1621. For the text on *Iucchi* I have used
Frianoro's 16th-cent. version. On this subject see also Pullan, 'Poveri, mendicanti e
vagabondi', 1011–14.

medicine at the University of Perugia, was himself in Perugia in 1484 as representative of the papal legate, Cardinal Giovanni Novariense. After two years spent in Perugia he was appointed governor of Todi, a post he held from the autumn of 1486 until the spring of 1488. He then returned to Perugia to assume the post of representative of the brother of Innocent VIII, Cardinal Maurizio Cybo, and remained there until the end of the following year.[20] So that if Bishop Santucci was indeed a source of inspiration to Teseo Pini, there can be little doubt that the *Speculum cerretanorum* reflects the social unease of the Umbrian territories during the years of Bernardino da Feltre's preaching. Pini paints a highly eclectic picture, seen from the streets and slums, and Jews are still present in it. But these were baptized Jews and *iucchi*, who walked the roads of Umbria in search of alms and stratagems for survival, against a background of bewildered and disintegrating communities.

THE POLICY OF ALMS

The Church's traditional attitude to the conversion of Jews, adopted by many Christian rulers, included the granting of gifts and provisions to those neophytes who had voluntarily had themselves baptized. It is already found in Gregory the Great (Epistles, 2: 38; 4: 31; 5: 7; 8: 23), in whose view the conversion of the Jews was to be made easier by granting them material goods. The third Lateran Council (1179) stated clearly that 'converts to the Christian faith should be put in a better condition than the one they had enjoyed before entering it'. Referring to neophytes Innocent III used a poetic metaphor, declaring that 'the young plant should not only be watered with the new doctrine, but that it must also be nourished with temporal goods'.[21] One constant policy among the Umbrian communes in the late Middle Ages towards converted Jews was to water the new plants with more or less abundant alms and other benefits, such as exemption from taxes and the right of citizenship.[22] In

---

[20] For the biography of Girolamo Santucci see A. Lazzari, *De' Vescovi d'Urbino concernenti il dominio temporale de' conti e duchi* (Urbino, 1806), 37–9; Camporesi, *Il libro dei vagabondi*, clviii–clx.

[21] On this subject see e.g. Grayzel, *The Church and the Jews*, 15–21; Blumenkranz, *Juifs et Chrétiens*, 95–7; id., *Les Auteurs chrétiens latins du Moyen Âge sur les juifs et le judaisme* (Paris–Hague, 1963), 73–5.

[22] There are still no adequate studies specifically concerning the problem of the conversion of Jews to Christianity in the communes of medieval Italy; for the 16th to 18th cents., however, cities such as Rome and Venice are documented by considerable research and extensive published archival material. See Milano, *Il Ghetto di Roma*,

September 1446 the commune of Perugia laid down that neophytes should be granted a charitable donation of 10 florins, 'in order to render further honour, propriety, praise, and magnificence to Almighty God, and to bring other Jews to convert to the Catholic faith'.[23] In subsequent years the sum was raised first to 12, then to 25 florins, until after 1474, at the height of the Minorite and Augustinian proselytizing campaigns, it reached the not inconsiderable ceiling of 30 florins. The resolution taken by the council of priors in May 1474 was inspired by the same motives as that of 1446, but its aggressive formulation betrayed a radical shift in mood in relations between Christian population and Jewish minority. It is fitting that alms be considerable, ran the document, 'in order that Jews should not be in fear of renouncing their goods and their perfidy and bad faith, and should convert to Christianity, serving as an example to other Jews'.[24] To provide the sums needed for such alms, the governors of the cities of Umbria generally drew upon funds administered by the charitable hospices. At Perugia the priors had recourse to the meagre funds of the Ospedale di S. Maria della Misericordia, of the old Ospedale di S. Giacomo, belonging to the Arte del Cambio, and of the Confraternity of S. Domenico at Porta S. Pietro. The governors of Spoleto drew the necessary funds from the Ospedale della Stella, belonging to the enclosed Augustinian convent, and from the Ospedale di S. Croce, outside Porta Romana. At Assisi the priors frequently made use of the assets of the Confraternity of S. Rufino.[25] Apart from the charitable donations and benefits given by the commune, which usually also provided them with

---

283–306; id., 'Battesimi di ebrei a Roma', 133–67; Pullan, *Jews of Europe*, 243–318; P. C. Ioly Zorattini, *Processi del S. Uffizio di Venezia contro ebrei e giudaizzanti*, i. *1548–1560* (Florence, 1980); ii. *1561–1570* (Florence, 1982); iii. *1570–1572* (Florence, 1984); iv. *1571–1580* (Florence, 1985). On conversionary writings in Italy by preachers and converts see F. Parente, 'Il confronto ideologico tra l'ebraismo e la Chiesa in Italia', *Italia Judaica*, Proceedings of the first international conference, held at Bari, 18–22 May 1981 (Rome, 1983), 303–81; R. Segre, 'Neophytes during the Italian Counter-Reformation: Identities and Biographies', *Proceedings of the World Congress of Jewish Studies*, 2 (Jerusalem, 1973), 131–42; M. Sanders, 'The Apostates in Italy during the Sixteenth Century and their Attitude towards Jews and Judaism' (Heb.), Ph.D. thesis, Bar Ilan University, Ramat Gan, 1985.

[23] AS Perugia, Con. e Rif., 82, fos. 121ᵛ–122ʳ (8 Sept. 1446). See also Fabretti, *Sulla condizione*, 43–5.

[24] AS Perugia, Con. e Rif., 110, fo. 78ᵛ (24 May 1474). See also Toaff, *Ebrei a Perugia*, 300–1.

[25] On the activity of the *ospedali* of Umbria in the medieval period see A. Grohmann, *Le città nella storia d'Italia: Perugia* (Bari, 1981), 65–7; id., *Città e territorio*, i. 89, 218, 232, 388, 402; L. Fausti, 'Degli antichi ospedali di Spoleto', 59–111; Ceccaroni, *La storia millenaria*.

white clothing for the baptismal ceremony, neophytes would receive gifts
in the form of clothing and trousseau items, as well as money collected
from the faithful on the occasion of the baptism.[26]
    In January 1475 the Jew Leone was baptized Michele Francesco in the
basilica of S. Francesco in Assisi by the Minorite fra Fortunato Coppoli,
the promoter of the local Monte di Pietà. On that occasion the priors
granted him citizenship of Assisi, together with a charitable donation of
8 florins, a house near the main square, and 20 *moggi* of cultivable land
near Castelnuovo, on the road to Spello. The donations collected from
the faithful present at the baptismal ceremony included the sum of 27
florins in cash, as well as rings, tablecloths, embroidered handkerchiefs,
and lengths of material of assorted shades and value.[27] When Benedetto
di Aleuccio da Genazzano converted at Spello in April 1470 with his wife
Stella and his three children, the municipality provided clothing for the
whole family, as well as the sum of 75 florins for the purchase of a house
in the town and a piece of cultivable land outside it. This considerable
sum was mostly made up of alms for the neophyte's family collected from
local citizens. However, the governors of Spello guarded against the possibility that Benedetto's conversion might not be sincere, but might
conceal a cunning scheme to defraud the commune: he was strictly forbidden to sell the property made available to him, and it was decreed it
should revert to the commune of Spello should he decide to move elsewhere.[28] In April 1525 the Jew Angelo converted at Spoleto with his wife
and one daughter, taking on the name Giulio. As was customary, the
commune provided him with white clothing for the ceremony, and alms
for the purchase of a farmhouse in the *contado* of Spoleto. A dowry of 20
florins, obtained from the property of the Ospedale di S. Croce, was set
aside for his daughter.[29] Two young Jewish girls, baptized Marta and
Maddalena on 10 September 1552 in Spoleto in the presence of an
Augustinian friar from Pontremoli, were granted citizenship by the
commune, and a house near the market square. They were also granted a
sum of 8 *scudi* in cash, drawn from the revenue of the Ospedale della
Stella, a *salma* of wine, and three measures of wheat over a period of ten
years, with the proviso that the wheat was to come from the municipal

[26] In 16th-cent. Venice Marin Sanuto used the expression 'to clothe a Jew' as a synonym for baptism; Pullan, *Jews of Europe*, 252.
[27] AC Assisi, H, Rif., 18, fos. 337ᵛ–339ᵛ (17 Jan.–13 Feb. 1475). See Toaff, *Jews in
Medieval Assisi*, 67–9, 168–70.
[28] AC Spello, Con. e Rif., env. 2, prot. 4, fos. 86ᵛ–88ᵛ (19–23 Apr. 1470).
[29] AC Spoleto, Rif., 77, fo. 51ʳ (10 Apr. 1525); ibid., Not., Sulpizio di Valerio,
173/II, fo. 73ʳ.

mills at Pissignano. Lastly, a dowry was set aside for each girl, to be handed over to them on their marriage to a Christian. The sum fixed for Marta was 30 florins, while Maddalena, who probably had some family property, was awarded 15 *scudi*.[30]

When an entire family converted, the local clergy could not resist the opportunity of further embellishing the baptismal ceremony. The newly baptized couple would then remarry, this time according to the Catholic rite, amidst great pomp and the active participation of the local population, even if the converts already had a long and happy married life behind them, with a number of children and grandchildren. An account of one such marriage, celebrated in the cathedral of S. Lorenzo in Perugia in 1467, is to be found in the chronicle of ser Giacomo di Pietro:[31]

Today [5 April] a Jewess received baptism in the church of S. Lorenzo at Perugia, at the hands of the canon ser Galeotto. She was given the name Caterina, and immediately afterwards her husband, who had been baptized on 29 March last and taken the name Lodovico, married her anew before a multitude of men and women, possibly as many as four thousand. Lodovico (as he had done before when both were Jews) took the woman to wife, and the wedding was celebrated by the sacristan of the church of S. Lorenzo, don Paolo Nicolai of Castel delle Forme, in the *contado* of Perugia. These Jews converted following the preaching of the famous friar *magister* Alessandro da Ancona, who gave his sermons in S. Lorenzo during Lent. On 29 March his two children had been baptized, together with their father: the boy was named Giovanni Francesco and the girl Maddalena. After the baptism, the family received alms from men and women.

Acceptance of the new religion entailed the assumption of different identities and the renunciation of the Jewish names the neophytes had previously borne. The Christian names taken on by converts at baptism often commemorated the churches or cathedrals where the ceremony had taken place, or the religious orders involved in their preparation and conversion. A Jewish woman baptized in the church of S. Lorenzo Maggiore in Perugia in August 1525 became Lorenza. The same name was taken by another young woman, Verena di Lazzaro, who converted in the cathedral of Perugia in April 1528.[32] Feliciano, the patron saint of Foligno, gave his name to many of the Jews baptized in Foligno

[30] Ibid., Rif., 11, fo. 172ʳ (12 Sept. 1552); ibid., fo. 295ʳ (30 Dec. 1552); ibid., 13, fo. 409ʳ (10 Sept. 1553); ibid., fo. 449ᵛ (15 Oct.–5 Nov. 1553).

[31] The text is quoted in Toaff, *Ebrei a Perugia*, 78–9, 299–300.

[32] AS Perugia, Con. e Rif., 130, fo. 208ʳ (20 Aug. 1525); ibid., Severo di Pietro, 464, fo. 201ᵛ (6 Apr. 1528).

cathedral. The Jew Angelo took on the name Feliciano on the occasion of his baptism in the church of the same name in 1479. The unusual choice of the name of the city's patron saint was also made by Leone di Angelo, who was converted together with his wife and daughter at Foligno in 1511.[33] The names most frequently taken on by neophytes were Giovanni, Giovanni Battista, Francesco, Giovanni Francesco, and Agostino for men, and Maddalena, Caterina, and Agnese for women. But some more exotic names are also found, biblical and oriental in flavour. Morbidella di Guglielmo, a Jewish girl baptized in Spoleto in 1394, was given the apparently immodest name Salomè,[34] though we have no reason to believe that it then had the connotations of exoticism, cruelty, and perversion given it by the literature of later centuries.

The construction of a typology of neophytes is fraught with problems. If, on the one hand, we should avoid the temptation of dividing the field into the simplistic categories of those who converted out of conviction and those who converted for advantage, we must avoid the opposite mistake of expanding the classification of converts on the basis of a multiplicity of real or presumed motives, or of their social and economic origins. It is not always true that the majority of converts came from the poor or very poor members of Jewish society.[35] Nor is it true that most converted for advantage, an inference which follows more or less explicitly from the above. In fact, if in normal times it was poor Jews who most often converted, there were also periods (particularly during the years of crisis in the second half of the fifteenth century and towards the middle of the sixteenth) when many wealthy Jews also voluntarily abandoned their faith, and apparently sincere converts were far from uncommon. However, it was also not unusual for Jews belonging to the class of bankers and rich merchants to decide to convert, in an attempt to safeguard their social status and economic security. Lastly, as we have seen, there was a sizeable category of neophytes who converted 'for love', or at least with matrimonial aspirations, and who saw conversion as offering a possible route towards fulfilling their amorous dreams of life with a Christian man or woman, or freedom from an inconvenient or importunate Jewish spouse.[36]

One category of poor, but in all probability sincere, converts was that

[33] AC Foligno, Not., Taddeo Angelelli, 11/3, fo. 65ᵛ (26 Feb. 1479); ibid., 22/22. fo. 42ᵛ (22–3 Oct. 1511).
[34] AC Spoleto, Rif., 12, fos. 86ʳ, 119ʳ, 156ʳ (1 July–11 Nov. 1394).
[35] See Simonsohn, *Jews in the Duchy of Mantua*, 524–5; Bonfil, 'Jewish Emigration', 152; Pullan, *Jews of Europe*, 244–5.   [36] See Ch. 1.

of Jews who, after conversion, chose to join a convent or monastery. A Jew from Perugia who converted in January 1298, taking the name Giovanni, became a monk and decided to withdraw to voluntary seclusion in the hermitage outside Porta S. Pietro. He was so poor that he did not even own a tunic to protect him from the winter cold, and the commune of Perugia felt impelled to intervene to provide him with clothing.[37] Cecca, daughter of Musetto, baptized in 1362 at Spoleto, withdrew shortly afterwards to the convent of S. Omobono, belonging to the Poor Clares. She was extremely poor, and for ten years continued to receive a charitable donation of 6 *lire* from the commune of Spoleto for the purchase of her monastic clothing.[38] One of Angelo da Foligno's daughters, baptized as Agnese in 1398, joined the convent of S. Agnese at Assisi,[39] and in January 1525 another Jewish woman from Foligno, baptized Maddalena, entered the convent of S. Benedetto at Assisi.[40] But, as I have said, the number of more or less sincere neophytes also included some who were rich and prosperous. Angelo di Salomone, a banker at Amelia, was baptized in 1328, along with a brother and a son. Two years earlier the commune had signed a charter with him, granting him a monopoly on moneylending in the town.[41] One of the richest cloth merchants of Foligno, Elia di maestro Salomone, known as Zucchero, converted in 1479 in the cathedral of S. Feliciano, taking the name Pietro Gaspare.[42] Later, around the middle of the sixteenth century, one of the sons of the well-known banker Leone da Montalcino converted in S. Lorenzo at Perugia, taking the name Paolo Siderchi. One of the richest Jews of Perugia, he was to continue to trade successfully in partnership with the noble family of the Orsini, and owned considerable landed property in Umbria and Tuscany.[43] The most famous Umbrian neophyte, recorded in Hebrew chronicles as Hananel da Foligno, and responsible, among other things, for the burning of the Talmud in various Italian cities, had been a banker before his

---

[37] AS Perugia, Con. e Rif., 12, fos. 111ʳ–112ʳ (25 Jan. 1298).
[38] AC Spoleto, Bollettari, 1362–3, fo. 11ᵛ; ibid. 1365–7, fo. 83ᵛ; ibid. 1372–3, fo. 100ᵛ.
[39] AC Assisi, Not., Girardo di Giovanni, C2, fo. 43ʳ (22 Dec. 1398).
[40] Ibid., Silvio Allegretti, R13, fo. 306ᵛ (5 Jan. 1525).
[41] AC Amelia, Rif., 1, fos. 136ʳ, 142ʳ (18–28 Oct. 1326); ibid., fos. 209ʳ–210ᵛ (19 Jan. 1328).
[42] AC Foligno, Not., Taddeo Angelelli, 11/3, fo. 268ᵛ (28 Sept. 1479).
[43] In 1555 Paolo Siderchi, 'a Jew become Christian', described as the son of Leone da Montalcino, was trading in Perugia in partnership with Fioravante Orsini (AS Perugia, Not., Amico Bonamici, 1393, fo. 86ᵛ).

conversion.[44] Graziadio di Angelo da Foligno, as his name is recorded in the archival documents, was baptized between 1541 and 1545, becoming Alessandro Franceschi; in the 1530s he had been engaged in official moneylending at Spoleto, Perugia, Foligno, and other Umbrian towns. The commune of Spoleto refused to grant alms to the former banker, now an ardent neophyte, possibly because it was unable to forgive him for the many long-running disputes he had previously had with the city authorities.[45] But certainly many of the converted came from the ranks of the poor and indigent, and were drawn to baptism by unrealistic prospects of social and economic betterment, not to mention alms. Possibly partly scenting a speedy solution to the problems they posed, the communes granted these converts written authority to beg in the streets, and from house to house. This practice, revealed by extensive documentation to have been widespread throughout Italy in the sixteenth century, may legitimately be seen as dating from at least two centuries earlier.[46] It was already widespread in Umbria at the beginning of the fourteenth century. In the winter of 1331 a band of paupers made its appearance on the streets of Todi, all converted Jews, and led by a certain Giovanni, said to be the son of the Jew Deodato da Roma. Giovanni claimed that he had brought other Jews to baptism in Perugia, and that they were now following him on his wanderings in pursuit of alms and provisions.[47]

'By the grace of almighty God, of blessed Mary mother of God, and all saints', said Giovanni, 'I converted last year at Perugia and had myself baptized in the faith of the Christians and holy mother Church. Thus today I belong by right to the Catholic religion. This year, and with Christ and Mary as my eyes, with cajolery and telling words, I managed to bring other Jews of the said city to baptism, who are now firmly rooted in the Christian religion. Unfortunately both I and the other Jews are poverty-stricken: lacking food and any means of support, we are forced to go from door to door to beg from Christians.'

[44] For an updated and well documented biography of Hananel da Foligno see Simonsohn, 'Some Well-known Jewish Converts during the Renaissance', *Ebrei e Cristiani nell'Italia medievale e moderna: Conversioni, scambi, contrasti*, proceedings of an international conference held at San Miniato, Pisa, 4–6 Nov. 1986 (Rome, 1988), 93–104.

[45] AC Spoleto, Rif., 4, fo. 222^r (14 June 1545); ibid., 7, fo. 12^r (27 Apr. 1548).

[46] On the various begging licences granted to Jewish converts in the Veneto in the 16th cent., see Pullan, *Jews of Europe*, 253–5.

[47] AC Todi, Rif., 27, fos. 21^v–23^r (19 Feb. 1331); ibid., fos. 103^v–104^v (16 June 1331); ibid. 35, fo. 40^v (19 Feb. 1335).

As I have said, in Umbria too the converts' custom of seeking municipal permission to beg persisted until the middle of the sixteenth century. In 1556 Giovanpaolo, a Jew baptized at Cascia, obtained the right of citizenship from the commune, along with exemption from payment of taxes, a subsidy of 1 florin, to be paid on All Souls' Day, 2 November, each year, and written licence to beg both at Cascia and in the surrounding countryside.[48]

Proselytizing preaching met with prompt success not only among the poor and dispossessed, but also among the exiled and disaffected. Following the expulsion of the Jews from France in 1394 some exiles had arrived in Italy, and various families had proceeded to the communities of Umbria. Unsurprisingly, they too had their converts. In March 1410 Abramo di Musetto di Francia, an 18-year-old exile who had been led to conversion by the Minorite Valentino da Rimini, was baptized in the cathedral of S. Feliciano at Foligno. The baptism had been performed by none other than the bishop of Foligno, Federico Frezzi.[49]

The archival documents concerning Umbria have yielded no evidence of 'enforced' conversions, or more precisely of conversions of minors against their parents' wishes, with the exception of one spectacular case which occurred in Spoleto in 1496, not surprisingly during one of the most intensive periods of the proselytizing of the Augustinian preachers.[50] At the beginning of June that year a young Jewish child of 5, named Chiarastella, disappeared from her home and was found a few weeks later in the Augustinian convent of S. Matteo, near Porta S. Lorenzo on the 'Roman road' to Carsulae. According to the abbess and nuns of the convent, the child had asked them for asylum, saying that she intended to convert; she had already begun instruction in Christian practices in preparation for her baptism. Chiarastella's parents, Abramo and Gentile, were firmly opposed to their daughter's conversion, and now embarked on a tough struggle to take her back home, out of the sphere of Christian influence. They claimed that the child was in no position to understand the meaning of the sacrament she was being prepared to take; in their view, she had been encouraged by their next-door neighbours, who had apparently led her astray and taken advantage of her extreme

---

[48] AC Cascia, Con. e Rif., 9, fo. 75ᵛ (23 Feb. 1556).

[49] AC Foligno, Not., Francesco di Antonio, I/B/v, fo. 178ʳ (5 Mar. 1410).

[50] On forced or *invitis parentibus* baptisms in Italy, esp. from the 16th cent. onwards, see C. Roth, 'Forced Baptisms in Italy', *Jewish Quarterly Review*, NS 27 (1936), 117–36; P. C. Ioly Zorattini, *Battesimi di fanciulli ebrei a Venezia nel Settecento* (Udine, 1984).

youth. The bishop of Spoleto, Costantino Eroli, agreed in part to their entreaty and ordered the abbess and nuns to release the child. However, she was not to return to her parents' house, but was to be lodged with a Christian woman of Spoleto until the religious authorities passed judgement on the whole matter, with a proper inquiry into her true intentions and degree of maturity. The nuns of S. Matteo vigorously contested the bishop's decision, claiming that it impugned their good faith, and appealed to Giovanni Oliver, deputy of Giovanni Borgia, the apostolic governor of the duchy of Spoleto.[51] After indignantly expressing their unwillingness to let the child out of the convent, they asked that the provincial father of the Hermits of S. Agostino, Paolo da Spoleto, should be consulted as to her fate. Finally the thorny question was drawn to the attention of the pope himself, Alexander VI. Clearly embarrassed at having to side either with Chiarastella's parents or the nuns of S. Matteo, he decided to hedge his bets: a brief of 9 July 1496 ordered that the child should be taken from the convent and given back to her parents. However, in accordance with the nuns' request, it enjoined that the provincial father of the Hermits of S. Agostino should open an inquiry to establish the child's real intentions, and look into the possibility of having her baptized when she came of age.[52]

THE PLIGHT OF THE 'CHRISTIANIZED' JEW

Whatever the reasons for their conversion, neophytes often became objects of hostility in Jewish circles, while at the same time finding themselves exposed to the distrust and suspicion of Christian society, which readily threw their Jewish origins back in their faces. If we cannot be certain that this happened throughout late medieval Italy, it was none the less sufficiently frequent to arouse concern in those ecclesiastical circles which saw it as one of the chief obstacles to the Church's proselytizing policy towards the Jews. Considerable pressure was therefore exerted on

[51] Pope Alexander VI (Rodrigo Borgia) had had his great-nephew Giovanni elected cardinal of S. Susanna in 1496. Two years earlier Giovanni had been appointed governor of Spoleto and apostolic legate, and in Apr. 1495 had entrusted the government of the city to Giovanni Oliver; see A. Sansi, *Storia del comune di Spoleto*, ii. 102–17; G. de Caro, 'Giovanni Borgia', in *Dizionario biografico degli Italiani* (Rome, 1970), xii. 715–17.

[52] The dossier on Chiarastella di Abramo da Spoleto is now in AC Spoleto, Suppliche, env. 1, fos 1ʳ–6ᵛ (4–9 July 1496). It is published in its entirety in my *Jews in Umbria*, iii. 1070–5.

communes not to abandon new converts to their fate, but to continue to protect them, and to try to ease their integration into Christian society. The measures taken by the priors of Terni in 1449 reflect these concerns, attempting as they did to neutralize possible threats to the long-term success of their proselytizing policy.[53] They included heavy fines for Christians and Jews offending converts as such; in addition, Jews might also be subjected to corporal punishment. 'Any Christian offending a convert to the Christian faith, reproaching him for having been a Jew, is liable to the penalty of one gold ducat. And if the offender be a Jew, he shall be punished with a fine of 25 ducats and ten strappados. Furthermore he shall be publicly whipped through the streets of the city.'

In many cases these fears proved unfounded, since Jewish society usually dealt with the problem of the conversion of one of its members—a distressing enough matter in itself—with admirable good sense and resignation, avoiding any show of recrimination. Not only did Jews refrain from ridiculing or cold-shouldering their former co-religionists—though they did not hesitate to show their disapproval—they also actually continued to associate and to do business with them.[54] Apostates who became implacable detractors of Judaism were a minority among the host of neophytes. Their presence was inevitably, and deliberately, much talked about, and often constituted a grave danger for the Jewish group, but this should not lead us to distort or overestimate their number.[55]

In Umbria too, the relatively extensive ranks of converts also included some who sought continued friendly personal and business relations with the Jewish circles from which they originally came. Even after being baptized at Foligno in 1479 as Pietro Gaspare, the merchant Elia di maestro Salomone continued to invest part of his profits in the bank of Abramo da Bevagna, in which he had previously been a partner.[56] Raffaele di Guglielmo, a Jew from Perugia, who converted around 1449, subsequently felt no obligation to break off his business dealings with

[53] AS Terni, Rif., 498, fos. 171ʳ–173ʳ (16 Mar. 1449).

[54] The picture of relations between Jews and neophytes in Umbria is basically not very different from that which emerges from the documentation concerning Rome during the same period; see Esposito, 'Ebrei a Roma nella seconda metà del Quattrocento', 52–5; id., 'Ebrei a Roma tra Quattro' e Cinquecento', 830.

[55] Respectful and sometimes cordial relations between Jews and converts also emerge from contemporary Hebrew sources, such as the ritual responsa of the Paduan rabbi Meir Katzenellenbogen; see Schwarzfuchs, 'I responsi di Rabbi Meir da Padova', 129–30.

[56] AC Foligno, Not., Taddeo Angelelli, 11/3, fo. 268ᵛ; AC Bevagna, Not., Gaspare di Angelo, 1523, fo. 13ʳ.

160   *Converts and Apostates*

other Jews of the city.[57] The Jewish community of Perugia found nothing unseemly in renting a house it owned in the district of Porta S. Angelo, adjacent to the synagogue building, to a convert called Michelangelo, a mattress-maker by trade, and from 1546 to 1548 he paid his rent to the heads of the Jewish community to which he himself had previously belonged.[58] A remarkable testimony to the pragmatic and tolerant attitude with which Jewish circles were often able to imbue relations with new converts to the Christian religion is found in a 1446 deed of gift made by a Jew of Perugia to the benefit of one of his nephews, who had been baptized two years earlier. Here Emanuele di Consiglio made over a house at Cannara, together with all the personal and landed property he owned at Collemancio on the river Arone in the *contado* of Perugia, to his nephew Elia di Venturello, living at Bettona, who had converted to Christianity with the name Agostino. The deed of gift ends with expressions which reveal Emanuele to be broad-minded and pragmatic, but far from faltering in his Jewish convictions. 'I wish to make this gift out of the great affection I bear Agostino, my blood nephew, from whom I have always received favours and kindnesses and whose merits I have had cause to appreciate. And thus I desire to proceed in this manner, although said Agostino has been baptized and become a Christian, and I desire that my promise be kept, swearing upon the law which almighty God gave to Moses on Mount Sinai and with my hands upon the sacred texts of Judaism.'[59]

In point of fact, the communes' efforts to disguise the converts' Jewish origins in order to ease their absorption into Christian society did not meet with much success. In practice, if without rancour or ill will, the Jewish past of a convert was remembered for many years; it served to identify him more easily, and did not generally arouse any sort of resentment or indeed any reaction at all in the now mature convert. A Jew from Spello, who had been baptized as a young man along with his whole family in 1470 with the name Giovanni Francesco, was still referred to by the townsfolk as 'the son of Leone the Jew'.[60] Elia di Venturello, the Jew who

---

[57] AS Perugia, Not., Mariano di Luca di Nino, 116, fo. 13ᵛ (25 Sept. 1449).

[58] Ibid., Giovanni Battista di Niccolò, 1149, fo. 281ʳ (8 Apr. 1546); ibid., Teseo di Antonio Baldella, 964, fo. 120ʳ (8 Mar. 1547); ibid., Bernardino di Angelo, 999, fo. 668ʳ (10 Mar. 1547) and 1000, fo. 85ᵛ (15 Mar. 1548).

[59] Ibid., Ospedale di S. Maria della Misericordia, Matteo di Guglielmo, 15, fo. 11ʳ (25 May 1447).

[60] AC Spello, Not., env. 7, Pier Tommaso Morichelli, 1, fo. 30ʳ (25 June 1470); ibid., env. 20, Domenico di Bartolomeo Micinelli, 2, fo. 147ʳ (24 Apr. 1501); ibid., env. 3, fo. 172ʳ (18 Mar. 1507).

converted at Bettona in 1444 under the name of Agostino, accompanied his daughter Monica to church in 1465 on the occasion of her marriage to a local peasant. Though more than twenty years had gone by since the day of his baptism, Agostino was described as 'a Jew who had become a Christian', a description which was not intended to single him out as in any way inferior, but which served simply to identify and characterize him more clearly.[61]

Conversion very rarely led to any actual change in an individual's social and economic position. If he had been poor before baptism, he would remain poor after it, and continue his life as as a marginal, begging and collecting alms. If he had belonged to a wealthy family, his integration would be easier, since Christian society did not attempt to hinder access to the more prestigious positions. Sometimes poor Jews or beggars were not merely supported by the commune with alms and charitable gifts but, after baptism, they were offered a position that might make their existence less precarious, though this was the exception rather than the rule. The fate of some converts already mentioned in Chapter 5 illustrates this. In 1456 Benigno, a poor Jew from Spoleto, was baptized in his native town, taking the name Giovanni. After his conversion, the governors took him on as a servant in the Palazzo dei Priori, with a monthly salary of 4 florins.[62] A Jewish beggar who had converted at Assisi around 1480, taking the name Menico, was subsequently employed by the town authorities as a municipal messenger.[63] Angelo, the young deaf-mute from Spoleto, was baptized in 1554 and given the position of bellringer in the tower of the Palazzo dei Priori, with a monthly salary of 2 florins.[64] The son of Vitale, the medical officer of Spoleto, on the other hand, who had converted in June 1394 taking the name Battista, was a wealthy Jew. At his baptism, celebrated with great solemnity in the cathedral of S. Maria Assunta, the priors granted him the ritual charitable donation, 'so that Battista, son of maestro Vitale, a Jew, who has abandoned the shadows of the perfidious Jewish faith and become reborn in the true faith by means of baptism, may devoutly persevere in the Christian religion and be a praiseworthy example to other Jews of the city of Spoleto, that they

[61] AC Bettona (at AS Perugia), Not., Acquisto Cioli, 3, fo. 117ʳ (1 Apr. 1444); ibid. 6, fo. 105ʳ (25 Apr. 1465).
[62] AC Spoleto, Camerario, 1456, fos. 27ʳ, 44ᵛ; ibid. 1457, fos. 35ᵛ, 53ᵛ, 62ʳ, and 96ʳ; ibid. 1458, fo. 81ʳ (28 Apr. 1456–28 Feb. 1458).
[63] AC Assisi, Not., Girolamo di Giovanni Portella, x7, file 7, fo. 23ʳ (7 Jan. 1500); ibid., Simone Paolozzi, N20, fo. 172ʳ (27 Nov. 1512).
[64] AC Spoleto, Camerario, Entrate e Uscite, 1554, III, fo. 65ᵛ (28 Dec. 1554).

too may convert'.[65] Battista, who was a pharmacist, and who is always referred to in municipal documents as 'a Jewish-born convert to Christianity', had a considerable career, and his rise was relatively rapid. He was first elected to the Consiglio Generale del Popolo of Spoleto, a post he was to hold several times during the following years, in 1416, when he was living in an elegant house in vaita Salamonesca. One of the prerogatives of the Consiglio, which consisted of 184 citizens, was to elect the captains of the guilds (two for each guild). Battista was called upon to be captain of the guild of pharmacists every year from 1416 to 1423. He reached the height of his public career in 1424, when he was elected a member of the Consiglio dei Priori which governed the city. The six-member council made him *priore delle bullecte* (prior of bills), that is, in charge of the commune's administrative policy, with responsibility for its finances.[66] The protocols of the sessions of the Consiglio del Popolo and the Consiglio dei Priori reveal Battista's active and committed approach to various aspects of city life, with its attendant problems. Not only did the Jews of Spoleto not seem worried about his increasing political influence, but they clearly felt that in Battista they had not an enemy, but rather a champion in the Palazzo del Consiglio. Here we have an apparently paradoxical phenomenon, with the convert constantly figuring among the supporters of Jewish requests and entreaties, unhesitatingly scuttling any proposals which might seem to threaten Jewish interests.

In the second half of the sixteenth century, by which time the Jewish community of Umbria was reduced to a few dozen families, Perugia too had a sort of Casa dei Catecumeni, modelled on the institution founded in Rome by Ignatius Loyola in 1543; it was followed by Venice in 1557, Mantua around 1580, and by many other Italian cities.[67] The Casa dei Catecumeni of Perugia was founded by the pious Camilla di Bernardino, a member of the Andreani family of rich Perugia merchants, with a palazzo in the Porta Sole district in the parish of S. Fiorenzo.[68] Numerous clauses of her will of 3 February 1562[69] are devoted to Jews awaiting

---

[65] AC Spoleto, Rif., 12, fo. 79ᵛ (8 June 1394).

[66] AC Spoleto, Rif., 24, fo. 41ʳ (23 Feb. 1416) and fo. 217ᵛ (27 Apr. 1416); ibid. 25, fo. 45ᵛ (4 Nov. 1423), fo. 57ʳ (25 Nov. 1423), fo. 92ᵛ (1 Jan. 1424), and fo. 104ʳ (10 Feb. 1424).

[67] On the aims and activities of the Casa dei Catecumeni in Rome, Venice, and Mantua, see Milano, *Il ghetto di Roma*, 283–306; id., 'Battesimi di ebrei a Roma', 133–67; Pullan, *Jews of Europe*, 248–92; Simonsohn, *Jews in the Duchy of Mantua*, 26–7, 524–5.

[68] On the Andreani family of Perugia see Grohmann, *Città e territorio*, i. 418.

[69] AS Perugia, Not., Amico Bonamici, 1397, fo. 32ʳ.

baptism, for whom she hoped to provide accommodation, together with spiritual and economic support. She bequeathed a house she owned in the district of Porta Sole 'for the use of Jews who are about to be converted to the true faith, in order that this house may always be used by them as a dwelling-place'. She also set aside a considerable sum 'in favour of Jews who have become Christians', providing an annual cash donation and an allocation of wine and oil. Religious and administrative responsibility for the new institution, and the management of the bequest, were entrusted to the friars of the Servite monastery of S. Fiorenzo, on the road leading from 'via delle Conce' up towards the Piazza di Sopramuro, adjacent to the house belonging to the Andreani which was intended to be the local Casa dei Catecumeni.[70] In practice it does not seem that more than three or four Jews in all were ever given hospitality in this institution, though it was still active in 1578, despite its scant success.[71] Nor did many converts ever actually enjoy the alms and other benefits, after the Protonotary Apostolic of Perugia, the Milanese Francesco Bossi, had given official notification of their baptism, as Camilla's will required. We know that in the winter of 1578 the Servites of S. Fiorenzo had only four Jews in their care, named in the registers as Donato, Francesco (previously Giuseppe di Manuele), Alessandro Vannucci ('son of Giacobbe the Jew'), and Salvatore Pacini. In 1611, almost forty years after his baptism, the monks were still giving Pacini 50 *scudi* of alms and his annual portion of wine and oil, as laid down in Camilla Andreani's will.[72]

Very occasionally the Rome Casa dei Catecumeni, the most influential in Italy, found ways of involving itself with the converted Jews of Umbria, intervening in the communes' affairs. One such case, possibly the most notorious, occurred in 1567. Angelo di Vitale da Camerino had begun his financial career at Trevi around 1530, becoming one of the wealthiest members of the Jewish community which, though numerically and economically impoverished, still lived on in the towns of Umbria in the first half of the sixteenth century.[73] The commune of

[70] See Grohmann, *Le città nella storia d'Italia: Perugia*, 48, 152; id. *Città e territorio*, i. 66.

[71] AS Perugia, Not., Giacomo Masci, 2012, fo. 379 (23 Oct. 1572); ibid., Francesco Torelli, 2047, fo. 171ʳ (28 June 1575); ibid., Ascanio Ugolini, 2099, fo. 35ʳ (18 Jan. 1576) and 2101, fo. 162ʳ⁻ᵛ (26 Feb. 1578).

[72] Ibid., Francesco Torelli, 2077, fo. 280ʳ (7 Sept. 1611).

[73] In the second *vigesima* imposed on the Jews by Clement VII in 1533 Angelo, 'a Jew from Trevi', paid a contribution of 32 florins. On 6 Jan. 1542 Angelo di Vitale, 'a Jewish banker at Trevi', paid Cardinal Ascanio Sforza a *vigesima* of 32 *scudi*; see *All'Illustrissima Congregazione*, republished as *Urkundliche Beiträge*, 77, 90.

Trevi borrowed from him to run its onerous municipal budget, to pay the taxes demanded by the papal authorities and to finance the frequent gifts made to ecclesiastical figures visiting the town.[74] Relations between the commune and the Jewish banker entered a period of crisis around 1555, following the application of the restrictive measures contained in Paul IV's bull *Cum nimis absurdum*, which included a sharp reduction in the interest rate for loans, now lowered to 12 per cent. Angelo da Camerino continued his activity as a banker for a few more years, but in the winter of 1564 he was forced to close down his bank. He left the town, thus arousing the wrath of the commune which, using alleged violations of the rules on moneylending as an excuse, requisitioned his property and expropriated the large palazzo he owned in the Castello district.[75] Angelo appealed against the decision at Perugia, presenting a memorandum to Francesco Bossi, the papal governor of Umbria, in which he claimed that he had not been repaid the huge sums he had formerly lent to the commune and citizens of Trevi. The dispute dragged on, and between March 1564 and October 1566 Angelo was summoned to Perugia on several occasions to plead his case, presenting the bank's books as evidence, but without obtaining satisfaction.[76] The apostolic governor failed to bring the parties to a friendly settlement. Then came the *coup de théâtre*, which has all the hallmarks of vengeance on the banker's part. At the beginning of 1567 Angelo di Vitale da Camerino had himself baptized and gave all his property to the Casa dei Catecumeni in Rome.[77] At this point the commune of Trevi unexpectedly found itself in dispute with this pious Jesuit institution, which was to prove a powerful and unbending adversary. Upon pressure from Paolo Strozzi, the representative of the Casa dei Catecumeni, the apostolic governor of Perugia ordered the commune of Trevi to pay the Casa the entire price of the palazzo formerly belonging to Angelo, valued at the huge sum of 750 florins. The commune, whose financial situation was already parlous, was in danger of going spectacularly bankrupt. Its frequent and desperate entreaties to the apostolic authority were systematically rejected, while the building, put

[74] AC Trevi, Tre Chiavi, env. 17, reg. 256, fo. 135ᵛ (11 June 1532) and fo. 208ᵛ (24 Aug. 1535); ibid., env. 20, reg. 289, fo. 87ᵛ (26 Feb. 1540), fo. 148ʳ (1 Feb. 1542), and fo. 156ᵛ (19 Apr. 1542); ibid., env. 20, reg. 306, fo. 27ᵛ (29 June 1545), and fo. 52ᵛ (16 Dec. 1545); ibid., env. 21, reg. 319, fo. 172ᵛ (8 May 1552); ibid., env. 22, reg. 330, fo. 97ᵛ (28 Sept. 1557); ibid., env. 22, reg. 343, fo. 52ʳ (10 July 1558).
[75] Ibid., env. 23, reg. 370, fo. 132ʳ (12 Mar. 1564).
[76] Ibid., env. 23, reg. 370, fo. 158ᵛ (23 July 1564); ibid., env. 23, reg. 379, fo. 79ʳ (3 June 1566), fo. 83ᵛ (14 July 1566), and fo. 94ᵛ (13 Oct. 1566).
[77] Ibid., env. 23, reg. 379, fo. 114ʳ (16 Mar. 1567).

on public sale on more than one occasion, remained unsold because of the high asking-price. The governors of Trevi were thus obliged to drop the price and seek the shortfall elsewhere, since the Casa dei Catecumeni was not remotely interested in reductions of any kind. The imposition of a special tax on the citizens of Trevi, and large-scale recourse to the funds of the local Monte di Pietà, finally enabled the commune to repay its debt. By April 1568, when its representatives paid the last instalment, the depleted coffers of the commune of Trevi were on the verge of collapse.[78]

[78] Ibid., env. 23, reg. 379, fo. 117ᵛ (20 Apr. 1567), fo. 119ᵛ (25 May–5 Aug. 1567), fo. 129ʳ (17 Aug. 1567), fo. 132ᵛ (7 Sept. 1567), fo. 135ᵛ (28 Sept. 1567), fo. 137ᵛ (2 Oct. 1567), fo. 139ᵛ (15 Oct. 1567), fo. 143ʳ (2 Nov. 1567), fo. 148ᵛ (6 Nov. 1567), and fo. 149ᵛ (7 Dec. 1567); ibid., env. 24, reg. 399, fo. 1ʳ (7 Jan. 1568); ibid., env. 23, reg. 379, fo. 161ʳ (8 Feb. 1568); ibid., env. 24, reg. 399, fo. 2ʳ (23 Feb. 1568), fo. 3ʳ (18 Mar. 1568), and fo. 4ʳ (3 Apr. 1568); ibid., env. 23, reg. 379, fo. 168ᵛ (4 Apr. 1568); ibid., env. 24, reg. 399, fo. 5ʳ (23 Apr. 1568).

8

The Pattern of Discrimination

PRIESTS AND JEWS

IT was always open season between Jews and Observant preaching friars. Church pulpits, market squares, and municipal council chambers were the chief battlegrounds. As in all long-drawn-out conflicts, there were slack periods, when the front seemed quiet and the two armies, so to speak, were engaged in digging communication trenches and reorganizing their own ranks. But there were other periods, at more or less the same times each year, when war would suddenly break out, cannon would thunder, and all weapons and ammunition would be used unstintingly. Trouble habitually erupted during Holy Week and the days immediately preceding it, for then the friars would deploy all their forces in the hope of gaining a definitive victory. For their part, Jews went on the defensive and waited for the dust to settle. Then, if they were still in a position to do so, they would lick their wounds and proceed to the counter-attack in order to regain lost ground, recruiting allies wherever they could. Relations with Minorite friars were always stormy, but the Jews' relations with their non-itinerant brothers— monks, priests, and friars—seem to have been much less turbulent and dramatic. Indeed, in everyday life they were often distinctly cordial, or at least unmarked by apparent prejudice or animosity.

The case of Assisi, the city of St Francis, is particularly informative in this context, offering us exceptionally wide-ranging documentation to illustrate Jewish–Christian relations in all their variety.[1] Here, towards the end of the fourteenth century, the friars of S. Francesco were treated by a Jewish doctor, Sabatuccio da Roma, and they were clearly not afraid that he might poison them either physically or spiritually. Furthermore, the good monks were not above drinking a glass of fine wine at his table, or buying the odd barrel of Sangiovese or vintage Vernaccia from him for the monastery. The friars of the Confraternity of S. Stefano were dedicated clients of the 'Osteria del Campo', run by another Jew from Assisi, who supplied them with cheaper, more workaday red wine.

[1] See Toaff, *Jews in Medieval Assisi*, 30–2.

When the roof of the church of S. Francesco was in danger of collapse in 1436, the friars turned to a Jewish ironmonger to provide the material for its restoration; in 1455 another Jew was called upon to unpick and flatten out the monastery's worn and lumpy woollen mattresses. Around 1430 transport from the convent of Assisi to other Umbrian towns, and to Perugia in particular, was regularly provided by a Jewish carter, and the energetic Franciscan friars—who paid little and were always in a hurry—habitually travelled in Aleuccio's carriage, drawn by a miserable nag. No Jewish hawker or pedlar arrived in Assisi in the fifteenth century without knocking on the doors of the monastery of S. Francesco to sell the bits of cloth and knick-knacks of which the monks seem to have been insatiable consumers.[2] Monks and priests were also some of the most loyal clients of the Jewish banks, turning to them for small loans, upon pledges such as books of hours, bibles, and breviaries. But religious institutions too—churches, monasteries, and hospitals—frequently and unhesitatingly used Jewish banks, blithely disregarding canonical bans and the blistering sermons of the Observants against usury. The loan charters signed with Jews generally contained a clause forbidding the offer or acceptance of sacred furnishings and objects of Christian worship as pledges. The clauses signed by the commune of Città di Castello with the Jews in 1449 warned the latter 'that they may not lend, at interest, nor in any way, upon pledges of church furnishings and particularly upon chalices, patens, missals and other sacred books, chasubles or other holy vestments'.[3] Everyone was aware of the canonical ban on giving or accepting objects sacred to Christian worship as pledges, and on trafficking in them; the Church authorities frequently referred to it, from Gregory the Great onwards.[4] But practice was another matter, and many priests, clerics, monks, and friars feigned ignorance, whether personally or as representatives of their respective ecclesiastical bodies. Examples are legion, and I shall limit myself to a random selection from the communes of Umbria.

In 1304 the canons of the church of S. Maria della Pieve at Cascia left an engraved silver chalice as a pledge with the local Jews to raise the

[2] Ibid. 30–6. The phenomenon cannot have been unusual, since in Rome too convents and hospitals often made use of Jewish craftsmen and purchased the wares of the omnipresent pedlars; see Esposito, 'Ebrei a Roma nella seconda metà del Quattrocento', 94.
[3] AC Città di Castello, Annali Comunali, 45, fo. 76ʳ. See Toaff, 'Ebrei a Città di Castello', 9, 48.
[4] See e.g. B. Blumenkranz, *Juifs et Chrétiens*, 318–19; Grayzel, *The Church and the Jews*, 34–5.

TABLE 8.1 Churches, religious communities, and hospitals in Umbria which maintained relations with Jews in the 14th and 15th centuries

Took loans from Jewish banks	Used Jewish labour (craftsmen, doctors)	Rented and sold property to Jews	Sold agricultural produce to Jews
Assisi	*Assisi*	*Assisi*	*Montefalco*
Convent of S. Francesco	Church of S. Rufino	Confraternity of S. Stefano	Monastery of the Madonna delle Lacrime
Church of S. Rufino	Confraternity of S. Stefano	Convent of S. Francesco	
Confraternity of S. Stefano	Convent of S. Francesco	*Città di Castello*	
Bevagna	*Spoleto*	Cathedral of S. Florido	
Church of S. Maria in Laurenzia	Monastery of S. Benedetto dei Celestini	Church of S. Egidio	
Cascia		Church of S. Martino	
Church of S. Maria della Pieve		Confraternity of the Disciplinati di S. Giovanni	
Monastery of S. Agostino		Monastery of S. Benedetto di Monte Oliveto	
Gualdo Tadino		Monastery of S. Domenico	
Church of S. Maria di Crocicchio		Monastery of S. Maria d'oltre Tevere	
Gubbio		*Gubbio*	
Church of S. Maria d'Alfiolo		Monastery of S. Croce, Fonte Avellana	
Church of S. Salvatore di Nerbisci			
Monastery of S. Bartolo			
Monastery of S. Benedetto			

Perugia
Church of S. Giovanni del Fosso
Church of S. Maria dei Servi at Porta Eburnea
Church of S. Simone at Porta Sole
Confraternity of the Disciplinati di S. Fiorenzo
Convent of S. Domenico at Porta S. Pietro
Convent of S. Fiorenzo at Porta Sole
Convent of S. Francesco del Monte
Convent of S. Francesco at Porta S. Susanna
Convent of S. Maria Novara at Porta Sole
Ospedale di S. Maria della Misericordia
Spoleto
Church of S. Maria Assunta
Confraternity of S. Maria della Candelora
Monastery of S. Benedetto dei Celestini
Todi
Church of S. Fortunato
Val di Ponte, Perugia
Convent of S. Maria

Foligno
Convent of S. Francesco
La Fratta
Monastery of S. Salvatore at Monte Acuto
Montone
Abbey of S. Bartolomeo da Camporeggio
Perugia
Church of S. Giovanni del Fosso
Church of S. Maria dei Servi at Porta Eburnea
Church of S. Simone at Porta Sole
Convent of S. Domenico at Porta S. Pietro
Convent of S. Fiorenzo at Porta Sole
Convent of S. Francesco del Monte
Convent of S. Francesco at Porta S. Susanna
Convent of S. Maria Novara at Porta Sole
Monastery of the Beata Colomba
Ospedale di S. Maria della Misericordia
Trevi
Monastery of S. Bartolomeo

Note: This list is naturally incomplete but serves as a general guideline.

money needed to pay a tax imposed on them by the bishop of Spoleto.[5] In 1309 the abbot of the monastery of S. Maria d'Alfiolo at Gubbio deposited various pieces of silver plate with the Jewish bankers of Assisi in order to obtain a loan.[6] In 1386 the monastery of S. Benedetto at Gubbio pawned three vestments of scarlet velvet, a banner with embroidered images of saints, and an engraved silver chalice (the latter belonging to the church of S. Salvatore di Nerbisci) with Matassia Scola, one of the most influential Perugian bankers of the time.[7] In 1418 the abbot of the monastery of S. Bartolo at Gubbio pawned various church furnishings with the main Jewish banks at Perugia.[8] In 1437 an elaborate bell from the church of S. Fortunato at Todi, the work of Luigi Bondi da Cortona, was given as a pledge to a bank at Spello, and ten years later this same bank is documented as being in possession of various sacred objects left as pledges by the monastery of S. Chiara.[9] In 1455 it was the turn of the church of S. Maria in Laurenzia, at Bevagna, which pawned an engraved silver chalice and a missal with the banker Abramo da Perugia, to raise the money to pay the rent on the house of the canon don Melchiorre.[10] At Cascia, at the beginning of the sixteenth century, the monks of the monastery of S. Agostino were regularly depositing 'religious pledges' at the bank of the local Jewish moneylender.[11] When they needed money in 1509, the canons of Spoleto cathedral, S. Maria Assunta, had no qualms about pledging a whole set of silver chalices, normally on display in the sacristy, with the Jewish bankers of the city.[12] The most sensational such case occurred in Assisi in 1385. In the spring of that year the municipality, requiring a huge loan of 1,200 florins, pledged nothing less than a portion of the wealth of the church of S. Francesco and the basilica of S. Rufino: precious liturgical objects and real works of art, including most notably a large and splendidly worked silver image of the Virgin, and the magnificent cope which had belonged

---

[5] AC Cascia, S. Maria della Pieve, MS 50/A (1304).

[6] AC Bevagna, Not., Giovanni di Alberto, env. 14C, file G, fo. 15ᵛ (7 July 1309). See Toaff, *Jews in Medieval Assisi*, 115–16.

[7] AC Gubbio, Not., Vanne di Cecco di Ubaldo, 12, fo. 5ᵛ (16 Nov. 1386). See Toaff, 'Ebrei a Gubbio', 177–8.

[8] AS Perugia, Ospedale di S. Maria della Misericordia, deeds of Gaspare di Luca, contr. 85, fo. 80ᵛ (6 Nov. 1418).

[9] AC Spello, Not., env. 4, Bartolomeo di Domenico, 1, fo. 190ᵛ (11 Dec. 1437); ibid., env. 3, Niccolò di Bartolomeo, 2, fo. 100ʳ (2 July 1447).

[10] AC Bevagna, Not., Bartolomeo di Gaspare, 1521, fos. 6ᵛ–7ʳ (6 July 1455).

[11] AC Cascia, Con. e Rif., 2, fos. 13ʳ, 15ᵛ.

[12] AC Spoleto, Rif., 69, fo. 290ʳ (11 Oct. 1509).

to pope Nicholas IV.[13] Only very rarely were canons, friars, and priests brought to trial and punished for such illicit 'sacred' pledging. In 1511 when a Jew from Gualdo Tadino was tried before the papal legate of Perugia, accused of having received a silver paten belonging to the church of S. Maria del Crocicchio as a pledge, and of having resold it at the fair in Recanati, he was acquitted for lack of evidence.[14]

If Jews often had holy ornaments and objects belonging to churches, monasteries, and convents in their possession, it was also not unknown for friars and clerics to be in possession of objects of Jewish worship. As noted in Chapter 4, in 1473 silver plate, lamps, and sacred furnishings were stolen from the Perugia synagogue on via Vecchia, at Porta S. Angelo. Several days later the repentant thieves confessed in the church of S. Agostino and returned their booty to the friars.[15] Antonio da Macerata, prior of the Ospedale di S. Maria della Misericordia, and Ercolano di Ugolino, who were the two front-ranking figures in the Augustinian order at Perugia at the time, called the representatives of the Jewish community into church and handed them back their sacred objects so that they might resume 'their divine offices' without further ado.[16]

Religious orders, churches, and convents frequently sold Jews their landed property, and rented them houses, land, and storehouses.[17] In Perugia in the fifteenth century, the institutions which regularly borrowed from Jewish bankers and rented them apartments and shops included the church of S. Simone at Porta Sole, the Ospedale di S. Maria della Misericordia, the convent of S. Francesco at Porta S. Susanna, the church of S. Maria dei Servi at Porta Eburnea, the convent of S. Francesco del Monte, the convent of S. Maria Novara at Porta

[13] AC Assisi, H, Rif., 4, file 5, fo. 40ʳ (16 Mar. 1385). See Toaff, *Jews in Medieval Assisi*, 24–5, 139–41; A. Fortini, *Assisi nel Medio Evo* (Rome, 1940), 357; C. Cenci, *Documentazione di vita assisana*, i. (Grottaferrata, 1974), 209–10.

[14] AS Perugia, Giud., Processus, env. 164, file 19 (5 Nov. 1511). Some scholars, even recently, have been naïve enough to believe that the ban on lending on security of sacred objects, or on pawning them in banks, was scrupulously observed by Jews and priests; see D. Carpi, 'The Account Book of a Jewish Money-lender in Montepulciano (1409–1410)', *Journal of European Economic History*, 14 (1985), 511.

[15] AS Perugia, Not., Tolomeo di Niccolò, 76, fo. 688ʳ. See Toaff, *Ebrei a Perugia*, 97, 281–2.

[16] On the Augustinian friars Angelo da Macerata and Ercolano da Perugia, see Majarelli and Nicolini, *Il Monte dei Poveri di Perugia*, 195.

[17] This also occurred frequently in Rome and the other centres of Latium in the 14th and 15th cents. See Maire Vigueur, 'Les Juifs à Rome', 23–7; Esposito, 'Ebrei a Roma nella seconda metà del Quattrocento', 93–4; Caciorgna, 'Presenza ebraica', 142.

Sole, the church of S. Giovanni del Fosso, the convent of S. Domenico at Porta S. Pietro and the convent of S. Fiorenzo at Porta Sole.[18] At Città di Castello in the same period the friars of the convent of S. Domenico, the monks of S. Benedetto di Monte Oliveto, the priors of the churches of S. Egidio, S. Martino, and S. Giuliano, and even the town's bishop, all sold landed property to Jews and rented them houses, storerooms, vegetable gardens, wells, vineyards and orchards. It was the friars of S. Domenico who, in 1450, provided the Jewish community with land to be used as a cemetery.[19] In the latter part of the fourteenth century the monks of S. Salvatore at Monte Acuto were renting land and vines on a long-term basis to Aleuccio da Perugia, a banker at La Fratta.[20] A century later the chapter of the convent of S. Francesco at Foligno sold vineyards and olive-groves to Jewish merchants of the city.[21] In 1475 the medical officer of Montone, Manuele da Padova, was living on via della Fonte, in a luxurious house owned by the monks of the abbey of S. Bartolomeo da Camporeggio, near the palazzo belonging to count Carlo Fortebracci, lord of the town.[22] In 1509 the Confraternità dei Disciplinati di S. Giovanni at Città di Castello unhesitatingly sold a fine house with a vegetable garden, in the district of Porta S. Giacomo, to Lazzaro di Samuele da Gubbio, one of the main bankers of the town; he then began to use the premises for his banking activities, against which the itinerant Minorites were currently thundering.[23] Around the middle of the sixteenth century the monastery of the Madonna delle Lacrime rented houses and land to the Jews of Trevi, and provided them with must and wine from its famous vineyards.[24] There therefore seems no possible doubt that daily business and general relations between Jews and the non-itinerant clergy in Umbrian communes in the late Middle Ages were close and constant. The tone of the dialogue between these two components of

---

[18] See the list in AS Perugia, Corporazioni religiose soppresse, Ospedale di S. Maria della Misericordia, contr. 107, fos. 72ʳ–75ʳ (26 Oct. 1457). For these Perugian institutions see Grohmann, *Le città nella storia dell'Italia: Perugia*.

[19] AC Città di Castello, Not., Bartolomeo di Antonio Bovari, 3, fos. 10ʳ, 47ᵛ (26 Sept. 1469); ibid., 16, fos. 39ʳ, 47ᵛ, 87ᵛ, 220ᵛ (22 Feb. 1470); ibid., Angelo di Battista, 3, fo. 81ʳ (1 Feb. 1471); ibid. 4, fo. 59ʳ (23 July 1472); ibid. 6, fo. 20ʳ (31 Aug. 1472).

[20] AC Umbertide, Not., Giunta Coli da Montone, 258/26, fos. 13ᵛ, 119ʳ (8 Nov. 1374, 14 July 1375).

[21] AC Foligno, Not., Taddeo Angelelli, 11/3, fo. 65ᵛ (1479).

[22] AC Gubbio, Not., Benedetto di Giuliano da Gubbio, prot. sine coll., fo. 24ʳ (28 Sept. 1475).

[23] AC Città di Castello, Not., Pietro Laurenzi, 7, fo. 142ʳ (12 Dec. 1509).

[24] AC Trevi, Tre Chiavi, env. 16, reg. 238, fos. M–N (1549).

Italian society in the age of the communes and *signorie* strikes me as unforced and often cordial, without any tell-tale signs of the damage worked by the antisemitic propaganda of Minorite preaching.

THE DISTINCTIVE BADGE

From the fifteenth century onwards, in the communes of Umbria as elsewhere in Italy, there was a proliferation of legislative measures obliging Jews to wear something that would distinguish them from Christians. The imposition of the so-called 'badge for Jews' (and Saracens) already figured in the articles of the Fourth Lateran Council of 1215, where it was justified by the hope that it would discourage sexual relations between infidels and Christians. Subsequent Church regulations, which frequently referred to this ruling, added a further justification: since the Jews' own religious rules required them to distinguish themselves from gentiles in certain customs and dietary matters, it was only right that this distinction should also be extended to their style of dress.[25] In practice it seems that the ruling concerning the badge was applied only very sporadically in Italy before the end of the fourteenth century.[26] We have no trace of it in Umbrian documents of the thirteenth and fourteenth centuries; at that time, even when Jews asked the commune for concessions and privileges, they do not ask for exemption

[25] For a thorough study of papal deeds and conciliar decrees concerning the distinctive badge for Jews, see Grayzel, *The Church and the Jews*, 61–70. The subject is also considered by e.g. G. Rezasco, *Del segno degli ebrei* (Genoa, 1889); V. Colorni, *Gli ebrei nel sistema del diritto*, 48–54; Abrahams, *Jewish Life in the Middle Ages*, 291–306; A. Milano, *Storia degli ebrei in Italia* (Turin, 1963), 585–9. See also the excellent study by D. Owen Hughes, 'Distinguishing Signs: Ear-Rings, Jews and Franciscan Rhetoric in the Italian Renaissance City', *Past and Present*, 112 (Aug. 1986), 3–59.

[26] The ruling was ratified in 1221 by Frederick II for the Jews of the Kingdom of Naples and Sicily, while in the following century the Angevins renewed it in 1307, 1310, and 1366; see B. and G. Lagumina, *Codice diplomatico dei Giudei in Sicilia* (Palermo, 1884), i. 17, 31–2, 80–1. The ruling was in force in 1333 in Pisa, the only commune in central Italy to have adopted it at this time; see F. Bonaini, *Statuti inediti della città di Pisa dal XII al XIV secolo* (Florence, 1854–70), iii. 89. Attempts to impose a distinctive badge or sign for Jews were made in Ferrara in 1310, in Rome in 1360, and in Siena in 1373, but apparently without concrete results; see C. Re, *Statuti della città di Roma del secolo XIV* (Rome, 1883), 190; V. Colorni, 'Ebrei in Ferrara nei secoli XIII e XIV', in E. M. Artom, L. Caro, and S. J. Sierra (eds.), *Miscellanea di studi in memoria di Dario Disegni* (Turin, 1969), 88–90; G. Mollat, 'Deux frères mineurs, Marc de Viterbe et Guillaume de' Gasconi, au service de la papauté', *Archivum Franciscanum Historicum*, 48 (1955), 69. The yellow circle seems to have been made obligatory for the Jews of Venice for the first time in 1394; see Ciscato, *Ebrei in Padova*, 165.

from wearing the distinctive badge. We find no mention of it until 1413, and then in connection with a dispensation from wearing it: the commune of Todi allowed all Jews living in town not to wear the badge which, significantly, is referred to as *novum habitum*.[27]

This privilege was confirmed for the Jews of Todi in 1420, and granted to those of Gubbio in 1421.[28] In this latter case too the badge is referred to as *novum habitum*, which leads us to believe that the first attempts to enforce the measure, hitherto regarded as strange and unusual, upon the Jews of Umbria, dates from the beginning of the fifteenth century. During the subsequent period it was taken up by numerous municipal statutes, and the resolutions of the governors of the towns of Umbria refer to it on several occasions. Yet the very proliferation of such rulings, so frequently repeated and referred to, confirms that here, as elsewhere in Italy, the regulation was rarely and unwillingly observed by Jews, while the communes reiterated it unenthusiastically and above all without much intention of seeing it obeyed.[29]

The nature of the badge was more or less the same in all the Umbrian cities: for men, it was a circle of yellow cloth, to be attached to the left-hand side of the garment, above the belt, and for women it was earrings, also circular in form. The rulings of the priors of Perugia passed in 1432 are extremely interesting and detailed in this

[27] AC Todi, Rif., 56, fos. 97ᵛ–99ʳ (24 Oct. 1413).
[28] Ibid. 58, fos. 52ʳ–54ʳ (4 Nov. 1420); AC Gubbio, Rif., 20, fos. 57ʳ–59ʳ (14 Dec. 1421).
[29] We find the proclamation on the wearing of the badge for Jews at Perugia in 1432, 1466, 1468, 1486, and 1519 (AS Perugia, Con. e Rif., 69, fos. 51ʳ–55ʳ; ibid., Copiario Privilegi, Bolle e Brevi, 3, fo. 10ʳ; ibid., Editti e Bandi, 2, fos. 18ʳ and 213ᵛ) ; at Assisi in 1453, 1456, 1457, 1468, and 1485 (AC Assisi, H, Rif., 11, file 1, fo. 116ʳ; ibid. 14, fos. 32ʳ and 111ᵛ; ibid. 17, fo. 133ᵛ; ibid. 9, file 4, fo. 31ᵛ) ; at Trevi in 1469, 1474, and 1483 (AC Trevi, Tre Chiavi, env. 9, reg. 127, fo. 8ʳ; ibid., reg. 139, fo. 1ʳ; ibid., env. 6, reg. 70, fo. 67ʳ); at Città di Castello in 1449, 1459, 1480, and 1507 (AC Città di Castello, Annali Comunali, 45, fo. 76ʳ; ibid. 46, fo. 44ʳ; ibid. 55, fo. 100ʳ; ibid. Arch. Segr., Con. e Rif., 33, 20 Sept. 1480); at Todi in 1436 and 1481 (AC Todi, Stat., 4, Add., rubric 224, fos. 323ᵛ–324ʳ; ibid., Rif., 82, fos. 43ᵛ–49ʳ); at Norcia in 1442 and 1478 (AC Norcia, Con. e Rif., 4, fos. 135ᵛ–137ʳ; ibid. 8, fos. 52ʳ–54ᵛ); at Foligno in 1456 and 1478 (AC Foligno, Rif., 30, fo. 94ᵛ; ibid. 38, fo. 126ʳ); at Amelia in 1468 (AC Amelia, Rif., 41, fo. 190ᵛ); and at Spoleto in 1451 (AC Spoleto, Rif., 36, fo. 205ʳ). Jews obtained official exemptions from wearing the badge at Todi in 1413 and 1420 (AC Todi, Rif., 56, fos. 97ᵛ–99ʳ; ibid. 58, fos. 52ʳ–54ʳ); at Gubbio in 1421 and 1431 (AC Gubbio, Rif., 20, fos. 57ʳ–59ʳ; ibid. 21, fos. 66ʳ–68ʳ); at Norcia in 1432 (AC Norcia, Con. e Rif., 4, fo. 135ᵛ); at Amelia in 1445 (AC Amelia, Rif., 38, fo. 74ʳ); and at Città di Castello in 1485, 1500, and 1510 (AC Città di Castello, Annali Comunali, 52, fos. 118ʳ–124ᵛ; ibid. 54, fos. 191ʳ–196ʳ; ibid. 55, fos. 222ʳ–230ʳ).

connection.[30] Noting that Jews living in the town, both men and women, had long dressed like Christians and were therefore indistinguishable from them, the governors of Perugia now required that they should wear a badge. The drafters of the document preferred the second of the classic justifications for the measure, namely, that Jews differed from Christians in their law, customs, and dietary rules, and that it was therefore right that they should also be distinguished from them in their dress. But no reference is made to the fact that the badge might serve to avert the danger of sexual relations between Jews and Christians. The ruling enjoins

that each Jew who has been living in the city or *contado* for eight years or more must wear a round yellow badge of the approved size sewn upon his coat or whatever outer garment he may be wearing, i.e. upon the chest . . . and that all Jewesses must wear the said rings in their ears, but they must wear short cloaks in the old style when they leave the house . . . except for widows, who shall not have to wear the said earrings, but must wear the short cloaks in the old style, of whatever colour they please, except for black, russet, or dark green.

The Perugia regulations were adopted in nearby Todi, and their text is quoted almost verbatim in the town statutes of 1436, accompanied by a full-size illustration of the badge and earrings.[31] When they went out, Jewish women were to wear *cerchi* (circles), known in Todi as *circillii*, in their ears, and a short cloak. Widows were exempt from wearing earrings, but they too were to wear the short cloak, provided it was not black or dark green, probably to avoid the embarrassment of being mistaken for nuns or sisters. In the fifteenth century earrings, regarded as the distinctive sign of the Jewish woman, gradually ceased to be worn by Christian women in the towns of central and northern Italy; general opinion, fuelled by Minorite preaching, now regarded them as symbols of luxury and loose living, common to Jewish women and prostitutes alike.[32] But although the wearing of such earrings is also mentioned as obligatory in later documents, for instance at Città di Castello in 1480, in

---

[30] AS Perugia, Con. e Rif., 69, fos. 51ʳ–55ʳ (10–17 Apr. 1432). See Fabretti, *Sulla condizione*, 32–5; Toaff, *Ebrei a Perugia*, 62–4.

[31] AC Todi, Stat., 4, Add. 224, fos. 323ᵛ–324ʳ (19 June 1436).

[32] See Hughes, 'Distinguishing Signs', 21–59. According to this respected American scholar, it was the Jewish women of southern Italy who popularized the custom of wearing earrings among northern Jewish women. The habit was subsequently adapted and used as a distinctive, and degrading, badge; her views are certainly interesting, but seem to me still to require conclusive proof.

practice Jewish women were mostly exempt from having to adopt this and other distinguishing signs.[33] Good sense almost always prevailed, despite the efforts of the fanatics who tried to enforce the compulsory wearing of the badge for women and children too. The governor of Spoleto, the Tuscan Giacomo Minutoli, sums up this pragmatic attitude when writing to the priors of Amelia in 1468: 'We wish Jewish women and children to be exempt from wearing the "O" badge or any other badge, because nowhere is it customary, and it is right that it should not be so.'[34]

Children were exempt from wearing the badge, but there was widespread confusion as to the age from which they should be obliged to do so. In the regulations of the priors of Città di Castello of 1449 the minimum age was set at 7, at Perugia in 1432 at 8, at Todi in 1436 at 10, and at Foligno in 1456 at 14.[35] In practice no one bothered to ascertain the ages of Jewish children found in the street without the badge in order to denounce them and oblige their parents to pay the statutory fine. Nor were women and children the only Jews to be exempt from the ban on going out dressed like Christians. Bankers travelling on business and doctors were usually exempt, as were all Jews when they were in or near their own homes. In the charter granted to the Jews of Città di Castello in 1449 and confirmed in 1459—which may be regarded as paradigmatic in this context—we read 'that no Jew shall incur any penalty if he shall venture out without a coat or otherwise without a badge when he is near to home, that is, in his own neighbourhood, and similarly if he returns without a badge from outside the city or *contado*'.[36] Lastly, foreign Jews were allowed an immunity, varying from one to ten days depending on the locality, before they were required to wear the badge.[37]

---

[33] 'No Jewish woman shall presume to go without rings in her ears' (AC Città di Castello, Arch. Segr., Con. e Rif., 33, 20 Sept. 1480). The compulsory use of hoop-shaped earrings as a distinctive badge for Jewish women is found in Avignon as early as 1243: Grayzel, *The Church and the Jews*, 66. In Italy in the second half of the 15th cent. earrings were used as a distinctive badge for Jewish women in the dominions of the Este: see Balletti, *Gli ebrei e gli Estensi*, 149–52; this was also the case in Ancona: see Rezasco, *Del segno degli ebrei*, 323–4.

[34] AC Amelia, Rif. 41, enc. with fo. 191ᵛ (letter of 9 Apr. 1468).

[35] AC Città di Castello, Annali Comunali, 45, fo. 76ʳ; AS Perugia, Con. e Rif., 69, fos. 51ʳ–55ʳ (17 Apr. 1432); AC Todi, Stat., 4, Add. 224, fos. 323ᵛ–324ʳ (19 June 1436); AC Assisi, H, Rif., 14, fo. 32ʳ (16 July 1456); AC Amelia, Rif., 41, fo. 190ᵛ (9 Apr. 1468); AC Foligno, Rif., 30, fo. 94ᵛ (29 June 1456).

[36] AC Città di Castello, Annali Comunali, 45, fo. 76ʳ (7 July 1449); ibid. 46, fo. 44ʳ (22 June 1459). See also Toaff, 'Ebrei a Città di Castello', 10–11.

[37] Exemption from wearing the badge for foreign Jews was granted for one day in Spoleto in 1451; two days in Perugia in 1432 and in Todi in 1436; three days in

When the ruling was in force, Jews in general avoided it in one of two ways: by paying the relevant fine in advance to the city authorities, who were usually perfectly amenable, or by going around 'with the badge concealed', that is, with the yellow circle hidden beneath their clothing, thus cocking a snook both at the measure and at those who had promoted it. The proceedings against a Jew of Gualdo Tadino in 1511 maintained, among other things, that 'Mosè goes out shamelessly in public without a badge, and even when he wears one, he has it hidden under his clothing, and so do all his family, so that it is impossible to distinguish them from Christians'.[38] Often the communes turned a blind eye and officially allowed Jews to go 'with the badge concealed', thus demonstrating the scant regard in which they held the measure. This happened, for example, at Foligno in 1456 and in Todi in 1481,[39] and naturally enraged the Observants, who felt that it made a mockery of the whole idea. It should therefore come as no surprise that the numerous proclamations inspired by their preaching should harp obsessively on the subject of the 'visible badge', that is, the obligation to wear the yellow circle so that it could indeed be seen. 'The Jews shall be obliged to wear the badge in the form of the letter O, in green or straw yellow on all their clothes, capes, tunics, overgarments and cloaks, above the belt and on the side where clothes are usually fastened around the waist, that is, on the left-hand side of the chest' (Norcia, 1478); 'no Jew may dare venture through the town or *contado* by day or night, without the badge of the O on his chest, openly and obviously displayed in a public and manifest fashion, so that all may see it' (Città di Castello, 1480); 'every Jew shall be obliged to wear the yellow O-shaped badge on his chest, clearly displayed on his outermost garment' (Assisi, 1485); 'all Jews are ordered to wear the badge visibly, so that they may be recognized by others thereby' (Perugia, 1486); 'all Jews living in the city must wear the badge visibly, so that they may be recognized and distinguished from Christians' (Perugia, 1519).[40] The anxiety not to be hoodwinked is

---

Foligno in 1456, in Trevi in 1469, and in Assisi in 1456; four days in Amelia in 1468 and in Città di Castello in 1449 and 1459; eight days in Norcia in 1478; and ten days in Trevi in 1474.

[38] AS Perugia, Giud., Processus, env. 164, file 19 (5 Nov. 1511).

[39] 'If the said Jews are found with the badge concealed, no penalty at all can be exacted' (AC Foligno, Rif., 30, fo. 94ᵛ, 29 June 1456). 'If any of the said Jews are found with the badge concealed, no penalty can be exacted' (AC Todi, Rif., 82, fos. 43ᵛ–49ᵛ, 28 Feb. 1481).

[40] AC Norcia, Con. e Rif., 38, fo. 74ʳ (16 Aug. 1478); AC Città di Castello, Arch. Segr., Con. e Rif., 33 (20 Sept. 1480); AC Assisi, H, Rif., 9, file 4, fo. 31ᵛ (14 Aug. 1485); AS Perugia, Editti e Bandi, 2, fo. 18ʳ (1 June 1486) and fo. 213ᵛ (20 Oct. 1519).

particularly evident in the legislation advocated by Minorite preachers at Spoleto in 1451, where once again we find a heavy-handed insistence on the 'visible badge': 'Each Jew shall wear the badge visibly on his chest in an obvious place, that is, he shall not wear it concealed, but on his chest, so that it may be clearly seen and may be visible to all who may wish to see it; and it must be visible in its entirety.'[41] It was probably the failure of the efforts to make Jews wear a 'visible' badge which led to the later alternative of replacing the cloth circle with a yellow cap for men, and a yellow veil for women, making subterfuge far more difficult. The new rulings on yellow caps and veils are found in Umbria from the beginning of the sixteenth century, appearing for the first time at Città di Castello, where the commune adopted them in 1507 at the insistence of the Minorite fra Cherubino da Spoleto.[42]

Regulations on the wearing of the badge were usually proclaimed by communes in the period following Holy Week, as the immediate outcome of Franciscan preaching during the Easter triduum. The antisemitic measures (including the badge) passed by the priors of Perugia in April 1432 were the fruit of Bernardino da Siena's preaching in the city.[43] In the spring of 1469 the wearing of the badge was made obligatory at Trevi under pressure from the Minorite Agostino da Perugia, while at Assisi it was advocated in 1468 by Fortunato Coppoli, the founder of the local Monte di Pietà.[44] The preaching of Bernardino da Feltre, too, led ineluctably to the renewal of proclamations concerning the badge in many towns, including Assisi in 1485 and Perugia one

[41] AC Spoleto, Rif., 36, fo. 205ʳ (13 Apr. 1451).

[42] 'In order to distinguish themselves from Christians, Jewish men shall be obliged to wear a yellow cap, and women a yellow veil' (AC Città di Castello, Annali Comunali, 55, fo. 100ʳ, 26 Mar. 1507). See Toaff, 'Ebrei a Città di Castello', 102–3. In Venice and on the Venetian mainland the yellow cap was introduced for the first time with a decree of 8 Apr. 1496: 'In order that Jews may clearly and manifestly be known by Christians through generally known signs . . . and since they are obliged to wear a circle of yellow cloth, so in Venice, as in all our territories on land and sea, they must wear the cap, or other manner of headgear, which must be bright yellow, which they are obliged to wear on their heads in both winter and summer'; see Ciscato, *Ebrei in Padova*, 273–4. In the same year the new distinctive badge was introduced at Brescia, Mantua, and in the lands of the Estensi; see Colorni, *Gli ebrei nel sistema del diritto comune*, 52; F. Glissenti, *Gli ebrei nel bresciano al tempo della dominazione veneta* (Brescia, 1890), 14; Balletti, *Gli Ebrei e gli Estensi*, 149–52.

[43] See Fantozzi, 'Documenta Perusina de S. Bernardino Senensi', 108–29; Majarelli and Nicolini, *Il Monte dei Poveri di Perugia*, 75–7; Toaff, *Ebrei a Perugia*, 60–4.

[44] See Cristofani, *Le Storie di Assisi*, 357–9; Toaff, *Jews in Medieval Assisi*, 60–4.

year later.[45] In their sermons the Minorites made no secret of their preference for the first of the Church's justifications for the need for Jews to wear distinctive clothing: namely, as a means of curtailing physical relations between Jews and Christians, regarded by them as one of the most serious and frequent blots upon Italian society in the fifteenth century. Fra Roberto Caracciolo visited Perugia in the winter of 1448;[46] in his sermons, subsequently collected in the *Spechio della christiana fede*, he referred to the *Decretali* of Gregory IX, resolutely concluding: 'That Jews must wear the badge in order that both men and women may easily be known, and that Christian men should not be led by error into sullying themselves with Jewish women, nor vice versa.'[47] But if the badge was to constitute an effective barrier discouraging those Jews and Christians who intended to continue with their close everyday relationships, its more or less obvious failure, with the tacit consent of both parties, also reveals to some degree the strong resistance met by the broader and more general aim so doggedly pursued by the Minorites: namely, that of isolating and discriminating against the Jewish minority within Christian society.

THE HOLY *SASSAIOLA*

The approach of the triduum of the Christian Holy Week brought the Jews no comfort: this was the period of the great 'performance' in which they figured among the protagonists. The script was always the same, its leading lights being the friars who mounted the pulpits to preach of Christ's passion, branding the deicides—the Jewish people who continued to suck innocent Christian blood through fraud and usury—with words of fire. Thus ran the inexorable prologue. This was followed by the processions of the faithful, banded into confraternities carrying the image of Christ and other holy relics through the streets. One character in the drama—the victim—was paraded through the town as though walking on the shoulders of the elated crowd. But there were other actors, who might or might not be sporting the yellow badge:

---

[45] See Wadding, *Annales Minorum*, xiv. 457–9, 468, 472–4, 518–20; Casolini, *Bernardino da Feltre*, 219–21; Marinelli, *La compagnia di S. Tommaso d'Aquino*, 19, 62; Toaff, *Ebrei a Perugia*, 80–1; id., *Jews in Medieval Assisi*, 69–71.

[46] See Toaff, *Ebrei a Perugia*, 66–7.

[47] Roberto da Lecce, *Spechio della christiana fede* (Venice, 1536), sermon XIX, fo. 137.

the Jews, cast as the murderers of the Messiah, deicides, doomed and unregenerate previous offenders. The friars had referred to them as 'ravening wolves', 'voracious curs', 'bloodsuckers of poor Christian blood', 'the devil's lackeys'. In the imagination of the faithful, the Jewish banker and his family, above all, followed by the other Jews who attended synagogue, were now seated in judgement in the Sanhedrin as Pilate's accomplices. Their very presence in the city streets constituted a mockery, a cruel insult. Anyone with pledges in the bank, or who had had them in the past, anyone who had a loan to repay or had just done so, anyone who was leasing an ox from a Jew, now identified with Christ and demanded that justice be done. And not just on behalf of the Christ Crucified whom they bore on their shoulders. This momentary identification with the Messiah, traduced and made an innocent victim, brought into focus images which, because they were normally kept in separate mental compartments, did not prevent the medieval Italian Christian from having 'much association, converse, company and familiarity with Jews . . . as though there were no prohibition upon this whatsoever'. Theological reflection on the Christian's position in relation to the Jew, together with respect for the canonical doctrine condemning usury, was usually no more than theoretical, pragmatically ignored in everyday economic and social transactions, and dealt with where necessary by useful compromises, which do not seem to have led to any sort of awkwardness on the moral plane.[48] But this delicate balance was invariably upset during Holy Week, when dramatic tension reached its height. The Jews, deicides and usurers, had to be punished: without its foregone conclusion, the story would remain a holy tragedy; punishment had to be exacted from the Jews in order for the Passion to be avenged and the historical balance restored. But the drama's villains, mindful of what was in store, were usually installed firmly in their houses with doors and windows barred, following the story-line as it unfolded outside in the streets and awaiting its preordained conclusion.

Medieval Italians were aficionados of the *sassaiola*, the fight with stones. No local event, whether joyful or mournful, funeral or fair, festival of a patron saint or settling of accounts between rival factions, game or competition, could be regarded as complete without stones being

---

[48] See Jacques Le Goff's important reflections on the psychology of medieval merchants and the sharp distinction they made between their religious and professional lives. Le Goff, 'Merchant's Time and Church's Time', 29–42.

thrown by young and old alike. These stonings were often bloodless events, serving to siphon off a pent-up violence which might otherwise have found far bloodier outlets.[49] The Easter procession too, the celebration of the drama of Christ and the race of deicides, performed by amateur actors, who were all nevertheless fully conversant with their respective roles, ended with the holy *sassaiola*. Jews' houses were targeted by the penitents of the confraternities and the processing faithful, and a hail of stones fell upon roofs and walls, to the accompaniment of much noise and, usually, little damage. The authorities countenanced the violence; to do otherwise would have been counter-productive, indeed dangerous. It was simply channelled into a cul de sac and controlled. The volley of stones against the windows avenged the Messiah, punished the Jewish loan-shark, satisfied those who threw them, and silenced the rantings of the Observant friars, at least temporarily. The drama was over, having been played out to everyone's satisfaction. Tomorrow normal life would resume. The banker would throw open the windows of his house and the doors of his bank, noting the damage; the pedlar would wheel his cartload of knick-knacks to the market, to be surrounded as usual by a motley flock of women customers from the town and surrounding *contado*; the old-clothes-seller would reopen his shop and the public would pour in; the usual crowd would gather at the inn on the town square: the Jewish carter, the friar, and the slaughterer, drawn together by their common love of wine; while the Jewish doctor–surgeon would resume the round of visits he had broken off during Holy Week. The performance was therefore a game: it had its set script, its rules, which were scrupulously observed by the whole cast, and a rigid framework which left no leeway for spontaneous action. No improvisation was allowed, and the town authorities supervised the performance intently, punishing anyone, whether Jewish or Christian, who violated the rules and thereby threatened long-established customs. The greatest danger was that the fuse lit by Minorite preaching might trigger uncontrolled violence against Jews, possibly leading to a pogrom and endangering their presence in the town, something which in reality no one wanted. Usually the game proceeded according to a tried and trusted pattern, and the religious rite was turned into a performance which was certainly violent and spectacular, but without dangerous and irreversible results. It was a show whose residue would be swept away

---

[49] On the widespread custom of stoning in the Middle Ages see esp. Bonazzi, *Storia di Perugia*, i. 446–8.

the following day, together with the assorted rubbish which had built up in the crowded streets over the Easter period.[50] The decrees of the Fourth Lateran Council (1215) include a ban on Jews going about the streets during Holy Week, but the ban's origin is certainly much older, possibly dating back to the sixth century.[51] At the end of the twelfth century Alexander III felt it appropriate to order Jews to close their doors and windows on Good Friday.[52] The Lateran Council ruling required that Jews 'should not appear in public during the days of lamentation and on Palm Sunday, for some of them do not hesitate to go around on those days dressed in festive attire, and do not fear to mock the Christians as they parade the memory of the holy Passion and exhibit signs of mourning'.[53] Innocent III was even more explicit in an epistle of 1205 addressed to the king of France, where the very presence of Jews on the streets during Holy Week was considered an insult to Christ's Passion: 'On Good Friday Jews walk up and down the streets and public squares, without regard for the age-old custom, everywhere making mock of the Christians who adore the figure of Christ upon the cross, and seeking through their insults to have them desist from their worship.'[54]

Just how disingenuous the accusation of sacrilegious arrogance really was emerges indirectly from the regulation keeping Jews out of public

[50] In his consideration of the Christian attitude to the Jews during the triduum of Holy Week, Dahan talks of a 'liturgy that has become a spectacle'; see G. Dahan, 'L'Église et les juifs au Moyen Âge, XIIème au XIVème siècles', *Ebrei e Cristiani nell' Italia medioevale e moderna: Conversioni, scambi, contrasti*, proceedings of an international conference held at San Miniato, Pisa, 4–6 Nov. 1986 (Rome, 1988). In a perceptive analysis of the more drastic aspects of the Church's proselytizing policy towards the Jews of Rome, such as the compulsory sermon, A. Foa, in a paper given at the same conference, describes them as 'proselytizing games', rightly stressing that this was 'a basic rite of reinforcement and stabilization, restraining violence by fixing it within codified and dramatized forms, and containing its extremes' ('Politica conversionistica e controllo della violenza contro gli ebrei nella Roma del Cinquecento e del Seicento', 154–9). A. similar conclusion is reached in a recent analysis of the Roman Jews' compulsory attendance at the Roman carnival; see M. Boiteux, 'Les Juifs dans le Carnaval de la Rome moderne, XVème au XVIIIème siècles', *Mélanges de l'École Française de Rome*, 88 (1976), 745–87.

[51] See Grayzel, *The Church and the Jews*, 81.

[52] On the origins of the ban on Jews appearing in the streets during Holy Week and its application in Avignon and Spain in the 13th and 14th cents., see ibid. 34; Dahan, 'L'Église et les juifs'.

[53] The text of the Lateran Council's decree is published in Grayzel, *The Church and the Jews*, pp. 308–9, document X.

[54] Innocent III's epistle to King Philippe-Auguste of France, dated 16 Jan. 1205, is published in Grayzel, *The Church and the Jews*, pp. 104–9, document XIV.

places during Holy Week, requested by the provincial councils from the second quarter of the thirteenth century onwards. Jews were prohibited from leaving their homes, except for emergencies, so as not to scandalize Christians. But the ecclesiastical legislators hastened to add 'that above all prelates shall protect them from harassment by Christians in the aforesaid week'.[55] Here Jews no longer appear as impious and arrogant bystanders at the ritual of the Passion, but as potential victims of the uncontrolled violence of the faithful, from which they need protection.

Like the obligatory distinctive sign, the enforced confinement of Jews to their homes during the triduum of Holy Week was a ruling applied all over Italy in the fifteenth century. In Umbria we find it for the first time in the measures issued by the priors of Perugia in the spring of 1432, which reflect the themes of Bernardino da Siena's preaching in the town: 'No Jew may leave his house, nor keep its doors and windows open, on Thursday, Friday, and Saturday of Holy Week, until the bells sound.'[56] In Foligno in 1456 the municipal authorities ordered that 'Jews shall be obliged to be confined to their houses during Holy Week, from Thursday evening until the bells sound on Saturday night'.[57] But usually the Jews saw to it, in the charters they signed with the communes, that the ban would be accompanied by an assurance that they would be protected from violence and excess. A typical example in this context was the charter granted by the commune of Città di Castello to the Jews in 1449, which contains the following ruling, whose text was to be reproduced unchanged in the subsequent agreements of 1459, 1485, 1500, and 1510: 'On Good Friday and Holy Saturday until the bells sound, no Jew may leave his house nor go through the town . . . and at the said time no one may perpetrate any damage, injury, or impediment upon their houses or persons.'[58] Protection from violence during Holy Week was explicitly extended to the Jews of Assisi by the town authorities in 1456, and confirmed one year later: 'On Good Friday, of whatever age and condition they may be, no harm shall be done to them in any way, either to their persons or to their dwellings, when they remain

---

[55] The ruling is found with this addition, for example, in the articles of the councils of Rouen (1223), Narbonne (1227), and Béziers (1246). See ibid. 316–19, 332–3.

[56] AS Perugia, Con. e Rif., 69, fos. 51ʳ–55ʳ (10–17 Apr. 1432). See Fabretti, *Sulla condizione*, 32–5; Toaff, *Ebrei a Perugia*, 62–4.

[57] AC Foligno, Rif., 30, fo. 94ᵛ (29 June 1456).

[58] AC Città di Castello, Annali Comunali, 45, fo. 76ʳ (1449); ibid. 46, fo. 44ʳ (1459); ibid. 52, fo. 118ʳ (1485); ibid. 54, fo. 191ʳ (1500); ibid. 55, fo. 222ʳ (1510). See Toaff, 'Ebrei a Città di Castello', 10–11.

within their houses.'⁵⁹ We find similar rulings at Todi in 1481 and at Trevi in 1483.⁶⁰ Excesses had therefore to be punished, and in practice they were. When a mob of toughs, returning from the triduum sermon in Assisi in April 1456, unleashed a hail of stones against a house belonging to some Jews in the district of S. Chiara, damaging the front door, windows, and roof, the municipal authorities promptly intervened, arresting the chief culprits and sentencing them to heavy fines.⁶¹ At Gubbio during Holy Week 1469, the door of the house of the banker Samuele di Consiglio was set on fire at night by persons unknown.⁶² Here too the town governors promptly imposed a heavy penalty upon those responsible, to dissuade others from engaging in 'copy-cat' activities and thus jeopardizing the fragile equilibrium of everyday relations between Christians and Jews, a balance which had been hard won but was now tempered by long habit.

When the authorities seemed to drag their feet in restraining violence, the Jews themselves reminded them of the need to respect the rules of the game, and of the inevitable consequences of any failure to do so. In Holy Week 1516 the Jews of Spoleto complained to the local governors of the damage habitually inflicted on them during Lent with the pretext of religious ceremonies and customs connected with Easter. As the time approached, many of them were not content with barricading themselves in their houses, with doors and windows barred, but actually left the city together with their families for greater safety. In the face of increasing abuse and thefts from their houses, they threatened to leave Spoleto for good, closing down their banks and ceasing their commercial activities.⁶³ In their petitions to the Consiglio Generale del Popolo they recalled how 'as everyone knows, each year, being in danger of being robbed during Lent, they are obliged to leave Spoleto to escape this danger, and to go to safe places, since they can no longer remain there because of the continual excesses done to them during those times, and at other times, with thefts of pledges and in other ways, so that they are

⁵⁹ AC Assisi, H, Rif., 14, fo. 32ᵛ (1456) and fo. 111ʳ (1457). See Toaff, *Jews in Medieval Assisi*, 52–3.
⁶⁰ AC Todi, Rif., 82, fo. 43ᵛ (1481); AC Trevi, Tre Chiavi, env. 6, reg. 70, fo. 67ʳ (1483).
⁶¹ AC Assisi, G, Libri mallefitiorum, box 1, file 4, fos. 1ʳ–4ᵛ (10–29 Apr. 1456). See Toaff, *Jews in Medieval Assisi*, 211–13.
⁶² AC Gubbio, Rif., 28, fo. 26ʳ (8 Apr. 1469).
⁶³ The petition of the Jews of Spoleto and the priors' reply are in AC Spoleto, Rif., 74, fo. 5ʳ (21 Apr. 1516).

left in a piteous state, and hence they adjudge it to be more expedient to abandon their home town rather than be subjected to these excessive dangers'. To avoid all possible misunderstanding, the Jews stressed that their stance was not motivated by any desire to challenge the rules of the game, and that they had nothing against the Easter *sassaiola*—when carried out by young boys—continuing as in the past, with the doors and windows of their houses as its target. They objected only to the involvement of adults, who took advantage of the traditional event to seize their pledges and to rob their dwellings. 'And the Jews are not complaining about young boys making the usual demonstration at the preordained time, but they object only that young men and grown men should join in, simply to rob them, and not with any other intention or zeal; and they do so in ways beyond what is due and decent; and similarly provision must be made that the pledges, upon which they make their loans, may not be taken from them by force and violence.' The governors of Spoleto accepted the Jews' request, regarding it as completely legitimate, and confirmed the set outlines of the script of the holy *sassaiola* for the information of Jews and Christians alike.

As is known, during the triduum of Holy Week and then alone, once the sacred office against the Jews is over, the Church allows the people to hurl stones against them, to commemorate the holy Passion of Christ and to rebuke their iniquity and obduracy; and since this tradition has become corrupted over time, and since there are some who take advantage of it (and who are certainly not moved by zealous faith) to rob and defraud the Jews, whose presence among Christians is tolerated by the Holy Roman Church; wherefore to repress and extirpate such abuses, we enjoin that no Christian, of whatever age and condition, who is above 15 years of age, shall throw stones at the Jews and their houses during Holy Week.[64]

The ruling of the governors of Spoleto ends with the warning that even those who may legitimately take part in the stoning 'must take care that they do not injure the Jews, their persons nor their houses, by using means other than stones alone'. These were the rules of a game whose violence had to be kept strictly within the set channels, so that the ritual spectacle would not degenerate into a seditious free-for-

---

[64] The custom of stoning Jews during Holy Week was widespread elsewhere in Italy too, but only boys were allowed to take part. At Savona in 1476 we read that 'on Good Friday the boys of the town attacked the houses of the said Jews, arousing much displeasure, but according to those who live in these parts, this is the common custom' (Motta, 'Ebrei in Como', 40–1).

all, but would actually act as an endorsement of stability and social restraint.

If Christians had to keep within the set guidelines for the spectacle to unfold as intended, the same, *a fortiori*, applied to Jews, who had to be on their guard not to provoke the faithful as they celebrated the Passion of the Messiah.[65] In 1510 Mosè, a Jew from Gualdo Tadino, was brought to trial at Perugia for having 'had the effrontery to stay at home with his family during the Easter triduum, keeping the windows open and standing at the balcony, making mock of the ecclesiastical ceremonies and performing other actions in contempt of the Christians'.

This was an accusation which we might easily dismiss as a calumny, were it not borne out to a surprising degree by the numerous testimonies of Jews and Christians at this unusual trial.[66] Basing my interpretation on the relevant documents, I have reconstructed the facts as follows. As the Confraternità dei Disciplinati di S. Bernardino was processing in front of Mosè's house at Gualdo on Good Friday, the latter was standing at his window with some other Jews enjoying the spectacle, in violation of the ecclesiastical rulings. At this point, to Mosè's fury, someone from among the group of flagellants began to hurl a volley of stones at the intrusive onlookers. Not in the least cowed, he picked up the stones that had rained down upon his house, and threw them back in turn down upon the heads of the amateur marksmen, together with a torrent of abuse. The procession with the crucifix and banners was forced to disperse, as the faithful sought refuge from the projectiles. The spectacle may have gained in interest as a result, but at the price of Mosè's flagrant infringement of the rules of the game, since he was thus disregarding the well-established pattern laid down by the script, which assigned him the part of meek and consenting victim. Fortunately for him, the judge in the case (the apostolic legate of Perugia) interpreted events in a lenient fashion, as an excess of legitimate defence, and granted him a dubious acquittal.

---

[65] e.g. in 1475 the Jews of Savona were accused of having hung 'certain enormous animal entrails, inflated and full of filth' at their windows while the Corpus Christi procession was passing by. Whether or not it was meant as an insult, the act was considered offensive and sacrilegious, and it earned the Jews a fine of 300 ducats; see Motta 'Ebrei in Como', 40.

[66] The proceedings of Mosè's appeal (he had been sentenced at first instance by the deputy of the bishop of Nocera) before the apostolic legate of Perugia, are in AS Perugia Giud., Processus, env. 164, file 19 (*Processus Moysis hebrei contra vicarium episcopi Nucerini*, 5 Nov. 1511).

JEWS AND GYPSIES IN THE GHETTO

Although there do not appear to have been any explicit ecclesiastical rulings limiting the Jewish presence to designated areas, or confining them to particular parts of town, a profusion of local ordinances was issued from the middle of the thirteenth century in France, Spain, and Italy obliging Jews to live exclusively in the localities they themselves had already chosen, often known as *giudecche* or *juderie*. The 1277 Council of Bourges forbade Jews, 'whose perfidy so often makes fraudulent mock of simple Christians and maliciously leads them into error, to live in towns, walled villages and other larger places, since this entails a danger of depravation'.[67] Cohabitation between Jews and Christians was seen as a threat to the town's moral health, and those who condoned such cohabitation were worthy of excommunication. The Jewish minority should be excluded or expelled in order to protect a closed and homogeneous Christian society, often deliberately browbeaten with the bogy of hypothetical and imaginary dangers.[68] The enforced segregation of the Jews and their world meant that they would no longer be absorbed into the city context, but simply embedded there, with all the ensuing implications. This was tantamount to admitting that efforts at assimilation had failed; and such efforts were now to be replaced by a calculated decision to exploit the Jews for all they were worth, while they still had something to offer. In many cases this was the prelude to expulsion. It expressed the desire of the majority to manipulate and humiliate a minority whose integration was now regarded as undesirable. The relative religious and socio-economic freedom Jews had often enjoyed now turned them into a symbol of destabilization for a sick Christian society in recession, an element which should be removed and hidden from sight because it had become a distorting mirror of society's woes and blemishes.[69] The establishment of ghettos marked a watershed in the

---

[67] Grayzel, *The Church and the Jews*, 59–60.

[68] 'From a sociological viewpoint, ghetto and expulsion are both forms of segregation intended to stabilize a closed and homogenous Christian society': H. A. Oberman, 'The Stubborn Jews: Changing Strategies in Late Medieval Europe, 1300–1600', *Ebrei e Cristiani nell'Italia medievale e moderna: Conversioni, scambi, contrasti*, proceedings of an international conference held at San Miniato, Pisa, 4–6 Nov. 1986 (Rome, 1988), 123–40.

[69] See T. S. Szasz, *The Manufacture of Madness* (New York, 1970), 310; A. di Nola, *Antisemitismo in Italia* (Florence, 1973), 67–8. On ghettos, see the classic and still helpful sociological study by L. Wirth, *The Ghetto* (Chicago, Ill., 1928), and Abrahams, *Jewish Life in the Middle Ages*, 62–82.

history of relations between Christians and Jews in a society that had shown the ability to be tolerant and pluralistic. It was a slow and constant process, which intensified in the second half of the fifteenth century, and which was to lead to the breakdown of reason in a dismal tribute to the Counter-Reformation. In point of fact, in Italy, attempts to confine Jews to a particular area were sporadic and short-lived until the middle of the fifteenth century. In 1312 Frederick III tried ordering the Jews of Palermo to leave the city and withdraw to a place outside the walls, 'so that they may be separated from the faithful in Christ'. But his measures were ineffective.[70] Roughly a century later, in 1427, Giovanna II followed suit under pressure from Giovanni da Capistrano, ordering the Jews of Lanciano in the Abruzzi to restrict their lodgings to a single outlying street.[71] But in this case too the ruling had a short life and was abrogated two months later, unenforced. The House of Savoy repeated the attempt to segregate the Jews resident in their territories on several occasions, and in 1430 Amadeus VIII gave the plan his backing 'so that the minds of the faithful may not be corrupted by the proximity of the Jews . . . and to avoid all damnable mingling between Christian and Jewish men and women'.[72] But it is extremely doubtful whether these Piedmontese ghettos were ever actually established.[73]

It was only in the second half of the fifteenth century, and more particularly towards its end, that efforts to impose specific areas of residence on Jews began to proliferate in Italy, driving them from the neighbourhoods they had previously lived in, often to worse parts of town. This happened in Bari in 1463, in Cesena in 1487, and probably in Ravenna in 1492.[74] Poliakov rightly observes that such confined areas

---

[70] See Lagumina, *Codice diplomatico dei Giudei di Sicilia*, i. *1884*, p. 35, document 35; Colorni, *Gli ebrei nel sistema del diritto comune*, 55.

[71] See N. Ferorelli, *Gli ebrei nell'Italia meridionale dall'età romana al secolo XVIII*, (Naples, 1990), 68–9.

[72] See M. D. Anfossi, *Gli ebrei in Piemonte* (Turin, 1914), 29–31; Colorni, *Gli ebrei nel sistema del diritto comune*, 55–6.

[73] In 1436 the Consiglio Generale of Cuneo decided 'to segregate the Jews . . . in a separate part of Cuneo, so that their close relations with Christians may be impeded'. A similar ruling was passed by the Council of Turin in 1447. But, as Segre points out, 'the impression gained from the text is that the ducal writ was not as cogent as expected, and that the Council was not considered fully committed to the enterprise' (*Jews in Piedmont*, i. 117, 203).

[74] At Bari, just before the city passed into the hands of the Sforza in 1464, a proposal was put forward to force the Jews 'to settle and take up their residence all together in one part of the city'; see Ferorelli, *Gli ebrei nell'Italia meridionale*, 100. For Cesena and Ravenna see respectively Muzzarelli, *Ebrei e città d'Italia*, 64–7, 182–3, and Maragi, 'La fondazione del Monte di Pietà di Ravenna', 247.

were the direct precursors of the ghettos, officially set up only from the sixteenth century.[75] So that if the first ghetto to be founded was that of Venice, in 1516, followed by the ghetto in Rome, founded at the end of 1555 at the orders of Paul IV, the warning signs immediately preceding them should be seen as dating from the end of the fifteenth century, in the period of the founding of the first Monti di Pietà and the concerted anti-Jewish preaching of the Minorites.[76]

From the beginnings of Jewish settlement in Umbria in the second half of the thirteenth century until the middle of the fifteenth, there is no evidence of any kind of attempt by the municipal authorities or ecclesiastical circles to confine Jews to a separate district. Both in the towns where the Jewish presence was relatively numerous, such as Perugia, Città di Castello, Spoleto, Foligno, Terni, and Assisi, and, more naturally, in the lesser centres where Jewish families could be counted on the fingers of one hand, Jews were allowed to settle in all areas of the city. The rich, understandably, chose houses in the more prestigious areas, as did the Perugian banker Matassia da Roma, the owner, at the end of the fourteenth century, of a sumptuous palazzo in the district of Porta Sole, on the street leading to the church of S. Lucia.[77] Others made do with buying or renting a house wherever one was available, according to their means. Some Jews actually lived in isolated farmhouses in the *contado* and went into the larger centres, where there was a synagogue, only on Jewish festivals. Indeed, wherever there was a Jewish community officially recognized as a *Universitas Judaeorum*, with its own institutions and a functioning place of worship, we see a natural concentration of many Jewish families in that part of town where the synagogue was situated. This was the case with Perugia, where many Jews chose to live in the district of Porta S. Angelo, along via Vecchia, where the synagogue was, beneath the Etruscan walls. In Spoleto many families lived in vaita Petrenga in the so-called 'street of the Jews', not far from the

[75] 'The ghettos set up officially in the sixteenth century were foreshadowed from the fifteenth by the prohibition on living in good districts in certain towns': Poliakov, *Jewish Bankers and the Holy See*, 127. See also Shulvass, *Jews in the World of the Renaissance*, 45–7.

[76] There is a vast bibliography concerning the founding of the ghettos of Venice and Rome; see e.g. C. Roth, *The History of the Jews in Venice* (Philadelphia, Pa., 1930), 39–104; Pullan, *Rich and Poor in Renaissance Venice*, 431–509; A. Toaff, 'Getto-Ghetto', *The American Sephardi*, 6 (1973), 70–7; Natali, *Il ghetto di Roma*; Milano, *Il ghetto di Roma*. See also V. Colorni, *Novissimo Digesto Italiano* (Turin, 1973), s.v. 'Ghetto'.

[77] See Toaff, *Jews in Medieval Assisi*, 20–7.

central Piazza del Foro or Piazza del Mercato. Their place of worship was a stone's throw from the church revealingly known as S. Gregorio della Sinagoga (St Gregory of the Synagogue), and it was here that they opened their slaughterhouses, those inexhaustible sources of evil-smelling debris.[78]

On 23 January 1493 the representatives of the commune of Spoleto went before the apostolic governor Giovanni Borgia, the great-nephew of Alexander VI, asking for Jews to be banned from living on streets in the city centre, and for them to be confined to an outlying area, well away from the houses of the Christians:

> Given that canon law forbids Jews from living among Christian citizens, which would be prejudicial to the Christian faith, since Christians might in some way be led by the Jews' wrongful beliefs into committing acts contrary to good custom and prejudicial to religion: it should therefore be laid down that Jews should go and dwell in an outlying place, separate from Christian citizens, on the outskirts of town, so that the latter shall not be obliged to witness their wicked customs.[79]

The governors of Spoleto had several concrete proposals to put forward in this connection:

> we propose that in future Jews should be forbidden to lend at interest . . . and that their charter privileges should be annulled, since a Monte di Pietà has been founded in Spoleto, to which poor and indigent citizens can have recourse for their needs; and therefore, for the steadying of the Christian faith, that they shall be obliged to transfer their dwellings within eight days to the place called 'le felici' at Spoleto, so that they may thus be kept away from Christian citizens.

Unco-operative Jewish families were to be punished with a huge fine of 200 ducats apiece. Via delle Felici, where the Jewish ghetto was to be set up, is still in existence; it runs under the medieval walls towards Monteluco, on the outskirts of town. This area, poor and virtually uninhabited at the time, stood under the shadow of the grim Rocca, and under the vigilant eye of the monks of the monastery of S. Marco, the

[78] See above, pp. 71–3.
[79] AC Spoleto, Not., Paride di Pierdonato, 112, fo. 176ʳ⁻ᵛ (23 Jan. 1493). Moved by similar thinking, on 8 Nov. 1491 the bishop of Città di Castello forbade the Jews of the town to receive Christians into their homes (AC Città di Castello, Not., Angelo di Battista di Angelo, 10, fo. 219ʳ).

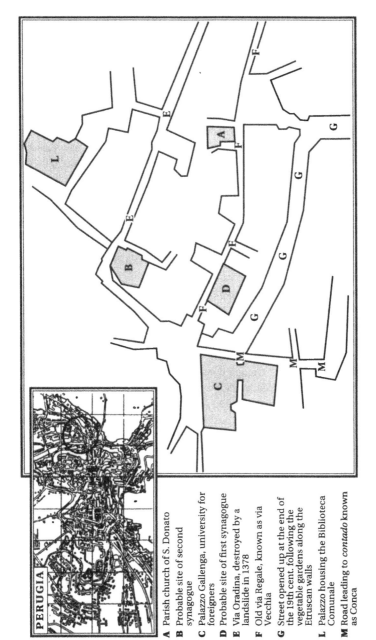

FIG. 8.1 The Jewish quarter of Perugia (14th–16th centuries)

A Parish church of S. Donato

B Probable site of second synagogue

C Palazzo Gallenga, university for foreigners

D Probable site of first synagogue

E Via Oradina, destroyed by a landslide in 1378

F Old via Regale, known as via Vecchia

G Street opened up at the end of the 19th cent. following the vegetable gardens along the Etruscan walls

L Palazzo housing the Biblioteca Comunale

M Road leading to *contado* known as Conca

only other important building in the district.[80] The Spoleto governors' petition to Borgia is significant because it links Jewish segregation and ghettoization to the founding of the Monte di Pietà. Given that they were no longer indispensable as financial providers, the problem of the Jews' enforced removal from the city fabric now loomed large. Christian society could not but suffer from cohabitation with Jews, now seen as enemies of the faith and corrupters of morals. The link between the foundation of the Monte di Pietà and Jewish segregation is not coincidental, and was undoubtedly one of the results of Minorite preaching, always supposing that the Observants were not directly responsible for the proposal. In this sense Balletti is right when he says that 'in the battle of the ghetto, just as in that of the Monte di Pietà, it was the friars who opened fire'.[81] The thesis of those scholars who have made a sophistic distinction between the two aims of Minorite preaching—the main one, namely the setting up of the Monte di Pietà, and the antisemitic polemic, presented as marginal and secondary, aimed at excluding and segregating Jews from Christian society—is thus clearly revealed as unsustainable.[82]

The Spoleto governors' petition to the apostolic governor was discussed again, a month later, in the presence of the representatives of the Jewish community, but it does not seem to have been accepted.[83] At all events, the Jews' expulsion from the town centre, and their enforced removal to the outskirts, did not take place in 1493 nor in the years immediately following, though the scheme was not abandoned, and continued to foment hatred in many hearts and minds. As the sixteenth century progressed, the problem of Jewish segregation was discussed ever more frequently and regarded as being of extreme urgency. On the eve of Easter 1539 the Consiglio dei Priori of Spoleto devoted numerous sessions to the plan to concentrate the Jews in an outlying part of town, or, secondarily, to forbid them to live on the streets of the

---

[80] On the position and history of the via delle Felici in Spoleto, see A. Gentili, L. Giacchè, B. Ragni, and B. Toscano, *L'Umbria: Manuali per il territorio—Spoleto* (Rome, 1978), 440–1, 482.

[81] See Balletti, *Gli ebrei e gli Estensi*, 169.

[82] 'All the Monti di Pietà arose in response to this prior situation: the desire to do away with usury. In the specific case of the poor, usury was practised particularly by Jews . . . the anti-usury campaign, of itself, was not inspired by racist and antisemitic ideas. It aimed simply at abolishing the monopoly of this form of lending' (A. Ghinato, 'I Monti di Pietà in Umbria', *Atti del VII Convegno di Studi Umbri*, proceedings of a conference held at Gubbio, 18–22 May 1969 (Perugia, 1972). A similar thesis was put forward by Meneghin in his biography of Bernardino da Feltre.

[83] AC Spoleto, Not., Paride di Pierdonato, 112, fos. 184ʳ–186ʳ (26 Feb. 1493).

centre.[84] As one of the priors of that year, Lorenzo Vicenzi, stated: 'Above all it is fitting that measures should be taken so that no Jew shall be allowed to live on the city's main streets and, secondly, that the Jews shall be assigned a special area of residence, chosen by the priors and approved by the citizens.' This time too the proposal was not implemented because of material difficulties; it was put forward again, with the same results, in the days leading up to Holy Week in 1543.[85]

Finally, towards the middle of the sixteenth century, the fate of the Jews became one with that of the gypsies, another category of marginals upon which Christian society, alarmed and suspicious, had decided to try out instruments of discrimination and repression. Moving in from the Rhineland and the Peloponnese, gypsies reached central Europe at the beginning of the fifteenth century. In 1419 they were sighted near Lyon, and by 1427 they had already reached Paris. There were many gypsies at Bologna, and then at Forlì, in 1442.[86] Their presence is attested in Umbria at the end of the fifteenth century; they were expelled from Perugia in 1486 with the pretext, put forward elsewhere in connection with Jews, that they were bearers of the plague; and gypsies found within the city walls were sent to the gallows.[87] To add spice to gypsy hunting, the governors of Perugia stated that 'on finding one of the aforesaid gypsies, it was permissible for all persons . . . to despoil and rob them, and to take possession of the things taken from them, when finding them in the said city or *contado* and district, with no penalty whatsoever'. Despite these measures, the gypsy community did not disband, nor move away from the regions of Umbria where it had previously settled. In 1516 a large group was encamped around Assisi, forming an organized community whose members were known as *fratres de Egypto seu melius zengari*, that is, gypsies or Egyptians, because they came from the Peloponnese or 'little Egypt'.[88] Bracketed by common opinion together with beggars and vagrants, and often with thieves and

[84] AC Spoleto, Rif., 91, fo. 17ʳ (9 Mar. 1539) and fo. 51ʳ (8 Apr. 1539).

[85] Ibid. 2, 2nd ser., fos. 57ʳ, 59ᵛ, 62ᵛ, 64ᵛ (1 Apr. 1543).

[86] See J. C. Schmitt, 'L'Histoire des marginaux'. B. Geremek, 'L'Arrivée des Tsiganes en Italie: De l'assistance à la repression', in G. Politi, M. Rosa, and F. della Peruta (eds.), *Timore e carità: I poveri nell'Italia moderna*, proceedings of the conference on poverty and social assistance in the medieval Italian states, held at Cremona, 28–30 Mar. 1980 (Cremona, 1982), 27–44.

[87] AS Perugia, Editti e Bandi, 2, fo. 23ᵛ (21 Oct. 1486). See A. Grohmann, *La fiera dei morti a Perugia* (Perugia, 1980), 112.

[88] See C. Cenci, *Documentazione di vita assisana*, ii. *1449–1530* (Grottaferrata, 1975), 1054.

criminals in general, towards the middle of the sixteenth century gypsies were in the same boat as Jews, adrift on an ever more storm-tossed sea. In 1552 the Consiglio del Popolo of Spoleto resolved to form a committee to deal with the problem of the presence of Jews and gypsies in the town. While for the Jews it envisaged enforced concentration within one area, for the gypsies the only option was expulsion. But, as we have said, ghettoization and segregation on the one hand, and expulsion on the other, were simply two sides of the same coin with which Christian society, now closed and homogeneous, hoped to deal with minority groups.[89] We are now on the eve of Paul IV's *Cum nimis absurdum* (1555). The building of the walls of the 'Jews' enclosure' of Rome, one of the first real ghettos in Italy or indeed anywhere, marked the definitive collapse of reason in Renaissance Italian society and of its attitude—contradictory in many ways, but generally open and tolerant—towards Jews. In 1569 Pius V expelled Jews from the Papal State, obliging those who remained to be confined in the ghettos of Rome and Ancona. Similar solutions were envisaged for gypsies. In 1566 Cardinal Chamberlain Vitellozzo Vitelli signed the decree expelling the gypsies from the Papal State, while some years later, in 1576, the council of Naples decreed that for them, as for Jews, the only alternative to expulsion was segregation within ghettos.[90]

[89] The committee had to choose 'ubi hebrei debeant habitare in civitate Spoleti . . . et habeant auctoritatem pro zingaris, qui non possunt stare et permanere in territorio spoletino [where the Jews should be allowed to live in the city of Spoleto . . . and have decreed that the gypsies shall not remain and live in the territory of Spoleto]' (AC Spoleto, Rif., 11, 2nd ser., fo. 183ᵛ, 18 Sept. 1552).

[90] See Geremek, 'L'Arrivée des Tsiganes en Italie', 40–1.

9

Merchants and Craftsmen

CARTERS AT SPOLETO, SAFFRON MERCHANTS AT CASCIA

At the beginning of the fifteenth century carters who transported goods and passengers from the city of Spoleto would park their vehicles in the district around Porta Ponzianina, and any passer-by would have noticed that there were many Jews among them. Carters and makers of pack-saddles, with the typically Jewish names of Mosè, Isacco, and Samuele, hired out their goods and conveyances for a daily or weekly rate. We know the names of at least three Jewish carters and one pack-saddle maker who transported goods or hired out their vehicles at Spoleto between 1422 and 1455. Guglielmo da Foligno had a small cart pulled by three nags which he often rented out to the municipality. Two other carters, Deodato di Elia and Mosè, each owned a one-horse cart and transported goods and foodstuffs with a tariff of 10 *soldi* per day or 3 *lire* a week. The pack-saddle-maker was Benedetto da Terni, whose work-shop was near Porta Ponzianina. Other Jewish carters plied their trade in Assisi at this same period; for example, we have the deed of partnership of a firm of Jewish carters signed at Perugia in 1461. This firm, which was to work both within the city and *contado* of Perugia and outside it, was made up of Manuello di Guglielmo da Montefalco and Dattilo di Manuele di Iesi, who had purchased a horse and vehicle for the sum of 4 ducats and committed themselves to dividing the profits equally, once the expenses of the horse's fodder and care had been subtracted.[1] Usually the carters accompanied the vehicle and goods to their destina-tion. The most usual route began outside Porta Ponzianina at Spoleto and climbed towards Vallo di Nera, which was a natural junction for anyone wanting to continue along the via Nursina towards Cerreto—

[1] AC Spoleto, Camerario, Uscita 1422, fos. 11ᵛ, 12ʳ; ibid. 1424, fo. 22ᵛ; ibid. 1428, fo. 2ʳ; ibid. 1431, fo. 15ʳ; ibid. 1453, fo. 34ᵛ; ibid., Entrata 1455, fo. 6ʳ; Toaff, *Jews in Medieval Assisi*, 31–2; AS Perugia, Not., Tomaso di Antonio, 391, fo. 503ᵛ. Jewish carters plied the route from Cesena to the fortress of San Marino during the last part of the 15th cent.; see A. A. Bernardy, 'Les Juifs dans le République de San-Marin du XIVᵉᵐᵉ au XVIIᵉᵐᵉ siècles', *Revue des études juives*, 48 (1904), 251–3.

dominating the upper Valnerina—and reach the three bridges over the Nera at Triponzo. Here the road, whose hairpin bends led up towards Cascia and Norcia divided, one branch passing through Sellano and climbing towards the upland plain of Colfiorito whose strategic position dominated the Marches and Ravenna. Here it met up with the via Plestina running from Foligno towards the duchy of Camerino. The other branch carried on along the bed of the Nera beyond the walled village of Triponzo, and led to Visso and Tolentino in the Marches.[2]

The carters taking the via Nursina would often come upon Jewish merchants from the Umbrian Apennines and the Marches, who went down the Valnerina to reach Spoleto, Terni, and the lower Tiber valley. These were cloth merchants from Camerino and Civitanova, the capsellers from Norcia transporting the characteristic hareskin hats with earmuffs to the market at Piazza Pellicciara at Spoleto, and saffron merchants from Cascia.[3] Saffron, a product of the crocus, was one of the most highly prized of spices, and was traded in small quantities. At Spoleto it was weighed out on the same precision balances used for florins and other gold coins, and towards the mid-fifteenth century it

---

[2] On the road network and traffic in goods around Spoleto in the Middle Ages and Renaissance see G. Fatteschi, *Memorie istoriche-diplomatiche riguardanti la serie de' duchi e la topografia de' tempi di mezzo del Ducato di Spoleto* (Camerino, 1801), 158–61; S. Nessi, *Spoleto, Campello sul Clitunno, Castel Ritaldi, Cerreto, Vallo di Nera, S. Anatolia di Narco, Scheggino* (Perugia, 1974); P. Grassini, 'Tra Roma e Spoleto non c'è più la Somma', *Spoletium*, 10 (1966), 12, 18–26; Gentili *et al.*, *L'Umbria: Manuali per il territorio—Spoleto*; G. Schmiedt, 'Contributo della foto-interpretazione alla conoscenza della rete stradale dell'Umbria nell'Alto Medioevo', *Atti del III Convegno di Studi Umbri*, proceedings of a conference held at Gubbio, 23–7 May 1965 (Perugia, 1966), 177–210; D. A. Bullough, 'La via Flaminia nella storia dell'Umbria', ibid. 211–33. On the activity of carters and muleteers on the roads of the Papal State in the Middle Ages and Renaissance see G. Cherubini, *Signori, contadini, borghesi: Ricerche sulla società italiana del basso medioevo* (Florence, 1974), 552–6; J. Delumeau, *Vita economica e sociale di Roma nel Cinquecento* (Florence, 1979), 25–60.

[3] Around 1470 Jewish merchants from Norcia and Cascia were active and skilled makers and traders of hareskin caps. In 1483 the chief dealer in caps on the marketplace of Foligno was Salomone da Fermo, who lived in Fabriano and Norcia. At the beginning of the 16th cent. a large company, made up of Jewish merchants from Cascia, Norcia, Camerino, and Fabriano, was dealing in wool, velvet, and silk, as well as the characteristic hareskin hats. The merchants' names were Angelo da Cascia, Dattilo da Camerino, Salomone da Poggibonsi, and Shalom da Fabriano; in autumn 1507 the value of their sales registered at Foligno was 700 ducats; AC Cascia, Not., Domenico di Marino di Angelello, 1, coll. 3, fo. 322^r; AC Norcia, Con. e Rif., 13, fo. 129^r; AC Foligno, Not., Taddeo Angelelli, 10, fos. 125^r, 213^r, 219^v; ibid. 12/2, fos. 129^r, 6^v, 8^v; ibid. 22/31, fo. 478^r.

was valued at 2½ to 3 florins per *libbra*.[4] All gifts presented by the Umbrian communes to popes and princes invariably included a certain quantity of saffron. In 1373 the papal governor Gomez Albornoz spoke highly of the quality of Umbrian capers and saffron, while in 1444 pope Eugenius IV obliged a delegation from Spoleto to present him with a tribute in the form of saffron, after Niccolò Piccinino had occupied the city. Severo Minervio tells us approvingly that the people of Spoleto 'get as much corn, wine, and oil as they need from the plain, and have almonds and saffron in abundance'.[5] In the fifteenth century the local saffron market was controlled by the Jews of Cascia, who sold the spice off in considerable quantities at the market-places of Perugia, Spoleto, Civitanova, and Camerino, and also at L'Aquila, which specialized in the saffron trade. The precious spice was taken to these markets on muleback from the merchants' shops in the district of S. Pancrazio and their storehouses in the walled village of Chiavano, carried in sacks never weighing more than 50 *libbre* apiece and whose commercial value varied from 130 to 150 florins.[6] Not infrequently the profits from the sale of this gold in plant form were actually greater than those of the bankers who travelled the same brigand-infested roads with their cargoes of valuable pledges and gold and silver coins.

The carters who took the road southwards from Vallo di Nera would come to S. Anatolia di Narco, from where the road from Monteleone and Leonessa climbed across the Abruzzi Apennines and the borders of the kingdom of Naples. The Vallinarca road, on the other hand, ran along the lower course of the Nera, leading to the walled village of Scheggino, skirting the Benedictine abbey of Ferentillo at the foot of Mount

---

[4] In Spoleto the tiny flowers and saffron were weighed on precision balances and a duty levied by weight; see A. Salzano, *Le finanze e l'ordinamento di Spoleto all'alba del Quattrocento* (Spoleto, 1941), 101–3; R. Rambaldi, 'Aspetti dell'economia spoletana nella seconda metà del XV secolo', Ph.D. thesis, University of Perugia, 1964, fos. 103–4, 115–35; P. Guaffacci, 'Il camerario del comune di Spoleto (secc. XIV–XV)', Ph.D. thesis, University of Perugia, 1970, fos. 86–7.

[5] See Sansi, *Storia del comune di Spoleto*, i. 250–1, ii. 19–20. The passage from Severo Minervio's chronicle, *De rebus gestis atque antiquiis monumentis Spoleti*, is in A. Sansi, *Documenti storici inediti in sussidio allo studio delle memorie umbre* (Foligno, 1879), 17–18.

[6] The main Jewish saffron merchants of Cascia were Salomone di Gaio da Perugia and Aleuccio di Sabato da Civitanova; their intensive activities are documented from the middle of the 15th cent. (AC Cascia, Not., Domenico di Marino di Angelello, 1, coll. 3, fos. 182ᵛ, 193ʳ, 209ʳ, 277ʳ, 343ᵛ, 346ᵛ, 349ʳ, 356ʳ, 364ʳ, 365ʳ, 386ᵛ, etc.). The most important saffron market in Italy was at L'Aquila, and its influence extended as far as Germany; see A. Grohmann, *Le fiere del Regno di Napoli in età aragonese* (Naples, 1969), 79–126.

Solenne, to continue towards Terni in one direction and Rieti in the other. This was the so-called *strada dei panni* (cloth route), constantly travelled by muleteers and carters as they transported their loads of cloth towards the territories of the Marsica and the Sabina and the area around Naples. The merchants of Spoleto, Foligno, and other Umbrian communes had storehouses at Scheggino where they stored their bales of cloth, awaiting the carts which would transport them over the mountain passes. In 1391, when Scheggino fell into the hands of the shepherds and mountain-dwellers of Monteleone who were rebelling against Spoleto, Parruccio Zambolini remarked reproachfully that 'Scheggino and its castle, in the Val di Narco, was taken by the Ghibellines . . . and that place housed a great quantity of cloth brought there . . . by the merchants of Spoleto prior to crossing the mountains, and the greater part of it was lost, for which reason Spoleto quickly took to arms, deeply divided and suspicious'.[7] For over two centuries, from the fourteenth to the beginning of the sixteenth, many of these cloth merchants were Jews, from Spoleto, Foligno, Terni, Perugia, Cascia, Norcia, Trevi, Todi, the communes of the upper Tiber valley, such as Città di Castello, and the Marches. In Perugia from 1383 Jews were enrolled in the guild of the cotton-waste and rag sellers, and had close relations with the wool guild, which they partly financed.[8] Such Jewish merchants often operated in some style: at Foligno and Terni, for example, at the end of the fifteenth century and the beginning of the next, they had set up companies together with Christian traders from Milan and Bergamo, investing thousands of florins in the wool, linen, and cotton trade.[9] The

[7] Parruccio Zambolini, 'Annali de Spuliti', cited in Sansi, *Documenti storici inediti*, 128. See also Sansi, *Storia del Comune di Spoleto*, i. 261–3.

[8] In Sept. 1383 Musetto di Deodato, who lived in the district of Porta S. Susanna, was enrolled in the guild of the cotton-waste dealers and paid an annual due of 2 florins and 4 *soldi* (AS Perugia, Not., Massarello di Pellolo, 15, fo. 88ᵛ). In 1443, also in Perugia, the partners in a firm selling decorative trimmings, both Jews and Christians, were also enrolled in the guild of cotton-waste dealers (AS Perugia, Not., Mariano di Luca di Nino, 113, fo. 22ʳ). Many Perugian Jews dealt in textiles and were members of the old-clothes-sellers' guild (AS Perugia, Giud., Processus, file 3, bundle 3; ibid., file 4, bundle 30). In 1435 when Perugia had once more become Florence's ally after years of hostility, Florentine artists were invited there to instil new life into the wool guild. The huge expenses incurred for the purchase of materials and machinery were partly covered by Jewish loans; see Toaff, *Ebrei a Perugia*, 64.

[9] A large company selling *guarnelli* (material made from tow and cotton waste and used for linings), with a base at Foligno, was formed in 1482 by Abramo da Matelica and the Tanti brothers, merchants from Milan. At Terni in 1514 there was a firm of Jewish and Bergamasque cloth merchants which paid a special tax to the commune (AC Foligno, Not., Taddeo Angelelli, 12/4, fo. 58ʳ; AS Terni, Rif., 511/1, fos. 8ᵛ, 30ᵛ).

communes often turned to them for the execution of big town-planning and building works which required large sums of ready cash. In 1440 the cloth merchant Giacobbe di Isacco received the contract for repairing the walls of Todi; in 1491 Raffaele di Isacco, who traded in wool and owned storerooms and warehouses along the via Nursina, provided materials for the brick paving for the large square of S. Maria at Spoleto.[10] At the end of the fourteenth century Jewish merchants from Urbino traded in cotton waste and imported light cotton veiling to Gubbio and the surrounding region.[11] At this time the Umbrian towns, and Perugia in particular, were important manufacturing centres of *veletti*, a popular and relatively inexpensive material, while the cotton waste usually came from Ancona, where it was one of the main items imported from the Near East.[12] The doctor David de Pomis tells us that in 1527, at the time of the sack of Rome, the troops of Sciarra Colonna had carried off a train of forty mules with a cargo of linen and wool cloth and silver coins weighing 700 *libbre* of refined silver, which his father Isacco, a cloth merchant, had sent from Spoleto along the road which led by way of Vallo di Nera and Cerreto to the duchy of Camerino.[13]

Other merchants, too, travelled the roads of Umbria: along the via Flaminia towards Rome, along the via Francigena towards the fairs of France and the countries of central Europe, along the great road network linking up with the Adriatic coast, along the post-roads running from Spoleto and Foligno to Camerino, Tolentino, Macerata, Recanati, and Ancona on the one hand, and to Fossato, Cagli, Fossombrone, and Fano on the other. They were the corn merchants, who provided the capital of the Papal State with the precious cereals from the rich agricultural provinces of the Marches, Romagna, and Umbria and from the towns of Fabriano, Tolentino, San Severino, Assisi, Foligno, and

[10] AC Todi, Rif., 63, fos. 97ᵛ–98ʳ; AC Spoleto, Depositario 1491–1500, fo. 25ʳ. In the documents Giacobbe di Isacco is described as *notabilis vir Iacob Isahac mercator judeus.*

[11] AC Gubbio, Camerlengato, 2, fo. 6ʳ. See Toaff, 'Ebrei a Gubbio', 159–60.

[12] On the trade in cotton waste and the cotton veiling industry at Perugia between the end of the 14th and beginning of the 15th cents., see F. Melis, *Aspetti della vita economica medievale* (Florence, 1962), 211–12; id., 'Uno sguardo al mercato dei panni di lana a Pisa nella seconda metà del Trecento', in id. (ed.), *Problemi economici dall'antichità ad oggi: Studi in onore di Vittorio Franchini* (Milan, 1959), 81. Cotton waste was brought to the port of Ancona by vessels from Turkey, Cyprus, Syria, and Egypt; see E. Ashtor, 'Il commercio levantino di Ancona nel basso medioevo', *Rivista Storica Italiana*, 88/2 (1976), 214–15, 243–4.

[13] David de Pomis, *Zemach David*, fo. 5ᵃ.

Spoleto. Some of them were Jews, for instance Sabato di Salomone da Nerola, who sent 400 *some* of corn from Foligno to Rome in September 1484, transporting it along the via Flaminia as far as Orte and Borghetto, where the Tiber became navigable.[14] This was a considerable quantity: one cart could carry an average of 1 to 4 *some* of corn, so we may imagine a convoy made up of over 100 vehicles, proceeding in columns along muddy and chaotic roads. The corn was sold at Foligno for 4 florins and 2 silver *bolognini* per *soma*, exclusive of transport, so that Sabato's overall profit would have been in excess of 1,600 florins. At the end of the fifteenth century and the beginning of the sixteenth, we also find Jewish banks in Umbria tending to 'put money on corn'. In other words, the bankers accepted and indeed often asked for the consignment of quantities of corn as pledges for loans or as payment for cash loans. In this latter case, and when the pledge had not been redeemed, they took on the role of corn merchants and exporters, which enabled them to make further and greater profits in periods of frequent and serious famine. At Spoleto at the beginning of the sixteenth century the Jewish bankers made loans to the commune at 7 per cent interest and had themselves paid in corn. Between 1513 and 1522 over 200 *some* of cereal piled up in their storehouses each year, with a value in excess of 800 florins, of which most was probably exported to the Roman market.[15]

CLOTH MERCHANTS, FAIR TRADERS, AND RAG-SELLERS

In the villages and larger Umbrian trading centres, Jewish cloth merchants had workrooms and shops where they received their town and country clientèle. They acquired their stock from the main local fairs, at Perugia, Foligno, Spoleto, Recanati, Macerata, and Senigallia, and sometimes from as far afield as Florence and Ancona. These merchants

[14] AC Foligno, Taddeo Angelelli, 9/1, fos. 132ᵛ, 133ʳ, 169ᵛ. On traffic in corn and cereals in the territories of the Papal State at the beginning of the 16th cent. see Delumeau, *Vita economica*, 25–36. The chronicler Beniamin Nehemia da Civitanova noted that the route taken by the Jewish merchants travelling to Rome from the Marches was the post-road passing through Ancona, Civitanova, Camerino, Foligno, Spoleto, Terni, Narni, Civita Castellana, Borghetto sul Tevere, and Castelnuovo di Porto. See Beniamin Nehemia b. Elnatan da Civitanova, 'Chronicle of Pope Paul IV', 66–9.

[15] AC Spoleto, Rif., 70, fo. 678ʳ; ibid., Camerario, 1514, fo. 95ᵛ; ibid., Rif., 73, fo. 52ᵛ; ibid. 74, fos. 273ʳ, 539ᵛ, 548ʳ.

formed companies which did not only sell woollen, linen, and cotton cloth but also actually wove it themselves.[16] At Perugia in the second half of the fifteenth century we find mention of these merchants being enrolled in the old-clothes guild.[17] The town authorities apparently had complete trust in their account books. As the guild treasurer wrote in 1470, 'these Jewish cloth merchants are not required to present evidence of their sales, because it is customary to have complete trust in their activity; indeed it is common practice in the city of Perugia to consider these traders on a par with old-clothes dealers, and the statutes enjoin that their account books recording the sale of their cloth should be trusted implicitly'.[18] We have information concerning the intensive activity of these city traders, and of their shops, not only at Perugia, the main Umbrian centre, but also at Città di Castello, Foligno, Spoleto, Todi, Norcia, and Cascia from 1430 until 1480.[19] All social classes used their services, but more particularly the country nobility and people of the *contado*, and in this sense their shops were crucially important distribution centres, in the small towns, villages, and *castelli*, for the cloth and fabrics which the cities produced or

---

[16] See e.g. the company *ad artem textendi pannos lini* (in the art of linen cloth weaving) set up in Perugia in 1511 by Bonaiuto da Città di Castello and Samuele di Spagna (AS Perugia, Not., Pacifico di Vico, 348, fo. 462ᵛ).

[17] AS Perugia, Not., Massarello di Pellolo, 15, fo. 88ᵛ; ibid., Bartolo di Lello, 252, fo. 250ʳ; ibid., Massarello di Brunaccio, 397, fo. 228ʳ; ibid., Tobaldo di Paolo di Balduccio, 506, fo. 57ʳ; ibid., Mariano di Luca di Nino, 113, fo. 22ʳ; ibid., Francesco di Giacomo, 206, fo. 202ʳ; ibid., Tolomeo di Niccolò, 78, fo. 640ʳ⁻ᵛ; ibid., Giud., Processus, file 3, bundle 3; ibid., file 4, bundle 30.

[18] AS Perugia, Giud., Processus, file 4, bundle 30 (30 July 1470). In this context it seems that scholars should reconsider the cliché according to which 'the rise of the Italian merchant class progressively edged Jews out of the commercial activities in which they had engaged fairly profitably during the whole of the late Middle Ages, thus becoming excluded from the city craft guilds'; see D. Carpi, 'Alcune notizie sugli ebrei a Vicenza', *Archivio Veneto*, 68 (1961), 18.

[19] In 1475 the merchants Dattilo and Bonaventura di Leone were running a shop selling woollen cloth and camlet (cloth made of goat's hair) at Città di Castello (AC Città di Castello, Not., Angelo di Battista, 6, fo. 248ʳ). In 1482 Abramo da Matelica had a large draper's shop at Foligno and a permanent stall at the Recanati fair (AC Foligno, Not., Taddeo Angelelli, 12/4, fo. 58ʳ); at Spoleto in 1439 Isacco di Elia had a shop near the market-place, selling fabrics (AC Spoleto, Camerario, Uscita 1439, fo. 15ᵛ); at Todi in 1440 the influential merchant Giacobbe di Isacco had a shop selling fine fabrics and silks (AC Todi, Rif., 63, fo. 97ᵛ); at Norcia at the end of the 15th cent. Angelo da Cascia had a large clothes-shop (AC Norcia, Con. e Rif., 13, fo. 129ʳ); in 1473 the dealers Leone da Camerino and Samuele da Civitanova were jointly running a shop selling cloth at Cascia (AC Cascia, Not., Domenico di Marino di Angelello, 2, coll. 4, fo. 268ᵛ).

imported from the great national and international traders. In 1438 the warehouse belonging to Mele dall'Aquila and Sabato da Anagni on Piazza di Sopramuro at Perugia was packed with a vast quantity of goods: woollen cloth worth 130 ducats, linen cloth worth 159 ducats, silks worth 168 ducats, cotton clothes (made of tow and cotton waste) worth 72 ducats, linen clothes worth 27 ducats, and—oddly enough—pepper worth 64 ducats.[20] The materials sold in the shop belonging to Manuele at Porta S. Susanna were more elegant and refined, as befitted the select clientèle for whom they were intended. They included variously decorated velvets and silks, embroidered with silver and pearls, for use by the fashionable tailors and dressmakers of the day, who particularly made clothes for women.[21] A vivid description of day-to-day events in one such emporium—the clothes-shop kept by the Jew Sabatuccio on via Vecchia, a few steps away from the church of S. Donato—is contained in the proceedings of a trial in 1470, when a peasant woman sued the merchant for failing to deliver a bodice she was said to have purchased from him:[22] 'In the month of July of this year, Donna Agnese went to Sabatuccio's shop to buy a bodice. Among the numerous items he had in stock and on show, Sabatuccio showed her a beautiful red doublet [a fine, straight, maroon-coloured jacket for use by a woman]. She tried it on and found it fitted perfectly, in both length and breadth. Seeing that it became her so well, she asked Sabatuccio how much he wanted for it. After lengthy haggling and much talk, they agreed upon the price of 12 *lire*.'

Apart from these settled merchants, there were also itinerant traders, stallholders who attended local markets on saints' days and at fairs; in Umbria there were fairs throughout the year, but particularly in summer. There is extensive documentation on the massive presence of Jews at the fairs of Ognissanti at Perugia and S. Florido at Città di Castello, at those of Assisi, Foligno, and Spoleto, and at the larger fairs in the Marches and the Abruzzi, at Recanati and Senigallia, L'Aquila and Lanciano; but no systematic research into this documentation has as yet been carried out for the late medieval period.[23]

[20] AS Perugia, Not., Bartolo di Lello, 252, fo. 250ʳ.

[21] Ibid., Massarello di Brunaccio, 397, fo. 228ʳ; ibid., Tobaldo di Paolo di Balduccio, 506, fo. 57ʳ.

[22] Ibid., Giud., Processus, file 4, bundle 30 (30 July 1470).

[23] On fairs and their economic function during the Middle Ages see A. Grohmann, *Le fiere del regno di Napoli*, with its extensive bibliography. On fairs in Umbria see G. Mira, 'Prime indagini sulle fiere umbre nel Medioevo', *Studi in onore di Ettore Corbino* (Milan, 1961), 541–62, and Grohmann, *La fiera dei morti*. An

Local fairs offered valuable opportunities for meetings between local and foreign merchants and for the exchange of national and imported goods; they were vital outlets for agricultural produce, cattle, raw materials from the *contado*, and the products manufactured in the towns. Many Jewish merchants followed every stage of the calendar of the fairs of Umbria and the Marches, arranging to meet from one event to another, acquiring wares at the Ognissanti fair at Perugia and paying for them at the Recanati fair, renting 'fair shops', wooden stalls for the seasonal sale of goods at Foligno, Spoleto, and Senigallia, and passing them on to one another if the need arose. Certain fairs were attended by so many Jews that the communes gave them permission to gather together on Saturdays and feast days in one of the stalls, turning it into an improvised synagogue.[24]

Around 1480, a Jewish merchant from the Marches could scarcely contain his enthusiasm at the approach of the Recanati fair, and he shared his emotions with a friend, writing to him in Hebrew: 'In the midst of my sorrows, I am consoled by the thought that the time of abundance and the remission of debts is upon us—the Recanati fair, where the redemption of the earth will be proclaimed . . . and we shall be able to select good-quality wares.'[25] Such stallholders were mainly selling to rural customers with limited needs; their activities took place at the margins of urban life and mainstream trade. Their stalls stocked everything, from low-quality wool and cotton cloth to cast-off clothes, from kitchen hardware to shoddy trimmings, from leather belts to hide

---

excellent general summary on country fairs and their trade is in Heers, *L'Occident aux XIVème et XVème siècles*, 140–7. On the involvement of Jewish merchants in the Ognissanti fair at Perugia, and in the fairs of Recanati, Senigallia, and Lanciano, see Grohmann, *La fiera dei morti*, 61–74; B. Ghetti, 'Gli ebrei e il Monte di Pietà in Recanati nei secoli XV e XVI, 19–20; A. Mancini, *Studi e saggi di storia medioevale del diritto e della economia* (Senigallia, 1943), 35–62, and S. Anselmi (ed.), *Ancona e le Marche nel Cinquecento*, 40 (both of which look at Senigallia); C. Marciani, *Scritti di Storia* (Lanciano, 1974), i. 266–300 (Jews at the fair of Lanciano).

[24] For the synagogue at the fair at Foligno see AC Foligno, Memorie diverse, inventari, ind. 201; for the synagogue at the Lanciano fair see Marciani, *Scritti di Storia*, i. 299–300.

[25] The phrase is quoted in the so-called *epistolario* (correspondence) of Obadiah da Bertinoro, a manuscript in the Biblioteca Casanatese in Rome (Heb. MS Casanatese 220, fo. 140^b, n. Heb. fo. 175^b, which reflects the problems of the mercantile world of the Jewish communities of Umbria and the Marches (Macerata, Cagli, Urbino, Matelica, Fossombrone, Civitanova, Pesaro, S. Ginesio, Fano, Recanati, Fabriano, Amatrice, Sassoferrato, Ascoli, Camerino, Città di Castello, Foligno) in the second half of the 15th cent.

204   *Merchants and Craftsmen*

and velvet bags, from fake jewels to cheap and fussy trinkets. They owned houses in town, at Perugia, Spoleto, and Terni, where they also had their storerooms, but for long periods of the year they were away travelling, semi-nomadic pedlars going from fair to fair, village to village, to farmhouses and *castelli*, cheek by jowl with jugglers, mountebanks, and ice-cream sellers.

As Jacques Heers observes, the pedlar was defined mainly in terms of the kind of life he led: active outside the usual framework of the commercial world of guilds and corporations, his work was closely bound up with the seasonal peasant markets.[26]

Jewish involvement in the economic life of the towns of Umbria in the late Middle Ages was extremely various and many-sided, though it has often been poorly served by studies which overemphasize the activity of bankers at the expense of craftsmen and traders, their less financially successful counterparts. It is now quite clear that not all Jews in central Italy in the fourteenth and fifteenth centuries were lenders on pledge or money traders, nor were they necessarily always linked to these activities in one way or another; the evidence suggests that the owners, managers, and employees of the banks probably only constituted a minority within each Jewish community, even though they had been its original founders. Sporadic but increasingly frequent references bear witness to the presence of Jewish artisans and professionals in a surprising variety of fields: as innkeepers and publicans at Assisi and Perugia,[27] as tailors and shearers at Spoleto and Perugia,[28] as stationers and bookbinders and sellers at Città di Castello and Perugia,[29] as phar-

[26] *L'Occident aux XIVᵉᵐᵉ et XVᵉᵐᵉ siècles*, 145.

[27] See Toaff, *Jews in Medieval Assisi*, 31; AS Perugia, Not., Tolomeo di Niccolò, 403, fo. 33ʳ. See also above, p. 82.

[28] The Jew Ventura, a tailor by profession, was employed by the commune of Spoleto in 1446 (AC Spoleto, Camerario, Uscita 1445–6, fo. 22ᵛ). In 1477 Tobia da Rimini practised as a tailor at Perugia in the district of Porta S. Pietro (AS Perugia, Catasti, group I, book 23, fo. 555ʳ). A company *ad artem cimatorum* (dedicated to the art of shearing) was formed in Perugia in 1473 by the Jew Elia di Dattilo and the Christian Benedetto Grassi (AS Perugia, Not., Guido di Paolo, 70, fos. 210ᵛ–211ʳ). The company was still operating in 1500 (ibid., Pierantonio di Giovanni, 590, fo. 202ᵛ).

[29] In 1511 a Jew from Fabriano, Salomone di Dattilo, opened a bookbinding establishment (*apotheca in arte ligandi libros*) on the Piazza di Sopramuro in Perugia, employing several young apprentices, all Jews: the German Joseph Levita, Mosè di Giacobbe from Fabriano, and Gabriele di Elia and Eliseo di Angelo from Perugia. Salomone was regularly enrolled in the Perugia guild of bookbinders and stationers (AS Perugia, Not., Gianfrancesco di Pietro, 556, fos. 132ʳ, 334ᵛ; ibid., Tolomeo di Niccolò, 406, fo. 307ʳ; ibid., Pietropaolo di Domenico, 571, fos. 299ᵛ, 442ʳ; ibid., Giud., Processus, env. 185, file 17, fo. 1ʳ). In 1515 another Perugian Jew, the bookseller Vitale di Mosè, opened a workshop with his son Giacobbe (AS Perugia, Not.,

macists at Spoleto and Perugia,[30] as ironmongers at Assisi,[31] as mattress-makers at Assisi and Perugia,[32] as carters at Perugia, Assisi, and Spoleto, as pack-saddle-makers at Spoleto,[33] as tanners and leather-dealers at Perugia.[34] Dattilo di Benedetto, a master goldsmith in the district of Porta Eburnea in Perugia, had his shop on the market square, near the church of S. Maria, and was recorded in the land registers in 1366.[35] At Città di Castello in 1431 a Jew named Musetto was making gunpowder for the commune's artillery.[36] At Perugia in 1471 competition from the dancing-master Deodato di Mosè threatened the best-known local expert, the trained dancer Mariotto Marchetti.[37] Deodato apparently ran

---

Ranaldo di Bartolomeo, 567, fos. 229ʳ, 447ʳ). Earlier, from 1507 to 1511, Salomone da Fabriano and Vitale da Perugia had run a firm of bookbinders (AS Perugia, Not., Gianfrancesco di Pietro, 554, fos. 176ʳ, 322ʳ). At the beginning of the 16th cent. a certain bookseller, Bonaventura, had a shop at Città di Castello (AC Città di Castello, Annali Comunali, 57, fo. 166ʳ).

[30] A son of Vitale, a medical officer at Spoleto at the end of the 14th cent., practised as a pharmacist; after converting to Christianity and taking the name Battista, he was elected on several occasions as a *capitano* of the city's guild (AC Spoleto, Rif., 24, fos. 41ʳ, 217ᵛ; ibid., 25, fos. 45ᵛ, 57ʳ, 92ᵛ, 104ʳ). A detailed description of the pharmacist's shop which the Jew Benemato di Lazzaro had opened on the Piazza del Comune in Perugia in 1342 is in AS Perugia, Ospedale di S. Maria della Misericordia, contr. 7, Giovanni di Pero da Porta Sole (11 Dec. 1342).

[31] The blacksmith Gabriele di Angelo was active in Assisi in the second half of the 15th cent. and was one of the last Jews to leave the city in 1487 after their expulsion; see Toaff, *Jews in Medieval Assisi*, 31–2, 71.

[32] A mattress-maker named Dattilo is documented at Assisi towards the middle of the 15th cent., working in the dormitories of the monastery of S. Francesco; see Toaff, *Jews in Medieval Assisi*, 31–2, 76. We find numerous companies of Jewish mattress-makers at Perugia from the end of the 15th to the middle of the 16th cent.; their members included local Jews and others from Prato, Orvieto, Cagli, and Montolmo, and their trade involved 'the art of making mattresses, covers, bolsters, pillows, and all the other accessories needed for beds' (AS Perugia, Not., Giacomo di Cristoforo, 430, fo. 794ʳ; ibid., Ranaldo di Bartolomeo, 568, fo. 55ᵛ; ibid., Giovanni Battista di Niccolò, 1149, fo. 387ʳ and 1151, fo. 337ᵛ).

[33] See the beginning of this chapter.

[34] On Jewish tanners and leather-dealers in Perugia, see below, pp. 208–14.

[35] *Magister Adactolus judeus* is recorded in the land register of Perugia on 22 Apr. 1366 as *auriflex et exercens artem aurificum* (goldsmith practising the art of goldsmiths) (AS Perugia, Catasto antico, group I, book 34, fo. 151ʳ).

[36] See L. Fumi, *Inventario e spoglio dei registri della tesoreria apostolica di Città di Castello*, 12; Toaff, 'Ebrei a Città di Castello', 6, 33.

[37] See Toaff, *Ebrei a Perugia*, 89, 301–2. On the numerous dancing-schools run by Jews in the Renaissance at Parma, Pesaro, Florence, and Venice, including that of the well-known Guglielmo da Pesaro, the author of the important *Trattato dell'arte del ballo* written around 1463, see Roth, *Jews in the Renaissance*, 274–81, and the extensive bibliography on the subject in my *Ebrei a Perugia*.

a successful school of dancing, 'conducting the classes in person and teaching every manner of dance to gentlemen and young ladies'. One century later, one of the most famous dancing-masters in Perugia was once again a Jew, known as 'maestro Leone'.[38] At the beginning of the sixteenth century we also find three Jews from Perugia enrolled in the painters' guild.[39] They were probably not followers or apprentices of Perugino, but part of the anonymous workforce which painted the fronts of houses and made banners for processions. Yet their presence in the guild's registers cannot fail to surprise those scholars who until recently regarded any Jewish presence in the figurative arts as exceptional and limited to eccentrics and converted Jews.[40] In our present state of documentation, it seems idle to speculate as to whether they were artists or house-painters.

Thus if the scene is indeed various and many-sided, its colours none the less vary in intensity. When the Monti di Pietà began to spring up in the towns of Umbria as Minorite preaching gathered momentum in the second half of the fifteenth century and the bankers' charters were systematically denounced, many Jews who had hitherto been involved in the money trade—often handling extremely modest capital sums—found themselves obliged to change profession. It was then that there was an increase in the number of woollen-cloth merchants, who now opened their shops in the towns and enrolled in the guilds of the cotton-waste dealers, shearers, weavers of woollen and linen cloth, and old-clothes dealers, probably purchasing many of their wares at the auction sales of the unredeemed pledges from the Monti di Pietà.[41] There were also artisans enrolled in the guilds of mattress-makers, inn-keepers, tanners, leather-dealers, drapers, stationers, booksellers, and waste-paper dealers, as well as of those who engaged in less legitimate activities, making playing-cards and dice.[42] In 1515 at Perugia an

[38] AS Perugia, Not., Giovanni Maria Senesi, 1661, fo. 196ᵛ (29 July 1574).

[39] Giacobbe di Vitale, Angelo di Elia, and David di Sabatuccio, whose names appear in the years 1507–8 among those enrolled in the guild and as paying their dues. See Gnoli, *Pittori e miniatori nell'Umbria*, 29, 130; Toaff, *Ebrei a Perugia*, 151–2, 164–5, 302–3.

[40] See Roth, *Jews in the Renaissance*, 191–5.

[41] See Toaff, *Ebrei a Perugia*, 73.

[42] On Jewish ragsellers in Perugia at the end of the 16th cent. see AS Perugia, Not., Giovanni Battista di Simone, 971, fo. 464ʳ. In 1508 a Christian artisan from Verona, Bianchino Bernardi, was called to Perugia by the Jewish innkeeper Vitale, whose tavern was on vicolo della Salsa, to form a company to manufacture playing-cards (*societas ad artem cartarum ad ludendum*); AS Perugia, Not., Benedetto di Massarello, 541, fo. 140ʳ.

attempt was made—probably unsuccessfully—to set up a Hebrew printing shop. In the winter of that year Giacobbe di Vitale, bookseller and bookbinder by profession, acquired printer's type and presses from a craftsman from Verona, but we do not know whether he ever put them at the service of a Jewish printing shop.[43] In this period many Jews who became rag merchants and second-hand clothes dealers often signed contracts bearing the high-sounding title of 'charters', which had previously been the privilege of the far wealthier Jewish bankers and doctors called to the service of the communes and *signorie*. At Trevi Jews had a monopoly on the sale of rags each year from 1475 to 1561, that is, during the period preceding their definitive exodus from the town.[44] They also often received the tax on wine dregs, whose tartar and tannin content was useful in dyeing and tanning.[45] Other Jews had a monopoly on *strazzeria* (rags) at Cascia from 1473 to 1536, at Spoleto from 1471 to 1551, and at Perugia from 1549 to 1560.[46] In the ragpicker's charter which Abramo da Camerino signed with the commune of Trevi in 1475 for a price of 28 florins, the Jew was granted the exclusive right to collect and buy rags in the town and *contado*, and to take his cart to the market of S. Maria delle Lacrime on the first Sunday of each month, without let or hindrance from the municipal authorities.[47]

Sometimes real firms of second-hand clothes dealers were formed,

[43] Ibid., Gianfrancesco di Pietro, 556, fo. 334ᵛ (10 Dec. 1515).

[44] AC Trevi, Tre Chiavi, env. 9, reg. 141. fo. 30ʳ; ibid., env. 10, reg. 164, fo. 74ʳ; ibid., env. 13, reg. 185, fos. 35ʳ and 175ʳ and reg. 187, fos. 34ʳ, 85ʳ, 132ᵛ, 194ʳ, 195ʳ, 251ʳ, and 265ᵛ; ibid., env. 17, reg. 256, fos. 20ᵛ and 74ᵛ; ibid., env. 20, reg. 289, fos. 114ᵛ, 159ᵛ, and 241ʳ; ibid., env. 21, reg. 319, fos. 40ᵛ, 208ᵛ, and 264ᵛ; ibid., env. 22, reg. 330, fo. 98ʳ and reg. 343, fos. 4ᵛ, 7ʳ, 235ᵛ, and 304ᵛ. The Jews who succeeded one another in the contract for the tax on rags at Trevi over a period of almost ninety years are named as Angelo da Camerino, Manuele, Benedetto di Mosè, Giuseppe, Michele, Gabriele di Michele, and Deodato.

[45] AC Trevi, Tre Chiavi, env. 13, reg. 187, fos. 258ʳ and 265ᵛ; ibid., env. 17, reg. 256, fo. 63ᵛ.

[46] AC Cascia, Not., Domenico di Marino di Angelello, 2, coll. 4, fo. 268ᵛ; ibid. 3, coll. 5, fo. 55ᵛ; ibid., Con. e Rif., 3, fo. 224ᵛ; AC Spoleto, Camerario, 1471, fo. 17ʳ; ibid. 1476, fo. 4ᵛ; ibid. 1478, fo. 24ʳ; ibid. 1479–80, fo. 26ʳ; ibid. 1524, fo. 1ʳ; ibid., Not., Eusebio Botontei, 181/1, fo. 24ʳ; AS Perugia, Not., Giovanni Battista di Niccolò, 1155, fo. 201ʳ; ibid. 1156, fo. 614ʳ; ibid., Francesco Gualterotti, 1370, fo. 79ᵛ; ibid., Giovanni Andrea di Antonio, 1573, fo. 507ʳ. These itinerant *stracciarii* (rag-dealers), who enjoyed a monopoly on rag-picking throughout the Umbrian territories, came from various towns in Umbria, the Marches, the Abruzzi, Emilia, and Romagna: Perugia, Spoleto, Foligno, Narni, Cerreto, Castel del Lago, Cascia, Norcia, L'Aquila, Camerino, Civitanova, Macerata, Ascoli, Ancona, Rimini, and Ferrara.

[47] AC Trevi, Tre Chiavi, env. 9, reg. 141, fo. 30ʳ.

with capital totalling hundreds of florins, and active over an area wide enough to take in many towns and rural centres. One of these financial trusts, set up in Spoleto around the middle of the sixteenth century with deeds drawn up by Christian notaries in Latin and by the rabbinical authority in Hebrew, had a dozen partners, all second-hand clothes dealers and pedlars who operated at Spoleto, Narni, Castel del Lago, L'Aquila, and Ascoli.[48] Given that the deed of enrolment required each partner to contribute a sum varying from 50 to 60 florins to the common capital, the funds administered by this company of rag merchants from Umbria, the Marches, and the Abruzzi were very healthy, and must have exceeded 500 florins.

THE LEATHER MARKET AT PERUGIA

In the Middle Ages and Renaissance, Perugia and the other Umbrian towns practised a thriving trade in raw and dressed hides, with numerous workshops linked more or less directly to leather and its associated industries, especially shoemaking and tanning. The centre of the Italian leather trade in the Middle Ages was Pisa, which imported large quantities of skins from Spain, southern France, and the Maghreb, and housed a flourishing industry that served a vast hinterland, including much of Tuscany and Florence, and whose influence was felt as far away as Perugia.[49] Pisa's leather guild was possibly even more important than its wool guild in the fourteenth century; next in importance came Genoa and Venice, ports of call for Spanish, Portuguese, and French ships, but also for schooners from Southampton, Bristol, and Flanders, laden with dressed leather and dried skins.[50] Ancona was one of the other Italian

48 AC Spoleto, Not., Eusebio Botontei, 181/1, fo. 24ʳ.

49 See A. Doren, *Storia economica dell'Italia nel Medioevo* (Padua, 1936), 288; D. Herlihy, *Vita economica e sociale d'una città italiana nel Medioevo: Pisa nel Duecento* (Pisa, 1973), 17, 61; J. Heers, *Le Travail au Moyen Âge* (Paris, 1968), 54–5; G. Volpe, *Studi sulle istituzioni comunali a Pisa: Città e contado, consoli e podestà, secoli XII–XIII* (Florence, 1970), 253–5; A. A. Ruddock, *Italian Merchants and Shipping in Southampton, 1270–1600* (Southampton, 1951), 76; T. Antoni, 'I costi industriali di un'azienda conciaria della fine del Trecento (1384–88)', *Bollettino Storico Pisano*, 42 (1973), 1–3.

50 See Ruddock, *Italian Merchants*, 76; G. Luzzatto, *Storia economica di Venezia dall' XI al XVI secolo* (Venice, 1961), 54, 65, 175–6, 197; F. Melis, *Documenti per la storia economica dei secoli XIII–XVI* (Florence, 1972), 304–8; J. Heers, *Gênes au XVᵉᵐᵉ siècle: Activité économique et problèmes sociaux* (Paris, 1961), 368, 462–4; id., 'Il commercio nel Mediterraneo alla fine del secolo XIV e nei primi anni del XV', *Archivio Storico Italiano*, 113 (1955), 169–70, 173, 178–9.

centres which attracted a flourishing market in local and imported leather, which came via Dubrovnik, on ships from the Peloponnese and the Aegean islands.[51] Here merchants could buy raw hides and semi-dressed leather, imported from the regions around the Black Sea, from Tana at the mouth of the Don, from Caffa in the Crimean peninsula, from Constantinople, the Balkan peninsula, and Romania.

As Federico Melis has noted,[52] Perugia and the other neighbouring Umbrian towns, particularly Foligno and Spoleto, were major junction-points on the main routes of the great international leather trade. Of the two main routes that passed through Perugia, one came from the Tyrrhenian Sea via Pisa, and the other from the Adriatic via Ancona and Fabriano. Perugia was an important centre for treating and trading in pelts as early as the fourteenth century, and this importance increased during the two following centuries.[53] Jewish activity in the trade and manufacture of leather is documented from the beginning of the sixteenth century. In 1514 Abramo da Ventura and Vitale di Mosè, two local Jews, set up a company for the tanning and dressing of hide.[54] The firm cannot have been very large, as it only treated hides from rural stock-farms destined for local markets. These were mainly lambskin, the so-called *cernie* of raw sheep- and goatskin, and cowhide which the two Perugian tanners imported from Marsciano, Compignano, and San Valentino in the countryside bordering the Orvieto region. The work-shop's suppliers also included some of the chief Perugian leather mer-

[51] On the leather trade at Ancona and in the Marches see P. Earle, 'The Commercial Development of Ancona, 1479–1551', *Economic History Review*, NS 22 (1969), 33–5; F. Gestrin,'Il commercio dei pellami nelle Marche del XV e della prima metà del XVI secolo', in S. Anselmi (ed.), *Le Marche e l'Adriatico orientale: Economia, società, cultura dal XII secolo al primo ottocento*, proceedings of a conference held at Senigallia, 10–11 Jan. 1976 (Ancona, 1978), 255–76. On the importation of cordwain to Ancona from the Peloponnese see Anselmi, *Ancona e le Marche nel Cinquecento*, 34–6. On the commercial activities of the Jews of Ancona during the late Middle Ages see E. Ashtor, 'Gli ebrei di Ancona nel periodo della repubblica', in Anselmi (ed.), *Le Marche e l'Adriatico orientale*, 331–68.

[52] See Melis, *Documenti per la storia economica*, 151.

[53] On the leather trade in the Middle Ages at Perugia see the excellent and exhaustive contribution by R. Pierotti, 'Aspetti del mercato e della produzione a Perugia fra la fine del secolo XIV e la prima metà del XV: La bottega di cuoiame di Niccolò di Martino di Pietro', *Bollettino della Deputazione di Storia Patria per l'Umbria*, 72/1 (1975), 79–185 and 73/1 (1976), 1–131. On the trade in and dressing of hides in the other Umbrian centres in the late medieval period see Salzano, *Le finanze e l'ordinamento di Spoleto*, 101–3; Menichetti, *Le corporazioni delle arti e mestieri medioevali a Gubbio*, 111–25.

[54] AS Perugia, Not., Pietropaolo di Ludovico, 824, fo. 75r (23 Mar. 1514).

chants.[55] In 1552 another Jew, Vitale di Simone, from Valentano in the Viterbo region, opened a tanning and dressing workshop in Perugia whose activity is documented over a couple of years.[56] Vitale was enrolled in the shoemakers' guild: his output, too, seems to have been modest, being destined mainly for the local market. He bought his raw materials cheaply from the main Perugian dealers: cowhide, lamb- and sheepskin, and dried and shaggy pelts.

From the 1540s the leather trade at Perugia and the other Umbrian centres, particularly in the better-quality skins, was supplied by Ancona. Cordwain, for example, a special type of leather treated according to the Andalusian tradition and made from hides imported from the Near East, was acquired largely by Jewish wholesalers in Ancona and other centres in the Marches—Pesaro, Osimo, Matelica, Fermo, Iesi, Cagli, and Camerino—and sent by them to Umbrian artisans. From 1540 to 1570 a firm of Jewish traders, including various members of the Stella, Romano, and Tedeschi families from Ancona, the Moscati from Osimo, and other traders from Pesaro and Matelica, provided considerable quantities of cordwain for the shoemakers of Perugia and Spoleto. The firm's chief members were Aron di Isacco Stella and Mosè di Salomone Romano and his sons: they went to the Umbrian centres to sell their wares, usually packed in bales of ninety-six pelts apiece or in bundles of ten, and to arrange the conditions of transport. At this period the price of a bundle of cordwain was around 5 *scudi*. In November 1540, for example, a Perugian shoemaker, Marcantonio Mariotti, was sold twelve bundles of cordwain for 60 *scudi* by Mosè Romano and his partners.[57] The same quantity of treated leather was purchased in December 1550 by an artisan from Spoleto belonging to the firm of Aron di Stella, and here too the agreed price was 60 *scudi*.[58] In January 1554 Aron di Isacco Stella supplied sixty large cordwain skins to this same Marcantonio Mariotti for 30

[55] AS Perugia, Not., Gianfrancesco di Pietro, 557, fo. 390ʳ (23 June 1514).

[56] Ibid., Giovanni Andrea di Antonio, 1573, fos. 46ᵛ, 111ᵛ, 112ʳ (25 Oct. 1552–29 Aug. 1553). Vitale da Valentano was enrolled in the *ars coraminis* (art of leather-work) and paid his dues. Earlier, in 1544, another Jew from Perugia, Abramo di Angelo, had a workshop for tanning goatskin (AS Perugia, Francesco Patrizi, 1326, fo. 1774ʳ, 26 Dec. 1544).

[57] Ibid., Giovanni Maffani, 560, fo. 51ᵛ (12 Nov. 1540). The members of the company of Jewish merchants included Mosè di Salomone Romano da Ancona, his brother Davide, and his son Sabato, as well as Rubino di Lazzaro, also from Ancona.

[58] AC Spoleto, Not., Bernardino di Pierlorenzo, 165, fo. 108ʳ (17 Dec. 1550). Other members of Aron di Isacco Stella's firm were David di Salomone da Pesaro and another merchant from Ancona, Vita di Viviano.

scudi.[59] These deliveries followed no particular seasonal pattern, but occurred throughout the year; the number of items in each load was always strictly limited, with a value varying from 15 to 80 *scudi*.[60]

From 1570 until the end of the century there was a marked rise in the export of hides and leather by Jewish merchants, particularly to Perugia; indeed, we gain the impression that the market was largely monopolized by them. Carts carrying these skins—starting from the port of Ancona and usually taking the post-road to Foligno, via Iesi and Fabriano, then the via Flaminia, with its turnings to Assisi and Perugia—arrived more and more frequently, and the quantity of goods carried in each individual load became larger. In this sense the Perugian market confirms observations made in connection with the fairs of Umbria, the Marches, and the Abruzzi area in the sixteenth century, when Jewish traders from the Marches 'had assumed a virtual monopoly in the sale of leather'.[61]

The partners in one firm which was very active in Perugia at this time were the merchants Leone di Laudadio da Iesi, Sabato Levi da Ancona, Dattilo di Sabato da Fermo, and Salomone di Sabato da Cagli, with their respective sons and relatives.[62] Towards the end of the century they

---

[59] AS Perugia, Not., Francesco Patrizi, 1345, fo. 132r (24 Jan. 1554). Giuseppe Moscati da Osimo and Vita di Salomone Tedeschi da Ancona appear as partners in the firm of Aron di sacco Stella.

[60] On 8 Feb. 1559 Vita di Durante da Ancona sent a load of cowhide to Perugia worth 37 *scudi* (AS Perugia, Not., Giovanni Maria Senesi, 1643, fo. 83r); on 11 Jan. 1563 Angelo di Salomone Tedeschi da Ancona and Isacco di Lazzaro da Matelica sold cow- and goat-hides at Perugia worth 19 *scudi* (ibid., Simonetto di Eusebio, 1123, fo. 858r); on 17 June 1566 these two merchants, in partnership with Mosè di Sabato Romano, sent a load of cordwain worth 77 *scudi* to Perugia (ibid., Amico Bonamici, 1400, fo. 196v).

[61] See Marciani, *Scritti di Storia*, 281. Some scholars maintain that towards the middle of the 16th cent. the monopoly on importing cordwain to Ancona and on trade in these skins in the regions of central Italy was in the hands of Portuguese Jews living in Ancona; see Gestrin, 'Il commercio dei pellami', 255–76; V. Bonazzoli, 'Ebrei italiani, portoghesi, levantini sulla piazza commerciale di Ancona intorno alla metà del Cinquecento', in G. Cozzi (ed.), *Gli ebrei e Venezia (secoli XIV–XVIII)*, proceedings of an international conference organized by the Istituto della Storia della Società e dello Stato Veneziano and the Cini Foundation, Venice, 5–10 June 1983 (Milan, 1987), 734.

[62] The following examples give sales of skins by this firm to Perugian shoemakers between 1579 and 1585. 20 Feb. 1579, sale of cordwain worth 98 *scudi* (AS Perugia, Not., Marcello Petrogalli, 1900, fo. 168r); 7 Nov. 1580, sale of cowhide worth *c*.31 *scudi* (ibid., Fulvio Fustini, 2193, fo. 287r), 16 Jan. 1581, sale of leather worth 71 *scudi* (ibid., Evangelista Evangelisti, 1817, fos. 38v–40r); 4 July 1585, sale of cordwain worth *c*.171 *scudi* (ibid., Silverio Rettabeni, 2481, fo. 222v and 2482, fo. 411r).

were joined by two other Jews from Ancona, Leone di Aron Cremisi and Leone Camerini.[63] Around 1590 there is also evidence of an attempt by a firm of Levantine Jewish merchants resident in Ancona to break into the Perugian leather trade, in competition with the Italian Jewish merchants. But the partners in this enterprise—Jacob Bacanin and Abramo Soria—ceased operations after the odd exploratory consignment of goods, leaving the field clear for the Jewish merchants from the Marches, who then dominated the trade until the beginning of the seventeenth century.[64]

We may gain some idea of the overall turnover in goods and cash achieved by the firm of Leone da Iesi and his partners through their imports to the Perugian market because we know that over one-and-a-half years, from June 1587 to December 1588, they imported hides to an overall value of around 1,300 *scudi* (see Table 9.1). These were largely cordwain, sometimes together with lesser quantities of cowhide and sheepskin. In the months of December 1587 and January 1588 alone, Leone da Iesi sold skins for a value of 615 *scudi* to shoemakers in Perugia, sending seven vehicles from Ancona with a load of fourteen bales of leather (about 1,350 skins). Part of the payment, in cash, was made to one of the firm's representatives, who went to Perugia to draw up the deed of sale for the goods, while the final settlement by the shoemaker would take place during the Recanati fair or, more often, during the

---

[63] The following list, almost certainly incomplete, gives sales on the Perugian market-place of skins by the Jewish merchants of Ancona between 1589 and 1602. The firm was made up of Sabato di Salomone da Cagli, his sons Salomone and Alfonso and his nephew Mosè, Isacco di Sabato Levi da Ancona and his cousin Chaim di Bonaiuto Levi, Israel di Sabato da Fermo and his brother Samuele, Leone Camerini, and Leone di Aron Cremisi. 9 Nov. 1589, sale of leather for 147 *scudi* (AS Perugia, Not., Ascanio Ugolini, 2120, fo. 395ʳ; 12 Feb. 1591, sale of leather for 33 *scudi* (ibid., Silverio Rettabeni, 2487, fo. 16ʳ); 18 Mar. 1591, sale of 130 cordwain skins for *c.*60 *scudi* (ibid., Contulo Contuli, 1962, fo. 167ᵛ); 7 Jan. 1592, sale of 300 cordwain skins for 129 *scudi* (ibid., Fulvio Faustini, 2246, fo. 32ʳ); 22 May 1592, sale of 140 cordwain skins for *c.*68 *scudi* (ibid., Agabito Toti, 2703, fo. 129ᵛ); 27 May 1592, sale of cordwain skins for 142 *scudi* (ibid., Orazio Franceschini, 2697, fo. 20ʳ); 20 July 1593, sale of leather for 68 *scudi* (ibid., Lorenzo Ferretti, 2550, fo. 170ʳ); 20 July 1593, sale of cordwain skins for 117½ *scudi* (ibid.); 28 Feb. 1595, sale of leather for 55 *scudi* (ibid., Ascanio Ugolini 2127, fo. 72ᵛ); 6 Nov. 1596, sale of cordwain skins for 23 *scudi* (ibid., Silverio Rettabeni, 2488, fo. 340ᵛ); 16 Jan. 1598, sale of cowhide for 47 *scudi* (ibid. 2490, fo. 118ʳ); 9 May 1602, sale of leather for 15 *scudi* (ibid., Antonio Grisaldi, 1723, fo. 85ʳ).

[64] On 12 July 1590 Jacob Bacanin, his son Jehudà, and Abramo Soria, Levantine merchants from Ancona, sold a Perugian shoemaker a consignment of leather valued at 41 *scudi* (AS Perugia, Not., Francesco Torelli, 2043, fo. 381ʳ).

TABLE 9.1 The Jewish merchants of Ancona and the Umbrian leather trade: sales to Perugian shoemakers

Date	Seller	Buyer	Goods	Price
1587				
10 June	Leone di Laudadio da Iesi Sabato Levi Dattilo di Sabato da Fermo Israel di Sabato da Fermo	Bonifacio Olivieri	cordwain skins	170 *scudi*
23 June	Israel di Sabato da Fermo	Giovanni Nicola da Montefalco	17 bales of cordwain	72 *scudi*, 20 *baiocchi*
10 July	Israel di Sabato da Fermo	Nicola and Michelangelo Pellegrini	cordwain	47 *scudi*
22 Dec.	Israel di Sabato da Fermo	Francesco and Cesare Fiorenzi	720 cordwain skins	359 *scudi*, 20 *baiocchi*
1588				
5 Jan.	Salomone di Sabato da Cagli	Piermatteo Vitali	4 bales of cordwain	192 *scudi*
5 Jan	Salomone di Sabato da Cagli Alfonso di Sabato da Cagli (father and son)	Nicola and Michelangelo Pellegrini	12 bales of cordwain	62 *scudi*, 40 *baiocchi*
5 July	Sabato Levi Dattilo di Sabato da Fermo Israel di Sabato da Fermo	Giovanni Antonio Radolini	cordwain	60 *scudi*
4 Oct.	Leone di Laudadio da Iesi Israel di Sabato da Fermo Samuele di Sabato da Fermo Salomone di Sabato da Cagli	Mencio Vincenzi	leather	68 *scudi*
3 Nov.	Salomone di Sabato da Cagli	Sebastiano Nicolai	150 cordwain skins	72 *scudi*, 75 *baiocchi*
	Salomone di Sabato da Cagli	Fabio Ippoliti	cordwain and sheepskins	52 *scudi*, 50 *baiocchi*
7 Nov.	Salomone di Sabato da Cagli	Ludovico Sebastiani	leather	108 *scudi*

Source: AS Perugia, Not., Angelo Tetii, 1621, fo. 400ʳ; ibid., Evangelista Evangelisti, 1817, fo. 100ᵛ; ibid., Simonetto Coppoli, 2401, fo. 233ᵛ and 2403, fo. 39ʳ; ibid., Antonio Grisaldi, 1721, fo. 267ʳ; ibid., Francesco Torelli, 2061, fo. 165ᵛ; ibid., Giuseppe Masci, 2599, fo. 133ʳ; ibid., Lorenzo Ferretti, 2547, fos. 326ᵛ–330ʳ.

fair at Foligno, whose most important sessions were during July and September.[65] The clients of the Jewish merchants on the market-place at Perugia included local artisans (thirty or so firms of shoemakers), but also craftsmen from further afield, who went there to stock their workshops with dressed leather. They came from various towns in Umbria and the Marches, such as Assisi, Montefalco, Fabriano, and San Severino, and even from important Tuscan centres such as Prato.[66] The outlets for the Jewish firms who dealt in hides and leather thus extended over a very wide area and were not limited merely to the market-place of Perugia. In this sense evidence of the continuity of a considerable Jewish presence in the commercial life of the Umbrian towns, over thirty years after their official expulsion from the region, tallies entirely with the observations made to pope Clement XI by the rulers of Perugia at the beginning of the eighteenth century, when they pleaded the cause of the Jews' permanent return to the city: 'Having reflected upon the positive and negative aspects of the matter, the positive would seem to outweigh the negative, with the conclusion that said city cannot continue to be without the Jews.'[67]

[65] AS Perugia, Evangelista Evangelisti, 1817, fo. 100ᵛ; ibid., Simonetto Coppoli, 2401, fo. 233ᵛ and 2403, fo. 39ʳ; ibid., Antonio Grisaldi, 1721, fo. 267ʳ; ibid., Francesco Torelli, 2061, fo. 165ʳ.

[66] In Feb. 1559 a shoemaker from San Severino acquired cowhide worth 37 *scudi* at Perugia from the merchants of Ancona (AS Perugia, Not., Giovanni Maria Senesi, 1643, fo. 83ʳ). In June 1587 a shoemaker from Montefalco bought seventeen bundles of cordwain worth *c.*75 *scudi* from the Jews in Perugia (ibid., Evangelista Evangelisti, 1817, fo. 100ᵛ). In summer 1590 a tanner from Fabriano bought leather worth 41 *scudi* from the Jews (ibid., Francesco Torelli, 2043, fo. 381ʳ). In May 1602 a shoemaker from Assisi bought cow- and goathide worth 15 *scudi* from Israel da Fermo and his partners (ibid., Antonio Grisaldi, 1723, fo. 85ʳ). In July 1585 a merchant from Prato went to Perugia and ordered a load of skins worth 170½ *scudi* from the firm of Leone da Fermo and Israel da Iesi (ibid., Silverio Rettabeni, 2481, fo. 222ᵛ and 2482, fo. 411ʳ).

[67] See Toaff, 'Una supplica degli ebrei di Lippiano alla città di Perugia', in Y. Colombo, U. Nahon, and G. Romano (eds.), *Scritti in memoria di Attilio Milano* (Rome, 1970), 452.

10

Doctors and Surgeons

THE QUEST FOR THE MEDICAL CONTRACT

FROM the mid-fourteenth century until the second half of the fifteenth, every Umbrian commune of any importance is documented as employing one Jewish doctor, or indeed several. From Trevi to Amelia, from Spello to Montone, from Spoleto to Città di Castello, from Assisi to Foligno, from Fratta to Narni, from Terni to Perugia, public records, notarial deeds, and contracts in Hebrew or Latin, all bear witness to the presence and activity of a host of Jewish doctors, hired by the communes to treat the people of any given town and *contado*. The practice appears to have been widespread throughout Italy, and its roots are to be sought less in the supposed Jewish penchant for medical studies than in the fact that such studies were virtually the only ones to which Jews had access in the Italian universities of the time.[1] Furthermore, the privileges and prestige which often accompanied the medical profession constituted an appreciable attraction for Jews in search of a social standing that might exempt them from the restrictions that went with their identity. Such advantages included above all the right of citizenship, with its attendant privileges, primarily that of being able to acquire property and enter it in the town's land register; exemption from payment of city tributes and

---

[1] Useful general works on Jewish doctors include the classic studies by E. Carmoly, *Histoire des médecins juifs anciens et modernes* (Brussels, 1844); Friedenwald, *The Jews and Medicine*; id., *Jewish Luminaries in Medical History* (Baltimore, Md., 1946). See also important additions by J. Shatzmiller, 'Notes sur les médecins juifs en Provence au Moyen-Âge', *Revue des études juives*, 128 (1969), 259–66; id., 'Doctors and Medical Practice in Germany around the Year 1200: The Evidence of Sefer Hasidim', *Journal of Jewish Studies*, 33, essays in honour of Y. Yadin (1982), 583–93; id., 'On Becoming a Jewish Doctor in the High Middle Ages', *Sefarad*, 43 (1983), 239–50; id., 'Doctors and Medical Practices in Germany around the Year 1200: The Evidence of Sepher Asaph', *Proceedings of the American Academy for Jewish Research*, 50 (1983), 149–64. For the situation in Italy in particular see C. Roth, 'The Qualifications of Jewish Physicians in the Middle Ages', *Speculum*, 28 (1953), 834–43; id., *Jews in the Renaissance*, 213–42. On the legal position of the Jewish doctor in medieval and Renaissance Italy see esp. V. Colorni, 'Sull'ammissibilità degli ebrei alla laurea anteriormente al secolo XIX', *La Rassegna Mensile di Israel*, 16, essays in honour of R. Bachi (1950), 202–16; id., *Gli ebrei nel sistema del diritto comune*, 28–31.

special taxes, authorization to carry defensive weapons; and dispensation from wearing the distinctive badge. In special cases it might bring with it the right to teach in the city university, a privilege enjoyed, for example, by Musetto di Guglielmo, professor of medicine at the University of Perugia from 1413 to 1417.[2] Several years earlier the rulers of the city had solemnly granted him the right of citizenship, further extended to his family and descendants with the following flattering justification: 'since maestro Musetto the Jew, living in the city of Perugia, is a courteous and upright person, and a doctor highly versed in the art of surgery, who practises his profession to the benefit of all citizens, prescribing excellent and effective measures and treatments which have earned him fame and well-deserved credit, we see fit to admit him to enjoyment of the privileges of Perugian citizenship.'[3] On previous occasions, too, doctors had been in the forefront of the Perugian Jews who obtained citizenship, for instance Gaudino di Bonaventura, *cerusico* (surgeon) to the commune from 1351, and Musetto di Salomone, its medical officer some years later.[4] In the second half of the fourteenth century Sabatuccio di Manuele da Roma, a surgeon from Assisi, enjoyed the rights of citizenship together with his sons; they were also authorized to own landed property and to bear arms.[5] Citizenship was granted in 1360 to Aleuccio di Dattolino, the surgeon at Spello, and also, in the years immediately following, to Vitale di Salomone, Ventura di Dattilo, and Guglielmo di Vitale, all Jews of Roman origin, medical officers respectively at Spoleto, Città di Castello, and Trevi, who were exempt from payment of city taxes.[6]

[2] AS Perugia, Conservatori della Moneta, 36, Entrate 1412–13, fo. 25ʳ. See Majarelli and Nicolini, *Il Monte dei Poveri di Perugia*, 74–5.

[3] AS Perugia, Con. e Rif., 202, fos. 19ʳ–20ᵛ (24 Feb. 1400); ibid., Catasto Antico, group 1, book 11, fo. 549ʳ (6 Aug. 1400). See Toaff, *Ebrei a Perugia*, 82, 269–73.

[4] AS Perugia, Catasto Antico, group 1, book 1, fo. 175ᵛ. See A. Rossi, 'Gaudino di Bonaventura, Albo dei professori nel terzo quarto del secolo XIV', *Giornale di erudizione artistica*, 6 (1877), 252; F. Momigliano, 'Un ebreo professore di medicina a Perugia nel secolo XIV', *Il Vessillo Israelitico*, 65 (1918), 384–7; Toaff, *Ebrei a Perugia*, 32–3. Musetto di Salomone and Gaudino di Bonaventura are recorded in the land registers in 1367 with the title of doctor. Gaudino is documented as active in Perugia as early as 1351 and continued to practise at least until the end of 1381. In 1367 he was described in the documents as a 'doctor authorized to practise the art of medicine and surgery in the city of Perugia and its surrounding district'.

[5] AC Assisi, P, Bollettari, reg. 3, fo. 41ʳ (6 July 1365); ibid., H, Rif., reg. 6, file 2, fo. 13ʳ (15 July 1383). See Toaff, *Jews in Medieval Assisi*, 32–6.

[6] AS Spello, Stat., B1, 1. IV, ch. 104, fo. 126ʳ; ibid., B2, 1. IV, ch. 104, fo. 175ʳ (1360); ibid., Not., env. 1, Antonio di Andreuccio di Bartolo, 1, fo. 79ʳ (27 Oct. 1376); AC Spoleto, Camerario, Uscite anni 1391–1406 (27 July 1391–27 Dec. 1406);

If the reasons which led many Italian Jews to embark upon a medical career in the Middle Ages appear fairly obvious, it is not always quite so clear why these towns and cities should have preferred to employ Jews rather than Christians as doctors. Setting aside the theory that Jewish doctors were preferred because of their supposed superior professional skills, I will look instead at the concrete factors which, in my opinion, often favoured the Jewish doctor and encouraged communes to employ him. The examination of dozens of medical contracts with their accompanying orders for payment, recorded in the municipal records, reveals without a shadow of doubt that the Jewish doctor usually cost far less than his Christian colleague. Granting a Jew a contract to work as a general practitioner (*fisico*), or surgeon (*cerusico*), committed the commune to an expense which rarely exceeded 25 florins a year and which was often even lower, while the same contract, if signed with a Christian, cost at least 35 florins a year, sometimes rising to as much as 100 florins when the doctor in question was famous and respected. The differential was therefore considerable, and in many cases might well have tipped the balance in favour of an equally skilled Jewish doctor in competition for the same post with a Christian who would not work for the low salary the Jew was prepared to accept. In 1383 the commune of Assisi employed the Jew Sabatuccio da Roma as a surgeon, paying him an annual salary of 12 florins.[7] A quick comparison with the salaries paid at the time by that commune to its Christian doctors reveals a marked inequality to the Jew's disadvantage: another Christian surgeon, Matteo Santori, was paid a salary of 36 florins a year, three times that of Sabatuccio, while Bartolomeo da Castel della Pieve, the town's 'physician', who was widely known and respected, was paid 125 florins a year, over ten times more than Sabatuccio.[8] Assisi was not the exception, but the rule. Elia and Ventura di Dattilo da Roma, both employed as surgeons by the commune of Città di Castello from 1396 to 1402,

---

ibid., Rif., 10, fo. 138ᵛ (11 Nov. 1393); ibid. 11, fo. 8ʳ (21 Jan. 1394); ibid. 12, fo. 19ʳ (11–31 Aug. 1394); ibid. 13, fo. 89ʳ (17 July 1395); ibid. 15, fo. 156ᵛ (9 Dec. 1397); ibid. 18, fos. 88ʳ, 91ᵛ (21–6 Aug. 1400); AC Città di Castello, Annali Comunali, 28, fos. 64ʳ, 172ᵛ (8 Apr. 1398); ibid., Libro dei Conti, Prov., 23, fo. 50ᵛ (26 Feb. 1399); ibid. 31, fo. 45ʳ (15 Apr. 1401); AC Trevi, Tre Chiavi, env. 4, reg. 35, fo. 235ᵛ (27 May 1380); ibid., env. 5, reg. 41, fo. 48ᵛ (14 Sept. 1393), fo. 103ᵛ (25 Aug. 1394), fo. 132ʳ (29 Apr. 1395), and fo. 140ᵛ (1 Aug. 1395).

[7] AC Assisi, P, Bollettari, reg. 3 (1383), fos. 166ᵛ–167ᵛ; ibid., reg. 2 (1384), fos. 17ʳ–18ᵛ; ibid., H, Rif., reg. 6, file 2, fo. 13ʳ (15 July 1383).

[8] See Cristofani, *Le storie di Assisi*, 218; Toaff, *Jews in Medieval Assisi*, 34–5.

received an annual salary of 25 florins.[9] Guglielmo da Spoleto, medical officer at Trevi from 1380 to 1395, was paid the same salary, with the additional payment of his rent on a house belonging to the commune.[10] In 1437 David da Montefiascone was employed by the commune of Amelia as a doctor 'versed both in general medicine and in surgery', with a salary of 35 florins a year, though it was reduced by one third two years later.[11] In 1416 even the famous Musetto di Guglielmo, medical officer and lecturer at the University of Perugia, received an annual salary of only 25 florins, reduced two years later to 20.[12] Only rarely were communes willing to pay more for a Jewish doctor. For instance, the influential and experienced Vitale di Salomone, medical officer at Spoleto from 1391 to 1402, and also sought after by Rieti and other cities of Campagna and the Patrimonio di San Pietro, received an annual salary of as much as 50 florins;[13] and Salomone di Bonaventura, the surgeon at Città di Castello and a protégé of Martin V, was paid a salary of 60 florins in 1417.[14]

The reason Jewish doctors were willing to work for the communes at virtually subsistence levels did not lie purely in a desire for social betterment at almost any price, nor in the prospect of the civic benefits they hoped would accompany the post. For a Jew, becoming a doctor opened the way to being licensed by the municipal authorities to operate as a local banker and thus to make a good living from the money trade. Even when he did not officially enjoy the benefits of a double contract, as doctor and banker, the Jewish doctor was always active in the town's credit sector, investing his capital, large or small, in loans to the commune and to private individuals. For the Jew who practised it, the medical profession would often turn out to be a marginal activity, at least from the economic point of view, though one which retained all its importance on the social plane.

In the second half of the fourteenth and the beginning of the fifteenth

[9] AC Città di Castello, Annali Comunali, 27, fos. 27ᵛ (26 Feb. 1396) and 113ʳ (28 Nov. 1396); ibid. 28, fo. 64ᵛ and fo. 172ᵛ (8 Apr. 1398); ibid., Libro dei Conti, Prov., 23, fo. 50ᵛ (26 Feb. 1399), fo. 71ᵛ (14 Feb. 1399); ibid. 31, fo. 45ʳ (15 Apr. 1401). See G. Muzi, *Memorie civili di Città di Castello* (Città di Castello, 1842), i. 227; Toaff, 'Ebrei a Città di Castello', 95–9.

[10] AC Trevi, Tre Chiavi, env. 4, reg. 35, fo. 235ᵛ (27 May 1380); ibid., env. 5, reg. 41, fo. 48ᵛ (14 Sept. 1393), fo. 103ᵛ (25 Aug. 1394), and fo. 132ʳ (29 Apr. 1395).

[11] AC Amelia, Rif., 19, fo. 59ʳ (12 Aug. 1437); ibid. 21, fos. 90ʳ–91ʳ (22 Oct. 1439).

[12] AS Perugia, Not., Nicola di Bartolo, 77, fo. 45ʳ (10 Sept. 1416), fo. 47ʳ (1418).

[13] AC Spoleto, Camerario, Uscite 1391–1406 (27 July 1391–27 Dec. 1406); ibid., Rif., 11, fo. 138ᵛ (11 Nov. 1393); ibid. 13, fo. 89ʳ (17 July 1395).

[14] AC Città di Castello, Annali Comunali, 38, fo. 137ʳ, and 39, fo. 201ᵛ (1416–18).

centuries, the various medical officers of Perugia, Città di Castello, Assisi, Trevi, Amelia, Terni, Foligno, and Spoleto were all active in the local money trade at various levels. When for some reason the municipal authorities failed to authorize their doctor to double as banker, the doctor acted swiftly to made good this unforgivable oversight. Matassia di Salomone, the medical officer of Spoleto, addressed a touching appeal to the priors in 1443: 'I have come to live in Spoleto, together with my family, with the intention of putting my expertise at the service of the community, both in general medicine and in surgery, but unhappily I have come to understand that it is difficult to live and support a wife and children purely upon the proceeds of the medical profession. I therefore find myself obliged to have recourse to a supplementary activity, asking permission to practise it in this city.'[15] It is not difficult to divine what supplementary activity Matassia was referring to, nor is it hard to guess at the commune's reply.

When a choice had to be made between expanding banking activities and a medical career with limited horizons, the Jewish doctor was forced off the fence, however unwillingly. In 1418 Salomone di Bonaventura, the surgeon at Città di Castello, asked for his medical contract to be rescinded so as to be able to devote himself entirely to moneylending, since his banking business had been expanding rapidly in recent years.[16] Sometimes a doctor preferred to turn banker without completely abandoning the medical profession, which he would continue to practise privately, once freed from his onerous commitment to the commune. Bonaiuto da Tivoli, a banker who had an official agreement with the commune of Assisi in 1457, continued to practise as a doctor, but only privately: 'and because the said maestro Bonaiuto is a doctor and intends to practise the said profession in the city of Assisi, without any salary from the commune, he asks and desires that he may treat anyone who requests he do so, and have himself paid by same, according to his desserts, or as agreed, without let or hindrance from any person.'[17]

Due weight should also be given to the fact that Jewish doctors could often round up their meagre municipal salaries by means of profitable medical contracts with religious institutions and wealthy Jewish families. Sabatuccio da Roma, the medical officer at Assisi who, as we have seen, was receiving an annual salary of only 12 florins from the commune around 1380, also treated the monks of the convent of S. Francesco, for

[15] AC Spoleto, Rif., 31, fo. 26ʳ (18 Aug. 1443).
[16] AC Città di Castello, Annali Comunali, 39, fo. 201ᵛ (16 Apr. 1418).
[17] AC Assisi, H, Rif., 14, fo. 112ᵛ (1457).

an annuity of a further 8 florins.[18] In 1498 Zaccaria di Abramo da Siena held the position of private doctor to the banking family of the de Pomis, who paid him an annual fee of 44 florins for treatment and medicines, well above what he was paid by the commune of Spoleto with which he had an official agreement.[19] Some years later, in 1502, he was replaced as the de Pomis's family doctor by Benedetto di Angelo da Viterbo, who was paid a similar annual fee.[20]

The employment of Jewish doctors by the communes was also furthered by the protection and support they received from influential political figures. Vitale di Salomone, surgeon to the commune of Spoleto at the end of the fourteenth century, was the personal doctor and protégé of Marino Tomacelli, the papal ruler of the duchy,[21] while Salomone di Bonaventura, the medical officer at Città di Castello in 1418, had the support of pope Martin V.[22] Abramo di Vitale, a doctor in the service of various Umbrian communes about the middle of the fifteenth century, held the post of personal doctor to Braccio Baglioni, the lord of Perugia.[23] Even if, since the first half of the thirteenth century, various church councils had forbidden the employment of Jewish doctors by Christians for fear that they might poison them both physically and spiritually, in practice this ruling was openly disregarded, and the employment of Jewish doctors by Italian communes became a widespread phenomenon.[24] Only from the second half of the fifteenth century, after the vicious antisemitic preaching of the Minorites, did those communes which were still disposed to employ Jews take the precaution, in the face of possible objections, of asking Jewish candidates to obtain a papal dispensation explicitly authorizing them to treat Christian patients. Elia di Manuele di Francia, appointed medical officer of Assisi

18 Toaff, *Jews in Medieval Assisi*, 33.
19 AC Spoleto, Not., Granato di Marco, 76, fo. 261ᵛ (14 Nov. 1498).
20 Ibid., Giovan Battista alias Moscato, 109, fo. 496ʳ (26 Sept. 1502).
21 AC Spoleto, Rif., 15, fo. 156ᵛ (9 Dec. 1397).
22 See Toaff, 'Ebrei a Città di Castello', 98–100.
23 AC Assisi, H, Rif., 16, fo. 121ʳ (9 Oct. 1461).
24 In the rulings of the Council of Trier (1227) Christians who had turned to Jews for treatment were threatened with excommunication. The ban was repeated in the resolutions of the Council of Béziers (1246), Albi (1254), and Exeter (1287). The Council of Avignon (1337) put Christians on their guard against the damage to their health which would ensue from using Jewish doctors and surgeons. The Council of Lavour (1368) repeated the ban. There is a vast bibliography on the subject: see e.g. V. Rocchi, 'Gli ebrei e l'esercizio della medicina di fronte alle leggi della Chiesa e del governo di Roma papale', *Rivista di Storia Critica delle Scienze Mediche e Naturali*, 1/2 (1910), 3–10; Grayzel, *The Church and the Jews*, 74–5, 318–19, 332–3, 336–7.

in 1474, presented the commune with two bulls from Sixtus IV authorizing him to treat Christian patients, commending him for his skill to the rulers of the communes of the Papal State, and exempting him from wearing the distinctive badge.[25] Daniele di Abramo da Castro, medical officer at Amelia in 1478, had a bull from Pius II dated twenty years earlier registered in the municipal records, praising his professional activity at Narni and Bagnoregio, authorizing him to treat Christians, and exempting him from wearing the distinctive badge.[26] A similar dispensation from the Piccolomini pope was presented to the rulers of Perugia and Assisi by the doctor Abramo di Vitale in 1459.[27] But, as we shall see, the period of papal dispensations was also the most difficult time for Jewish doctors employed by the communes in the Papal State, where their presence was systematically disputed and opposed.

PRO CORPORE MORTUO: A LET-OUT CLAUSE

The contract regulated the professional relationship between doctor and commune, establishing his obligations and responsibilities down to the last detail, together with his salary and the conditions of treatment of the citizens, peasants, and visitors who were to be in his care. In 1474 the priors of Assisi engaged the doctor Elia di Manuele di Francia with the following enjoinders:

You are committed to offering your medical services scrupulously, in good faith and without deceit, to all the citizens, peasants, and officials of this commune, of both sexes and all ages, without claiming payment of a fee or any other reward. If you are called to the *contado* to treat a patient, you shall betake yourself thither without delay. If some urgent impediment prevents the other Christian medical officer from going to care for the sick in the *contado*, you shall go in his place, providing yourself with a mount; but you may ask for reimbursement of expenses for yourself, for the servant who accompanies you, and for the horse. You may not absent yourself from the city for any reason whatsoever, and particularly should the city and *contado* be struck by plague.[28]

[25] AC Assisi, H, Rif., 18, fo. 335ʳ (bull of 22 Nov. 1474, from Rome), fo. 341ᵛ (bull of 3 Feb. 1474, from Rome).
[26] AC Amelia, Rif., 46, fo. 280ʳ (bull of 1 Mar. 1459, from Perugia).
[27] AC Assisi, H, Rif., 16, fo. 121ʳ (bull of 13 Mar. 1459, from Perugia).
[28] Ibid., 18, fo. 330ᵛ (26 Oct. 1474). On medical contracts in Renaissance Italy see C. M. Cipolla, *Contro un nemico invisibile: Epidemie e strutture sanitarie nell'Italia del Rinascimento* (Bologna, 1985), 297–301.

The rulers of Amelia were even more explicit in 1478 when they addressed their medical officer, Daniele di Abramo da Castro: '. . . you are enjoined to examine the peasants' urine free of charge, and also offer your advice so that they may regain their health, whereas for pilgrims and visitors you may claim payment of your medical fee . . . you will also be obliged to care for those stricken with the plague, giving them your professional assistance, though we shall not oblige you to go and visit them in person.'[29] In 1430, on his return from a period as medical officer at Sangemini, Giacobbe di Mele da Terni was also given permission by the commune of Amelia to visit patients at night: 'maestro Giacobbe, together with his servant, shall also be authorized to carry out visits to the sick at night, after the third stroke of the bell, lighting his way through the streets of the town with a torch.'[30]

When the patients were private, the doctor could justifiably claim a fee. He could also do so when he had not signed a contract with the commune which obliged him to offer his services free of charge. Information concerning the daily activities of the Jewish doctors in the communes of Umbria, the type of patients with whom they had to deal, the treatment they were asked to provide, the diagnoses they gave, and the fees they claimed, are given us by an extensive series of notarial deeds, dating mainly from the first half of the fifteenth century. When a sick or seriously wounded person, in need of urgent treatment or a delicate surgical operation, was brought to him by a relative or friend, the doctor and the patient's family signed a standard contract, whose clauses were virtually identical in all cases. The doctor agreed to take on the patient *pro corpore mortuo*, that is, without assuming any responsibility if the patient were to die as a result of the treatment or operation. After giving a diagnosis—necessarily somewhat approximate—of the seriousness of the illness or injury he was being called upon to treat, and the possible ensuing complications, the doctor would fix his fee 'for restoring the patient to health', requesting two alternative sums: the first, naturally the higher, to be paid should the treatment be successful; the second, lower, sum was to be paid by the family whatever the outcome.[31]

---

[29] AC Amelia, Rif., 46, fos. 279ʳ–281ʳ, 282ᵛ (27 Sept. 1478).

[30] Ibid., 15, fos. 277ᵛ–279ᵛ (7 Aug. 1430).

[31] I examine this type of medical contract (a large number are now in the notarial archive in Assisi) at length in my *Jews in Medieval Assisi*, 87–90, 175–85. Similar notarial contracts, stipulating the payment of two alternative sums depending on the success or otherwise of the treatment, were also used by Jewish doctors in southern Italy in the 15th cent; see C. Colafemmina, 'Presenza ebraica a Bitetto e Palo del Colle nel secolo xv', *Brundisii Res*, 11 (1979), 44, 50–1. An interesting contract,

The receipts of the actual payments, appended at the foot of these contracts, often enable us to reconstruct the results of each case, and to
ascertain the effectiveness of the treatment and operations carried
out; though this in no way allows us to pronounce on the professional
capacities of the doctors of the time, since even in our own day medical
practice seems to teach that a patient can die even after a 'successful'
operation.

In 1439 the Assisi notary ser Evangelista di Francesco sent for the
surgeon Abramo di Sabatuccio because he felt unwell and was having
difficulty breathing. The diagnosis was serious: 'the patient has a
tumour of the throat [*quoddam nascitum in gula*] which is seriously weak-
ening him'. The treatment was surgery, and the doctor prepared to
perform it. But first he made sure that he would be paid a fee 'of one
good, sound gold florin, even should said ser Evangelista die following
the incision and the removal of the tumour'. This fee was also to be paid
'even if the family should decide to call in another doctor to perform the
surgical operation'.[32] In 1434 the Assisi nobleman Sebastiano Celli summoned the same Abramo to his palazzo at Porta S. Pietro, asking him to
tend his servant Antonio, who had a serious head wound. The pro-
cedure was more or less the same, and a notary was called to draw up the
standard contract, in which the doctor accepted the patient *pro corpore
mortuo*. 'Bearing in mind that the wound inflicted to the head of said
Antonio has entailed the fracture of the bone, that is, the skull, and is
therefore dangerous, and since it is necessary to bare the wound with
surgical instruments in order to examine it, and that there is a reasonable possibility that the patient may not survive the operation, I maestro
Abramo, a doctor, do not intend to make an incision to bare this wound
unless said Antonio is consigned to me *pro homine mortuo*, meaning by
this that if the patient should die as a result of the operation, I shall not
be apportioned any responsibility and that no penalty shall be imposed
upon me, since I intend to operate on the wound and treat it with surgical instruments to restore the sufferer to good health.' If the operation

---

signed between a Jewish doctor and a Tuscan peasant in 1462, is studied by M. Luzzati in 'Il medico ebreo e il contadino: Un documento pisano del 1462', *La Rassegna
Mensile di Israel*, 45 (1979), 385–92. For similar contracts signed by Christian doctors
see A. Chiappelli, *Medici e chirurghi pistoiesi nel Medio Evo: Con documenti—Contributo alla storia professionale della medicina in Italia* (Pistoia, 1909), 186; M. S. Mazzi,
Salute e società nel Medioevo (Florence, 1978), 92–4; I. Naso, *Medici e strutturè sani-
tariè nella società tardo-medievale* (Milan, 1982), 198–9.

[32] AC Assisi, Not., B11, file 3, Giovanni di Cecco Bevignate, fo. 77ᵛ (11 Sept. 1439).

succeeded, the doctor could claim a fee of 4 florins; otherwise, should the hapless Antonio die, he would be content with one.[33] In 1440 Gaio di Sabatuccio, a doctor at Spello, went to the bedside of a woman who had a serious head wound inflicted by her husband after a fit of jealousy. Here too the surgeon, before embarking on treatment, made sure that the relatives agreed to entrust the patient to him *pro corpore mortuo*, freeing him from all responsibility should treatment not have the desired result.[34]

Such contracts signed by Jewish doctors with their patients' families reveal that they were very often asked to perform operations to the skull, necessitated by serious and dangerous fractures, and to treat and dress wounds from swords and daggers. In May 1413 Abramo, whom I have already mentioned, received a fee of 4 florins for treating a citizen of Assisi 'who had fallen and fractured his skull'. In September of the same year, he was paid 5 florins for treating a woman who had been knifed by her brother-in-law. In 1429 Abramo treated a peasant from Cannara whose skull had been fractured by a kick from a donkey. In February 1431 he treated another peasant, this time from Armenzano, for a serious fracture to the skull: 'this man has a wound to the head which must be regarded as very dangerous; to treat and dress it, his hair will have to be shaved, and the wound laid bare, in order to examine the skullbones.' In 1435 the doctor was called to stanch the bleeding of a citizen of Assisi who had 'bloody wounds' all over his body, for which task he asked a fee of 2 florins.[35] In 1419 Gaio di Sabatuccio, who practised at Assisi and then at Spello, was called out to tend a peasant from Poggio Morico 'with wounds to the throat and left leg'. When the treatment was concluded, the patient paid him with 2 *some* of kosher wine and two *caldarelli* (builder's buckets) of olive oil. In 1433 the doctor operated on a woman of Assisi 'who had fallen from a height and fractured her skull'. In 1436 Gaio received a fee of 3 *lire*, equivalent to the annual rent of his house, from a woman of Spello whom he had treated for a head wound. In 1442 Gaio received a payment of 5 florins for medical attentions to a patient with a serious wound to the skull requiring a surgical operation.

---

33 AC Assisi, Not., B14, file 2, Giovanni di Cecco Bevignate, fo. 79ᵛ (8 Aug. 1434).

34 AC Spello, Not., env. 5, Pascuccio di Giacomo, 1, 256ʳ (29 Dec. 1440).

35 AC Assisi, Not., C20, Francesco di Benvenuto Stefani, fo. 84ᵛ (21 May 1413); ibid., C7, file 1, Gerardo di Giovanni, fo. 149ᵛ (19 Sept. 1413); ibid., R4, file 1, Angelo di Nicoluccio di Vanne, fo. 86ʳ (15 June 1429); ibid., B12, Giovanni di Cecco Bevignate, fo. 39ᵛ (2 Feb. 1431); ibid., R5, Angelino di Nicoluccio di Vanne, fo. 29ʳ (8 Feb. 1431); ibid., B14, file 2, Giovanni di Cecco Bevignate, fo. 13ʳ (28 Mar. 1434) and fo. 176ʳ (8 Mar. 1435).

'He is wounded and the shell of his pate is broken', says the medical contract drawn up for the occasion.[36] These doctors' clients came from all levels of society—citizens and peasants, merchants and craftsmen, clerics and artists. The fees they received were those laid down in the official price-lists 'for the offices of surgeon' in force in the various communes, of which the one approved in Gubbio in 1548 is a late example: its text follows those of similar documents published earlier.[37] The price-list quoted a fee of 5 *scudi*

for treating head wounds with open fractures; and if the person should have several wounds to the head, open or otherwise, the doctor shall receive 1 *scudo* for each one; for head wounds without open fractures, 2 *scudi* and, should the patient have more than one, 1 *scudo* each; for open chest wounds, 4 *scudi* and, should the patient have more than one, 1 *scudo* each; for chest wounds that are not open, 1 *scudo*; for wounds with broken bones and tendons, 2 *scudi*; for the treating of broken bones without wounds, 2 *scudi*, and for wounds where bones and flesh are broken, 3½ *scudi*, with one more *scudo* each for every additional such wound; for verminous and malignant abscesses of any kind, and for serious fistulas and gangrene, 3 *scudi* and, should the patient have more than one, 1 *scudo* each thereafter.

Sometimes the commune itself consulted the doctor to hear his professional opinion in cases with complex legal implications, or to entrust him with the treatment of special patients. In the summer of 1371 Ugolino Petrucci, the count of Montemarte, deputy of the governor of Perugia, sentenced a German mercenary soldier, a certain Teio, guilty of theft and pillage, to have his right hand amputated. After this grim operation had been performed by the executioner, the municipal officials called upon the medical officer Gaudino di Bonaventura to dress the soldier's wound, paying him a fee of 40 *soldi*.[38] In 1413 a citizen of Assisi was tried before the Podestà, accused of having seriously wounded a woman. The judge called to witness Abramo, the municipal surgeon, together with another, Christian, medical officer, asking for their professional opinion on the seriousness of the victim's injuries. Such an opinion was regarded as crucial for gauging the severity of the punishment

---

[36] Ibid., B18, Giovanni di Cecco Bevignate, fo. 428ᵛ (10 May 1419); ibid., R6, Angelino di Nicoluccio di Vanne, fo. 58ᵛ (30 Mar. 1433); AC Spello, Not., env. 3, Niccolò di Bartolomeo, 1, fo. 13ᵛ (29 Apr. 1436); ibid., env. 5, Pascuccio di Giacomo, 2, fo. 46ᵛ (7 Aug. 1442).

[37] This text is published in Menichetti, *Le corporazioni delle arti*, 39–40.

[38] AS Perugia, Computisteria, Massari, file 89, fo. 2ʳ (4 Aug. 1371).

to be meted out to the aggressor, though in this case the woman had pardoned him.[39] In 1440 Gaio, the municipal surgeon at Spello, and the other, Christian, medical officer, were asked to treat a woman whose life was in danger as a result of wounds inflicted upon her by her husband. In this case too the doctor's intervention was considered necessary for the purposes of the aggressor's trial.[40]

Doctors also had their preferred pharmacies, to which they sent their patients to obtain the medicaments they had been prescribed. Often their preference for particular pharmacies was not purely professional. Musetto di Guglielmo, medical officer at Perugia at the beginning of the fifteenth century, had links with that of Nicola Marcucci at Porta S. Pietro, which he financed in part, sharing the profits on the sale of medicaments with the pharmacist.[41] Elia di Matassia, the medical officer at Foligno around 1475, made exclusive use of the pharmacy of the Ospedale della Stella of Spoleto, where he bought sugar with which to make his medicines.[42] This peculiarity had earned him the nickname Zucchero among the people of Spoleto and Foligno. The communes did not look kindly upon these combined firms of surgeons and pharmacists, created as they clearly were in order to make money at the expense of the sick. The priors of Amelia addressed an explicit warning to their medical officer, Daniele da Castro, in this connection in 1478: 'you must take care not to come to any agreement with any pharmacist and herbalist of the city'.[43] But such admonishments went unheeded, and their effectiveness in curbing ingenious dealings to the detriment of the sick is somewhat to be doubted.

Very often the medical profession was handed down from father to son in Jewish families; we have evidence of numerous medical 'dynasties' in the Umbrian cities of the period, and indeed the practice was widespread in the rest of Italy. One of the most famous such clans was that of Mosè da Rieti, a doctor, rabbi, and man of letters and a protégé of Pius II Piccolomini; he practised at Terni, Narni, Fabriano, and other centres in Umbria and the Marches around the middle of the fifteenth century.[44] Mosè was at Perugia in 1436, and it was here that he copied

[39] AC Assisi, Not., C7, file 1, Gerardo di Giovanni, fo. 97ʳ (29 May 1413).
[40] AC Spello, Not., env. 5, Pasucccio di Giacomo, 1, fo. 256ʳ (29 Dec. 1440).
[41] AS Perugia, Giud., Processus, file 23, bundle 1 (15 May 1427).
[42] AC Spoleto, Not., Ponziano di Giordano, 30, fo. 261ᵛ (10 June 1479).
[43] AC Amelia, Rif., 46, fos. 279ʳ–281ʳ (27 Sept. 1478).
[44] On Mosè di Isacco da Rieti see Toaff, *Ebrei a Perugia*, 82–5 and the extensive bibliography.

the Hebrew version of Averroës's *Robur coelorum* for his own library, which housed a large number of medical and philosophical texts.[45] At his death his books went to his son Gaio, who had followed in his father's footsteps and practised medicine at Narni.[46] In his will of 1475 Gaio expressed his desire that the great medical library of the Rieti family should not be dispersed, but should pass to his young nephew Mosè, who had made an encouraging start on his medical studies: 'I enjoin that all my books, both those I inherited from my father, maestro Mosè, and those I purchased with my own money, should not be divided up after my death . . . and if my nephew Mosè successfully completes his studies in the sciences of philosophy and medicine, he may use these books freely and, should he wish to acquire them, my sons shall be obliged to sell them to him at half their market value, particularly those which have to do with the sciences and, in particular, with the art of medicine.'[47] Gratitude to the medical profession is also in evidence in the will of Gaio, medical officer of Spello, drawn up in 1439: here he made a generous bequest to the town's hospital, where he had worked for many years.[48] Gaio belonged to another illustrious family of Jewish doctors, originally from Rome, which had been active in Umbria for almost two centuries: his father Sabatuccio had been medical officer at Assisi in the second half of the fourteenth century, while his two brothers, Abramo and Daniele, had been surgeons at Assisi, Trevi, and Perugia.[49]

OPPOSITION TO JEWISH DOCTORS

From the mid-fifteenth century onwards the employment of Jewish doctors by the communes began to be hotly and openly contested. The Minorite argument did not end with the sitting target of the

[45] See G. B. de Rossi, *MSS Codices Hebraici* (Parma, 1803), iii. 158, no. 1376.

[46] The estate of Mosè da Rieti was distributed among his three sons Gaio, Leone, and Bonaiuto on 17 Dec. 1466. Gaio, who was the eldest, was left a double share of the inheritance, in accordance with Jewish law, and this included his father's medical library (AS Perugia, Not., Simone di Giovanni di Giacomo, 295, fos. 7ʳ–8ᵛ). Leone, the second son, was also a doctor, and on 15 July 1445 he received the contract for the post of surgeon at Amelia (AC Amelia, Rif., 38, fo. 74ʳ).

[47] AC Spoleto, Not., Antonio di Pietro, 142, fos. 147 24ʳ–25ʳ (5 June 1475).

[48] AC Spello, env. 4, Bartolomeo di Domenico, 1, fo. 238ʳ (1 July 1439).

[49] On the family of Sabatuccio and his activity as a doctor see my *Jews in Medieval Assisi*, 32–6, 87–90.

banker–usurer, but embraced the whole problem of the legality of any Jewish presence in city life. In particular there was now dogged opposition to the opportunities for social betterment offered to certain elements within the Jewish community, and to doctors first and foremost; they were now declared to be unlawful from the viewpoint of Christian doctrine, and dangerous for the community at large. Entrusting the care of one's body to a Jewish doctor meant jeopardizing one's physical and spiritual health. Every medical contract signed by a commune with a Jew placed the life of its citizens in thrall to their mortal enemies, for whose likely misdeeds the improvident rulers thus made themselves jointly responsible. Reference to the baneful presence of Jewish doctors at Christian patients' bedsides, a presence which many official Church interventions had unsuccessfully attempted to guard against since the thirteenth and fourteenth centuries, became a stock item in the dextrous verbal swordsmanship of the itinerant preachers.[50] In his pamphlet *Contra perfidiam modernorum judecorum*, written at the beginning of the sixteenth century, the Minorite Giacomo Ongarelli thundered against 'Jewish doctors who dispatch not only the body but also the soul of the Christian to perdition'.[51] For fra Roberto Caracciolo, Jewish doctors 'are full of all manner of iniquity and ruthlessness'; as though this were not enough, he adds that, being Jews, they give out an unbearable stench. In this connection the friar recalled an experience he himself had had when, 'preaching one summer, I felt a slight pain in my chest, brought on by sweating and then cooling down; when I was in my room, a Jewish doctor came up to me unbidden'. But when the doctor had tried to approach the stricken friar to offer his assistance, fra Roberto had been seized with such nausea at the stench coming from the Jew, that he recovered only when he had driven him from the room. 'I said to him: go away, bother me no further. As soon as the Jewish doctor had withdrawn, the turbulence in my stomach ceased.' On another occasion—as fra Roberto da Lecce told his mesmerized listeners—a Jewish doctor, one Abramo, had sent him a present of some fowl. But although the friar was blessed with a hearty appetite, the succulent birds, once cooked, proved uneatable. 'When they were brought to the table, I felt so nauseous that I had them taken away.' Unsurprisingly, Caracciolo concluded that Jewish doctors not only offended the sense of smell ('I, a

---

[50] See n. 24, above, on the Church's attitude towards Christians using Jewish doctors.

[51] See Fioravanti, 'Polemiche antigiudaiche nell'Italia del Quattrocento', 35.

sinner, have learned how Jews stink'), but that they actually tainted and corrupted everything they laid their hands on.[52]

After busying themselves with the usurers who 'sucked Christian blood', the preachers now directed their viciously graphic tirades at Jewish doctors, and the communes were obliged to take defensive action. Now, when they still wanted or needed to employ Jewish medical officers, they did their best to cover themselves as far as possible. On the one hand they required the doctor to arm himself with a papal dispensation authorizing him to treat Christian patients, relieving the communes intending to use his services of all moral and religious responsibility. On the other, they dreamed up a new and extravagant justification for the employment of Jews, aimed all too transparently at softening aggressive Minorite opposition: the Jewish doctor's contact with Christian patients would hasten his conversion to Christianity, opening his eyes to the light of the true faith. Now the situation was dramatically reversed: all of a sudden the Jew's possible negative influence on the Christians who were entrusted to his care, and the attendant danger of their being poisoned in flesh and spirit, receded into the background. Now, it seemed, it could be hoped that contact might act as an effective instrument for the Jew's conversion, with the Christian patients' influence suddenly and infallibly in the ascendant. A diagnosis of gangrene or the setting of a fracture might serve as a prelude to a surprise baptism. But this disingenuous ploy could not hope to silence the opposition of the preachers, who were now adopting increasingly hectoring tones, particularly after the successful founding of the first Monti di Pietà. Vacillating and bombarded with polemics, an ever larger number of communes now felt obliged to dismiss their Jewish doctors, often rescinding their contracts prematurely. Now medicine too—once one of the most sought-after and respected professions in late medieval Italian Jewish society—was characterized by fear and uncertainty. Another symbol of successful Jewish integration into Christian society was thereby undermined, if not actually destroyed.

In Umbria, hostilities began at Trevi around the mid-fifteenth century. Following the Minorite offensive culminating with the Easter sermons of 1442, Trevi made a unilateral decision prematurely to terminate the medical contract signed with Abramo da Assisi, who had served

[52] Roberto da Lecce's dealings with Jews are recorded in his *Spechio della christiana fede*, sermo II, 48[a]–49[b]. On this subject see Semeraro, 'Fra Roberto Caracciolo e gli ebrei', 58–9.

the local population as a surgeon for several years.[53] Some years later, in 1456, when the Priors' Council was presented with a proposal to take on another Jew as medical officer, argument raged yet again, fired as always by the Franciscan friars. At last, after a brief tussle, the friars carried the day and the rulers of Trevi solemnly vowed not to employ the services of a Jewish doctor. It was a promise they observed scrupulously during the following years.[54]

At Assisi, objections to the Jewish presence in the town gathered momentum during the years following the founding of the Monte di Pietà in 1468. In the autumn of 1474 the commune decided to employ Elia di Francia to be their medical officer, as both general physician and surgeon; his family had lived in the town for several generations and was one of the most respected among the small local Jewish group. As a condition of signing the contract, the priors urged him to obtain a papal dispensation authorizing him to treat Christian patients. At the same time they tried to sweeten the bitter pill for the inevitably hostile friars, seasoned opponents of the employment of the Jewish doctor, by loudly proclaiming their firm conviction that Elia's familiarity with his Christian patients would finally lead him to see the light and accept the waters of baptism. 'We may hope that familiarity with good Christians will convert him, so that he may know the light of truth, and that the divine spirit, which bloweth where it listeth, may also blow within him.'[55] The Minorites responded to this blatant attempt to get round the law with the respect they felt it deserved. Although Elia had promptly presented the commune with the necessary dispensation, signed by Sixtus IV, the preachers let fly with their usual vicious insults from squares and pulpits, spitting disdain upon the choice of medical officer.[56] His pernicious and diabolical attitudes, they said, constituted a mortal danger to the simple flock of the faithful, hoodwinked as they were by dishonest and corrupt rulers. Excommunication hung like the sword of Damocles over the offending town, clearly bent on its own destruction. In the hope of placating the protesters who had selected him as their target, the doctor appealed once again to the pope and obtained a bull solemnly

53 The commune of Trevi revoked the contract of maestro Abramo di Sabatuccio da Assisi on 5 May 1442 (AC Trevi, Tre Chiavi, env. 5, reg. 100, fos. 70ʳ, 116ᵛ–117ᵛ, 15 Oct. 1441–5 May 1442).
54 Ibid., env. 8, reg. 112, fo. 10ᵛ (19 Sept. 1456).
55 AC Assisi, H, Rif., 18, fo. 330ʳ⁻ᵛ (2–26 Oct. 1474).
56 Elia presented the commune with Sixtus IV's dispensation on 22 Nov. 1474 (AC Assisi, H, Rif., 18, fo. 335ʳ).

reaffirming his right to practise his profession freely among Christians in all the territories under the rule of the Church, and also granting him exemption from wearing the yellow badge. Sixtus IV's document ended with a stern warning that attempted to forestall the inevitable objections: 'Let no one have the audacity to infringe the contents of this page of concessions and privileges, or the temerity to gainsay it. Should anyone have the presumption to try to do so, he should know that he will incur the wrath of God and of the blessed apostles Peter and Paul.' The rulers of Assisi, emboldened by the papal bull and now sure of having obtained effective cover, registered it in the town hall in the spring of 1475.[57] The preaching friars, however, were far less impressed; heedless of the wrath of God and the apostles, they refused to tone down their attacks upon Elia and his employers. The most rancorous among them was Antonio da Vercelli who, hot-foot from a blazing Easter sermon, commanded the rulers of the city to annul the contract granted to the Jewish doctor, on pain of excommunication.[58] It was Elia himself who took the step which let the dithering rulers of Assisi off the hook: with great dignity he resigned from his post, observing, with a touch of bitter sarcasm, that he had learned with regret that his condition as a Jew made his work as a doctor unwelcome to the population: 'I do not intend to continue to take your money, because I have realized that the people do not wish to be served by me, who am a Jew.'[59] The preachers could thus chalk up a new victory in the struggle which was to lead to the expulsion of the Jews from the city ten years later.[60]

The example of Assisi was soon followed by other communes embarking more or less unwillingly upon the same course. In the autumn of 1478 the Jew Daniele da Castro was employed as a medical officer by the commune of Amelia. He had been trained in both general medicine and surgery, and had previously practised successfully at Narni and Bagnoregio, bringing with him warm letters of recommendation which seemed likely to ensure him a very favourable contract with Amelia. As usual, the commune asked Daniele to obtain the papal dispensation authorizing him to treat Christian patients, so as to proceed to the signing of the document. At the same time the commune was careful

---

[57] Sixtus IV's new bull supporting the Jewish doctor was registered in the chancellery of the commune on 5 Mar. 1475 (AC Assisi, H, Rif., 18, fos. 341ʳ–343ᵛ).

[58] AC Assisi, H, Rif., 18, fos. 373ʳ–374ᵛ.

[59] Elia gave up his post as medical officer on 23 Mar. 1476 (ibid., fo. 376ʳ).

[60] On the last years of the Jewish community in Assisi see Toaff, *Jews in Medieval Assisi*, 65–71.

to justify the Jew's employment on the now customary grounds of his possible conversion, going some way to countering the preachers' stock opposition. 'Through his conversation and familiarity with the faithful, the Jewish doctor will be able to cast aside his blindness and recognize and fear the light of truth.' As mentioned above, Daniele had registered a bull from Pius II in the town hall, authorizing him to treat Christians in all the cities of the Papal State and exempting him from wearing the distinctive badge.[61] Despite these precautionary measures, Minorite wrath immediately broke out in the town, and the friars uttered ringing demands from the church pulpits that the Jew's medical contract be rescinded. A few months after the doctor's appointment, the rulers of Amelia had come to an agreement with the people and appointed a committee of citizens 'to verify the complaints concerning the Jew's professional inadequacies'.[62] Finally, at the beginning of the summer of 1479, the municipal authorities decided unilaterally to terminate Daniele's contract and, after offering him a gratuity to avoid the inconvenience of any appeal, they asked him to leave the town.[63]

The polemic against the communes' employment of Jewish doctors now spread throughout the territories of Umbria, moving first from Amelia to nearby Terni. Here it was once again the Minorite preachers, Serafino da Todi and Cherubino da Perugia in particular, who in 1482 set matters in train by mounting a campaign against the medical officer Emanuele di Mosè, who had served the population for over thirty years. Threatened by excommunication and popular unrest, the municipal officials saw themselves forced to dismiss Emanuele, even though he had appealed to Sixtus IV and obtained his protection.[64] At the end of the fifteenth century the number of Umbrian cities willing to employ Jewish medical officers had therefore dropped sharply.[65] In the following

61 AC Amelia, Rif., 46, fos. 279ʳ–281ʳ, 282ᵛ (27 Sept. 1478).
62 Ibid. 47, fos. 22ʳ–27ʳ, 57ᵛ–58ʳ (13 Feb. 1479).
63 Ibid., fo. 94ʳ (28 June 1479).
64 AS Terni, Rif., 505, ɪɪ, fo. 123ᵛ (7 Oct. 1482). Emanuele was practising as a doctor at Terni from at least 1452 (ibid. 498, ɪɪɪ, fo. 322ʳ). On these events see Ghinato, *Studi e documenti*, ii. 84, 93–4.
65 In 1484 and 1485 we find Manuele di Angelo da Padova as medical officer at Fratta (AC Umbertide, Not., Giovanni di Bartolomeo da Perugia, 296/64, fo. 27ʳ; ibid. 299/67, fo. 41ʳ). Between 1498 and 1502 Zaccaria di Abramo da Siena and Benedetto di Angelo da Viterbo were practising medicine at Spoleto (AC Spoleto, Not., Granato di Marco, 76, fo. 261ᵛ; Giovanni Battista alias Moscato, 109, fo. 496ʳ). In 1498 and 1499 Giacobbe da Forlì was medical officer at Città di Castello (AC Città di Castello, Libro dei Conti, Prov., 1498–9, fo. 329ᵛ; ibid., Not., Angelo di Battista, 12, fo. 205ʳ).

century too, with the exceptions of Spoleto, Perugia, and Città di Castello, there is no evidence of any commune in Umbria being ready to risk giving a medical contract to a Jewish doctor.

11

Banks and Bankers

ITALY AND UMBRIA: THE GENERAL PICTURE

'IN these regions the practice of giving credit is more widespread than in the rest of the Jewish diaspora . . . In these parts, now that money-lending is a common profession, the need arises for a treatise briefly outlining the various laws governing credit.' Thus wrote the banker Jechiel (Vitale) Nissim da Pisa in 1559, in the introduction to his treatise on credit (*Ma'amar ḥayei olam al inyan haribit*), giving succinct expression to two important truths: that in Italy above all the loan banks of the Jewish companies had found ideal conditions to thrive in; and that a considerable number of Jews living in Italy were now involved in this activity.[1] Jechiel Nissim da Pisa's observations were made bearing in mind the situation that existed during the first years of the Counter-Reformation (when the credit system had already entered a period of crisis and was subject to severe restrictions); but they acquire an even greater significance if we apply them to the earlier periods of the late Middle Ages and Renaissance.

There is no doubt that, from the end of the thirteenth century, the communes of central and northern Italy held a powerful attraction for Jewish financiers from Rome and beyond the Alps, and that the origins of many Italian Jewish communities, whose history often continues down to our own day, are linked to the migrations of these first Jewish merchants and bankers. At the end of the thirteenth century and the beginning of the fourteenth, Jewish financiers of varying degrees of wealth left Rome, where the Curia had attracted large investments of capital and where these merchants and bankers had forged valuable connections and attained positions of some importance. They travelled along the great consular roads towards northern Italy, stopping in those places where their capital was most in demand, where investment was more rewarding, and where the general financial climate was favourable.

---

[1] See G. S. Rosenthal, *Banking and Finance among Jews in Renaissance Italy* (New York, 1962), 9–10. Rosenthal has published the critical edn. of the *Maamar ḥayei olam* of Jechiel Nissim of Pisa.

Their first appearance is usually made known to us by a large loan to the relevant commune.[2]

In central Italy—Latium, Umbria, the Marches, Romagna, and Tuscany—a constellation of tiny Jewish communities was formed at an early date. The northbound flow of bankers from Rome did not stop at these central regions: in the second half of the fourteenth century it spread northwards, giving birth to new communities in the Po valley. In the first years of the fifteenth century, another wave of Jewish bankers arrived, this time across the Alps. These Jews, from the Rhine and Main valleys, had been the object of virtually constant persecution. Some families had sought refuge in Italy from the very beginning of the fourteenth century, while massacres of Jews following the Black Death in 1348 had led the survivors to abandon Germany for new horizons. Many decided to follow the earlier pioneers, who had found a less troubled life in the Italian communes, especially in Friuli, Istria, and the northern Veneto, where they were able to use their financial expertise to make a living. Immigrants from beyond the Alps, who had already founded numerous communities in northern Italy, swelled the wave of those who had moved northwards from Rome, and gave life to new Jewish communities in the Po valley and in the communes and *signorie* of Emilia, the Veneto, and Lombardy.[3] Lastly, following the expulsion of the Provençal Jews in 1394, a third, though smaller, wave of bankers crossed the Alps, settling mainly in the regions of Piedmont and Savoy. Despite attempts to restrict them, Jewish bankers and moneylenders continued to be active, often increasingly so, in thirteenth- and fourteenth-century Italy. It is misleading to emphasize, as do some commentators, the economic 'segregation' of Italian Jews in this period, or to generalize about a situation which tended to vary with local conditions and from region to region and town to town. Plentiful opportunities always awaited them in favourable political situations. In view of the religious constraints on joining guilds in the Middle Ages, Jews had to be discerning in their search for sectors where they could do business. But there was no shortage of cities whose priors were relatively free

[2] See Colorni, 'Prestito ebraico e comunità ebraiche'; Milano, 'I primordi del prestito ebraico in Italia'; Poliakov, *Jewish Bankers and the Holy See*.

[3] See A. Toaff, 'Convergenza sul Veneto di banchieri ebrei romani e tedeschi'; M. Luzzati, 'I legami fra i banchi ebraici toscani ed i banchi veneti e dell'Italia settentrionale', in G. Cozzi (ed.), *Gli ebrei e Venezia (Secoli XIV–XVIII)*, proceedings of a conference organized by the Istituto della Storia della Società e dello Stato Veneziano and by the Cini Foundation, Venice, 5–10 June 1983 (Milan, 1987), 571–94.

from the meddlings of guilds or mendicant orders, of rulers who intended somehow to make use of capable and trustworthy men, nor indeed of guilds interested in reliable financing, the introduction of new techniques (linked to the availability of daring investments), and the conquest of distant markets.

Umbria received one of the earliest, and largest, waves of migrating Jewish bankers from Rome: here, introduced and supported by the circles of the Roman Curia, whose political and economic interests they often represented, these bankers were invited by the communes to invest their capital in the local economy.[4] The priors gave them official status in the money-market, binding them to the strict observance of charters laying down permitted charges and other regulations protecting prospective borrowers, but also granting them the rights of citizenship and numerous privileges of a legal and religious kind. The presence of Jewish bankers on local financial markets led to a general lowering of the cost of money, the loan of which had previously been monopolized by Christian usurers, mostly from Florence and Arezzo, who tended to demand higher interest rates than the Jews.[5] The latter soon succeeded in completely ousting the Tuscan financiers in average and small-scale credit dealings.

In the second half of the thirteenth century and the first years of the fourteenth we thus find many companies of Jewish bankers of Roman origin working in the Umbrian communes: at Perugia above all, but also at Todi, Terni, Assisi, Cascia, Amelia, Trevi, Gubbio, Deruta, Montefalco, Gualdo Cattaneo, and Visso. Gaps in municipal archival holdings sometimes prevent us from going back to the first years of the Jewish presence in these towns, so the pattern of settlement has not yet been fully charted. None the less, we can say with some degree of certainty that the Jews arrived in almost all the Umbrian centres at the end of the thirteenth century, and were to be active there over the following centuries until their expulsion in 1569. At Perugia, where their activity is documented from the 1250s, Jewish bankers seem completely to have supplanted Christian moneylenders (particularly those from Arezzo) on the local credit market as early as the beginning of the fourteenth

---

[4] On the links between the Roman Curia and these first Jewish bankers see Toaff, 'Gli ebrei romani e il commercio del denaro', 183–96.

[5] I agree with Reinhold Mueller that one of the main factors in the success of Jewish bankers in relation to their Lombard and Tuscan competitors 'was that they stormed the market, by virtue of being able to lend at lower interest rates'; see Mueller, 'Prestatori ebrei e banchi di pegno a Venezia e nel Dominio', in G. Cozzi (ed.), *Gli ebrei e Venezia (secoli XIV–XVIII)*, 691–2.

century. During the following years they consolidated their position, enjoying a virtual, and unbroken, monopoly in the money trade until the second half of the fifteenth century; at this point, first in Perugia in 1462 and then in other Umbrian centres, the Monti di Pietà were founded and the charters of the Jewish bankers were systematically denounced by the town councils.

THE STRUCTURE AND FUNCTIONING OF THE BANKS

Throughout the regions of central and northern Italy the great banking and trading companies of the Jews of Roman origin developed powerful and flexible structures, linked to the popes and local governors by preferential relations, although these were not always explicit. These companies extended their trade to the main cities of Latium and Tuscany, Umbria and the Marches, Emilia and Romagna—to Florence and Siena, Perugia and Ancona, Fano, Rimini, and Bologna. Like the great Tuscan companies,[6] these firms had four main characteristics: their relative stability (their charters were renewed every five to ten years, on which occasion the list of the partners, too, might alter); their inter-familial character, guaranteeing solidarity between the members (the firms' *grands commis* were usually chosen from within the one or two families with the greatest wealth and prestige); their capitalistic structure, which divided profits in proportion to the capital invested (the firms also received considerable deposits from Christians, which enabled them also to profit from the money trade, something which was forbidden them by canon law); their deliberate geographic dispersal, which allowed them to reduce the risks attendant upon possible shifts in the political situation, and consequent changes in Jewish standing in the various Italian states (apart from their main headquarters, the companies of Jewish bankers also preferred to open branch offices in various towns). These were features also shared by the Tuscan companies of

[6] On the structure of the Tuscan companies see e.g. A. Fanfani, *Le origini dello spirito capitalistico in Italia* (Milan, 1933); R. de Roover, *The Rise and Decline of the Medici Bank (1397–1494)* (Cambridge, Mass., 1963); A. Sapori, *La crisi delle compagnie mercantili dei Bardi e dei Peruzzi* (Florence, 1936); id., 'Storia interna della compagnia mercantile dei Peruzzi', *Studi di Storia Economica*, 2 (1955), 653–94; F. Melis, *Note di storia della banca pisana nel Trecento* (Pisa, 1955); id., *Aspetti della vita economica medievale*. On the structure of the Jewish loan companies, esp. in Tuscany, see the recent work by A. Toaff, 'The Jewish Bank in Central Italy in the Thirteenth to Fifteenth Centuries' (Heb.), in H. Beinart (ed.), *Jews in Italy: Studies Dedicated to the Memory of U. Cassuto* (Jerusalem, 1988), 109–30.

moneylenders, but the Jewish bankers had one additional characteristic
of their own: namely, they belonged to the community of Jews originating in Rome which, with its shared historical–religious traditions and
customs, constituted a further and by no means unimportant bond
between its members.

It was above all between the end of the fourteenth century and the
beginning of the fifteenth that these firms developed in a thoroughly
capitalistic direction. Indeed, as Gino Luzzatto has noted, the banks,
opened supposedly to serve the poor, were in reality also used (in many
cases markedly so) by merchants, landed nobility, the communes, and
even princes. While poor people made use of the more oppressive
system of lending on pledge, wealthier borrowers used these banks to
take out large loans on mere debenture.[7] The income from this activity
gave the banker room to manœuvre, and his company gained in stability,
often employing paid workers, administrators, and clerks in the
branches while the owner managed affairs in his home town. The capital
was rationally divided up: shares would be transfered to other investors
and further investments were made, principally in trade. Each bank had
average investments of the order of 4,000–5,000 florins, sometimes
rising to as much as 9,000–10,000 florins. Bearing in mind that the
networks of these large Jewish companies included on average a dozen
or so lesser branches, the sums involved must have been considerable. A
cluster of clients of all social classes gathered around these Jewish banks:
specialized workers, commercial agents, brokers, and notaries. The
Jewish banker was usually free to operate as he thought fit, within the
broad limits set by his charter, even if he was subject to the all-powerful
and self-interested authority of the state. The Observants' preaching
against usury made no noticeable impression until the second half of the
fifteenth century; and even where it did set restrictive measures in
motion, these were short-lived or easily circumvented. Curiously
enough, despite their otherwise forward-looking attitude, a certain antiquated character persisted in the account books of these bankers (though
they were not alone in this, since fifteenth-century French and Tuscan
merchants worked in the same way), bearing witness to the primitive
nature of their techniques. The book was used purely to register the
debts and pledges of each client, often entered in an extremely disorderly way, and described in the most pedantic fashion.[8]

[7] See G. Luzzatto, *I banchieri ebrei in Urbino nell'età ducale* (Padua, 1902), 16.

[8] On the account books of the Jewish bankers see S. de Benedetti, 'Un manoscritto cavense in caratteri rabbinici', *Archivio Storico per le Province Napoletane*, 8

For their frequent loans to other companies (but also to private individuals), the Tuscan merchant banks had invented the system of bills of exchange, but also a newer, more flexible and dynamic method, namely the letter of credit. The Jewish bankers, however, who had a much larger, less cohesive, and typically 'retail' clientèle, preferred to use the concrete, movable guarantee, the pledge, which had the advantage of simplifying the system.[9] The pledge was linked to the payment of interest, rather than committing the borrower to the repayment of the initial sum. In the late Middle Ages and Renaissance pledges included all those items which made up the movable capital goods of the various social classes of the time: jewels, gold and silver plate, cloth, and goods of various kinds. Items of clothing were particularly common: unlike today's equivalents, they were intended to last, representing a costly investment and having considerable value, being exchanged and handed down among the bourgeoisie through wills and donations. As Carlo Cipolla stresses, in pre-industrial Europe the purchase of a garment, or the cloth to make it, was a luxury which ordinary people could afford only a few times in a lifetime, so that clothing had a symbolic value in the European society of the time. Anyone who dressed well was rich, and since the price of material was high in relation to current incomes, even the length of the garment was largely determined by social status.[10] The pledges deposited by the foremost families of the town at Angelo da Ferrara's bank at Assisi in 1456 included richly embroidered garments (both men's and women's) and valuable furs worth hundreds of florins.[11] The pledges registered at the bank of Raphael di Isacco de Pomis at Spoleto in 1483 included women's garments worth 20 florins apiece,

---

(1883), 766–74; A. Medin and G. Tolomei, 'Per una storia aneddotica dell'Università di Padova nel secolo XVI', *Atti e memorie della Regia Accademia di Scienze, Lettere e Arti di Padova*, 26 (1911), 103–5; U. Cassuto, 'Alcune note ebraiche di contabilità del secolo XVI', *Rivista Israelitica*, 8 (1911), 54–64; id., *Ebrei a Firenze*, 160–71; Carpi, 'The Account Book of a Jewish Money-lender'. See also F. Patroni Griffi, *Il banco di pegni di Cava dei Tirreni del 1495* (Cava dei Tirreni, 1985).

[9] Todeschini has made a stimulating and intelligent contribution on the typically Jewish economic approach to the pledge, which differed from and in many ways conflicted with the Christian one. See G. Todeschini, *La ricchezza degli ebrei: Merci e denaro nella riflessione ebraica e nella definizione cristiana dell'usura alla fine del Medioevo* (Spoleto, 1989).

[10] See C. M. Cipolla, *Prezzi, salari e teoria dei salari in Lombardia alla fine del Cinquecento* (Rome, 1956), 14; id., *Storia economica dell'Europa pre-industriale* (Bologna, 1974), 48–50.

[11] AC Assisi, Not., s2, file 2, Polidoro di Ludovico, fo. 25^r. See Toaff, *Jews in Medieval Assisi*, 54.

valuable weapons with silver hilts, gold and silver rings with opals and precious stones, and gold and coral necklaces. Eleven years later the list of pledges at the bank of this same Raphael included breastplates, silver helmets, and saddles with silver trimmings.[12]

The official formulas of the charters often stress that the credit system of such Jewish banks had been accepted by the governors of the city 'to meet the needs of the poor'. The authorities preferred to be seen to regard moneylending as a social necessity, even though this also brought with it inconvenient implications of a moral and religious order, rather than as vital backing for the town economy.[13] This attitude—though never made explicit in writing—was born of a logic which was averse to the concept of profit, and which indeed condemned it. It would be incorrect to compare the activity of the Jewish banks which lent on interest (particularly the larger ones), or their position in the credit system of fourteenth- and fifteenth-century Italian capitalism, with either the more restricted activities of the small moneylenders who lent on pledge, or to the later dealings of the Monti di Pietà. Suffice it to say that in 1438 the Florentine Jewish banks invested at least 40,000 florins in loans. We also know that at the beginning of the fourteenth century the annual debt, 'irrecoverable or contested', or at all events uncollected, of the commune of Perugia to the Jewish bankers of the city, varied from 8,000 to 10,000 florins.[14] Although we

[12] AC Spoleto, Not., Ponziano di Giordano, 34, fo. 166r (5 June 1483); ibid., Giovanni Bancaroni, 64, fo. 518r (12 Oct. 1494).

[13] In a recent study aimed at minimizing the importance and influence of Jewish lending, Bonfil was still maintaining that Jewish bankers were necessary to lords and princes only as instruments of social control, in order to allay poverty, while their role in the overall financial context of Italian cities and states was negligible; see R. Bonfil, 'Società ebraica e società cristiana nel Medioevo e nel Rinascimento: Significato e limiti di una convergenza', *Ebrei e Cristiani nell' Italia medievale e moderna: Conversioni, scambi, contrasti*, proceedings of an international conference held at San Miniato, Pisa, 4–6 Nov. 1986 (Rome, 1988), 231–60. In contrast, see Kellenbenz's considered view: 'For a time during the fifteenth century Jewish bankers began to compete with the large banking institutions . . . They too worked with the savings of the wealthy, thus creating competition with the "discretionary deposits" of the Christian bankers. The decline of the Arte del Cambio in Florence probably has a connection with the flourishing of Jewish banking operations'. H. Kellenbenz, 'Lo stato, la società e il denaro', in A. de Maddalena and H. Kellenbenz (eds.), *La repubblica internazionale del denaro tra XV e XVII secolo* (Bologna, 1986), 346.

[14] These figures are taken from the land register of Musetto di Dattilo (29 July 1334) and Beniamino di Bonaventura (27 July 1335), where the commune of Perugia's debts to the Jewish loan companies in the city are recorded; AS Perugia, Catasto Antico, group 1, book 27, fos. 248v–252v; ibid., book 4, fos. 97v–101v. See also G. Mira, 'Note sulla presenza di una comunità ebraica in Perugia e sulla sua attività

have only sporadic documentation, which does not offer us very precise data, the general situation does not seem to have changed much by the end of the century, when the commune was contracting huge loans with the Jewish bankers, whose repayment must have been somewhat problematic. Bonaventura di Meluccio, the chief Jewish banker at Foligno at the end of the fourteenth century, has left us the registrations of his loans to the local populace in the period 1380–1412. The overall sums lent varied between 1,000 and 1,600 florins per annum.[15] These were exclusively loans on debenture or mortgage security, based on notarial deeds, but we do not have either the registrations of loans to the commune, or of those on pledge, which in all likelihood constituted the greater part of the bank's operations. We may therefore reasonably suppose that Bonaventura was investing no less than 4,000–5,000 florins a year in the money trade at Foligno and in the *contado*, a far from negligible sum. In 1385, on his death in Perugia, the banker Matassia di Sabatuccio was honoured by the council of the priors not by allusion to his activities in favour of the poor of the city, but more realistically because 'he proved much concerned for the interests of the city of Perugia, coming to the help of the commune with his money and advice and, clearly foreseeing the impending harm and perils threatening our state, he duly and zealously informed the priors and citizens, so that they might adopt opportune remedies'.[16]

Many historians argue that the main activity of the officially established Jewish banks was on a retail level, lending small sums for short periods. This underestimates the importance of these institutions. It should be stressed that the loans were not limited to consumer credit. Jewish banks naturally loaned small sums on a short-term basis to less wealthy clients—artisans and the petty bourgeoisie—who used the money for daily needs and to bolster their cash-flow. But they also lent

---

creditizia nella seconda metà del secolo XIII e nella prima metà del XIV', in F. Borlandi (ed.), *Fatti e idee di storia economica nei secoli XII–XX* (Bologna, 1976), 107–8.

[15] The contracts relating to the operations of the bank of the brothers Bonaventura and Salomone di Meluccio, situated in the rione Contrastanga at Foligno, are to be found in the registers of the Foligno notaries Angelo di Francesco, Francesco di Antonio, and Masseo di Gervisa; AC Foligno, Not., Angelo di Francesco, prot. 2B; ibid., Francesco di Antonio, prots. I/BII, I/B/III, I/B/V; ibid., Masseo di Gervisa, prots. 5/4, 5/5, 5/6, 5/7, 5/8, 5/9, 5/10. The number of loans registered varies from 220 to 300 per annum, of which 30% are for sums under 10 florins, 50% for sums between 10 and 25 florins, and 20% for sums greater than 25 florins (loans of over 50 florins account for 5%).

[16] See Toaff, *Ebrei a Perugia*, 230.

much larger amounts to commercial firms and to the nobility, and we have significant documentation from within the system of officially recognized Jewish banks in Italy that reveals a wide range of investment in trade and industry: in cloth and clothing, metals and spices, and agricultural goods.[17]

We have already said that part of the money at the disposal of the Jewish banks came from deposits made by Christians, who could thus avoid income tax on the one hand, and the ecclesiastical censure of so-called usurious lending on the other. Fra Cherubino da Spoleto harshly condemned the many Umbrian citizens who were secretly investing their capital in Jewish banks, warning them that sooner or later they would be found out and punished, 'for even foxes get found out'.[18] But the custom was widespread. In March 1460, in the negotiations between Pius II and Francesco Sforza in connection with the *vigesima*, a tax of 20 per cent which the pope was demanding from the Jews for the financing of the crusade against the Turks, the duke of Milan instructed his ambassador to the Holy See to remind Pius II 'that much of the Christians' money is in the hands of Jews, *cum quo advertendum est* [therefore I have to warn you] that to try and oblige said Jews to pay more than a twentieth of their profits would mean dissatisfying a large number of people, so that *diligenter considerandum est* [we have to consider carefully] whether too many malcontents might not thus be created'.[19] A similar situation obtained at the court of Ferrara, and probably also in Florence, where the beginnings of the Jewish monopoly of credit on authorized interest coincided with the rise to power of the Medici group, led by Cosimo. In the second half of the fifteenth century deposits with the Florentine Jewish banks were taxed at 10 and 12 per cent, but anonymity was permitted. After the fall of the Medici, the 'reformer' Domenico Cecchi called for the expulsion of the Jews, who were guilty of shielding the 'usurious' speculations of many Christian families of the city behind their own banking activities. In 1457 the commune of Siena ordered the Jewish banks to give the authorities the list of

---

[17] Thus the claim of those who appear to believe that Jewish lending in central and northern Italy was characterized 'above all by the short-term loan of small sums to the lower classes' can be seen to be inaccurate; see Carpi, 'Account Book of a Jewish Moneylender', 508.

[18] Cherubino da Spoleto, *Sermones quadragesimales* (Venice, Giorgio Arrivabene, 20 Oct. 1502), 259ª.

[19] The document is published in G. B. Picotti, 'D'una questione tra Pio II e Francesco Sforza per la ventesima sui beni degli ebrei', *Archivio Storico Lombardo*, 40 (1913), 206–7, and repr. in Simonsohn, *Jews in the Duchy of Milan*, i. 300–1.

Christian citizens and dwellers in the *contado* who had money deposited on loan.[20]

I have already referred to the sense of community shared by those Jews, including the bankers, whose origins lay in Rome; this cohesive force was in evidence wherever they moved to, even several decades after they had left the city. Throughout the first half of the fifteenth century the representatives of the Jewish communities of Roman origin probably met officially and at regular intervals to establish what steps should be taken to ensure papal protection, and to collect funds for this purpose by means of a form of taxation which would involve not just the Jewish community of Rome, but also the other Jews with Roman origins and their communities scattered throughout the peninsula. At such meetings the hegemony of Rome, the mother community, was never in doubt, as we see from the resolutions adopted by the congress of the 'Roman' Jewish communities held at Forlì in 1418, which bear unequivocal witness to the strength of their links with the Jewish 'mother city'.[21]

THE MAJOR BANKING FAMILIES

The chief banking family in Perugia in the second half of the fourteenth century was that of Matassia di Sabatuccio da Roma. Matassia's name appears for the first time in the list of the twenty-eight bankers with whom the commune established agreements on 26 December 1381.[22] On his death in the summer of 1383, the priors granted his son, Salomone, and his other relatives permission to wear mourning for the funeral.[23] This was an unusual privilege for a Jew at this time, and it was granted

[20] See Cassuto, *Ebrei a Firenze*, 155–6; Poliakov, *Jewish Bankers and the Holy See*; N. Piccolomini and N. Mengozzi, *Il Monte dei Paschi di Siena* (Siena, 1891), i. 152; S. Boesch Gajano, 'Il Comune di Siena e il prestito ebraico nei secoli XIV e XV', in id. (ed.), *Aspetti e problemi della presenza ebraica nell'Italia centrale–settentrionale* (Rome, 1983), 214–15. There is significant, if sporadic, documentation on Christian deposits in many other areas, e.g. in the Po delta, at Parma and its *contado*, and at Monza. See B. Rigobello, 'Gli ebrei in Polesine: I primi banchi di prestito', *Rassegna degli Archivi di Stato*, 41 (1981), 87; A. Antoniazzi Villa, 'Ebrei a Parma e nel contado parmense nella seconda metà del XV secolo', *Rivista Storica Italiana*, 95 (1983), 119–28; id., 'Aspetti e momenti della presenza ebraica'.

[21] On the meetings of the delegates of the Jewish communities of Roman origin and the Congress of Forlì in 1418 see Finkelstein, *Jewish Self-Government*, 281–95; I. Sonne, 'I congressi delle comunità israelitiche italiane nei secoli XIV–XVI e il sinodo dei quattro paesi in Polonia', *L'idea sionistica*, 1 (Mar.–Apr. 1931), 5–9.

[22] See Fabretti, *Sulla condizione degli ebrei in Perugia*, 9.

[23] AS Perugia, Con. e Rif., 31, fo. 229ʳ.

in view of the esteem the dead man had earned in the eyes of the commune of Perugia. The priors praised Matassia's qualities: he had shown himself *verus zelator* (zealous counsellor) of the city *opere et sermone* (by his deeds and words), and had supplied money for its numerous needs, giving the governors sound advice on political decisions, and supporting them courageously in their struggle against rebel factions. Matassia's solemn funeral set off from the sumptuous towered palazzo which the family owned in the district of Porta Sole, proceeding along the road to the church of S. Lucia, to arrive at the church of S. Trinità and the monastery of S. Tommaso, whose land the Jewish cemetery abutted.

Matassia and his father Sabatuccio had also been the chief bankers in Assisi around the middle of the century. They owned a house in the district of Porta S. Chiara and were the most highly taxed Jews of the commune (paying almost 520 *lire* in 1368, while the total taxes paid by the Jews living in the city barely reached 1,500 *lire*).[24] In February 1381, after the death of his father, the governors of Assisi had signed a loan charter with Matassia on extremely favourable terms.[25] Though enjoying rights of citizenship in Assisi, Matassia had preferred to live in Perugia, handing over the running of the bank at Assisi to a partner, Dattilo di Abramo da Norcia, who managed it until at least 1385.[26] Later, in 1401, after Assisi had come under Visconti rule, Matassia's bank charter was transferred, at the request of his son Salomone, who had inherited his father's estate, to his cousin Abramo di Musetto da Camerino.[27] In the mean time, Salomone had risen to a front-ranking position in the money trade in Perugia (his name, *Salomon Matassie Sabbatutii Salamonis*, heads the list of the signatories to the charter granted to the Jews on 10 May 1385, followed by those of a further thirty-one bankers).[28] We know that his business was particularly large, employing a considerable number of administrators, assistants, and relatives, because this same list (and it is the only such case documented) explicitly mentions the 'dependents and managers of the affairs of Salomone, son of Matassia di Sabatuccio'. On 29 June 1389 Salomone di Matassia, still living in the Porta Sole district in the parish of S. Lucia,

24 AC Assisi, N, Dative, reg. 3, file 2, fo. 4ʳ (1356); ibid. file 3 (1363), fos. 6ʳ, 12ʳ, 19ʳ; ibid., reg. 4, file 8 (1368), fos. 16ʳ, 25ʳ, 26ᵛ.
25 Ibid., H, Rif., reg. 6, file 3, fo. 31ʳ.
26 See Toaff, *Jews in Medieval Assisi*, 20–7.
27 AC Assisi, H, Rif., reg. 8, file 1, fo. 29ʳ.
28 AS Perugia, Con. e Rif., 191, fos. 31ʳ–37ᵛ.

was registered in the restricted list of the six main bankers from whom the priors were asking for an enforced loan of 700 florins to supply the city with grain.[29]

Salomone had earlier been associated with a large company of bankers from the Marches and Umbria which had extended its interests as far as the southern Veneto, and which signed a charter for the opening of a bank at Montagnana in the autumn of 1383, investing a capital of 3,800 ducats.[30] The prosperous state of investments in the Po valley led Salomone to leave Perugia and move to Bologna, whence he could follow the activity of the new banks more closely.[31] But for the moment he did not withdraw from the activities he had already established at Perugia and Assisi, which constituted a back-up should the new enterprises in the north of Italy meet with failure. However, his fears were to prove groundless, and in 1390 Salomone featured among the partners of the Paduan bank of S. Lucia, together with two other bankers of Perugian origin and other Jewish financiers from Tuscany and the Marches.[32] Subsequently, on 20 January 1393, most of the partners in the banks of Montagnana and S. Lucia at Padua, Salomone among them, signed a charter for the opening of a bank at Modena with the marquis Alberto d'Este.[33] At this time Salomone, who was living in Bologna, also appears to have had interest in banks in Siena, Arezzo, Pisa, and Prato.[34] Later, he moved with his family to Ferrara. On 14 November 1437 Salomone must already have been dead, because at that date his heirs, before a notary from Assisi, handed over the shares they had invested in the Umbrian banks and sold their splendid palazzo in Perugia to the banker Consiglio di Abramo da Gubbio for the huge sum of 800 florins.[35] Salomone's heirs were his sons Giacobbe and David and his nephew Isacco, who represented the other son, Samuele, who had died at an early age. In the same year, 1437, the first two sons, who were then living in Ferrara, figured among the partners in the first Jewish

[29] See Fabretti, *Sulla condizione degli ebrei in Perugia*, 18–21.
[30] See Ciscato, *Ebrei in Padova*, 21–2.
[31] On the moneylending activity of Salomone di Matassia at Bologna see A. I. Pini, 'Famiglie, insediamenti e banchi ebraici a Bologna e nel Bolognese nella seconda metà del Trecento', *Quaderni Storici* 22/54, issue on Jews in Italy (1983), 797, 800, and 812.
[32] D. Carpi, 'The Jews of Padua during the Renaissance, 1369–1509' (Heb.), Ph.D. thesis, University of Jerusalem, 1967, fo. 29.
[33] See Balletti, *Gli ebrei e gli Estensi*, 16.
[34] See Luzzati, 'Banchi ebraici toscani', 573.
[35] AC Assisi, Not., B15, Giovanni di Cecco Bevignate, fo. 139ʳ.

bank in Florence, whose founder, as we shall see, was the well-known Abramo da San Miniato (Abramo di Dattilo di Matassia Scola da Perugia).[36] The British Museum manuscript 626, containing the formulary of prayers according to the Roman rite, was completed for the two brothers at Florence in August 1441 by the scribe Gaio di Servadio da Forlì (Izchaq b. Obadiah).[37] We know that in 1450 Giacobbe, David, and Isacco were also partners in the bank at Borgo S. Sepolcro.[38] Giacobbe, the first-born son of Salomone di Matassia da Perugia, also figures among the partners in the Jewish bank in Fano, which was set up in 1439 with a capital of 3,000 ducats.[39] Other members of the banking company included Italian Jewish bankers from Ancona, Arezzo, and Montalcino, as well as the Finzis of Vicenza, whose recent dealings with the Paduan money market had not caused them to break their links with Ancona and the other centres in the Marches where they had worked for so many years.

As we have seen, the important Perugian bank of Salomone di Matassia had been taken over by Consiglio di Abramo; at the beginning of the fifteenth century he moved to Perugia from Gubbio, where his family had been engaged in moneylending since 1385.[40] Consiglio was a typical example of the *nouveau riche* banker from among the Jews of Roman origins. Leaving his son Samuele and his brother Elia to run the Gubbio bank, on which the family's fortunes had been based, but which was now no longer adequate for his needs, Consiglio lost no time in stepping into the position vacated by the house of Matassia di Sabatuccio at Perugia.[41] As we have seen, together with the bank, and regardless of expense, Consiglio had also acquired the landed property owned by Matassia's family, including the lordly palazzo 'with the tower' at Porta Sole. In the first half of the fifteenth century, he also forged himself a position in Perugia's *Universitas Judaeorum*, setting his sights upon the highest and most prestigious posts and rising through the ranks with meteoric speed. On 4 November 1420 Consiglio signed a charter for the

[36] See Cassuto, *Ebrei a Firenze*, 33–6.

[37] See G. Morgoliouth, *Catalogue of the Hebrew and Samaritan Manuscripts in the British Museum* (London, 1899), no. 626; L. Belleli, 'Sopra un libro di preghiere fiorentino del secolo XV', *Corriere Israelitico*, 42 (1904), 165–7, 225–38.

[38] See Luzzati, 'Banchi ebraici toscani', 573.

[39] See Luzzatto, I. *banchieri ebrei in Urbino*, 30.

[40] See Toaff, 'Ebrei a Gubbio', 153–92.

[41] The last charter signed by the governors of Gubbio with Consiglio dates from 13 Apr. 1404; AC Gubbio, Rif., 16, fos. 106ᵛ–108ʳ.

opening of a loan bank at Todi, giving its management over to Salomone di Consiglio da Viterbo.[42] In 1436, together with a group of rich and influential Jews, including the well-known doctor Elia di Sabato Beer and the banker Isacco da Pisa, Consiglio da Gubbio obtained permission from pope Eugenius IV to visit the Holy Land with his family and relatives.[43] Little is known of these. His son, Guglielmo, who had followed his father to Perugia, seems to have distinguished himself only as a debauchee with a long tally of misadventures; his nephew Lazzaro was involved in moneylending at Città di Castello, an important centre at the time, while another nephew, Consiglio, the son of his brother Elia, like many others, was seeking his fortune in the Po valley and settled at Quistello, in the Mantua region.[44]

Another important figure among the Jewish bankers operating at Perugia was Leone di Consiglio, who appears in the loan charters drawn up by the commune with the Jews in 1381 and 1385. Leone had arrived in Perugia from Camerino in the summer of 1378, and had rented a large house in the district of Porta S. Angelo, not far from the church of S. Fortunato.[45] On 29 July 1389 his name figures in the list of the city's main Jewish financiers, from whom the priors demanded an enforced loan of 700 florins to supply the city with grain. On 17 January 1392 the commune asked for a further loan of 500 florins, from Leone and five other Jewish bankers, to finance the defence of Perugia, now under attack by the mercenaries of Biordo Michelotti. His name figures twice in the select list of Jewish bankers from whom the priors asked for enforced loans: of 500 florins on 13 September 1392 and 400 florins on 27 August 1393.[46] We know that Leone was still in Perugia in 1401, because at that time the copyist Consiglio di Vitale (Jechiel b. Jequtiel) was completing a manuscript for him (now no. 605 in the Bibliothèque Impériale in Paris), containing the formulary for Jewish religious feast days according to the Roman rite; Leone's Hebrew name, Jehudah b.

---

[42] AC Todi, Rif., 58, fos. 52ʳ–54ᵛ.

[43] See Sh. Simonsohn, 'Divieto di trasportare ebrei in Palestina', *Italia Judaica*, ii. *Gli ebrei in Italia tra Rinascimento ed età barocca*, proceedings of the second international conference, held at Genoa 10–15 June 1984 (Rome, 1986), 50–1.

[44] In 1435 Consiglio figures as deputy for the Jewish community of Perugia; as such, he took steps to acquire a site to extend the Jewish cemetery; AS Perugia, Not., Mariano di Luca di Nino, 110, fo. 85ʳ. For the biography of Consiglio da Gubbio and his family see Toaff, 'Ebrei a Gubbio', 160–2.

[45] AS Perugia, Not., Massarello di Pellolo, 4, fo. 101ᵛ (4 June 1378).

[46] Ibid., Con. e Rif., 194, fos. 46ʳ–47ᵛ; ibid. 196, fos. 14ʳ–15ʳ, 21ʳ–22ʳ, and 206ᵛ–208ᵛ; ibid., Not., Bartolomeo di Giovanni, 35, fo. 2ᵛ.

Jequtiel, appears in the colophon.[47] At this same period, in association with other Jewish financiers, Leone di Consiglio was also investing his capital in loan banks operating at Padua, Rovigo, Lonigo in the Vicenza district, S. Andrea, and Ascoli, as well as in the headquarters in Perugia.[48] But by far the most significant figure among the Jewish bankers active in Umbria in the last part of the fourteenth century was Matassia di Sabato Scola (or Bethel), the founder of the da Pisa family, generally regarded as the most powerful and influential Jewish clan of the Italian Renaissance.[49] Already well established in the financial markets of Perugia, Gubbio, and other Umbrian centres, in 1393, together with his sons Vitale, Dattilo, Sabato, and Consiglio, Matassia drew up a bank charter with the town of San Miniato, thus extending his influence to Florentine territory. This was followed by charters with the important commune of Prato, then with Pescia and Colle Val d'Elsa. Vitale di Matassia subsequently set himself up in Pisa as the owner of the city's Jewish bank. Matassia Scola, who lived in the Porta Eburnea district in Perugia, figures among its main bankers in the lists compiled by the priors in 1381, 1385, and 1389.[50] During those years he was working alongside a group of bankers, the Montalcino family, to whom he was undoubtedly related, and who, judging by the name they adopted, may be assumed to have lived for some time in the Sienese republic, a key centre in the money trade.[51]

THE BANKER'S SERVANTS

As we have seen, wealthy bankers and merchants usually had a number of people directly or indirectly in their service, and who thus found

[47] See H. Zotenberg, *Manuscrits orientaux: Catalogues des manuscrits hébreux de la bibliothèque impériale* (Paris, 1866), no. 605.

[48] See Colorni, 'Prestito ebraico', 38; Cassuto, *Ebrei a Firenze*, 261; Ciscato, *Ebrei in Padova*, 18–19; Carpi, 'The Jews of Padua', 25, 150, 158, 160–2.

[49] Of the vast bibliography on the da Pisa family, see esp. D. Kaufmann, 'La Famille de Yehiel de Pise', *Revue des études juives*, 26 (1893), 83–110, 220–39; id., 'Notes sur l'histoire de la famille de Pise', *Revue des études juives*, 29 (1894), 142–7; id., 'La Famille de Pise', *Revue des études juives*, 31 (1895), 62–73; id., 'Abraham ben Isaac de Pise', *Revue des études juives*, 32 (1896), 130–4; U. Cassuto, 'La famiglia da Pisa', *Rivista Israelitica*, 5–7 (1908–10); id., 'Ancora sulla famiglia da Pisa', *Rivista Israelitica*, 10 (1913–15), 48–59, 123–7; id., *Ebrei a Firenze*; Luzzati, *La casa dell'ebreo*, 117, 246–7; F. Pisa, 'Parnassim: Le grandi famiglie ebraiche italiane dal secolo XI al XIX', *Annuario di Studi Ebraici*, 10 (1984), 414, 433–4.

[50] See Toaff, *Ebrei a Perugia*, 27–30; id., 'Ebrei a Gubbio', 154.

[51] See Toaff, *Ebrei a Perugia*.

themselves in the position of dependents. They included administrators, bank employees, apprentices, and clerks, whose privileges and rights, when they had any, were an extension of those granted to the bankers by the communes. Indeed the loan charters always stated that the clauses they contained were applicable not only to the banker whose name was explicitly mentioned, but also to the unnamed troop 'of his administrators, family, and companions'. In addition to the bank's employees and dependents, who rarely lived with the owner and who usually had an independent family life of their own (though there are exceptions), the banker also had in his pay a number of servants who lived with him in his house. Despite the stream of ecclesiastical and civil enjoinders issued from the beginning of the Middle Ages, and forbidding Jews to use the services of Christian nurses and servants, the rule was ignored in Italy at least until the Counter-Reformation.[52] We find such a prohibition, for example, in the laws promulgated by Amedeo VIII in 1430 concerning the Jews of Piedmont, and in the privileges granted to the Jews of the duchy of Milan by Francesco Sforza in 1456.[53] At Perugia, too, the ordinances passed by the commune in 1439 state that 'no Jew or Jewess can or may take a Christian woman as a wet-nurse for their children, nor have them fed or suckled by one such in any way'.[54] But in fact, as I have said, such prohibitions were royally disregarded, and scarcely anyone raised an eyebrow if Christian maidservants and wet-nurses were employed by Jewish families, particularly the more wealthy ones: indeed, it was a widespread practice in Italian town life in the Middle Ages, and regarded as completely normal. Accusations concerning such cases rarely led to court actions, and when they did these were almost always brought by the preaching friars and their circles; court cases which appear to have ended with guilty verdicts were rarer still.

We know, for instance, that in 1466 Angelo di Guglielmo, a banker at Perugia, who already employed a large number of servants, had taken on a Christian wet-nurse, a certain Marta Margherita, a peasant girl from Colle Fontana, to suckle one of his baby daughters.[55] In 1511 Mosè di Abramo, a banker at Gualdo Tadino, was tried, among other things, for

---

[52] On the Church's attitude from the third Lateran Council (1179) onwards towards the problem of the legitimacy of Christians acting as domestic servants in Jewish households, see e.g. Grayzel, *The Church and the Jews*, 25–6, 73; Colorni, *Gli ebrei nel sistema del diritto comune*, 36–9.

[53] See Anfossi, *Gli ebrei in Piemonte*, 35–7; C. Bonetti, *Gli ebrei a Cremona* (Cremona, 1917), 11–12; Simonsohn, *Jews in the Duchy of Milan*, i. 194–6.

[54] See Fabretti, *Sulla condizione degli ebrei in Perugia*, 42.

[55] AS Perugia, Giud., Sentenze del Podestà, 1467, orig. A, fo. 73ʳ (9 Dec. 1467).

having taken on Christian wet-nurses for his children, having them nursed both at his own house and at theirs, and also for having employed Christian manservants, whom he had lodged in his own home. During the course of the trial, which ended with his acquittal, the witnesses, all from Gualdo Tadino, stated that one of Mosè's Christian servants, named Valentino, 'habitually went to fetch wood with the Jew's donkey, which he tended personally, and went to work every day in the banker's vineyard, being lodged in his house and carrying out the duties proper to servants and household retainers'.[56]

While bankers do often seem to have employed Christian servants, the latter were frequently helped by Jewish workers, who were better qualified to cater for the needs of families for whom the observance of Jewish dietary and other laws was fundamental. We thus find a large body of Jewish servants, mostly from families in difficult financial circumstances, either poor or *déclassé*, who earned their bread in the service of the richer bankers and merchants. In the towns of Umbria, particularly in the fifteenth century, many of these seem to have been Ashkenazi or French, more or less recent fugitives to Italy from beyond the Alps, or from the centres of the Po valley, where their chief communities were now being established. This aspiring German and French workforce travelled down the via Francigena and the Cassia, often settling for the humble goal of a contract as a general servant in the houses of the rich Italian Jews who had become established in the prosperous centres of Romagna, the Marches, Tuscany, and Umbria. Ventura di Abramo was the most important Jewish banker in Perugia at the end of the fifteenth century, and he employed many servants, both Jewish and Christian.

Angelo of Germany, a Jewish servant working for the banker, died in 1485; but it was only three years later that one of his brothers, Isacco, made his appearance at Ventura's house in Perugia to collect the servant's personal possessions and the money he was owed. Isacco did not speak Italian and had therefore brought with him another German Jew, Paltiel di Michele Alemanno, to act as interpreter, since apparently Hebrew could not serve as a common language. Ventura probably spoke only Italian, while Isacco spoke only German and Yiddish. The banker finally gave the dead servant's brother the equivalent of the four most recent annual salaries owing to him, which amounted to 14 ducats.[57]

---

[56] Ibid., Processus, env. 164, file 19 (Perugia, 5 Nov. 1511).

[57] The Jewish servant is named as Angelo di Consiglio 'de Allemania'; AS Perugia, Not., Francesco di Giacomo, 221, fo. 404ᵛ (1 July 1488).

In 1490 another of Ventura's servants, Falcone da Cremona, also of German origin, was paid an annual wage of 3 ducats, as well as his board and lodging.[58] The maid, or more accurately housekeeper, of Ventura's large house on via Vecchia, near Porta S Angelo, was a Jewess from Bologna, Benvenuta di Guglielmo Finzi, whom the documents refer to as *famula et servitrice*: in 1494 she was receiving an annual wage of 3 ducats.[59] She clearly belonged to a branch of the Finzi family which had fallen on hard times: the Finzis had been a famous banking family, originally from Rome and Ancona, which had moved to Bologna and the main centres of the Po valley at the end of the fourteenth century.[60] Benvenuta was a typical *déclassée*, forced by poverty to become a servant in the house of a master who, in earlier times, had probably been the social and economic equal of her own family.

In her will of 1457 Ora di Giuseppe, a rich Jewess living in Perugia, in the district of Porta Sant' Angelo, made a bequest of 20 florins in favour of her own Jewish servant, Gentilina da Assisi, who had served her attentively and devotedly. The sum was to be added to the items forming the girl's dowry.[61] Mosè da Gualdo, whose trial in 1511 I have mentioned several times, gave houseroom to various Christian servants and wet-nurses, but also to several Jews, including one Raffaele, employed by the banker as *shohet*, or ritual slaughterer.[62] Apart from providing Mosè's family with the quarters of beef, lamb, and poultry fit to be eaten by observant Jews, Raffaele was also employed as tutor and religious instructor to the banker's children, now weaned and back from their stay with the local wet-nurse. In 1445 a rabbi from Chambéry in Savoy, Mosè di Vitale (Moshè b. Jechiel) was employed as tutor in the house of Giacobbe di Elia, a Jew of French origin who had banks at Perugia and Assisi. In his employment contract, signed before a Perugian notary, the rabbi pledged himself 'to serve Giacobbe for one year, instructing his children in religion, while Giacobbe, for his part, was to provide him with bed and board, as well as some payment in florins'.[63]

[58] On 20 July 1490 Ventura paid Falcone di Mosè da Cremona his wages for two years, amounting to 6 ducats; AS Perugia, Not., Francesco di Giacomo, 223, fo. 304ʳ.
[59] Ibid., Mariotto di Giovanni detto Calcina, 474, fo. 569ᵛ (17 Nov. 1494).
[60] On the Finzi family and their banking activities at Ancona, Bologna, Padua, Vicenza, and Mantua see V. Colorni, 'Genealogia della famiglia Finzi: Le prime generazioni', in id., *Judaica Minora* (Milan, 1983), 329–42. On the Bolognese branch of the family see also Pini, 'Famiglie, insediamenti e banchi ebraici', 809–10.
[61] AS Perugia, Not., Giovanni di Costante, 119, fo. 347ʳ (25 May 1457).
[62] Raffaele is explicitly described as 'slaughterer' in the records of the trial; AS Perugia, Giud., Processus, env. 164, file 19 (5 Nov. 1511).
[63] Maestro Mosè di Vitale from Chambéry in Savoy received his first wages from

A banker, particularly if he was wealthy, would usually have one or two individuals among his servants who acted as bodyguards and escorts, both to protect him from the attentions of ill-wishers and to recover the more problematic debts, deterring and discouraging default-ers and swindlers by fair means or, more often, by foul. These profes-sional 'heavies', who acted as the banker's debt-collectors, were naturally *au fait* with his most secret and delicate dealings; their position was one of great trust, and some danger, and their wages were therefore relatively high, or at least always much higher than those of the servants and bank apprentices. Giovanni, a hefty peasant from S. Cristoforo di Piscille, near Ponte S. Giovanni, was employed in Perugia for many years in the service of the banker Angelo di Guglielmo, with the delicate position of 'strongman' to the financier and, when the occasion required, as debt collector in the more obstinate cases. These somewhat tricky duties earned him a wage of 25 florins a year, a considerable sum, which could be justified only by the skill and discretion with which he was required to operate. During a court case in 1480, Giovanni explained to the judge of the Podestà of Perugia that he earned his living in the house of the Jewish businessman:

For over eighteen years I have accompanied Angelo to many regions and towns outside Perugia, and he keeps me in his service as a bodyguard to defend him from his enemies in these places. Needless to say, my position obliges me constantly to lay myself open to grave dangers, risks, and incon-veniences. Furthermore, when he is here in Perugia, Angelo is wont to send me, Giovanni, out of town on a wide variety of missions, and he derives great benefit from my services, because it is common knowledge that I always carry out the banker's business with extraordinary efficiency and benefit to his affairs, running grave risks, including attempts on my life from the many enemies whom Angelo has in these parts.[64]

Despite the relative scarcity of surviving documents on the subject, we may in all likelihood conclude that, in the households of Jewish bankers, as in those of Italian nobles and rich merchants of the time, expenditure on servants was one of the chief forms of conspicuous con-sumption; the number of housekeepers, servants, wet-nurses, tutors,

---

Giacobbe di Elia di Francia at Perugia on 7 Sept. 1445; AS Perugia, Not., Antonio di Cecco, 283, fo. 38r.

[64] The case brought by Giovanni da S. Cristoforo di Piscille against Angelo di Guglielmo for the failed payment of an annual wage of 25 florins was heard at Peru-gia on 8 Feb. 1480; AS Perugia, Giud., Processus, file 17, bundle 61.

errand boys, slaughterers, and bodyguards whether Jewish or Christian, living in the house constituted an obvious sign of the family's social standing. Furthermore, the servants who were part of the banker's domestic community each played a part within their master's working organization, on either a professional or an apprentice level, as well as participating in the daily running of the household and the preparation of its food, activities which entailed knowledge of and respect for those religious practices that underpinned Jewish family life in medieval Umbria.[65]

[65] Among the few studies on domestic staff in Italy and the other European countries in the pre-industrial period see esp. J. P. Gutton, *Domestiques et serviteurs dans la France de l'Ancien Régime* (Paris, 1981); P. Guardacci and V. Ottanelli, *I servitori domestici della casa borghese toscana nel basso Medioevo* (Florence, 1982); G. Casarino, *I giovani e l'apprendistato: Iniziazione e addestramento* (Genoa, 1982). See also Barbagli, *Sotto lo stesso tetto*, 216–38; Hinrichs, *Einführung in die Geschichte*, 22 and 25–6.

Bibliography

ARCHIVAL SOURCES

Archive of the Cathedral of S. Rufino, Assisi
Archive of the Collegio del Cambio, Perugia
Archive of the Convent of S. Francesco, Assisi.

Civil Archives (AC)
Amelia; Bevagna; Cascia; Città di Castello; Gubbio; Foligno; Norcia;
Spello; Spoleto; Trevi; Todi; Umbertide

State Archives (AS)
Foligno; Perugia; Spoleto; Terni; Vatican Archive

PUBLISHED SOURCES

ABBONDANZA, R., *Il notariato a Perugia* (Perugia, 1973).
ABRAHAMS, I., *Jewish Life in the Middle Ages* (New York, 1973).
ALBINI MANTOVANI, G., 'La comunità ebraica in Crema nel secolo XV e le origini del Monte di Pietà', *Nuova Rivista Storica*, 59 (1975), 378–406.
All'Illustrissima Congregazione particolare deputata dalla Santità di Nostro Signore Pio PP. VI . . . per l'Università degli ebrei di Roma (Rome, 1789).
ALLONY, N., 'Old Booklists in the Vatican Library' (Heb.), *Areshet*, 4 (1966), 213–33.
ALTAVILLA, E., *I giochi d'azzardo* (Milan, 1963).
AMORE, O., 'L'apporto degli atti privati alla conoscenza della società medioevale', *Studi Romani*, 28 (1980), 467–73.
ANFOSSI, M. D., *Gli ebrei in Piemonte* (Turin, 1914).
ANNIBALDI, G., 'I banchi degli ebrei ed il Monte di Pietà di Iesi', *Picenum Seraphicum*, 9 (1972), 89–129.
ANSELMI, S. (ed.), *Ancona e le Marche nel Cinquecento* (Ancona, 1982).
ANTONI, T., 'I costi industriali di un'azienda conciaria della fine del Trecento (1384–88)', *Bollettino Storico Pisano*, 42 (1973), 1–27.
ANTONIAZZI VILLA, A., 'Ebrei a Parma e nel contado parmense nella seconda metà del XV secolo', *Rivista Storica Italiana*, 95 (1983), 119–28.
—— 'Aspetti e momenti della presenza ebraica nell'Italia settentrionale del basso medioevo: I banchieri dei domini sforzeschi', in J. Shatzmiller (ed.),

Les Juifs dans la Méditerranée médiéval et moderne, proceedings of a conference held at Nice, 25–6 May 1983 (Nice, 1986), 53–77.

ANTONIAZZI VILLA, A., *Un processo contro gli ebrei nella Milano del 1488* (Bologna, 1986).

——' Di un falso matrimonio: Note di vita ebraica nella Lombardia quattrocentesca', *Studi di storia medievale e di diplomatica*, 9 (1987), 165–92.

ARIÈS, P., *The Hour of our Death* (Harmondsworth, 1983).

ASAF, S., *Sources for the History of Education among the Jewish People* (Heb.) (Tel Aviv, 1930).

ASHTOR, E., 'Il commercio levantino di Ancona nel basso medioevo', *Rivista Storica Italiana*, 88/2 (1976), 214–50.

——'Gli ebrei di Ancona nel periodo della repubblica', in S. Anselmi (ed.), *Le Marche e l'Adriatico orientale: Economia, società, cultura dal XIII secolo al primo ottocento*, proceedings of a conference held at Senigallia, 10–11 Jan. 1976 (Ancona, 1978), 331–68.

BACHI, R., and DELLAPERGOLA, S., 'Did Characteristics of Pre-Emancipation Italian Jewry Deviate from a General Demographic Paradigm for Jewish Traditional Communities?' in V. O. Schmelz and S. DellaPergola (eds.), *Contemporary Jewry: Essays in Honour of Moshe Davis* (Jerusalem, 1984), 159–89.

—— —— 'Gli ebrei italiani nel quadro della demografia della diaspora', *Quaderni Storici*, 19/55 (1984), 155–91.

BAER, Y., *A History of the Jews in Christian Spain* (Philadelphia, Pa., 1961).

BALESTRACCI, D., *La zappa e la retorica: Memorie familiari di un contadino toscano del Quattrocento* (Florence, 1984).

BALLETTI, A., *Gli ebrei e gli Estensi* (Reggio Emilia, 1930).

BARBAGLI, M., *Sotto lo stesso tetto: Mutamenti della famiglia in Italia dal XV al XX secolo* (Bologna, 1984).

BAROJA, J. C., *The World of the Witches* (London, 1964).

BARTOLUS A SAXOFERRATO, *Omnia quae extant opera*, 9 vols. (Venice, 1603).

BATO, J. L., 'L'immigrazione degli ebrei tedeschi in Italia dal Trecento al Cinquecento', in U. Nahon (ed.), *Scritti in memoria di Sally Meyer* (Jerusalem, 1956), 11–18.

BATTISTI, E., *L'antirinascimento* (Milan, 1962).

—— and BATTISTI, G., *La civiltà delle streghe* (Milan, 1964).

BEC, CH, 'La figura del contadino nella novellistica toscana del secondo Trecento e del primo Quattrocento', in id., *Cultura e società a Firenze nell'età della rinascenza* (Rome, 1981), 79–103.

BELLELI, L., 'Sopra un libro di preghiere fiorentino del secolo XV', *Corriere Israelitico*, 42 (1904), 165–7, 225–38.

BERNARDY, A. A., 'Les Juifs dans le République de San-Marin du XIVème au XVIIème siècles', *Revue des études juives*, 48 (1904), 241–64.

BLUMENKRANZ, B., *Juifs et Chrétiens dans le monde occidental* (Paris–Hague, 1960).

—— *Les Auteurs chrétiens latins du Moyen Âge sur les juifs et le judaisme* (Paris–Hague, 1963).

BOCCATO, C., 'Testamenti di israeliti nel fondo del notaio veneziano Pietro Bracchi seniore (secolo XVII)', *La Rassegna Mensile di Israel*, 42 (1976), 281–95.

BOESCH GAJANO, S., 'Il Comune di Siena e il prestito ebraico nei secoli XIV e XV', in id. (ed.), *Aspetti e problemi della presenza ebraica nell'Italia centrale–settentrionale (secoli XIV e XV)* (Rome, 1983), 175–225.

BOIS, G., 'Marxisme et nouvelle histoire', in J. Le Goff (ed.), *La Nouvelle Histoire* (Paris, 1978), 255–75.

BOITEUX, M., 'Les Juifs dans le Carnaval de la Rome moderne, XVème au XVIIIème siècles', *Mélanges de l'École Française de Rome*, 88 (1976), 745–87.

BOKSENBOIM, Y. (ed.), *Responsa of Rabbi Azriel Diena* (Heb.), 2 vols. (Tel Aviv, 1977).

—— (ed.), *Responsa Mattanot ba-adam* (Tel Aviv, 1983).

—— (ed.), *Parashiot: Some Controversial Affairs of Renaissance Italian Jews* (Heb.) (Tel Aviv, 1986).

BOMBE, W., 'Dokumente und Regesten zur Geschichte der Peruginer Miniaturmalerei', *Repertorium für Kunstwissenschaft*, 33 (1910), 1–114.

BONAINI, F., *Statuti inediti della città di Pisa dal XII al XIV secolo*, 3 vols. (Florence, 1854–70).

BONAZZI, L., *Storia di Perugia*, 2 vols. (Città di Castello, 1960).

BONAZZOLI, V., 'Ebrei italiani, portoghesi, levantini sulla piazza commerciale di Ancona intorno alla metà del Cinquecento', in G. Cozzi (ed.), *Gli ebrei e Venezia (secoli XIV–XVIII)*, proceedings of an international conference organized by the Istituto della Storia della Società e dello Stato Veneziano and by the Cini Foundation, Venice, 5–10 June 1983 (Milan, 1987), 727–70.

BONETTI, C., *Gli ebrei a Cremona* (Cremona, 1917).

BONFIL, R., 'Aspects of the Social and Spiritual Life of the Jews in the Venetian Territories at the Beginning of the XVI Century' (Heb.), *Zion*, 41 (1976), 68–98.

—— 'Jewish Emigration to Italy in the Late Middle Ages' (Heb.), in A. Shinan (ed.), *Emigration and Settlement in Jewish and General History* (Jerusalem, 1982), 139–53.

—— 'The Historian's Perception of the Jews in the Italian Renaissance: Towards a Reappraisal', *Revue des études juives*, 143 (1984), 59–82.

BONFIL, R., 'La sinagoga in Italia come luogo di riunione e di preghiera', in A. Neppi Ventura (ed.), *Il centenario del Tempio Israelitico di Firenze* (Florence, 1985), 36–44.

—— 'A Proposal for the Foundation of a Rabbinic Academy in Southern Italy at the End of the Fifteenth Century' (Heb.), *Studies in Memory of Rabbi Isaac Nissim*, 4 (Jerusalem, 1985), 185–204.

—— 'Una enciclopedia di sapere sociale', *Rivista di storia della filosofia*, 1 (1985), 127–30.

—— 'Società ebraica e società cristiana nel Medioevo e nel Rinascimento: Significato e limiti di una convergenza', *Ebrei e Cristiani nel Italia medievale e moderna: Conversioni, scambi, contrasti*, proceedings of an international conference held at San Miniato, Pisa, 4–6 Nov. 1986 (Rome, 1988), 231–60.

—— *Rabbis and Jewish Communities in Renaissance Italy*, trans. Jonathan Chipman (London, 1993).

BONOMO, G., *Caccia alle streghe: La credenze nelle streghe dal sec. XIII al XIX con particolare referimento all'Italia* (Palermo, 1959).

BRAGAZZI, G., *La rosa dell'Umbria* (Foligno, 1864).

BRAUDEL, F., *Capitalism and Material Life, 1400–1800* (New York, 1973).

BRUCKNER, G., (ed.), *The Society of Renaissance Florence: A. Documentary Study* (New York, 1977).

BRUTI, PIETRO, *Victoria adversus Judaeos* (Mantua, 1489).

BULLOUGH, D. A., 'La via Flaminia nella storia dell'Umbria', *Atti del III Convegno di Studi Umbri*, proceedings of a conference held at Gubbio, 23–7 May 1965 (Perugia, 1966), 211–33.

BURCKHARDT, J., *The Civilization of the Renaissance in Italy* (London, 1928).

BURKE, P., *The Historical Anthropology of Early Modern Italy: Essays on Perception and Communication* (Cambridge, 1987).

CACIORGNA, M. T., 'Presenza ebraica nel Lazio meridionale: Il caso di Sermoneta', in S. Boesch Gajano (ed.), *Aspetti e problemi della presenza ebraica nell'Italia centrale–settentrionale (secoli XIV e XV)* (Rome, 1983), 127–73.

CAMMAROSANO, P., 'Aspetti delle strutture familiari nelle città dell'Italia comunale: Secoli XII–XIV', in G. Duby and J. Le Goff (eds.), *Famille et parenté dans l'Occident médiéval* (Paris, 1977), 109–23.

CAMPORESI, P., *Il libro dei vagabondi* (Turin, 1980).

CAPSALI, ELIYAHU, *Seder Eliyahu Zuta: History of the Ottomans of Venice and that of the Jews in Turkey, Spain and Venice* (Heb.), ed. A. Shmuelevitz, 3 vols. (Jerusalem, 1976–83).

CARMOLY, E., *Histoire des médecins juifs anciens et modernes* (Brussels, 1844).

CARPI, D., 'Alcune notizie sugli ebrei a Vicenza', *Archivio Veneto*, 68 (1961), 17–23.

—— 'The Jews of Padua during the Renaissance, 1369–1509' (Heb.), Ph.D. thesis, University of Jerusalem, 1967.

—— 'The Account Book of a Jewish Money-lender in Montepulciano (1409–1410)', *Journal of European Economic History*, 14 (1985), 501–13.

CASARINO, G., *I giovani e l'apprendistato: Iniziazione e addestramento* (Genoa, 1982).

CASOLINI, E., *Bernadino da Feltre: Il martello degli eretici* (Milan, 1939).

CASSUTO, U., 'La famiglia da Pisa', *Rivista Israelitica*, 5 (1908), 227–38; 6 (1909), 21–30, 102–13, 160–70, 223–32; 7 (1910), 9–19, 72–86, 146–50.

—— 'Alcune note ebraiche di contabilità del secolo XVI', *Rivista Israelitica*, 8 (1911), 54–64.

—— 'Ancora sulla famiglia da Pisa', *Rivista Israelitica*, 10 (1913–15), 48–59, 123–7.

—— *Gli ebrei a Firenze nell'età del Rinascimento* (Florence, 1918).

CASTELLANI, G., 'Gli ebrei a Verona', *Studi Storici Veronesi*, 6–7 (1955–6), 70–82.

CECCARONI, S., *La storia millenaria degli ospedali della città e della diocesi di Spoleto* (Spoleto, 1978).

CENCI, C., *Documentazione di vita assisana*, 3 vols. (Grottaferrata, 1974–5).

CERONI, R., *Legislazione statutaria e condizione femminile a Narni nel basso Medio Evo* (Terni, 1983).

CHERUBINI, G., *Signori, contadini, borghesi: Ricerche sulla società italiana del basso medioevo* (Florence, 1974).

CHIAPPELLI, A., *Medici e chirurghi pistoiesi nel Medio Evo: Con documenti— Contributo alla storia professionale della medicina in Italia* (Pistoia, 1909).

CHIUPPANI, G., *Gli ebrei a Bassano* (Bassano, 1907).

CHOJNACKI, S., 'Dowries and Kinsmen in Early Renaissance Venice', *Journal of Interdisciplinary History*, 5 (1975), 571–600.

CIAVARINI, M., *I banchieri ebrei in Firenze nel secolo XV* (Borgo S. Lorenzo, 1907).

CIPOLLA, C. M., *Prezzi, salari e teoria dei salari in Lombardia alla fine del Cinquecento* (Rome, 1956).

—— *Storia economica dell'Europa pre-industriale* (Bologna, 1974).

—— *Contro un nemico invisibile: Epidemie e strutture sanitarie nell'Italia del Rinascimento* (Bologna, 1985).

CISCATO, A., *Gli ebrei in Padova (1300–1800)* (Padua, 1901).

COHN, N., 'The Myth of Satan and his Human Servants', in M. Douglas (ed.), *Witchcraft* (London, 1970).

COLAFEMMINA, C., 'Presenza ebraica a Bitetto e Palo del Colle nel secolo XV', *Brundisii Res*, 11 (1979), 39–51.

—— 'Documenti per la storia degli ebrei in Campania', *Sefer Yuhasim*, 2 (1988), 125–40.

COLORNI, V., 'Prestito ebraico e comunità ebraiche nell'Italia centrale e settentrionale', *Rivista di Storia del Diritto Italiano*, 8 (1935), 1–55.

—— *Legge ebraica e leggi locali* (Milan, 1945).

—— 'Sull'ammissibilità degli ebrei alla laurea anteriormente al secolo XIX',

La Rassegna Mensile di Israel, 16, essays in honour of R. Bachi (1950), 202–16.

COLORNI, V., *Gli ebrei nel sistema del diritto comune fino alla prima emancipazione* (Milan, 1956).
—— 'Ebrei in Ferrara nei secoli XIII e XIV', in E. M. Artom, L. Caro, and S. J. Sierra (eds.), *Miscellanea di studi in memoria di Dario Disegni* (Turin, 1969), 69–106.
—— 'Ghetto', *Novissimo Digesto Italiano* (Turin, 1973), 830–1.
—— 'Genealogia della famiglia Finzi: Le prime generazioni', in id., *Judaica Minora* (Milan, 1983), 329–42.

Corpus statutorum italicorum, i/4. *Statuti di Perugia del 1342*, ed. G. degli Azzi (Rome, 1913).

CORTONESI, A., 'Le spese in victualibus della Domus Helemosine Sancti Petri di Roma: Contributo alla storia del consumo alimentare in area romanolaziale fra XIII e XIV secolo', *Archeologia medievale*, 8 (1981), 220–30.

COULET, N., 'Juif intouchable et interdits alimentaires', in M. de Combarieu *et al.*, *Exclus et systèmes d'exclusion dans la littérature et la civilisation médiéval: Sénéfiance* (Aix-en-Provence, 1978) 207–21.

CRISTOFANI, A., *Le Storie di Assisi* (Venice, 1959).

DA CIVITANOVA, BENIAMIN NEHEMIA B. ELNATAN, 'Chronicle of Pope Paul IV' (Heb.), in I. Sonne (ed.), *From Paul IV to Pius V* (Jerusalem, 1954), 3–93.

DA LECCE, ROBERTO, *Spechio della christiana fede* (Venice, 1536).

DA MODENA, LEON, *Letters* (Heb.), ed. Y. Boksenboim (Tel Aviv, 1984).

DA SIENA, BERNARDINO, *Le prediche volgari*, ed. P. Bargellini, 4 vols. (Milan–Rome, 1936).

DA SPOLETO, CHERUBINO, *Sermones quadragesimales* (Venice, 1502).

DAHAN, G., 'L'Église et les juifs au Moyen Âge, XIIème au XIVème siècles', *Ebrei e Cristiani nell' Italia medievale e moderna: Conversioni, scambi, contrasti*, proceedings of an international conference held at San Miniato, Pisa, 4–6 Nov. 1986 (Rome, 1988), 19–43.

DAVIS, J. C., *The Decline of the Venetian Nobility as a Ruling Class* (Baltimore, Md., 1962).

DAVISO DI CHARVENSOD, M. C., 'Coltivazione e reddito della vigna a Rivoli nel secolo XIV', *Bollettino storico bibliografico subalpino*, 3 (1950), 1–13.

DE BENEDETTI, S., 'Un manoscritto cavense in caratteri rabbinici', *Archivio Storico per le Province Napoletane*, 8 (1883), 766–74.

DE COMBARIEU, M., *et al.*, *Exclus et systèmes d'exclusion dans la littérature et la civilisation médiéval: Sénéfiance* (Aix-en-Provence, 1978).
—— (ed.), *Les Marginaux et les exclus dans l'histoire* (Paris, 1979).

DE LA RONCIÈRE, CH., 'Le Vin et la vigne dans le contado de Florence au XIVème siècle', *Le Vin: Production et consommation*, proceedings of the sec-

Bibliography 261

ond conference of the Société des Historiens Médiévistes de L'Enseignement Publique (Grenoble, 1971).

—— 'Alimentation et ravitaillement à Florence au XIVème siècle', *Archeologia medievale*, 8 (1981), 183–92.

DE POMIS, DAVID, *Zemach David* (Venice, 1587).

DE ROOVER, R., *The Rise and Decline of the Medici Bank (1397–1494)* (Cambridge, Mass., 1963).

DE ROSSI, G. B., *MSS Codices Hebraici*, 3 vols. (Parma, 1803).

DEI VEGHI, ANTONIO, 'Diario', in A. Fabretti (ed.), *Cronache della città di Perugia*, 2 vols. (Turin, 1888), 1–30.

DELLAPERGOLA, S., *La trasformazione demografica della diaspora ebraica* (Turin, 1983).

DELUMEAU, J., *Vita economica e sociale di Roma nel Cinquecento* (Florence, 1979).

DI NOLA, A., *Antisemitismo in Italia* (Florence, 1973).

DION, R., *Histoire de la vigne et du vin en France des origines au XIXème siècle* (Paris, 1959).

DIOTALLEVI, D., 'Ultimi momenti della presenza ebraica a Fano', *Fano*, 1/1 (1978), 85–96.

DITO, O., *La storia calabrese e la dimora degli ebrei in Calabria dal sec. V alla seconda metà del sec. XVI* (Rocca S. Casciano, 1916).

Dizionario biografico degli Italiani, 12 vols. (Rome, 1970).

DOREN, A., *Storia economica dell'Italia nel Medioevo* (Padua, 1936).

DORIO, D., *Historia della famiglia Trinci* (Foligno, 1636).

DOUGLAS, M., (ed.), *Witchcraft* (London, 1970).

EARLE, P., 'The Commercial Development of Ancona, 1479–1551', *Economic History Review*, NS 22 (1969), 33–71.

ECKERT, W. P., 'Il beato Simonino negli atti del processo di Trento contro gli ebrei', *Studi Trentini di Scienze Storiche*, 44 (1965), 193–221.

Enciclopedia delle Religioni, ed. A. di Nola, 6 vols. (Florence, 1973).

ESPOSITO, A., 'Gli ebrei a Roma nella seconda metà del Quattrocento attraverso i protocolli del notaio Giovanni Angelo Amati', in S. Boesch Gajano (ed.), *Aspetti e problemi della presenza ebraica nell'Italia centrale-settentrionale (secoli XIV e XV)* (Rome, 1983), 29–125.

—— 'Gli ebrei a Roma tra Quattro' e Cinquecento', *Quaderni Storici*, 18/54 (1983), 815–45.

FABBRI, P., 'Il Monte della Pietà a Spello', *Bollettino della Deputazione di Storia Patria per l'Umbria*, 14 (1908), 161–92.

FABRETTI, A., *La prostituzione in Perugia nei secc. XIV e XV* (Turin, 1885).

—— *Sulla condizione degli ebrei in Perugia dal XIII al XVIII secolo* (Turin, 1891).

FANFANI, A., *Le origini dello spirito capitalistico in Italia* (Milan, 1933).

FANTOZZI, A., 'Documenta Perusina de S. Bernardino Senensi', *Archivum Franciscanum Historicum*, 15 (1922), 103–54, 406–75.

FARINE, A., 'Charity and Study Societies in Europe of the Sixteenth to Eighteenth Centuries', *Jewish Quarterly Review*, NS 64 (1973–4), 16–47.

FATTESCHI, G., *Memorie istoriche-diplomatiche riguardanti la serie de' duchi e la topografia de' tempi di mezzo del Ducato di Spoleto* (Camerino, 1801).

FAUSTI, L., 'Degli antichi ospedali di Spoleto', *Atti dell'Accademia Spoletina*, 1 (1922), 59–111.

FERORELLI, N., *Gli ebrei nell'Italia meridionale dall'età romana al secolo XVIII* (Naples, 1990).

FERRAI, C., 'Gergo e frodi in giocatori d'azzardo', *Archivio di psichiatria, scienze penali e antropologia criminale*, 19 (1898), 118–53.

FERRERO, E., *I gerghi della malavita dal Cinquecento a oggi* (Milan, 1972).

FERRETTI, M., 'Ai margini di Dosso', *Ricerche di storia dell'arte*, 17 (1982), 70–82.

FINKELSTEIN, L., *Jewish Self-Government in the Middle Ages* (New York, 1964).

FIORAVANTI, G., 'Aspetti della polemica antigiudaica nell'Italia del Quattrocento', in Paolo Sacchi (ed.), *Atti del secondo convegno dell'Associazione Italiana per lo studio del Giudaismo*, conference held at Idice, Bologna, 4–5 Nov. 1981 (Rome, 1983), 35–57.

—— 'Polemiche antigiudaiche nell'Italia del Quattrocento: Un tentativo di interpretazione globale', *Quaderni Storici*, 22/64 (1987), 19–37.

FOA, A., 'Politica conversionistica e controllo della violenza contro gli ebrei nella Roma del Cinquecento e del Seicento', *Ebrei e Cristiani nel Italia medievale e moderna: Conversioni, scambi, contrasti*, proceedings of an international conference held at San Miniato, Pisa, 4–6 Nov. 1986 (Rome, 1988), 154–69.

FORTINI, A., *Assisi nel Medio Evo* (Rome, 1940).

FRIEDENWALD, H., *The Jews and Medicine*, 2 vols. (Baltimore, Md., 1944).

—— *Jewish Luminaries in Medical History* (Baltimore, Md., 1946).

FUMI, L., 'I registri del Ducato di Spoleto', *Bollettino della Deputazione di Storia Patria per l'Umbria*, 3 (1897), 491–548; 4 (1898), 137–44; 5 (1899), 142–64.

—— *Inventario e spoglio dei registri della tesoreria apostolica di Città di Castello* (Perugia, 1900).

—— 'L'Inquisizione Romana e lo Stato di Milano', *Archivio Storico Lombardo*, 37 (1910), 5–124, 285–414.

GAUDIOSO, M., *La comunità ebraica di Catania nei secoli XIV e XV* (Catania, 1974).

GENTILI, A., GIACCHÈ, L., RAGNI, B., and TOSCANO, B., *L'Umbria: Manuali per il territorio—Spoleto* (Rome, 1978).

GEREMEK, B., 'L'Arrivée des Tsiganes en Italie: De l'assistance à la repression', in G. Politi, M. Rosa, and F. della Peruta (eds.), *Timore e carità: I poveri nell'Italia moderna*, proceedings of the conference on poverty and social assistance in the medieval Italian states, held at Cremona, 28–30 Mar. 1980 (Cremona, 1982), 27–44.

GESTRIN, F., 'Il commercio dei pellami nelle Marche del XV e della prima metà del XVI secolo', in S. Anselmi (ed.), *Le Marche e l'Adriatico orientale: Economia, società, cultura dal XIII secolo al primo ottocento*, proceedings of a conference held at Senigallia, 10–11 Jan. 1976 (Ancona, 1978), 255–76.

GHETTI, B., 'Gli ebrei e il Monte di Pietà in Recanati nei secoli XV e XVI', *Atti e memorie della R. Deputazione di Storia Patria delle Marche*, 4/2 (1907), 11–39.

GHINATO, A., 'Fondazione e statuti del Monte di Pietà di Amelia', *Archivum Franciscanum Historicum*, 48 (1955), 345–70.

—— 'Apostolato religioso e sociale di S. Giacomo della Marca di Terni', *Archivum Franciscanum Historicum*, 49 (1956), 106–42, 352–90.

—— *Vita religiosa nel Quattrocento italiano* (Rome, 1956).

—— *Studi e documenti intorno ai primitivi Monti di Pietà: I primordi del Monte di Pietà di Terni (1464–1489)*, 3 vols. (Rome, 1956–60).

—— 'I Monti di Pietà in Umbria', *Atti del VII Convegno di Studi Umbri*, proceedings of a conference held at Gubbio, 18–22 May 1969 (Perugia, 1972), 7–62.

GILIANI, B., *Compendium iuris municipalis civitatis Perusiae*, apud Angelum Bartolum (Perugia, 1635).

GINZBURG, C., 'Stregoneria e pietà popolare: Note a proposito di un processo modenese del 1519', *Annali della Scuola Normale di Pisa*, 30 (1961), 269–87.

—— *The Night Battles: Witchcraft and Agrarian Cults* (London, 1983).

GLISSENTI, F., *Gli ebrei nel bresciano al tempo della dominazione veneta* (Brescia, 1890).

GNOLI, U., *Pittori e miniatori nell'Umbria* (Spoleto, 1923).

GOLDSCHMIDT, E. D. (ed.), *The Passover Haggadah: Its Source and History* (Jerusalem, 1969).

GRASSINI, P., 'Tra Roma e Spoleto non c'è più la Somma', *Spoletium*, 10 (1966), 12–26.

GRAYZEL, S., *The Church and the Jews in the Thirteenth Century* (New York, 1966).

GRAZIANI, 'Cronaca della città di Perugia dal 1309 al 1491', in F. Bonaini, A. Fabretti, and F. Polidori (eds.), *Archivio Storico Italiano*, 16/1. *Cronache e storie della città di Perugia dal 1150 al 1563* (Florence, 1850), 580–623.

GROHMANN, A., *Le fiere del Regno di Napoli in età aragonese* (Naples, 1969).

GROHMANN, A., *La fiera dei morti a Perugia* (Perugia, 1980).

—— *Città e territorio tra medioevo ed età moderna: Perugia, secc. XIII–XVI*, 3 vols. (Perugia, 1981).

—— *Le città nella storia d'Italia: Perugia* (Bari, 1981).

GRUNDMAN, J. P., *The 'Popolo' at Perugia (1139–1309)* (St Louis, Miss., 1974).

GUAFFACCI, P., 'Il camerario del comune di Spoleto (secc. XIV–XV)', Ph.D. thesis, University of Perugia, 1970.

GUALANDI, M., *Memorie originali riguardanti le belle arti*, ser. 4 (Bologna, 1843).

GUARDACCI, P., and OTTANELLI, V., *I servitori domestici della casa borghese toscana nel basso Medioevo* (Florence, 1982).

GUTTON, J. P., *Domestiques et serviteurs dans la France de l'Ancien Régime* (Paris, 1981).

HEERS, J., 'Il commercio nel Mediterraneo alla fine del secolo XIV e nei primi anni del XV', *Archivio Storico Italiano*, 113 (1955), 162–97.

—— *Gênes au XVème siècle: Activité économique et problèmes sociaux* (Paris, 1961).

—— *L'Occident aux XIVème et XVème siècles: Aspects économiques et sociaux* (Paris, 1963).

—— *Le Travail au Moyen Âge* (Paris, 1968).

HERLIHY, D., 'Vieillir au Quattrocento', *Annales ESC*, 24 (1969), 1338–52.

—— *Vita economica e sociale d'una città italiana nel Medioevo: Pisa nel Duecento* (Pisa, 1973).

—— 'The Medieval Marriage Market', *Medieval and Renaissance Studies*, 7 (1976), 3–27.

—— and KLAPISCH, CH, *Tuscans and their Families* (London, 1985).

HINRICHS, ERNST, *Einführung in die Geschichte der frühen Neuzeit* (Munich, 1980).

—— *Alle origini dell'età moderna* (Bari, 1984).

HUPPERT, G., *Les Bourgeois Gentilshommes* (London, 1977).

IBN VERGA, SHELOMOH, *Shevet Yehudah* (Heb.), ed. A. Shochat (Jerusalem, 1947).

IOLY ZORATTINI, P. C., *Battesimi di fanciulli ebrei a Venezia nel Settecento* (Udine, 1984).

—— *Processi del S. Uffizio di Venezia contro ebrei e giudaizzanti*, i. *1548–1560* (Florence, 1980); ii. *1561–1570* (Florence, 1982); iii. *1570–1572* (Florence, 1984); iv. *1571–1580* (Florence, 1985).

—— 'Il testamento di Caliman Belgrado', *East and Maghreb*, 5 (1986), pp. vii–xxix.

ISRAEL, J. I., *European Jewry in the Age of Mercantilism, 1550–1750* (Oxford, 1985).

JORDAN, W. C., 'Problems of the Meat Market of Béziers, 1240–1247: A Question of Anti-Semitism', *Revue des études juives*, 135 (1976), 31–49.

—— 'Jews on Top: Women and the Availability of Consumption Means in Northern France in the Mid-Thirteenth Century', *Journal of Jewish Studies*, 29 (1978), 39–56.

JUVAL, J., 'Ordinances against the Frequency of Divorce in Germany in the Fifteenth Century' (Heb.), *Zion*, 48 (1983), 175–215.

KAUFMANN, D., 'La Famille de Yehiel de Pise', *Revue des études juives*, 26 (1893), 83–110, 220–39.

—— 'Notes sur l'histoire de la famille de Pise', *Revue des études juives*, 29 (1894), 142–7.

—— 'La Famille de Pise', *Revue des études juives*, 31 (1895), 62–73.

—— 'Abraham ben Isaac de Pise', *Revue des études juives*, 32 (1896), 130–4.

KELLENBENZ, H., 'Lo stato, la società e il denaro', in A. de Maddalena and H. Kellenbenz (eds.), *La repubblica internazionale del denaro tra XV e XVII secolo* (Bologna, 1986), 333–83.

KLAPISCH-ZUBER, CH., *Women, Family and Ritual in Renaissance Italy* (Chicago, Ill., 1985).

KRIEGEL, M., 'Un trait de psychologie sociale dans les pays méditerranéens du bas Moyen Âge: Le Juif comme intouchable', *Annales ESC*, 31 (1976), 326–30.

—— *Les Juifs à la fin du Moyen Âge dans l'Europe méditerranéenne* (Paris, 1979).

KUPFER, E., 'Further Clarifications Concerning the Scandal of the Tamari–Venturozzo Divorce' (Heb.), *Tarbiz*, 38 (1969), 54–60.

LAGUMINA, B., and LAGUMINA, G., *Codice diplomatico dei Giudei in Sicilia*, 3 vols. (Palermo, 1884).

LANDSMAN, L., 'Jewish Attitudes Towards Gambling', *Jewish Quarterly Review*, 57 (1967), 298–318, and 58 (1968), 34–62.

LARIVAILLE, P., *La vita quotidiana in Italia ai tempi del Machiavelli* (Milan, 1984).

LAUTS, J., *Die 'Madonna della Vittoria'* (Stuttgart, 1960).

LAZZARI, A., *De' Vescovi d'Urbino concernenti il dominio temporale de' conti e duchi* (Urbino, 1806).

LE GOFF, J., 'Merchant's Time and Church's Time in the Middle Ages', in id., *Time, Work and Culture in the Middle Ages* (London, 1980), 29–42.

—— *L'Imaginaire médiéval* (Paris, 1981).

—— *Medieval Civilization* (Oxford, 1988).

LE ROY LADURIE, E., *Love, Death and Money in the Pays d'Oc* (London, 1982).

Le Vin: Production et consommation, proceedings of the second conference of the Société des Historiens Médiévistes de L'Enseignement Public (Grenoble, 1971).

LEONIJ, L., 'Decreti del comune di Todi contro gli ebrei e giustizia loro resa da Francesco Sforza', *Archivio Storico Italiano*, 7/4 (1881), 25–8.

LÉVI-STRAUSS, C., *Structural Anthropology* (London, 1968).

LIONTI, V., 'La rotella rossa', *Archivio Storico Siciliano*, 8 (1883), 156–69.

LOMBARDO, M. L., *La dogana minuta a Roma nel primo Quattrocento* (Rome, 1983).

LUZIO, A., 'La Madonna della Vittoria di Mantegna', *Emporium*, 10 (1899), 340–60.

LUZZATI, M., 'Per la storia degli ebrei italiani nel Rinascimento: Matrimoni e apostasia di Clemenza di Vitale da Pisa', *Studi sul medioevo cristiano offerti a Raffaello Morghen* (1974), 427–73.

—— 'Il medico ebreo e il contadino: Un documento pisano del 1462', *La Rassegna Mensile di Israel*, 45 (1979), 385–92.

—— 'Ebrei in Umbria', *Annali della Scuola Normale di Pisa, Classe di Lettere*, 10 (1980), 1859–66.

—— 'Ebrei, chiesa locale, principi e popolo: Due episodi di distruzione di immagini sacre alla fine del Quattrocento', *Quaderni Storici*, 22/54 (1983), 847–77.

—— *La casa dell'ebreo* (Pisa, 1985).

—— 'I legami fra i banchi ebraici toscani ed i banchi veneti e dell'Italia settentrionale', in G. Cozzi (ed.), *Gli ebrei e Venezia (secoli XIV–XVIII)*, proceedings of an international conference organized by the Istituto della Storia della Società e dello Stato Veneziano and by the Cini Foundation, Venice, 5–10 June 1983 (Milan, 1987), 571–94.

—— Introduction to *Ebrei e Cristiani nell'Italia medievale e moderna: Conversioni, scambi, contrasti*, proceedings of an international conference held at San Miniato, Pisa, 4–6 Nov. 1986 (Rome, 1988), 9–17.

LUZZATTO, A., and TAGLIACOZZO, A., 'Gli ebrei a Bagnoregio', *Archivio della Società Romana di Storia Patria*, 101 (1978), 221–309.

LUZZATTO, G., *I banchieri ebrei in Urbino nell'età ducale* (Padua, 1902).

—— *Storia economica di Venezia dall'XI al XVI secolo* (Venice, 1961).

MAIRE VIGUEUR, J. C., 'Les Juifs à Rome dans la seconde moitié du XIVème siècle', in S. Boesch Gajano (ed.), *Aspetti e problemi della presenza ebraica nell'Italia centrale–settentrionale (secoli XIV e XV)* (Rome, 1983), 19–28.

MAJARELLI, S., and NICOLINI, U., *Il Monte dei Poveri di Perugia: Periodo delle origini (1462–1474)* (Perugia, 1962).

MANCINI, A., *Studi e saggi di storia medioevale del diritto e della economia* (Senigallia, 1943).

MANCINI, G., *Cortona nel Medioevo* (Florence, 1897).

MANDROU, R. R., *Magistrats et sorciers en France au XVIème siècle* (Paris, 1968).

MANZINI, V., *La superstizione omicida e i sacrifici umani* (Turin, 1925).

MARAGI, M., 'La fondazione del Monte di Pietà di Ravenna e la situazione economico–sociale ravennate alla fine del secolo XV', *Studi Ravennati*, 17 (1966), 235–52.

MARCIANI, C., *Scritti di Storia*, 2 vols. (Lanciano, 1974).

MARESCALCHI, A., and DALMASSO, G., *Storia della vite e del vino in Italia* (Casale Monferrato, 1931).

MARINELLI, O., *La compagnia di S. Tommaso d'Aquino a Perugia* (Rome, 1960).

MARINI, G., *Degli Archiatri Pontifici*, 2 vols. (Rome, 1784).

MATTHEW-GRIECO, S. F., 'Mogli ribelli e mariti picchiati nel sec. XVI', in G. Duby (ed.), *L'amore e la sessualità* (Bari, 1986), 321–31.

MAZZI, M. S., *Salute e società nel Medioevo* (Florence, 1978).

—— 'Consumi alimentari e malattie nel basso Medioevo', *Archeologia medievale*, 8 (1981), 328–42.

MEDIN, A., and TOLOMEI, G., 'Per una storia aneddotica dell'Università di Padova nel secolo XVI', *Atti e memorie della Regia Accademia di Scienze, Lettere e Arti di Padova*, 26 (1911), 103–201.

MELIS, F., *Note di storia della banca pisana nel Trecento* (Pisa, 1955).

—— 'Uno sguardo al mercato dei panni di lana a Pisa nella seconda metà del Trecento', in id. (ed.), *Problemi economici dall'antichità ad oggi: Studi in onore di Vittorio Franchini* (Milan, 1959).

—— *Aspetti della vita economica medievale* (Florence, 1962).

—— *Documenti per la storia economica dei secoli XIII–XVI* (Florence, 1972).

MENEGHIN, V., *Bernardino da Feltre e i Monti di Pietà* (Vicenza, 1974).

MENICHETTI, P. L., *Le corporazioni delle arti e mestieri medioevali a Gubbio* (Città di Castello, 1980).

MESSINI, A., *Le origini e i primordi del Monte di Pietà di Foligno (1463–1488)* (Foligno, 1940).

MILANO, A., 'I primordi del prestito ebraico in Italia', *La Rassegna Mensile di Israel*, 19 (1953), issued in instalments: 221–30, 272–80, 306–19, 360–71, 398–406, 450–60.

—— *Storia degli ebrei in Italia* (Turin, 1963).

—— *Il Ghetto di Roma* (Rome, 1964).

—— 'Battesimi di ebrei a Roma dal Cinquecento all'Ottocento', in D. Carpi, A. Milano, and U. Nahon (eds.), *Scritti in memoria di Enzo Sereni* (Jerusalem, 1970), 133–67.

Minutes-Book of the Council of the Jewish Community of Padua (Heb.), ed. D. Carpi, 2 vols. (Jerusalem, 1973).

MIRA, G., 'Prime indagini sulle fiere umbre nel Medioevo', *Studi in onore di Ettore Corbino* (Milan, 1961), 541–62.

—— 'Note sulla presenza di una comunità ebraica in Perugia e sulla sua attività creditizia nella seconda metà del secolo XIII e nella prima metà del XIV', in F. Borlandi (ed.), *Fatti e idee di storia economica nei secoli XII–XX* (Bologna, 1976), 93–109.

MIRA, G., 'Contribuzione alla conoscenza dei consumi nell'età di mezzo: Il consumo di vino a Perugia', *Studi in memoria di P. M. Arcari* (Milan, 1978), 525–32.

MOLLAT, G., 'Deux frères mineurs, Marc de Viterbe et Guillaume de' Guasconi, au service de la papauté', *Archivum Franciscanum Historicum*, 48 (1955), 68–92.

MOLLAT, M., *The Poor in the Middle Ages* (London, 1986).

MOMIGLIANO, F., 'Un ebreo professore di medicina a Perugia nel secolo XIV', *Il Vessillo Israelitico*, 65 (1918), 384–7.

MONTANARI, M., *L'alimentazione contadina nell'alto Medioevo* (Naples, 1979).

—— *Campagne medioevali: Strutture produttive, rapporti di lavoro, sistemi alimentari* (Turin, 1984).

MORENO KOCH, Y., 'The Taqqanot of Valladolid of 1432', *The American Sephardi*, 9 (1978), 58–145.

MORGHEN, R., *Medioevo cristiano* (Bari, 1974).

MORGOLIOUTH, G., *Catalogue of the Hebrew and Samaritan Manuscripts in the British Museum* (London, 1899).

MORTARA, M., 'Notizie di alcune collezioni di consulti MSS di rabbini italiani', *Mosè*, issued in instalments: 5 (1882), 125–6, 155–6, 191–3, 231–2, 265–6, 306–7, 377–9; 6 (1883), 52–3, 133–4, 191–3, 263–5, 337–8.

MOTTA, E., 'Ebrei in Como ed in altre città del ducato milanese', *Periodico della Società Storica per la provincia e antica diocesi di Como*, 5 (1885), 7–44.

MUELLER, REINHOLD, 'Prestatori ebrei e banchi di pegno a Venezia e nel Dominio', in G. Cozzi (ed.), *Gli ebrei e Venezia (secoli XIV–XVIII)*, proceedings of an international conference organized by the Istituto della Storia della Società e dello Stato Veneziano, and by the Cini Foundation, Venice, 5–10 June 1983 (Milan, 1987), 687–700.

MUZI, G., *Memorie civili di Città di Castello*, 2 vols. (Città di Castello, 1842).

MUZZARELLI, M. G., *Ebrei e città d'Italia in età di transizione: Il caso di Cesena dal XIV al XVI secolo* (Bologna, 1984).

NADA PATRONE, A. M., *Il cibo del ricco ed il cibo del povero: Contributo alla storia qualitativa dell'alimentazione—l'area pedemontana negli ultimi secoli del Medio Evo* (Turin, 1981).

NAHON, G., 'Pour une approche des attitudes devant la mort au XVIIIème siècle: Sermonnaires et testateurs juifs portugais à Bayonne', *Revue des études juives*, 86 (1977), 3–123.

NASO, I., *Medici e strutture sanitarie nella società tardo-medievale* (Milan, 1982).

NATALI, E., *Il ghetto di Roma* (Rome, 1887).

NESSI, S., 'La coltivazione della vite e la produzione del vino a Montefalco attraverso i secoli', *Spoletium*, 15 (1973), 31–8.

—— *Spoleto, Campello sul Clitunno, Castel Ritaldi, Cerreto, Vallo di Nera, S. Anatolia di Narco, Scheggino* (Perugia, 1974).

NIGRO, S. S., *Le brache di San Griffone: Novellistica e predicazione tra '400 e '500* (Bari, 1983).

NORSA, P., *Una famiglia di banchieri: La famiglia Norsa (1350–1950)* (Naples, 1953).

OBERMAN, H. A., 'The Stubborn Jews: Changing Strategies in Late Medieval Europe, 1300–1600', *Ebrei e Cristiani nell'Italia medievale e moderna: Conversioni, scambi, contrasti*, proceedings of an international conference held at San Miniato, Pisa, 4–6 Nov. 1986 (Rome, 1988), 123–40.

OWEN HUGHES, D., 'Distinguishing Signs: Ear-Rings, Jews and Franciscan Rhetoric in the Italian Renaissance City', *Past and Present*, 112 (Aug. 1986), 3–59.

PAPAGNO, G. (ed.), *Il vino e l'uomo* (Florence, 1984).

PARENTE, F., 'Il confronto ideologico tra l'ebraismo e la Chiesa in Italia', *Italia Judaica*, proceedings of the first international conference, held at Bari, 18–22 May 1981 (Rome, 1983), 303–81.

PATRONI GRIFFI, F., *Il banco di pegni di Cava dei Tirreni del 1495* (Cava dei Tirreni, 1985).

PELLINI, P., *Del Historia di Perugia*, 2 vols. (Venice, 1664).

PICCOLOMINI, N., and MENGOZZI, N., *Il Monte dei Paschi di Siena*, 2 vols. (Siena, 1891).

PICOTTI, G. B., 'D'una questione tra Pio II e Francesco Sforza per la ventesima sui beni degli ebrei', *Archivio Storico Lombardo*, 40 (1913), 184–213.

PIEROTTI, R., 'Aspetti del mercato e della produzione a Perugia fra la fine del secolo XIV e la prima metà del XV: La bottega di cuoiame di Niccolò di Martino di Pietro', *Bollettino della Deputazione di Storia Patria per l'Umbria*, 72/1 (1975), 79–185; 73/1 (1976), 1–131.

PINI, A. I., 'La viticoltura italiana nel Medioevo: Cultura della vite e consumo del vino a Bologna dal X al XV secolo', *Studi Medioevali*, ser. 3, no. 15 (1974), 795–884.

—— 'Famiglie, insediamenti e banchi ebraici a Bologna e nel Bolognese nella seconda metà del Trecento', *Quaderni Storici*, 22/54, issue on Jews in Italy (1983), 783–814.

PIPERNO BEER, G., 'Gli ebrei di Roma nel passaggio dal governo pontificio allo stato liberale italiano', in E. Toaff (ed.), *1870: La breccia del Ghetto* (Rome, 1971), 145–93.

PISA, F., 'Parnassim: Le grandi famiglie ebraiche italiane dal secolo XI al XIX', *Annuario di Studi Ebraici*, 10 (1984), 291–491.

POLIAKOV, L., *Jewish Bankers and the Holy See* (London, 1977).

POLITI, G., ROSA, M., and DELLA PARUTA, F. (eds.), *Timore e carità: I poveri nell'Italia moderna*, proceedings of the conference on pauperism and social security in the old Italian states, held at Cremona, 28–30 Mar. 1980 (Cremona, 1982).

PORTIOLI, A., 'La Chiesa e la Madonna della Vittoria di Mantegna a Mantova', *Archivio Storico Lombardo*, 10 (1883), 447–73.

—— 'La Chiesa e la Madonna della Vittoria', *Atti e Memorie dell'Accademia Virgiliana di Mantova*, 10 (1884), 60–70.

POWER, E., *Medieval People* (London, 1946).

PULLAN, B., *Rich and Poor in Renaissance Venice* (Oxford, 1971).

—— 'Poveri, mendicanti e vagabondi', *Storia d'Italia*, i. *I marginali* (Turin, 1978), 981–1047.

—— *The Jews of Europe and the Inquisition of Venice, 1550–1670* (Oxford, 1983).

RAMBALDI, R., 'Aspetti dell'economia spoletana nella seconda metà del XV secolo', Ph.D. thesis, University of Perugia, 1964.

RE, C., *Statuti della città di Roma del secolo XIV* (Rome, 1883).

REYDELLET-GUTHINGER, CH., *L'Administration pontificale dans le Duché de Spolète* (Florence, 1975).

REZASCO, G., *Del segno degli ebrei* (Genoa, 1889).

RIGOBELLO, B., 'Gli ebrei in Polesine: I primi banchi di prestito', *Rassegna degli Archivi di Stato*, 41 (1981), 74–91.

RINALDI, E., 'Gli ebrei a Forlì nei secoli XIV e XV', *Atti e Memorie della R. Deputazione di Storia Patria per le Province di Romagna*, ser. 4, no. 10 (1920), 295–324.

RINALDI, R., 'Un inventario di beni dell'anno 1503: Abramo Sforno e la sua attività di prestatore', *Il Carrobbio*, 9 (1983), 313–27.

ROCCHI, V., 'Gli ebrei e l'esercizio della medicina di fronte alle leggi della Chiesa e del governo di Roma papale', *Rivista di Storia Critica delle Scienze Mediche e Naturali*, 1/2 (1910), 3–10.

ROCHE, D., 'Un letto per due', in G. Duby (ed.), *L'amore e la sessualità* (Bari, 1986), 169–74.

ROSENBERG, C., *Alcuni cenni bibliografici di rabbini e letterati della comunità israelitica di Ancona* (Ancona, 1932).

ROSENTHAL, G. S., *Banking and Finance among Jews in Renaissance Italy* (New York, 1962).

ROSSI, A., 'Gaudino di Bonaventura, Albo dei professori nel terzo quarto del secolo XIV', *Giornale di erudizione artistica*, 6 (1877), 252–60.

ROSSI, L., 'Ebrei in Todi nel secolo XIII', *Bollettino della Deputazione di Storia Patria per l'Umbria*, 67 (1970), 31–71.

ROSSIAUD, J., *Medieval Prostitution* (Oxford, 1988).

ROTH, C., *The History of the Jews in Venice* (Philadelphia, Pa., 1930).

—— 'Forced Baptisms in Italy', *Jewish Quarterly Review*, NS 27 (1936), 117–36.

—— 'Will and Bequests of a Woman of Verona in 1642' (Heb.), *Zion*, 2 (1937), 125–36.

—— 'The Qualifications of Jewish Physicians in the Middle Ages', *Speculum*, 28 (1953), 834–43.

—— The Jews in the Renaissance (New York, 1965).

RUDDOCK, A. A., Italian Merchants and Shipping in Southampton, 1270–1600 (Southampton, 1951).

RUDERMAN, D. B., 'The Founding of a Gemilut Hasadim Society in Ferrara in 1515', Association of Jewish Studies Review, 1 (1976), 234–58.

SACERDOTE, G., Catalogo dei codici ebraici della biblioteca Casanatense di Roma (Florence, 1897).

SALZANO, A., Le finanze e l'ordinamento di Spoleto all'alba del Quattrocento (Spoleto, 1941).

SANDERS, M., 'The Apostates in Italy during the Sixteenth Century and their Attitude towards Jews and Judaism' (Heb.), Ph.D. thesis, Bar Ilan University, Ramat Gan, 1985.

SANSI, A., Documenti storici inediti in sussidio allo studio delle memorie umbre (Foligno, 1879).

—— Storia del Comune di Spoleto dal secolo XII al XVII, 2 vols. (Foligno, 1884).

SAPORI, A., La crisi delle compagnie mercantili dei Bardi e dei Peruzzi (Florence, 1936).

—— 'Storia interna della compagnia mercantile dei Peruzzi', Studi di Storia Economica, 2 (1955), 653–94.

—— Studi di storia economica, 2 vols. (Florence, 1962).

SASSI, R., 'Un famoso medico ebreo a Fabriano nel secolo XV', Studia Picena, 6 (1931), 113–20.

SCHMIEDT, G., 'Contributo della foto-interpretazione alla conoscenza della rete stradale dell'Umbria nell'Alto Medioevo', Atti del III Convegno di Studi Umbri, proceedings of a conference held at Gubbio, 23–7 May 1965 (Perugia, 1966), 177–210.

SCHMITT, J.-C., 'L'Histoire des marginaux', in J. Le Goff (ed.), La Nouvelle Histoire (Paris, 1978), 257–87.

SCHWARZFUCHS, SH., 'I responsi di Rabbi Meir da Padova come fonte storica', in D. Carpi, A. Milano, and A. Rofé (eds.), Scritti in memoria di Leone Carpi (Jerusalem, 1967), 112–32.

SEGRE, R., 'Gli ebrei e il mercato delle carni a Casale Monferrato nel tardo Cinquecento', in E. M. Artom, L. Caro, and S. J. Sierra (eds.), Miscellanea di studi in memoria di Dario Disegni (Turin, 1969), 219–37.

—— Gli ebrei lombardi nell'età spagnola (Turin, 1973).

—— 'Neophytes during the Italian Counter-Reformation: Identities and Biographies', Proceedings of the World Congress of Jewish Studies, 2 (Jerusalem, 1973), 131–42.

—— 'Bernardino da Feltre, i Monti di Pietà e i banchi ebraici', Rivista Storica Italiana, 40 (1978), 818–33.

SEGRE, R., 'La società ebraica nel tardo Medioevo', *Italia Judaica*, proceedings of the first international conference, held at Bari, 18–22 May 1981 (Rome, 1983), 239–50.

—— *The Jews in Piedmont*, 3 vols. (Jerusalem, 1986).

—— 'Gli ebrei a Ravenna nell'età veneziana', in D. Bolognesi (ed.), *Ravenna in età veneziana* (Ravenna, 1986), 168–9.

SEMERARO, M., 'Fra Roberto Caracciolo e gli ebrei', in C. Colafemmina (ed.), *Studi Storici* (Bari, 1974), 43–60.

SENSI, M., *Vita di pietà e vita civile in un altopiano tra Umbria e Marche (secc. XI–XVII)* (Rome, 1984).

SETTIS, S., 'Artisti e committenti fra Quattrocento e Cinquecento', *Storia d'Italia*, iv. *Intellettuali e potere* (Turin, 1981), 712–22.

SHAHAR, SH., *The Fourth Order: A History of Women in the Middle Ages* (Heb.) (Tel Aviv, 1983).

SHATZMILLER, J., 'Notes sur les médecins juifs en Provence au Moyen-Âge', *Revue des études juives*, 128 (1969), 259–66.

—— 'Doctors and Medical Practice in Germany around the Year 1200: The Evidence of Sefer Hasidim', *Journal of Jewish Studies*, 33, essays in honour of Y. Yadin (1982), 583–93.

—— 'Doctors and Medical Practices in Germany around the Year 1200: The Evidence of Sepher Asaph', *Proceedings of the American Academy for Jewish Research*, 50 (1983), 149–64.

—— 'On Becoming a Jewish Doctor in the High Middle Ages', *Sefarad*, 43 (1983), 239–50.

SHULVASS, A., *The Jews in the World of the Renaissance* (Leiden, 1973).

SIMONSOHN, SH., 'The Scandal of the Tamari–Venturozzo Divorce' (Heb.), *Tarbiz*, 28 (1959), 375–92.

—— 'Alcune note sugli ebrei a Parma nel '400', in E. Toaff (ed.), *Studi sull'ebraismo italiano in memoria di Cecil Roth* (Rome, 1974), 227–60.

—— *History of the Jews in the Duchy of Mantua* (Jerusalem, 1977).

—— *The Jews in the Duchy of Milan*, 4 vols. (Jerusalem, 1982).

—— 'Divieto di trasportare ebrei in Palestina', *Italia Judaica*, ii. *Gli ebrei in Italia tra Rinascimento ed età barocca*, proceedings of the second international conference, held at Genoa 10–15 June 1984 (Rome, 1986), 39–53.

—— 'Some Well-known Jewish Converts during the Renaissance', *Ebrei e Cristiani nel Italia medievale e moderna: Conversioni, scambi, contrasti*, proceedings of an international conference held at San Miniato, Pisa, 4–6 Nov. 1986 (Rome, 1988), 93–104.

SOLÈ, J., *Storia dell'amore e del sesso nell'età moderna* (Bari, 1979).

SOLOVEITCHIK, H., 'Can Halakhic Texts Talk History?', *Association of Jewish Studies Review*, 3 (1978), 153–96.

SONNE, I., 'I congressi delle comunità israelitiche italiane nei secoli XIV–XVI e il sinodo dei quattro paesi in Polonia', *L'idea sionistica*, 1 (Mar.–Apr. 1931), 5–9.

Statuta Illustrissimae Civitatis Narniae (Narni, 1716).

STEINSCHNEIDER, M., *Hebräische Bibliographie*, 19 vols. (Berlin, 1879).

STERN, M. *Urkundliche Beiträge über die Stellung der Päpste zu den Juden* (Kiel, 1893).

STOW, K. R., *Catholic Thought and Papal Jewry Policy, 1555–1593* (New York, 1977).

—— *Taxation, Community and State: The Jews and the Fiscal Foundations of the Early Papal State* (Stuttgart, 1982).

SZASZ, T. S., *The Manufacture of Madness* (New York, 1970).

TABARRINI, M., *L'Umbria si racconta: Dizionario*, 3 vols. (Foligno, 1982).

TENENTI, A., *Il senso della morte e l'amore della vita nel Rinascimento* (Turin, 1957).

TOAFF, A., 'Una supplica degli ebrei di Lippiano alla città di Perugia', in Y. Colombo, U. Nahon, and G. Romano (eds.), *Scritti in memoria di Attilio Milano* (Rome, 1970), 441–52.

—— 'Documenti sulla storia degli ebrei a Perugia nei secoli XIII e XIV', *Michael*, 1 (1972), 316–25.

—— 'Getto-Ghetto', *The American Sephardi*, 6 (1973), 70–7.

—— 'Gli ebrei a Città di Castello dal XIV al XVI secolo', *Bollettino della Deputazione di Storia Patria per l'Umbria*, 72/2 (1975), 1–105.

—— *Gli ebrei a Perugia* (Perugia, 1975).

—— *The Jews in Medieval Assisi (1305–1487)* (Florence, 1979).

—— 'Gli ebrei a Gubbio nel Trecento', *Bollettino della Deputazione di Storia Patria per l'Umbria*, 78 (1981), 153–92.

—— 'Gli ebrei romani e il commercio del denaro nei comuni dell'Italia centrale alla fine del Duecento', *Italia Judaica*, proceedings of the first international conference, held at Bari, 18–22 May 1981 (Rome, 1983), 183–96.

—— 'Commercio del denaro ed ebrei romani a Terni (1296–1299)', *Annuario di Studi Ebraici*, 10 (1984), 247–90.

—— *The Roman Ghetto in the Sixteenth Century: Ethnic Conflicts and Socioeconomic Problems* (Heb.) (Ramat Gan, 1984).

—— 'Convergenza sul Veneto di banchieri ebrei romani e tedeschi nel tardo medioevo', in G. Cozzi (ed.), *Gli ebrei e Venezia (secoli XIV–XVIII)*, proceedings of an international conference organized by the Istituto della Storia della Società e dello Stato Veneziano, and by the Cini Foundation, Venice, 5–10 June 1983 (Milan, 1987), 595–613.

—— 'Conversioni al cristianesimo in Italia nel Quattrocento, movimenti e tendenze: Il caso dell'Umbria', *Ebrei e Cristiani nell'Italia medievale e moderna: Conversioni, scambi, contrasti*, proceedings of an international conference held at San Miniato, Pisa, 4–6 Nov. 1986 (Rome, 1988), 105–12.

TOAFF, A., 'The Jewish Bank in Central Italy in the Thirteenth to Fifteenth Centuries' (Heb.), in H. Beinart (ed.), *Jews in Italy: Studies Dedicated to the Memory of U. Cassuto* (Jerusalem, 1988), 109–30.

—— *Jews in Umbria*, 3 vols. (Leiden and New York, 1993–4): i. *1245–1345*, pp. 1–460; ii. *1435–84*, pp. 461–978; iii. *1484–1736*, pp. 979–1466.

TODESCHINI, G., *La ricchezza degli ebrei: Merci e denaro nella riflessione ebraica e nella definizione cristiana dell'usura alla fine del Medioevo* (Spoleto, 1989).

TRACHTENBERG, J., *The Devil and the Jews: The Medieval Conception of the Jew and his Relation to Modern Antisemitism* (New Haven, Conn., 1943).

URBANI, R., and ZAZZU, G., *Ebrei a Genova* (Genoa, 1984).

VAUCHEZ, A., 'Richesse spirituelle et matérielle du Moyen Âge', *Annales ESC*, 25 (1970), 1566–73.

VOGELSTEIN, H., and RIEGER, P., *Geschichte der Juden in Rom*, 2 vols. (Berlin, 1896).

VOLLI, G., 'I Processi Tridentini e il culto del beato Simone da Trento', *Il Ponte*, 19 (1963), 1396–408.

—— 'Contributo alla storia dei Processi Tridentini del 1475', *La Rassegna Mensile di Israel*, 31 (1965), 570–8.

—— 'Il beato Lorenzino da Marostica presunta vittima d'un omicidio rituale', *La Rassegna Mensile di Israel*, 34 (1968), 513–26, 564–9.

VOLPE, G., *Studi sulle istituzioni comunali a Pisa: Città e contado, consoli e podestà, secoli XII–XIII* (Florence, 1970).

VOVELLE, M., *Piété baroque et déchristianisation: Attitudes provençales devant la mort* (Paris, 1973).

WADDING, L., *Annales Minorum*, xiv. *1472–91* (Ad Claras Aquas, 1933).

WIRTH, L., *The Ghetto* (Chicago, Ill., 1928).

YAARI, A., *Letters from the Holy Land* (Heb.) (Tel Aviv, 1943); 2nd edn. published as *Letters from the Land of Israel* (Ramat Gan, 1971).

ZAMBOLINI, PARRUCCIO, 'Annali de Spuliti', in A. Sansi (ed.), *Documenti storici inediti* (Foligno, 1879), 122–6.

ZAPPERI, R., *The Pregnant Man* (London, 1991).

ZAVIZIANO, G. A., *Un raggio di luce: La persecuzione degli ebrei nella storia* (Corfu, 1891).

ZOTENBERG, H., *Manuscrits orientaux: Catalogues des manuscrits hébreux de la bibliothèque impériale* (Paris, 1866).

Index

290   *Index*

nted and bound by CPI Group (UK) Ltd, Croydon, CR0 4YY

09/06/2025

14685814-0001